The Contours of Agency

The Contours of Agency

Essays on Themes from Harry Frankfurt

edited by Sarah Buss and Lee Overton

A Bradford Book

The MIT Press
Cambridge, Massachusetts
London, England

This book was set in Sabon on 3B2 by Asco Typesetters, Hong Kong and was printed and bound in the United States of America.

Library of Congress Cataloging-in-Publication Data

The contours of agency : essays on themes from Harry Frankfurt / edited by Sarah Buss and Lee Overton.
    p.   cm.
"A Bradford book."
Includes bibliographical references and index.
ISBN 978-0-262-02513-3 (hc. : alk. paper)
1. Act (Philosophy)—Congresses. 2. Agent (Philosophy)—Congresses.
3. Frankfurt, Harry G., 1929– —Congresses. I. Buss, Sarah. II. Overton, Lee.
B105.A35 C665   2001
191—dc21
                                                                    2001044505

10 9 8 7 6 5 4 3 2

Contents

Acknowledgments

Many of the essays in this book were read and discussed at a conference held at Wake Forest University in the fall of 1999. The conference was sponsored by the Wake Forest Department of Philosophy and funded by the department's A. C. Reid Philosophy Endowment. We are grateful for this very generous support.

We would also like to thank the contributors to this volume. Not only did they write new essays for the occasion, but they responded promptly and patiently to the many requests we sent their way during the editing process. To Jonathan Vogel we owe a special debt of gratitude. Always "on call," he offered support and advice from the moment this book was just an idea to the final days of its production. The idea, of course, was to combine in one volume a collection of new essays in which leading philosophers engage with the work of Harry Frankfurt. This book is about Harry. And it is for him, too. It acknowledges his importance to philosophy—and to us, his students.

Contributors

Michael Bratman, Philosophy Department, Stanford University

G. A. Cohen, All Souls College, Oxford University

John Martin Fischer, Department of Philosophy, University of California, Riverside

Harry Frankfurt, Department of Philosophy, Princeton University

Barbara Herman, Department of Philosophy, University of California, Los Angeles

Jonathan Lear, Department of Philosophy, The University of Chicago

Richard Moran, Department of Philosophy, Harvard University

Joseph Raz, Balliol College, Oxford University

T. M. Scanlon, Department of Philosophy, Harvard University

Eleonore Stump, St. Louis University

J. David Velleman, Department of Philosophy, University of Michigan

Gary Watson, Department of Philosophy, University of California, Riverside

Susan Wolf, Department of Philosophy, Johns Hopkins University

Introduction

In a recent paper Harry Frankfurt describes human beings as "generally hard to pin down, difficult to sort out, and just about impossible to sum up." He might have been describing his own work. For over thirty years, in language at once elegant and direct, Frankfurt has been exploring the contours of human agency. The power of his insights is due, in part, to his refusal to sum up his complex, elusive subject. He calls attention to the complexity, acknowledges that much eludes him, and, in the process, prods us to continue the exploration ourselves. As he explains in the preface to the second collection of his papers, his goal as a philosopher has always been to grapple with "lines of thought" that confront him "as a human being trying to cope in a modestly systematic manner with the ordinary difficulties of a thoughtful life." This is why we cannot read his essays without acknowledging to ourselves that what he says matters, whether we agree with him or not.

The difficulties of a thoughtful life—or at least many of them—can be traced to one central fact about human beings: we are capable of reflecting on ourselves; indeed, there are few things that come more naturally to us. This reflexivity generates problems because it divides us from ourselves. It splits us into the one who reflects and the one who is the object of this reflection. And this split makes us vulnerable to real rifts in our psyche—to inner strife and self-alienation—which must be overcome if we are to become whole.

The chief "ordinary difficulty" of human life is that we are not whole. As Frankfurt puts it, most of us find it difficult to identify wholeheartedly with all of our emotions, desires, and inclinations. This self-alienation takes two forms that especially interest Frankfurt. First, we are often filled with uncertainty about whether we really ought to care as we do about what we care about; we are often ambivalent. Second, we often discover that we have desires, or inclinations, that we really would prefer *not* to have; and this can reduce us to being "passive bystanders" to our own wills.

The latter form of self-alienation preoccupies Frankfurt in his earlier work. It is, he argues, the key to understanding moral responsibility. According to Frankfurt, we are responsible for what we do if and only if our motives for doing it are truly our own. Contrary to what many have thought, whether our motives are truly our own does not depend on their causal history; nor does it depend on whether we have the power to replace them. When moral responsibility is at issue, what matters is whether the motivating force of our desires is in harmony with our attitudes toward being moved in this way.

Insofar as our attitudes conflict, we are ambivalent. And insofar as we are ambivalent, we lack confidence in our own "take" on things. In his more recent work, Frankfurt has become especially interested in those attitudes which are immune to doubt because we identify with them "wholeheartedly." In effect, he has shifted his focus from the self-control sufficient for moral responsibility to the self-integration that, he claims, is an implicit goal of every human agent. With this shift, he has become less concerned about how our power as *agents* is manifested in the power of our *desires*, and more interested in how our wholehearted psychic investments in people, institutions, and projects impose authoritative limits on the power of our own wills.

According to Frankfurt, the most fundamental ideal of human agency is wholeheartedness. Unless one cares wholeheartedly about something—unless, that is, one is fully satisfied with the fact that one cares about it—one's life lacks balance, continuity, and structure. Caring about something "guides [a person] in supervising the design and the ordering of his own purposes and priorities." And to care wholeheartedly about something is to trust the guide without reservation. Someone who wholeheartedly endorses his motives is as actively involved in producing his own actions as an agent can possibly be.

Frankfurt tells us that the defining characteristic of persons is that they care about things. And, following Hume, he insists that whatever we have reason to do (or refrain from doing) depends on what, in particular, we care about. Love, he says, is a special kind of care. When one loves something, or someone, one cannot help caring about this thing, or person. More important, one cannot doubt the authority of the reasons that are grounded in this care. In short, the authority that turns certain facts into reasons for action is the authority of love; the "ought" of practical reason is grounded in love's nonrational "must."

To discover that one cannot help caring about something (and that one cannot help being satisfied with the fact that one cannot help caring) is to come up against a "volitional necessity." A person who is subject to volitional necessity "accedes to [a constraint on his will] because he is *unwilling* to oppose it and because, furthermore, his unwillingness is *itself* something which he is unwilling to alter." On Frankfurt's account, such necessities are the key to self-integration, and to the self-confidence that is tied to wholeheartedness as both cause and effect. In giving us reasons, volitional necessities are also the source of values. And because they are constitutive of who we are, they determine the conditions under which we succeed in governing ourselves.

When we truly govern ourselves—when we are truly autonomous—this is not, Frankfurt insists, because there is more than one possible way we can act. Rather, it is because certain possibilities are closed off by what we truly care about. Being truly autonomous is one and the same thing as being truly wholehearted. An autonomous agent "identifies himself fully and uninhibitedly with the volitional configurations that define his final ends.... There is no part of him—no part with which he identifies—that is opposed to or that resists his loving what he loves." Just as being at war with oneself is incompatible with self-government, so, according to Frankfurt, self-love is a defining characteristic of the autonomous agent.

The themes that are central to coping with the difficulties of a thoughtful human life are among the themes of greatest philosophical importance. This is evident in the essays collected here. Written to honor a distinguished colleague, these essays cover a wide range of topics in metaphysics, metaethics, normative ethics, and action theory. They are the work of eminent philosophers who defend their own original philosophical positions at the same time that they respond to Frankfurt's.

In his contribution to this volume, John Martin Fischer addresses Frankfurt's claim that causal determinism poses no threat to moral responsibility. Frankfurt has two reasons for taking this position: he does not believe that the history of an agent's motives is relevant to whether they are truly her own; and he does not believe that moral responsibility requires alternate possibilities. Fischer rejects the antihistorical aspect of Frankfurt's conception of moral responsibility. But he joins Frankfurt in attacking the assumption that an agent is responsible for her action only if she could have done otherwise. Fischer concedes that even if Frankfurt is right on this score, there are other reasons one might have for thinking that an agent cannot be responsible for an action that was causally determined by the state of the world in the far distant past, together with the laws of nature. He examines these additional considerations, argues that they are not compelling, and thus concludes that whether an act is causally determined is irrelevant to whether the agent is morally responsible for performing it.

Eleonore Stump shares Fischer's sense that Frankfurt's account of moral responsibility attributes too little importance to the history of an agent's motives. But she raises concerns about Fischer's attempt to reconcile the relevance of history with the irrelevance of causal determinism. She argues that the most compelling argument for the incompatibility of causal determinism and moral responsibility relies on a principle that Fischer has not succeeded in undermining. And she strengthens her case against approaches like Fischer's by showing how they do no better than Frankfurt's ahistorical approach in distinguishing causally determined action from action caused by direct brain manipulation.

Even incompatibilists concede that being free from determination by events in the past does not *suffice* for being morally responsible for one's actions. In developing his own compatibilist account, Frankfurt introduces a notion that many others have found suggestive. An agent is morally responsible for his act, he says, if and only if he *identifies* with the desire that moves him to perform it. Otherwise, the desire is just a motivational force he suffers passively, like a reflex bodily movement that occurs in spite of himself. In his essay Michael Bratman focuses on this elusive notion of identification. What is it exactly? On Bratman's reading of Frankfurt, to identify with a given desire D is to have "higher-order attitudes in support of D." Bratman believes that the sort of identification that is especially important to agency involves a proattitude toward D's providing a justifying reason for action; and he devotes most of his essay to analyzing this attitude and its propositional content. Frankfurt, he notes, suggests that "treating D as reason-providing" can be reduced to "D's functioning as an effective motive because of the higher-order attitude in favor of that functioning." Like many other contributors to this volume, however, Bratman is skeptical of any such reduction. After all, he points out, "A desire for E may motivate action without any thought that E is a justifying consideration." He thus recommends an alternative analysis: to identify with some desire D is to have a higher-order attitude toward D's "functioning as end-setting for practical reason." The relevant attitude, he claims, is a "higher-order self-governing policy." Such policies have authority to represent the agent's standpoint because of the essential role they play in the unity of agency. In offering this analysis of identification, Bratman aims to call attention to the significant role that higher-order attitudes and policies play in our agency. He brings his essay to a close by reviewing additional ways in which such attitudes and policies can support our motives.

Bratman's interest in identification is an interest in the attitudes an agent has *qua* practical reasoner. This reflects the fact that our intentional actions are actions we perform for a reason. David Velleman also believes that the "self whose participation in causing behavior is necessary and sufficient" for intentional agency is the self conceived as the point of view from which reasons for action are assessed. Velleman argues that this participating, identifying self need not persist over time in order for a person to remain in existence. In other words, one can betray even one's deepest evaluative commitments without ceasing to be the person one was. Persons, Velleman argues against Frankfurt, do not have volitional essences. If we are tempted to think that they do, this may well be because it is comforting to dissociate ourselves from aspects of ourselves we find threatening, or otherwise painful. With reference to Freud, Velleman reminds us of the psychic damage that such dissociation can cause.

The theme of Gary Watson's essay is the volitional necessities that are, allegedly, grounded in our volitional essences. To gain an understanding of this special sort of limit on one's will, Watson compares it with many other "constraints on one's ability to do something." To be subject to volitional necessity is *not* to be constrained by psychic impediments, such as phobias. Nor is it the same thing as "normative necessity," or the constraint imposed by the conclusions of practical reasoning. Turning also to Bernard Williams's discussion of "moral incapacity," Watson examines two candidate conceptions of volitional necessity, each of which he finds in Frankfurt's work. According to the first, we are subject to volitional necessity when we are constrained by what we regard as choiceworthy—or, as Watson puts it, what we "stand behind." According to the second conception, the relevant constraint is imposed by what we are "invested in or bound up with," where this need not reflect our judgments about which commitments we are most *justified* in making. Watson points out that each conception of volitional necessity implies something different about the agent's relation to his own will. If the incapacity constitutive of one's own will reflects one's evaluations, then one could not possibly have a reason to try to change one's will. If, on the other hand, the necessities of one's will can diverge from one's evaluations, then one has reason to try to resist them; and the possibility of doing so "exhibits a source of agency that is independent of [the limits of one's own will]." Watson concludes his comparison by affirming a view that is interestingly similar to both Bratman's and Velleman's: when what we care about is at odds with our evaluations, the latter are "more central to agency." This does not mean, he hastens to add, that they are more central to who we really are.

T. M. Scanlon and Richard Moran also express sympathy for the thesis that insofar as the concept of identification helps us to delimit the contours of agency, it has something essential to do with the agent's evaluative judgments, and with the perception of reasons these judgments express. They defend this connection in the context of exploring the different respects in which an agent's attitudes can "belong" to him. Moran probes Frankfurt's suggestion that to "identify with" one's motives is to be "active" in relation to their motivating force. What is required in order for us to be active in the relevant sense? Frankfurt's own remarks might seem to encourage the picture of an agent exerting influence over the effectiveness of his motivating attitudes by approving of some and disapproving of others. Moran argues, however, that we need not exercise direct control over the attitudes to whose motivating force we actively contribute. Indeed, as Frankfurt himself stresses, the attitudes with which we most deeply identify cannot be adopted "at will." Nor does it suffice that we *approve* of our attitudes. After all, our approval of someone *else's* motives does not make them our own. The sense in which we are especially active in relation to some of our motives is similar, Moran suggests, to the sense in which we are active when we are in the "process of thinking." Genuine thinking (as opposed to mere free associating) is a norm-governed activity. So, too, we are active in relation to our motives when and only when these motives are responsive to "specific norms." A motive passes this test when it is the product of our reasoning about what is worth doing; but we can also be responsive to norms without engaging in any reasoning whatsoever.

In defending a very similar view, Scanlon notes that many of an agent's attitudes are "attributable" to him because they "fall within the rational authority of his judgment"; they reflect his judgment regarding what he has reason to do. Other attitudes, however, belong to an agent in an additional way: they are responsive to his voluntary choice. Scanlon argues that most of an agent's desires belong to him in the first way. That is, contrary to Frankfurt's assumption, they involve "something's seeming to be a reason." According to Scanlon, this is precisely why most desires to do something (most "first-order desires") are capable of entering into the sort of inner conflicts that interest Frankfurt. Psychological states which imply nothing about reasons cannot oppose our deepest, most confident value assessments; if they stand in the way of our doing what we most want to do, this is simply because they are an external (albeit psychological) impediment. On Scanlon's account, if our desires have a claim to be satisfied, this is partly a function of the desirability judgments implicit in them. Scanlon's critique thus goes to the heart of Frankfurt's account of love: love's authority depends, he argues, on the value of the loved object.

Like Scanlon, Susan Wolf and Barbara Herman are uneasy about Frankfurt's attack on the objectivity of values. Wolf reminds us of how we think and talk about values in nonphilosophical contexts. She reviews the phenomenology of evaluation and caring, and concludes that it does not support Frankfurt's position. Frankfurt is right, Wolf says, to stress that what we have reason to care about cannot be settled by what is objectively valuable. Indeed, it would be unseemly to base one's love of one's children on an objective assessment of their characteristics. On the other hand, there are constraints on what we have reason to care about, and these constraints are not merely a function of our own psychic capacities. "Worth," Wolf suggests, "figures in, somehow, to what it is desirable to care about, but not exclusively or perhaps decisively." To determine whether we have reason to care about something, we do need to discover whether we have an "affinity" for it, and whether in caring about it we will be able "to create or bring forth experiences, acts, or objects of further value." But we must also consider its objective worth. In other words, the justifiability of our commitments depends, in part, on the truth of the evaluations they presuppose. Because Frankfurt neglects this fact, Wolf argues, he overvalues wholeheartedness, and misconceives the nature of autonomous agency.

Herman raises additional concerns about the fact that Frankfurt rules out the possibility of valuing what is not really of value. To be sure, on his account, it is possible for someone to discover that he is not satisfied with the role a given value plays in his life. But, on his account, the value of X cannot itself be a reason. *Moral* values seem to pose a special challenge to Frankfurt's conception of rational agency as "a system of beliefs and desires, organized hierarchically through a process—acts—of reflections and identification." In search of a picture of the human mind that is better able to accommodate the constraints imposed by such values, Herman turns to Kant, and to his "more metaphysically contentful notion of will," in particular. According to Kant, rational willing involves deriving an action from a principle, or law, which is constitutive of the will's causal power. What an agent has reason to do depends on what this principle of volition implies. If someone acts in a manner that contradicts the principle, then he makes a "deliberative error"; he makes a mistake about what is valuable that does not presuppose any additional motive on his part. Herman concedes that the Kantian account rests on metaphysical assumptions that many are anxious to deny. Her aim, however, is to convince us that we have good reason to take a closer look at these assumptions: unless they can be defended, we cannot do justice to the motivating role of values—and of moral values, in particular.

Like Scanlon, Jonathan Lear argues that love's authority depends on the fact that it "aims at the good." And like Wolf and Herman, he warns that someone might achieve wholeness at the expense of his "connection to the world." In making his case, Lear also continues the exploration of volitional necessity pursued in such different ways by both Velleman and Watson. We need, he urges, to distinguish an agent's *psychological* needs from the needs that are essential to his will. And he argues that Frankfurt is wrong to think that the human will has a more basic need for unity than for connectedness to external reality. According to Lear, "love is a fundamental force that promotes the growth of ever-more differentiated unities." But it does so by promoting "ever more sophisticated relations to worldly objects"; and the significance of these relations cannot be entirely determined by the lover himself if they are to have their transformative effect.

Of all our connections to the world, none is more important than our connection to other people. It is widely agreed that there is something about people—something about the *value* of *persons*—that constrains how we have reason to treat them. This thought is expressed by the claim that persons deserve to be treated with respect. In his contribution to the volume, Joseph Raz examines this assumption and considers whether Frankfurt's account of respect for persons can help us make sense of it. He sets the stage for this examination by posing a question. If, he asks, there are reasons against treating people in certain ways, why do these reasons need to be supplemented with an appeal to the special moral status of persons? In other words, how can there be "special reasons for respecting persons"—reasons that are not a "by-product" of whatever considerations determine what one "ought anyway to do"? Frankfurt's answer, Raz notes, is that when a person is not treated as he ought to be treated, he is hurt by this very fact. He is hurt because disregarding the reasons to treat him otherwise is equivalent to "denying his reality." Raz points out that in order for this answer to be satisfactory, we need to say more about what is involved in "denying the reality of others"; and he concludes with a brief outline of the sort of account he favors. Whatever the correct account may be, however, it appears, as Raz suggests, to be committed to the value of persons. If the "reality" of persons is not simply a function of how they appear to others, then it would seem to be a basis of reasons that do not depend on what anyone happens to care about. Frankfurt's discussion of how it is "appropriate" to treat other persons thus provides an interesting focal point for the debate over the relationship between what we care about and what is really worth caring about.

In evaluating this debate, we cannot ignore Frankfurt's remarks about bullshit. As a substitute for "disinterested efforts to determine what is true and what is false," "sincerity itself is," he warns us, "bullshit." Sincerity as bullshit takes the following form: "Rather than seeking primarily to arrive at accurate representations of a common world, the individual turns toward trying to provide honest representations of himself. Convinced that reality has no inherent nature, which he might hope to identify as the truth about things, he devotes himself to being true to his own nature. It is as though he decides that since it makes no sense to try to be true to the facts, he must therefore try instead to be true to himself." This is bullshit because self-knowledge depends on knowledge of the world. Accordingly, indifference to what is true and what is false is inimical, if not to caring about anything, then to knowing both what one really cares about and the real nature of what one cares about.

Gerald Cohen addresses Frankfurt's account of bullshit. He singles out two respects in which the account appears to be incomplete. First, in claiming that indifference to truth is the essence of bullshit, Frankfurt overlooks a second mode of discourse—"unclarifiable unclarity"—to which, according to Cohen, the term also applies. Second, Frankfurt misrepresents the relationship between even his variety of bullshit and lying; and this reflects his failure to distinguish the bullshitter's *tactics* from his *goals*. To the extent that some bullshit presupposes an indifference to truth, Cohen argues, the indifference is at the level of tactics: though the bullshitter is indifferent to whether he utters the truth, he may have a keen interest in whether he causes others to believe something false. Having raised these issues regarding Frankfurt's account, Cohen turns, in his essay's concluding pages, to examine the unclarifiable discourse that especially interests him.

At the conclusion of his own essay on bullshit, Frankfurt writes, "As conscious beings, we exist only in response to other things, and we cannot know ourselves at all without knowing them." But which responses to other things are warranted? What is the basis of this warrant? To what extent is it located in us? And to what extent in the things themselves? What is the relationship between the power of our responses and their authority? And under what circumstances are these responses truly our own?

The essays in this volume address these questions. And in each of his replies, Frankfurt responds to the challenge to clarify and defend his own answers. As we, the readers, follow the many overlapping discussions, the claims and counterclaims enter our own reflections. They force these reflections to take new directions, directions no introduction can possibly sum up.

1

Frankfurt-Style Compatibilism

John Martin Fischer

I Introduction

Many philosophers have worried that God's existence (understood in a certain way) or causal determinism (the doctrine that nonrelational features of the past, together with the laws of nature, are causally sufficient for all truths about the present and future) would rule out moral responsibility. One influential reason for this discomfort, although certainly not the only reason, is that it is plausible to suppose that God's existence (construed in a certain way) or causal determinism would rule out "genuine" alternative possibilities. If moral responsibility requires this sort of alternative possibility (at least at some relevant point along the path to behavior), then it would seem that God's existence or causal determinism would be incompatible with moral responsibility.

The thought that moral responsibility requires genuine alternative possibilities—the freedom to will, choose, or do otherwise—has been and continues to be an important motivation for incompatibilism about such doctrines as God's existence or causal determinism and moral responsibility. It is quite natural to suppose that if we have only one option that is genuinely available to us, then we *have* to do what we actually do, and that if we have to do what we actually do, we are *compelled* so to behave. But if we are compelled to behave as we actually do, then surely we cannot legitimately be held morally responsible for what we do.

Joel Feinberg employs the analogy between an individual making decisions about his life and a train going down the railroad tracks. Having genuine freedom—the sort that grounds our moral responsibility— corresponds, on Feinberg's model, to a train's having more than one track available to it. If our lives correspond to a train chugging down a track which is the only track it can take, then it follows, according to Feinberg, that we "could take no credit or blame for any of [our] achievements, and [we] could no more be responsible for [our] lives than are robots, or the trains in our ... metaphor that must run on 'predestined grooves.'"[1] Feinberg here articulates the powerful and influential idea that in order to be morally responsible, we must have more than one option. The future must be a branching, treelike structure; following Borges, the future must be a "garden of forking paths."

Because of the presupposed link between moral responsibility (and even personhood) and alternative possibilities, an extraordinary amount of attention has been given to arguments purporting to establish that God's existence or causal determinism do indeed rule out the relevant sorts of alternative possibilities. Much ingenuity has been displayed on both sides. But today, after literally thousands of years of debates about these issues, there is still heated disagreement about whether God's existence (understood in certain ways) or causal determinism rules out alternative possibilities.

Given this disagreement, and the fact (I believe it to be a fact) that rational people can disagree about whether the doctrines in question are indeed incompatible with the relevant sort of alternative possibilities (that is, the fact that there is no *knockdown* argument for incompatibilism), we seem to have arrived at a certain kind of stalemate. In my view, Harry Frankfurt has helped us to make considerable progress in this dialectic context. Frankfurt has presented a set of examples that appear to show that moral responsibility does not after all require alternative possibilities. If he is correct about this, then we can admit that it is plausible that God's existence or causal determinism would rule out alternative possibilities but still maintain that we can reasonably be thought to be morally responsible (even in a causally determined world or a world in which an essentially omniscient, temporal God exists). Slightly more carefully, Frankfurt has helped us to shift the debate away from issues pertaining to alternative possibilities to issues related to the actual sequence of events leading to the behavior in question. In my view, this is an important contribution, even if it does not in itself decisively establish compatibilism about (say) causal determinism and moral responsibility.

In this essay I shall begin by sketching a "Frankfurt-type example." I shall then lay out a disturbing challenge to the claim I have made above that these examples help us to make significant progress in the debates about the relationship between moral responsibility and causal determinism. (In the discussion that follows, I focus mainly on causal determinism, although I believe the points will in most instances apply equally to God's existence.)[2] I then will provide a reply to this challenge, and the reply will point toward a more refined formulation of the important contribution I believe Frankfurt has made to defending a certain sort of compatibilism.

II   Frankfurt-type Examples

Here is a particular version of a "Frankfurt-type example."[3] In this sort of case, a crucial role is played by some kind of involuntary sign or indication of the agent's future choices and behavior.[4] So suppose Jones is in a voting booth deliberating about whether to vote for Gore or Bush. (He has left this decision until the end, much as some restaurant patrons wait until the waiter asks before making a final decision about their meal.) After some reflection, he chooses to vote for Gore, and does vote for Gore by marking his ballot in the normal way. Unbeknownst to him, Black, a liberal neurosurgeon working with the Democratic party, has implanted a device in Jones's brain that monitors Jones's brain activities. If he is about to choose to vote Democratic, the device simply continues monitoring and does not intervene in the process in any way. If, however, Jones is about to choose to vote (say) Republican, the device triggers an intervention that involves electronic stimulation of the brain sufficient to produce a choice to vote for the Democrat (and a subsequent Democratic vote).

How can the device tell whether Jones is about to choose to vote Republican or Democrat? This is where the "prior sign" comes in. If Jones is about to choose at t_2 to vote for Gore at t_3, he shows some involuntary sign—say a neurological pattern in his brain—at t_1. Detecting this, Black's device does not intervene. But if Jones is about to choose at t_2 to vote for Bush at t_3, he shows an involuntary sign—a different neurological pattern in his brain—at t_1. This brain pattern would trigger Black's device to intervene and cause Jones to choose at t_2 to vote for Gore, and to vote for Gore at t_3.

Given that the device plays no role in Jones's deliberations and act of voting, it seems to me that Jones acts freely and is morally responsible for voting for Gore. And given the presence of Black's device, it is plausible to think that Jones does not have alternative possibilities with regard to his choice and action. Thus Frankfurt-type cases seem to sever the putative connection between moral responsibility and alternative possibilities; they appear to show the falsity of the Principle of Alternate Possibilities (PAP): A person is morally responsible for what he has done only if he could have done otherwise. And if moral responsibility does not require alternative possibilities, then if causal determinism threatens moral responsibility, it would not do so in virtue of ruling out alternative possibilities.

III   The Challenge

The idea that Frankfurt-type examples help to pave the way for compatibilism has been challenged by various philosophers.[5] The challenge can usefully be put in terms of a dilemma: the Frankfurt-type stories presuppose either that causal determinism is true, or that it is false. If the former, then the claim that the relevant agent is morally responsible is question-begging, and if the latter, then the claim that the agent lacks alternative possibilities is false.

Let us start with the presupposition that causal determinism obtains. It does appear as if the relevant agent—Jones, in the example above—cannot choose or do otherwise (cannot choose at t_2 to vote for Bush or vote for Bush at t_3). This is because the "counterfactual intervener"—the liberal neurosurgeon, Black—can know, given the prior sign exhibited by Jones at t_1, that Jones will indeed choose to vote for Gore at t_2. If Jones were to choose at t_2 to vote for Bush, the prior sign would have had to have been different; thus Jones cannot at t_2 choose to vote for Bush. But the problem is that the contention that Jones is morally responsible for choosing to vote for Gore, and actually voting for Gore, is put in doubt, given the assumption of causal determinism.

That is, if causal determinism is assumed, it does not seem that someone could say that Jones is obviously morally responsible for his actual choice and action in a context in which the relationship between causal determinism and moral responsibility is at issue. To do so would appear to beg the question against the incompatibilist.

Laura Ekstrom is a good example of a philosopher who insists that if causal determinism is assumed to be true, then one cannot infer that the agent in question is morally responsible for his behavior.[6] Ekstrom says:

[Let us] focus our attention on the fact that causal determinism might be true. If it is true, then past events together with the laws of nature are together sufficient for Jones's making the particular decision he makes.... So Jones's subjective perception of available options is irrelevant; in fact, the past pushes him into one particular decision state, the only state physically possible at the time, given the past and the laws of nature.... In fact, according to the incompatibilist, if determinism is true, Jones should not be judged as morally responsible for his decision and his act, given the pushing feature of determinism ... so P.A.P. is not defeated.[7]

In further support of her view, Ekstrom says:

Whether or not determinism is true *ought* to be relevant [to our intuitions concerning Jones's moral responsibility]—this is precisely what incompatibilist arguments are designed to show. According to the incompatibilists, our everyday notions concerning our own and others' freedom and moral responsibility in acting can be shown to be, upon reflection, in need of revision if the thesis of causal determinism is true.[8]

Now consider the other horn of the dilemma: that is, suppose that indeterminism (of a certain relevant sort) obtains. Under this supposition it would not be dialectically inappropriate to claim that Jones is morally responsible for his actual choice at t_2 to vote for Gore and his vote for Gore at t_3. But now the contention that Jones cannot choose at t_2 to vote for Bush at t_3 is called into question. This is because there is no deterministic relationship between the prior sign exhibited by Jones at t_1 and Jones's subsequent choice at t_2. So, if we consider the time just prior to t_2, everything about the past can be just as it is consistently with Jones's choosing at t_2 to vote for Bush. Someone might think that if it takes some time for Jones to make the choice, Black can intervene to prevent the completion of the choice; but then Jones will still have the possibility of "beginning to make the choice."

The proponents of the Frankfurt-type examples contend that they are non-question-begging cases in which an agent is morally responsible for his choice and action and yet has no sufficiently robust alternative possibilities. But the challenge appears to show that the examples in question are either not uncontroversial cases in which the agent is morally responsible for his choice and subsequent behavior, or not cases in which the agent lacks alternative possibilities.

IV   Reply

The Assumption of Indeterminism

In giving my strategy for replying to the challenge, I want to start with the assumption of causal indeterminism. The idea behind the worry here is that although the agent can legitimately be deemed morally responsible, there are ineliminable alternative possibilities (given the assumption of indeterminism). I will only sketch the sort of reply I would be inclined to pursue, because I want to focus here on the assumption of causal determinism.

The first thing to say is that various philosophers, including Eleonore Stump, Alfred Mele and David Robb, and David Hunt, have argued that one can indeed construct versions of the Frankfurt-type examples in which it is both the case that indeterminism obtains and there are *no* alternative possibilities.[9] As I have discussed these versions of the Frankfurt-type examples in some detail elsewhere, I shall here simply say that I find these examples, and similar indeterministic Frankfurt-type examples, intriguing and highly suggestive.[10] They may indeed show that one can construct Frankfurt-type examples that explicitly presuppose indeterminism in which there are *no* alternative possibilities.

It may, however, turn out that even in these examples there emerge alternative possibilities of certain sorts; here I would, however, pursue the argument (which I have developed elsewhere) that the alternative possibilities in question are not sufficiently *robust* to ground attributions of moral responsibility.[11] That is, I would argue that it is not enough for the critic of the Frankfurt-type examples to argue that there exist *some* alternative possibilities in the cases, no matter how flimsy or exiguous; if one grounds moral responsibility in alternative possibilities, I believe they must be *of a certain sort*. Someone who believes in the "garden of forking paths" picture (according to which alternative possibilities are necessary for moral responsibility) should also believe that those alternative possibilities are sufficiently robust. The mere possibility of unintentional or involuntary behavior—behavior for which the agent is not morally responsible—does not seem to me to offer sufficient substance on which to base one's attributions of moral responsibility. As in the debates about the relationship between libertarianism and control, there is a crucial difference between the *ability* to do otherwise and the *mere possibility* of something different happening. The same point applies to the debates about the Frankfurt-type cases.

So my view is that either one can entirely expunge alternative possibilities—even in the context of indeterminism in the actual sequence—or the remaining alternative possibilities will not be sufficiently robust. This is not surprising, because I would suggest that what we *value* in action for which an agent can legitimately be held morally responsible is *not* that he makes a certain sort of difference to the world, but rather, that he expresses himself in a certain way. And this sort of self-expression does not require alternative possibilities. I have argued elsewhere that adopting this view about the intuitive picture behind our ascriptions of moral responsibility—that what we value, in behavior for which the agent can fairly be held morally responsible, is a distinctive kind of self-expression—can make it considerably more plausible that moral responsibility does not in fact require alternative possibilities.[12]

The Assumption of Causal Determinism

Let's now suppose that causal determinism is true. Under this assumption, it is unfair and question-begging simply to assert that the relevant agent—say, Jones—is morally responsible for his behavior. But the proponent of Frankfurt-style compatibilism should not—and need not—make such an assertion at this point.[13] Rather, the argument is in two parts. The first step is to argue—based on the Frankfurt-type examples—that intuitively it is plausible that alternative possibilities are irrelevant to ascriptions of moral responsibility. If one agrees with this point, the preliminary conclusion could be stated as follows: if the agent (say, Jones) is not morally responsible for his behavior, this is *not* in virtue of his lacking alternative possibilities. That is, the proponent of Frankfurt-style compatibilism does *not* assert, simply on the basis of Frankfurt-type examples, that the relevant agent is morally responsible for his behavior. Such a compatibilist should not take any stand about the responsibility of the agent simply on the basis of reflection on the Frankfurt-type examples. He should just say, "I don't know at this point whether the agent is morally responsible for his behavior, but *if* he is not, it is *not* because he lacks alternative possibilities."

Thus Frankfurt-type examples have the important function of *shifting the debate* away from considerations pertinent to the relationship between causal determinism and alternative possibilities. What now becomes important is to consider whether causal determinism in the actual sequence can plausibly be thought *directly* to rule out moral responsibility, independently of considerations relating to alternative possibilities. It is important to see that the issues here are different. That is, causal determinism is alleged to rule out alternative possibilities in virtue of deeply plausible principles encapsulating the "fixity of the past" and the "fixity of the natural laws." If causal determinism is true, then the past, together with the natural laws, entails all truths about the present and future. So, if the past is fixed and the natural laws are fixed, it would seem that this leaves room for only one present and one future.[14] But such principles (encapsulating the fixity of the past and natural laws) can be embraced by a "semicompatibilist"—a compatibilist about causal determinism and moral responsibility who separates this claim from the claim of the compatibility of causal determinism and alternative possibilities. The factors that would allegedly show that causal determinism directly rules out moral responsibility are *different* from those that appear to show that causal determinism rules out alternative possibilities.

Some philosophers have evidently thought that Frankfurt-type compatibilism must fail insofar as the Frankfurt-type examples in themselves do not decisively establish the compatibility of causal determinism and moral responsibility. Michael Della Rocca argues that the relevance of alternative possibilities—even if they are mere flickers of freedom—is that they are a *sign* of the existence of actual-sequence indeterminism. If causal determination obtains in the actual sequence, then Della Rocca claims that one cannot conclude that the relevant agent is morally responsible.[15] Similarly, recall that Ekstrom has claimed that if causal determinism is assumed to be true, one cannot assert that the relevant agent is morally responsible, and thus "PAP is not defeated."

But the success of the Frankfurt-type strategy should not be judged on the basis of whether the Frankfurt-type cases in themselves decisively establish that moral responsibility is compatible with causal determinism.

That they do not do *all* the work does not show that they do not do *some* important work. For example, I believe that the Frankfurt-type cases *do* show the following principle false: (PAP*): Lacking alternative possibilities is a condition which in itself—and apart from anything that accompanies it (either contingently or necessarily)—makes it the case that an agent is not morally responsible for his behavior. That (PAP*) is shown to be false is real progress: now we should turn to the issue of whether something that (perhaps) accompanies the lack of alternative possibilities—actual-sequence causal determination—rules out moral responsibility *directly*. Of course, if the reasons to think that causal determination in the actual sequence rules out moral responsibility directly are just as strong as the reasons to think that causal determinism rules out alternative possibilities, then the progress would be illusory; but I shall be arguing in the rest of this paper that the reasons are *not* as strong.

V   Causal Determination in the Actual Sequence

The question now is this: does causal determination in the actual sequence *directly* rule out moral responsibility (i.e., does causal determinism rule out moral responsibility apart from ruling out alternative possibilities)? In my book, *The Metaphysics of Free Will: An Essay on Control*, I considered a number of reasons someone might think that causal determination directly rules out moral responsibility.[16] For example, an incompatibilist might insist that the presence of causal determination in the actual sequence is inconsistent with notions of "initiation," "origination," "being active rather than passive," or "creativity," where some (or all) of these notions are requirements of moral responsibility. On this approach, the incompatibilist does not rest his case on principles encapsulating the fixity of the past and the fixity of the laws (or modal "transfer principles" of any sort); rather, he rests his case on factors whose presence in the actual sequence allegedly directly rules out moral responsibility.

None of these notions, however, provides a compelling reason to opt for incompatibilism about causal determinism and moral responsibility. My argument (in *The Metaphysics of Free Will: An Essay on Control*) was that with respect to each of the notions in question—origination, initiation, activity, creativity, and so forth—there are compatibilist and incompatibilist interpretations, and, further, that there is no strong reason to opt for the incompatibilist interpretation, *apart from considerations pertaining to alternative possibilities*.[17] Thus there is no reason that a fair, reflective, and reasonable person not already committed to incompatibilism should conclude that causal determinism, in itself, and apart from considerations about alternative possibilities, is incompatible with moral responsibility. In the rest of this paper, I want to consider some other reasons it might be thought that causal determinism directly rules out moral responsibility; basically I will be defending and developing my view that there is no good reason a fair-minded person (not already committed to incompatibilism) should be convinced that causal determination in the actual sequence directly precludes moral responsibility.

Robert Kane's book, *The Significance of Free Will*, together with related articles, is perhaps the most comprehensive and thoughtful presentation of the motivation of incompatibilism (and also a positive account of libertarian freedom) of which I am aware.[18] Kane distinguishes two separate motivations for incompatibilism: a worry about alternative possibilities, and a worry about "ultimacy." To have "ultimate responsibility," according to Kane, agents must

have the power to be the *ultimate* producers of their own ends. . . . They have the *power to make choices which can only and finally be explained in terms of their own wills* (i.e., character, motives, and efforts of will). No one can have this power in a determined world.[19]

Thus Kane contends that quite apart from issues about alternative possibilities, the presence of causal determination in the actual sequence would be inconsistent with an agent's being "ultimately responsible" and so would rule out the agent's being morally responsible.

But why exactly must an agent have this sort of ultimate responsibility in order to be morally responsible? Someone could say that on reflection we have a deep preference not to be intermediate links in a deterministic causal chain that begins in events prior to our births. Perhaps *this* is the reason causal determinism rules out moral responsibility (quite apart from threatening alternative possibilities).

I find this answer puzzling and difficult to assess. One reason is that it seems to me to be dangerously close to, if not identical with, simply asserting that on reflection we have a deep preference that causal determinism (as applied to us) not be true. The question at issue is why exactly causal determinism in the actual sequence rules out moral responsibility *directly*. The answer that is proposed is that we can just see that we do not want it to be the case that our deliberations are simply intermediate links in a causally deterministic chain that begins before our births. But this answer does seem to me to be the assertion that we do not want it to be the case that causal determinism is true and thus that our behavior be causally determined. Perhaps this answer could be deemed "question-begging," or perhaps it is simply dialectically unhelpful. In any case, if the question at issue is why there is some reason to suppose that causal determination in the actual sequence directly rules out moral responsibility, and the dialectical context is one in which it is supposed that it is not *immediately obvious* that mere causal determination in the actual sequence directly rules out moral responsibility, then one must say more than that we object to being intermediate links in a deterministic causal chain.

When it is not the case that a person's choice and action are produced by a deterministic causal chain that starts with factors "external" to the person, Kane points out that it can be said of the person, "The buck stops here." Quite apart from wanting alternative possibilities, Kane suggests that we want it to be the case that the buck stops here. But, obviously, in this context, "The buck stops here" is a metaphor. If it simply stands for not being an intermediate link in a deterministic causal chain, then we are back to the problem that this does not make any dialectic progress.

A similar problem afflicts the view of Derk Pereboom, who claims that "if all of our behavior was 'in the cards' before we were born, in the sense that things happened before we came to exist that, by way of a deterministic causal process, inevitably result in our behavior, then we cannot legitimately be blamed for our wrongdoing."[20] Our behavior's "being in the cards" is obviously a metaphor. Pereboom means by this that conditions prior to our births "inevitably result in our behavior by a deterministic causal process." If the problematic notion of inevitability simply implies the notion of entailment, then Pereboom's claim just comes down to the unargued-for assumption that causal determination in the actual sequence rules out responsibility. Again, this is dialectically unhelpful. If "inevitability" also implies some sort of actual-sequence compulsion, this is question-begging within the dialectic context. *Why* exactly is it the case that one's behavior's being "in the cards," in the relevant sense, involves problematic compulsion and thus directly rules out moral responsibility?

I think it is interesting that, once the debate is shifted away from the relationship between causal determinism and alternative possibilities, it is difficult to present a non-question-begging reason why causal determinism rules out moral responsibility. I can however identify various additional resources in Kane's work which could be employed to explain why it is that we would object to the presence of causal determination in the actual sequence (apart from worries about alternative possibilities). The first idea seems to be that if we allow for moral responsibility when there is actual-sequence causal determination, then we will need to say that agents who are covertly manipulated in objectionable ways are also morally responsible.

Kane distinguishes between "constraining" and "nonconstraining" manipulation or "control."[21] Constraining control thwarts preexisting desires, values, ends, and purposes. But nonconstraining manipulation (or, in Kane's term, "control") actually implants the desires, values, ends, and purposes. When the nonconstraining control is covert (CNC), the agent is unaware of it. Kane says:

We are well aware of these two ways to get others to do our bidding in everyday life. We may force them to do what we want by coercing or constraining them against their wills, which is constraining or CC control. Or we may manipulate them into doing what we want while making them feel that they have made up their own minds and are acting "of their own free wills"—which is covert non-constraining or CNC control. Cases of CNC control in larger settings are provided by examples of behavioral engineering such as we find in utopian works like Aldous Huxley's *Brave New World* or B. F. Skinner's *Walden Two*. Frazier, the fictional founder of Skinner's Walden Two, gives a clear description of CNC control when he says that in his community persons can do whatever they want or choose, but they have been conditioned since childhood to want and choose only what they can have or do.[22]

As Kane points out, the citizens of Walden Two are "satisfied" with themselves; they do not have inner motivational conflicts and they are marvelously "wholehearted" in their attitudes and engagements.[23] Indeed, Frazier, the founder of Walden Two, describes it as the "freest place on earth."[24]

Kane's point is that someone who allows for moral responsibility in the presence of actual-sequence causal determination will also have to allow for it in contexts like Walden Two. His suggestion is that once one concerns oneself with the *sources* of one's purposes and ends, this will necessarily lead to incompatibilism.[25] But I disagree. A compatibilist will certainly insist that not all causal chains are relevantly similar. The kind of manipulation that takes place in Walden Two does indeed rule out moral responsibility; for a compatibilist, this can be in virtue of the *specific nature* of the causal sequences that issue in behavior, rather than the *mere fact* of causal determination.

For example, on the approach to compatibilism I favor, one looks carefully at the *history* of the behavior in question. If there is unconsented-to covert manipulation of certain sorts, this can be the sort of historical factor that rules out moral responsibility. On my approach, one demands that the behavior issue from the agent's own suitably reasons-sensitive mechanism. That is, the agent must—in a specified sense—have "ownership" of the process that leads to the behavior, and this process must be appropriately sensitive to reasons. These conditions are not met in the objectionable cases of CNC, and yet I would argue that they can be met in a context of mere causal determination.[26]

One might press all sorts of worries about the particular account I have simply gestured at here. But the key point is that a compatibilist can offer a robustly historical theory of moral responsibility. A compatibilist may well offer plausible ways of distinguishing between objectionable sorts of manipulation and mere causal determination. In reply to this sort of point, Kane says that in the cases of CNC and mere causal determination, the agents are *equally* unable to choose or do otherwise; that is, alternative possibilities are expunged as effectively by mere determination as by problematic manipulation.[27] I am willing to grant this, but this point is irrelevant to the issue of whether causal determination in the actual sequence *directly* rules out moral responsibility. It is in no way obvious that a compatibilist cannot usefully distinguish between the *actual sequences* involved in problematic manipulation and those involved in mere causal determination.

It is helpful to see how the sort of compatibilism envisaged here—semicompatibilism—differs from old-style compatibilism. Both sorts of compatibilism insist on the point that not all causal sequences are relevantly similar. But old-style compatibilism sought to defend the idea that when the causally deterministic sequence is not "problematic," then the agent has a genuine ability or freedom to choose and do otherwise. In contrast, semicompatibilism concedes that the mere fact of causal determination rules out alternative possibilities; nevertheless, it seeks to sort through the actual pathways to the behavior in question, distinguishing between those pathways that confer responsibility and those that do not. In doing so, the view can look carefully at the *sources* of an agent's values, preferences, purposes, and ends; it can attend to how the agent got to be the way he is.[28]

Kane gives great emphasis to a second point, which is related to his view that a compatibilist cannot adequately account for contexts of covert nonconstraining control. He claims that the causal determination of all of an agent's behavior is inconsistent with the agent's having "objective worth."[29] To develop the notion of objective worth, Kane tells the story of Alan the artist:

Alan has been so despondent that a rich friend concocts a scheme to lift his spirits. The friend arranges to have Alan's paintings bought by confederates at the local art gallery under assumed names for $10,000 apiece. Alan mistakenly assumes his paintings are being recognized for their artistic merit by knowledgeable critics and collectors, and his spirits are lifted. Now let us imagine two possible worlds involving Alan. The first is the one just described, in which Alan thinks he is a great artist, and thinks he is being duly recognized as such, but really is not. The other imagined world is a similar one in which Alan has many of the same experiences, including the belief that he is a great artist. But in this second world he really is a great artist and really is being recognized as such; his rich friend is not merely deceiving him to lift his spirits. Finally, let us imagine that in both these worlds Alan dies happily, believing he is a great artist, though only in the second world was his belief correct.[30]

Kane points out that although Alan would feel equally happy in both worlds, most of us would say that there is an important difference in value in the two worlds for Alan. To say this, for Kane, is to accept some notion of "objective worth," according to which value is not simply a function of subjective states or experiences. So far so good. But Kane goes on to say:

I want to suggest that the notion of ultimate responsibility is of a piece with this notion of objective worth. If, like Alan, we think that the objective worth of our acts or accomplishments is something valuable over and above the felt satisfaction the acts have or bring, then I suggest we will be inclined to think that a freedom requiring ultimate responsibility is valuable over and above compatibilist freedoms from coercion, compulsion, and oppression. . . . [I]f objective worth means little to us, or makes no sense—if we believe that the final perspective Alan or anyone should take is *inside* the worlds, in which subjective happiness is all that counts (even if it is based on deception)—we are likely to see no point or significance as well in ultimate responsibility and incompatibilist freedom.[31]

But, again, I disagree with Kane's contention that the compatibilist is saddled with the unattractive view. It is admittedly the case that some compatibilist views focus solely on structural arrangements of mental states.[32] But this is not essential to compatibilism. As I pointed out above, the view I favor is *historical.* I have argued elsewhere that there are two problems with purely structural accounts of moral responsibility (such as the hierarchical model): they are ahistorical, and they do not attend to the *connections* between the agent and the world.[33] My compatibilist account of moral responsibility is sensitive to history and it demands certain connections between the agent and the reasons provided by the world.[34] Just as a compatibilist account of moral responsibility can have these features (in virtue of which it is not purely structural), so a compatibilist can certainly agree with the view that there is "objective" worth in the sense that value is not purely a function of experiences— one must be connected to the world in the right way. (I also do not see why even a purely structural or "internalistic" compatibilist could not have an objective view about value, which is, after all, a *different* notion from moral responsibility.) There is absolutely *nothing* about compatibilism that requires a purely subjective account of value.

The attempts discussed above to argue that causal determination of behavior rules out moral responsibility apart from considerations pertinent to alternative possibilities are unconvincing. I now want to explore what Kane takes to be a related theme—the idea of independence. Kane says:

. . . when one traces the desires we have for incompatibilist free will to their roots, by way of [the idea of ultimate responsibility], one eventually arrives at two elemental (and I think interrelated) desires—(i) the desire to be independent sources of activity in the world, which is connected, I maintain, from the earliest stages of childhood to the sense we have of our uniqueness and importance as individuals; and (ii) the desire that some of our deeds and accomplishments (such as Alan's paintings in my example) have objective worth. . . .[35]

But what exactly is it to be an "independent" source of activity? At this point in the dialectical context, one cannot say that the relevant notion of independence requires that, given the agent's past and environmental niche, he has alternative possibilities; and as we have seen, one cannot simply argue that the relevant notion of independence is captured by the claim that we prefer not to be an intermediate link in a deterministic causal chain.

Alfred Mele has offered a useful suggestion here.[36] This is the idea: an agent is independent, in the relevant sense, according to the incompatibilist, insofar as he makes an explanatory contribution to his behavior, the making of which cannot be fully explained by the laws of nature and the state of the world at some time prior to his having any sense of the apparent options.[37] If an agent's making a contribution to his behavior is fully explained by reference to prior conditions and the laws of nature, then he is not independent in the relevant sense; and of course if there is causal determination in the actual sequence leading to behavior, then the agent's contributions can in fact be entirely explained by prior conditions and the laws of nature. The desire for this sort of independence can then be offered as a reason why causal determination in the actual sequence would rule out moral responsibility quite apart from issues pertaining to alternative possibilities.

Kane attributes great importance to the requirement of incompatibilistic independence. As we saw above, Kane connects this sort of independence to one's "uniqueness and importance as an individual." Kane says, "What determinism takes away is a certain sense of the importance of oneself as an individual."[38] In a further elaboration of this view, Kane quotes William James, from his essay, "The Dilemma of Determinism": "The great point [about the incompatibilist view] is that the possibilities are really *here*. At those soul-trying moments when fate's scales seem to quiver [we acknowledge] that the issue is decided nowhere else than *here* and *now*. *That* is what gives the palpitating reality to our moral life and makes it tingle ... with so strange and elaborate an excitement."[39] About this passage from James, Kane says, "It may be easy to ridicule James's assertion that a certain passion and excitement would be taken out of present and future choice situations if we believed their outcomes were determined. But many ordinary persons and philosophers, myself included, would say that it is true."[40]

If causal determinism were true, would our importance as individuals be diminished? Would the passion, the thrill of life be gone? I don't have any inclination to think so. Imagine that a consortium of scientists from

Cal Tech, Stanford, and MIT announced that despite the previous scientific views, it turns out that the equations that describe the universe are deterministic. That is, the previous indeterministic views—which posited tiny residual indeterminacies at the macro-level based on quantum indeterminacies at the micro-level—were based on inadequacies in our understanding of nature, and the new view is that the equations are universal generalizations. Would you conclude that your life lacks importance, that its importance is significantly diminished, or that your deliberations are empty and meaningless? I certainly would not.

I grant that those who are strongly predisposed to incompatibilism will cling to the requirement of independence (interpreted as above). They think of us as having what might be called the "importance of independence." But there is another sort of importance, which is, in my view, at least as compelling; let us call this the "importance of indispensability." Note that even if causal determinism obtains, invocation of prior states of the world plus the natural laws cannot explain our behavior and its upshots without *also* explaining that *we make a certain sort of contribution to them*. That is, the prior conditions and laws of nature explain what happens only by also explaining that we make a certain sort of contribution—that our deliberations have a certain character, for example. The very factors that explain what happens cannot explain the way the world actually unfolds without *also* explaining that we make a certain sort of contribution through (for example) our unhindered deliberations.[41]

Thus, in a causally deterministic world, although we would lack the importance of independence (interpreted as above), we could have the importance of indispensability. By "unhindered" deliberations I mean deliberations not impaired by factors *uncontroversially* thought to rule out moral responsibility, such as certain sorts of hypnosis, manipulation, subliminal advertising, coercion, and so forth.[42] I believe that when one engages in unhindered deliberation in a causally deterministic world, one can exercise a certain sort of control; this is a kind of "actual-sequence" control, which does not require the presence of alternative possibilities. If this view is correct, then in a causally deterministic world, invocation of prior conditions together with the laws of nature cannot explain what happens without also explaining that the agent exercises a certain sort of control in contributing to it. Such an agent can surely be important, and—leaving aside the tingling sensation referred to by James—his deliberations can certainly have all the passion and engagement that it is reasonable to want.

Recall Robert Kane's metaphor, "The buck stops here." With apologies to Harry Truman, the compatibilist can suggest an alternative metaphor. To quote—or perhaps I should concede, paraphrase—the former Green Bay Packer, Ray Nitschke (not to be confused with the philosopher, Friedrich Nietzsche!), "To get there from here, you have to go through me, baby."

Now the dialectical situation is as follows. We have discussed two different notions of importance related to the explanatory role of prior conditions, the laws of nature, and the self—the importance of independence and the importance of indispensability. I suppose that certain people who are strongly predisposed to incompatibilism will insist on the requirement of independence (as interpreted above) for moral responsibility. But it seems to me that the importance of indispensability is at least an equally attractive notion. It is not obvious that one should prefer the requirement of independence (as interpreted above) to the requirement of indispensability. Given the compatibilistic notion of the importance of indispensability, I do not think that a fair-minded, reasonable person not already committed to incompatibilism will conclude that incompatibilistic independence is a requirement of moral responsibility. The compatibilist, then, can offer an attractive account of the sort of importance related to the explanatory role of prior conditions. Further, it is clear that the compatibilist can offer his own account of "independence," which would posit a freedom from certain *objectionable* kinds of influences (but not necessarily all prior states of the universe and the laws of nature).

Return now to Laura Ekstrom's contention that, if there is causal determination in the actual sequence, "the past pushes [the agent] into one particular decision state, the only state physically possible at the time, given the past and the laws of nature...." It seems to me that Ekstrom's idea faces the same problems as the various suggestions discussed above. There is a commonsense notion of "pushing," according to which there is a difference between (say) being pushed by a strong gust of wind and simply walking normally down a trail. On this notion of "pushing," one would not necessarily be pushed by the past and laws of nature, given causal determinism. Of course, one could adopt a special incompatibilist notion of pushing, but this will only be attractive to those already strongly inclined toward incompatibilism, and not to reasonable and fair-minded persons not already strongly committed to a particular view about the compatibility issue.

I suppose Ekstrom could seek to argue that on the commonsense notion of "pushing," the laws of nature push. But there are various different accounts of what makes a generalization a law of nature. On many of these accounts, which have considerable plausibility, there would be no inclination whatsoever to say that laws of nature must "push." On some views, laws of nature do not "necessitate";[43] on other views, laws of nature necessitate, but this necessitation may be cashed out in ways which should not incline one to say that the laws push. So, for example, some would argue that one feature that makes a generalization a law of nature is that it "supports its counterfactuals" in a certain way; surely, however, this feature in itself does not entail problematic "pushing."

To elaborate. On the Stalnaker/Lewis account of the semantics for counterfactuals, the truth of a counterfactual is determined by the similarity-relations among possible worlds.[44] (Very roughly, "If P were the case, then Q would be the case" is true, on this approach, just in case Q is true in the possible world or worlds most similar to the actual world in which P is true.) Employing this approach to the truth conditions for counterfactuals, one could say that what helps to distinguish between mere generalizations and the laws of nature is the similarity-relations among various possible worlds. But this in itself does not seem to imply that the laws of nature "push" in any objectionable way, and it is hard to see how this, in combination with other factors, would have this sort of implication. Thus, as far as I can see, there is *no* reason that would compel a person not already committed to incompatibilism to think that causal determination in the actual sequence rules out moral responsibility *directly* (i.e., apart from ruling out alternative possibilities).

VI Conclusion

I said above that the Frankfurt-type examples have helped to shift the debates about free will and moral responsibility from considerations about alternative possibilities to factors present in the "actual-sequence." I now want to return explicitly to the issue of whether this is genuine—or merely illusory—progress. The progress would be merely illusory if the reasons to think that causal determination in the actual sequence rules out moral responsibility are just as strong as the reasons to think that causal determinism rules out alternative possibilities.

But I do *not* think that this is so. I believe that a reasonable person, having fairly considered the arguments, should conclude that causal determinism rules out alternative possibilities. The argument to this conclusion from the principles encapsulating the fixity of the past and the fixity of the natural laws seems to me to be strong. I do not think that the argument here is knockdown, or that any rational person needs to accept it simply in virtue of his rationality. But I believe that the argument that causal determinism rules out alternative possibilities is a valid argument based on premises that any fair-minded and reasonable person really *should* accept: the relevant notions of the fixity of the past and laws are deeply embedded in common sense.

In contrast, I do not think that any reasonable and fair-minded person, not already strongly predisposed to or antecedently committed to incompatibilism, should conclude that causal determination in the actual sequence *directly* rules out moral responsibility. There are various factors one might consider here: initiation, creativity, activity, freedom from objectionable manipulation, objective value, importance, and so forth. But for each notion there is a compatibilist account as well as an incompatibilist account. And it seems to me that there is no good reason to think that a reasonable and fair-minded person, not already committed to incompatibilism, should embrace the incompatibilist notion. Of course, the arguments sketched above will not convince a person who comes to the discussion with strong incompatibilist inclinations or is already firmly committed to incompatibilism; but I don't think any argument could do that, and this is certainly not a fair test of success.

So we should not accept the conclusion of the party-poopers who claim that Frankfurt-style compatibilism is not successful. Frankfurt-style compatibilism does represent a genuine advance; Frankfurt has helped to shift the debates from a context in which incompatibilism has an advantage to one in which incompatibilism has no such advantage.[45] If one believes—as I do—that there is a good "positive" reason to adopt compatibilism insofar as our basic views about ourselves—our views of ourselves as persons and as morally responsible—should not be held hostage to the discoveries of a consortium of scientists about the precise nature of the equations that describe the universe, then the progress made by Frankfurt can at least help to clear the way to embracing compatibilism.[46]

Acknowledgments

I am indebted to thoughtful questions and comments by Michael Zimmerman, Win-Chiat Lee, and Harry Frankfurt at the conference, "Contours of Agency: The Philosophy of Harry Frankfurt," Wake Forest University, November 1999. I am especially grateful to the probing and detailed written comments by the editors, Sarah Buss and Lee Overton. I am privileged to be included among such distinguished philosophers in this volume in honor of a man whose work sets the standard for originality and elegance: Harry Frankfurt.

Notes

1. Joel Feinberg, "The Interest of Liberty on the Scales," in his *Rights, Justice, and the Bounds of Liberty: Essays in Social Philosophy* (Princeton: Princeton University Press, 1980), 36–40.

2. Whether this is the case will depend on how one understands God's attributes, and, in particular, whether God's providential activities involve causation of the human will.

3. The classic presentation is in Harry Frankfurt, "Alternate Possibilities and Moral Responsibility," in *The Importance of What We Care About* (Cambridge: Cambridge University Press, 1988).

4. For this kind of Frankfurt-type case, see David Blumenfeld, "The Principle of Alternate Possibilities," *Journal of Philosophy* 67 (1971): 339–344.

5. For such skepticism, see (among others) David Widerker, "Libertarian Freedom and the Avoidability of Decisions," *Faith and Philosophy* 12 (1995): 113–118; and "Libertarianism and Frankfurt's Attack on the Principle of Alternative Possibilities," *Philosophical Review* 104 (1995): 247–261; Robert Kane, *Free Will and Values* (Albany: State University of New York Press, 1985), 51; and *The Significance of Free Will* (New York and Oxford: Oxford University Press, 1996), esp. 142–145; Carl Ginet, "In Defense of the Principle of Alternative Possibilities: Why I Don't Find Frankfurt's Argument Convincing," *Philosophical Perspectives* 10 (1996): 403–417; Keith D. Wyma, "Moral Responsibility and Leeway for Action," *American Philosophical Quarterly* 34 (1997): 57–70; and Laura Ekstrom, "Protecting Incompatibilist Freedom," *American Philosophical Quarterly* 35 (1998): 281–291.

6. Ekstrom, "Protecting Incompatibilist Freedom."

7. Ibid., 284–285.

8. Ibid., 284.

9. Hunt employs what might be called a "blockage" case, rather than a "prior-sign" case. This sort of case takes its cue from John Locke's example of a man who is, unbeknownst to him, locked in a room and decides voluntarily to remain in the room. In Hunt's case, although the brain actually works by an indeterministic process, all other neural pathways (all neural pathways not actually taken) are blocked (as in the locked door of John Locke's example). David P. Hunt, "Moral Responsibility and Unavoidable Action, " *Philosophical Studies* 97 (2000): 195–227. Mele and Robb present a case in which there are two actually operating sequences—one indeterministic and the other deterministic—which simultaneously result in the agent's decision (in which case the indeterministic sequence preempts the deterministic sequence). Alfred R. Mele and David Robb, "Rescuing Frankfurt-Style Cases," *Philosophical Review* 107 (1998): 97–112. And Stump employs the plausible idea that one could correlate a certain stream of neural events with mental events such as choices or decisions; in her cases, the "counterfactual interveners" (the analogues to Black) can anticipate an impending mental event (of the relevant sort) by "reading" or detecting the *beginnings* of the neural sequence. Stump argues that they can thereby cut off the *mental event* (as opposed to the correlated neural sequence) before it even begins. Eleonore Stump, "Non-Cartesian Dualism and Materialism with Reductionism," *Faith and Philosophy* 12 (1995): 505–531; "Libertarian Freedom and the Principle of Alternate Possibilities," in *Faith, Freedom, and Rationality: Philosophy of Religion Today*, eds. Daniel Howard-Snyder and Jeff Jordan (Lanham, Maryland: Rowman and Littlefield, 1996), 73–88; and "Alternative Possibilities and Responsibility: The Flicker of Freedom," unpublished manuscript delivered at the American Philosophical Association Pacific Division Meetings, March 1998, Los Angeles, California.

10. For a more careful description and evaluation of these sorts of indeterministic Frankfurt-type cases, see John Martin Fischer, "Recent Work on Moral Responsibility," *Ethics* 110 (1999): 93–139, esp. 113–123.

11. John Martin Fischer, *The Metaphysics of Free Will: An Essay on Control* (Oxford: Blackwell Publishers, 1994), 131–159; and "Responsibility and Self-Expression," *Journal of Ethics* 3 (1999): 277–297.

12. Fischer, "Responsibility and Self-Expression."

13. I sketch this sort of reply in Fischer, "Recent Work on Moral Responsibility."

14. For a development and discussion of such arguments, and the parallel argument with respect to God's foreknowledge, see Fischer, *The Metaphysics of Free Will*.

15. Michael Della Rocca, "Frankfurt, Fischer and Flickers," *Nous* 32 (1998): 99–105. Indeed, he begins the article with the statement, "In this paper, I argue that John Martin Fischer's most recent argument for the compatibility of causal determinism and moral responsibility does not succeed" (99).

16. Fischer, *The Metaphysics of Free Will*, esp. 149–154.

17. For an elaboration of this argument, see Fischer, *The Metaphysics of Free Will*, 147–154.

18. Kane, *The Significance of Free Will*.

19. Robert Kane, "Two Kinds of Incompatibilism," *Philosophy and Phenomenological Research* 50 (1989), 254.

20. Derk Pereboom, "Alternative Possibilities and Causal Histories," chapter 1 of *Living without Free Will* (Department of Philosophy, University of Vermont, Burlington, unpublished manuscript).

21. Kane, *The Significance of Free Will*, 64–71.

22. Ibid., 65.

23. Ibid., 65.

24. B. F. Skinner, *Walden Two* (New York: MacMillan, 1962), 297; as cited in Kane, *The Significance of Free Will*, 65.

25. A similar point is made by Ekstrom:

But the model of a person as chugging along on a certain line of straight train tracks, without any forks in the path, is the antithesis of a deep-seated and pervasive image of ourselves as free agents. The idea that we can direct our behavior by our thoughts (desires, beliefs, intentions) is welcome, but it is only superficially comforting. It comforts until we think about the possibility that even our thoughts are driven to be what they are by previous neurophysiological events which themselves stand in a chain of events (between which there are deterministic causal links), a chain going backward through events in our childhood brains and to events prior to our birth. (Ekstrom, "Protecting Incompatibilist Freedom," 285)

Also, Kane says:

But, as Martha Klein has pointed out, an interest in ultimacy adds a different set of concerns [from those pertaining to alternative possibilities] about the "sources," "grounds," "reasons," and "explanations" of actions and events—that is, concerns about where they came from, what produced them, and who was responsible for them. It is by focusing on such concerns about origins and responsibility, I would argue, and not merely on alternative possibilities, that one arrives at incompatibilism. (Kane, *The Significance of Free Will*, 74)

26. For developments of this sort of view, see Fischer, *The Metaphysics of Free Will*; and John Martin Fischer and Mark Ravizza, *Responsibility and Control: A Theory of Moral Responsibility* (Cambridge: Cambridge University Press, 1998). The conditions on ownership of the mechanism that issues in behavior are set out in *Responsibility and Control*, 207–239; the sort of reasons-sensitivity required for moral responsibility is developed on pp. 62–150. Throughout the book we argue that the conditions on reasons-sensitivity and mechanism ownership can indeed be met in a causally deterministic world; for a discussion of the relevant sorts of "manipulation," and how they would run afoul especially of the ownership condition, see pp. 230–236.

27. Kane, *The Significance of Free Will*, 67–69.

28. In her review of my book, *The Metaphysics of Free Will: An Essay on Control*, Sarah Buss says:

... I do not see how [Fischer's] semicompatibilism differs in any very important way from good old-fashioned compatibilism. Compatibilists have always readily conceded that if causal determinism is true, then no one has the ability to do-otherwise-even-when-the-past-and-the-laws-are-held-fixed. They have simply insisted that agents do not need *this* ability to be morally responsible for their behavior. According to the familiar compatibilist view, the ability to do otherwise relevant to moral responsibility is the ability to do otherwise *if* certain counterfactual conditions obtain—if, for example one chooses to do otherwise.... (Sarah Buss, "Review of *The Metaphysics of Free Will*, by John Martin Fischer," *Philosophical Books* [1997]: 117–121, esp. 120)

I admit that there has been some confusion about the "target" of various compatibilist analyses of "could" or "ability." Some compatibilists have indeed taken the relevant notion to be a *conditional ability*, corresponding to "can, if the agent were to choose differently," or something like this. But this seems to me to open the compatibilist to an obvious and devastating objection; it is simply irrelevant that the agent would have been able to do the thing in question *under different circumstances*. What one is interested in is whether the agent can do the thing in question in the particular circumstances he is in. Most compatibilists have understood their project to be to give an analysis of precisely this notion of "can, in the agent's particular circumstances." They take it that they are giving an account of the intuitive notion of "can"—what Austin called the "all-in sense of 'can'"—that corresponds to the notion of "can" that plays a role in our deliberations as agents (where we take it that we have more than one path into the future genuinely available to us—here and now). Given this project, however, their analyses do not necessarily embrace the fixity of the past or the fixity of the natural laws. It is important to distinguish between taking some sort of conditional ability to be the target of one's compatibilist analysis of an unconditional ability, on the one hand, and denying the fixity of the past or the fixity of the natural laws as part of one's compatibilist analysis, on the other. For good examples of such compatibilist approaches, see Keith Lehrer, "'Can' in Theory and Practice: A Possible Worlds Analysis," in *Action Theory: Proceedings of the Winnipeg Conference on Human Action*, eds. M. Brand and D. Walton (Dordrecht: D. Reidel, 1976), 241–270; and Terence Horgan, "'Could,' Possible Worlds, and Moral Responsibility," *Southern Journal of Philosophy* 17 (1979): 345–358.

29. Kane, *The Significance of Free Will*, 97–98.

30. Ibid., 97.

31. Ibid., 98.

32. Harry Frankfurt's "hierarchical" view of moral responsibility is a salient and important example of such a view. The classic presentation is in Harry Frankfurt, "Freedom of the Will and the Concept of the Person," in *The Importance of What We Care About*.

33. See, for example, Fischer and Ravizza, *Responsibility and Control*, esp. 252–253.

34. I believe that a mechanism becomes the "agent's own" in virtue of the process whereby he "takes responsibility" for it; this renders my approach to moral responsibility a historical theory: *Responsibility and Control*, 170–239. Further, the reasons-responsiveness requirement ensures the appropriate sort of connection between the agent and the world.

35. Kane, *The Significance of Free Will*, 98.

36. Alfred R. Mele, "Soft Libertarianism and Frankfurt-Style Scenarios," *Philosophical Topics* 24 (1996): 123–142; "Flickers of Freedom," *Journal of Social Philosophy* 29 (1998): 144–156; "Kane, Luck, and the Significance of Free Will," *Philosophical Explorations* 2 (1999): 96–104; and "Ultimate Responsibility and Dumb Luck," *Social Philosophy and Policy* 16 (1999): 274–293.

37. Mele, "Ultimate Responsibility and Dumb Luck," 285–287.

38. Kane, *Free Will and Values*, 178.

39. William James, "The Dilemma of Determinism," in *The Will to Believe and Other Essays* (New York: Dover, 1956), 183; as cited in Kane, *The Significance of Free Will*, 88.

40. Kane, *The Significance of Free Will*, 88.

41. Michael Zimmerman has pointed out that in a case of actual (as opposed to preemptive) overdetermination, reference to one's (unhindered) deliberations may not be necessary in order to explain the fact that some state of affairs obtains, given that the same state of affairs is caused to obtain by some other route, as well as by one's deliberations. But it is nevertheless true that reference to one's unhindered deliberations is essential to an explanation of *how the actual sequence unfolds*, and thus, *of how it comes about* that the state of affairs obtains. The intended notion of explanation is not simply an explanation *that* a state of affairs obtains; it is an explanation of how it comes about that the state of affairs obtains.

42. Of course, an incompatibilist will contend that causally determined deliberations are not *unhindered*. I cannot here argue against the incompatibilist's contention; I am not here seeking to "prove" that my notion of "unhindered" is somehow the "correct" notion. Rather, I am employing what I admit to be a compatibilist notion. My claim is that this notion can be employed to present something—the importance of indispensability—that is at least as attractive (to the target audience—reasonable and fair-minded people not already committed to incompatibilism) as the incompatibilistically construed importance of independence.

43. For such a view, and its role in rendering compatibilism more appealing, see Bernard Berofsky, *The Metaphysical Basis of Responsibility* (New York: Routledge and Kegan Paul, 1987).

44. Robert Stalnaker, "A Theory of Conditionals," in *Studies in Logical Theory*, *American Philosophical Quarterly* Series, ed. N. Rescher (Oxford: Blackwell Publishers, 1968): 98–112; and David Lewis, *Counterfactuals* (Cambridge: Harvard University Press, 1973).

45. In Della Rocca, "Frankfurt, Fischer, and Flickers," he says:

... I should like to call attention to a connection between my criticism of Fischer and what is, perhaps, Fischer's guiding insight in his approach to moral responsibility. For Fischer, in accounting for moral responsibility, we should focus not directly on any alternative sequence of events there may be, but on properties of the actual sequence, including especially facts about the actual causes of the relevant action. In criticizing Fischer, I have, in effect, used this insight or at least an implication of it against Fischer himself. The problem I have raised stems from his focusing on what the flicker of freedom shows about the alternative scenario (viz. that Jones does not do A freely in the alternative scenario), but not on what the flicker shows about the actual situation (viz. that Jones' action is not externally determined in the actual situation). If my objection to Fischer succeeds, it does so in virtue of drawing our attention to a connection between the presence of the flicker and a feature of the actual causal sequence. My procedure here thus reinforces, in a way that is perhaps not entirely welcome to Fischer, his exhortation to focus on the actual sequence. (103–104)

But Della Rocca's "procedure" is not at all unwelcome to me. If his point is that once one focuses on the actual sequence, there will be no *knockdown* argument (acceptable even to those already strongly inclined toward incompatibilism), I do not disagree. Rather, my point is that the debate will have been shifted to terrain considerably more hospitable to compatibilism. This is why I think it is useful to see that the presence of alternative possibilities does not *in itself* ground ascriptions of moral responsibility, and why I welcome the focus on the actual sequence.

46. I do not believe that our personhood and moral responsibility should be insulated from *every* empirical discovery about the world. Rather, I believe that these central notions should be resilient with respect to this particular issue— whether the equations that describe the macroscopic universe are universal generalizations or probabilistic generalizations with extremely high probabilities attached to them. For discussions, see Fischer and Ravizza, *Responsibility and Control*, 253–254, and Fischer, "Recent Work on Moral Responsibility."

REPLY TO JOHN MARTIN FISCHER

Harry Frankfurt

1. Fischer defends the view that agents may be morally responsible for what they have done even if they could not have done otherwise. Needless to say, I share this view with him.[1] He also argues that establishing its truth is a genuine advance in our efforts to understand whether determinism is compatible with moral responsibility. I am with him there too. Moreover, I think his ways of rebutting a variety of objections against these two views are on the whole sound. However, my agreement with him concerning these matters is not unqualified. I will mention two points on which we are not in accord.

2. First, I do not go along with his response to the familiar claim that compatibilists are unable to explain how it is that moral responsibility may be undermined when a person's conduct has been manipulated by behavioral engineering or by other modes of influencing someone's preferences and decisions. He says that the way for compatibilists to explain this is by looking at the causally pertinent antecedents of the behavior in question in order to see how the behavior was produced. My own opinion is that while this historical approach may be suggestive, it is not indispensable or determinative. What we need most essentially to look at is, rather, certain aspects of the psychic structure that is coincident with the person's behavior.

Briefly, it seems to me that if someone does something because he wants to do it, and if he has no reservations about that desire but is wholeheartedly behind it, then—so far as his moral responsibility for doing it is concerned—it really does not matter how he got that way. One further requirement must be added to this: the person's desires and attitudes have to be relatively well integrated into his general psychic condition. Otherwise they are not genuinely his, but are merely disruptive intruders on his true nature. As long as their interrelations imply that they are unequivocally attributable to him as his desires and his attitudes, it makes no difference—so far as evaluating his moral responsibility is concerned—how he came to have them.

A manipulator may succeed, through his interventions, in providing a person not merely with particular feelings and thoughts but with a new character. That person is then morally responsible for the choices and the conduct to which having this character leads. We are inevitably fashioned and sustained, after all, by circumstances over which we have no control. The causes to which we are subject may also change us radically, without thereby bringing it about that we are not morally responsible agents. It is irrelevant whether those causes are operating by virtue of the natural forces that shape our environment or whether they operate through the deliberately manipulative designs of other human agents. We are the sorts of persons we are; and it is what we are, rather than the history of our development, that counts. The fact that someone is a pig warrants treating him like a pig, unless there is reason to believe that in some important way he is a pig against his will and is not acting as he would really prefer to act.

3.   The second aspect of Fischer's rebuttal from which I demur has to do with his reliance on the notion of a "reasons-responsive mechanism." Against Kane, he argues that the assumption that an agent's choices and actions are determined does not rule out regarding the agent as morally responsible as long as what the agent does "issues from the agent's own suitably reasons-responsive mechanism." I do not believe that the mechanism has to be reasons-responsive. The mechanism is constituted by desires and volitions and, in my view, what counts is just whether what the agent wills is what he really wants to will. In philosophical accounts of our psychic lives, the role of reasons tends to be considerably exaggerated. People do not necessarily have reasons for what they want, or for accepting or even for approving their desires. Someone who is wholeheartedly behind the desires that move him when he acts is morally responsible for what he does, in my judgment, whether or not he has any reasons for his deeds or for his desires. But this is a long story, and I will leave the matter here.

4.   Fischer makes what I regard as the quite important observation that counterexamples to the Principle of Alternate Possibilities do not actually show that attributions of moral responsibility are compatible with determinism. They do go a long way, I think, to making compatibilism

plausible; but the only thing that they show at all definitively is that a person may be morally responsible for what he does even if there are no alternatives to his doing it. This leaves open the possibility that determinism may entail other conditions, besides the absence of alternatives, which preclude regarding people as morally responsible for what they do.

Fischer deals very effectively with a number of conditions that may be suggested to be entailed by determinism and to preclude moral responsibility. I agree with his overall claim that determinism does not entail any condition that undermines attributions of moral responsibility. However, what I think people find most basically disturbing about determinism is its apparent implication that human choice and behavior cannot genuinely originate anything. I want to take this occasion to say that, in my judgment, there can be no finally satisfactory vindication of the compatibilist doctrine without an adequate account of agency.

Neither Fischer nor I accept the view that, since the events in our lives are merely the outcomes of causal processes extending back to the beginning of time, we must therefore recognize that we are moved by forces other than our own in such a way that we are essentially passive. Determinism surely does not require us to think of ourselves merely as locales in which various events are caused to occur. The trouble is that no good account of the difference between being passive and being active is available. We are agents, even if it is a fact that everything in our lives is caused. But until it has been explained what being an agent means, the compatibility of determinism with our agency (and hence with our moral responsibility) cannot be decisively established or fully understood.

5.   There is something else that must be cleared up if we are to be confident about the compatibilist view of the relationship between determinism and moral responsibility. We need to arrive at a better understanding than we now have of what holding people morally responsible is all about. We cannot expect to reach a satisfactory conclusion concerning whether determinism is or is not compatible with moral responsibility unless we know what it is with which its compatibility is in question. We require a clear idea, in other words, of the nature of this "moral responsibility" whose relationship to determinism is at issue.

My colleague Gideon Rosen said to me one day that the concept of moral responsibility is "the soft underbelly" of the whole discussion of freewill and related topics. That observation strikes me as correct. It sometimes seems that blaming someone for what he has done, as distinct from simply observing that his conduct has done unjustifiable harm or has violated certain valuable rules, is nothing more than a rather complicated way of being angry at him or of punishing him. That is pretty clearly what we are doing to ourselves when we blame ourselves for our own conduct and feel guilty about it.

Our inclinations to get angry and to punish are firmly entrenched in our nature. This does not mean that they are rationally warranted; nor, more particularly, does it mean that they make sense if determinism is true. Our common practices and intuitions about moral responsibility, which philosophical discussions of these matters so frequently invoke as important evidence, may not be very reliable indications of what we have good enough reason to believe or to do. In any case, we can certainly not hope to find out how reliable they are until we know just what it is that we are believing and doing when we hold people morally responsible.

6.   I am uncertain about Fischer's suggestion that counterexamples to the Principle of Alternate Possibilities are to be construed as effective against a principle to which he refers as PAP*. He says that PAP* asserts the following: "Lacking alternative possibilities is a condition which in itself—and apart from anything else that accompanies it (either contingently or necessarily)—makes it the case that an agent is not morally responsible for his behavior." His claim that the counterexamples in question are effective against this principle strikes me as correct. What I do not quite understand is just how PAP* differs from PAP.

PAP says that an agent who could not have done otherwise is not morally responsible for what he did. PAP* appears to say just that the fact that an agent could not have done otherwise entails that the agent is not morally responsible for what he did. It is true that PAP* emphasizes, by saying it in so many words, that an inability to do otherwise entails the absence of moral responsibility regardless of any other consideration. So far as I can see, this entailment is already quite strictly conveyed—albeit in a less elaborately explicit manner—in the formulation of PAP.

Note

1. I would propose a small emendation to his statement that "what we value in action for which an agent can legitimately be held morally responsible is ... that he expresses himself in a certain way ... [that] does not require alternative possibilities." I suppose that the point Fischer wishes to make is not about what we *value* in actions but about what it is about them that we *evaluate* when we are considering the moral responsibility of the agent. We evaluate something about the person that his action reveals.

2

Control and Causal Determinism

Eleonore Stump

Introduction

Harry Frankfurt's account of the nature of moral responsibility has been enormously influential; it has generated considerable discussion, and it has opened up new ways of looking at old problems in more than one area of philosophy. Frankfurt's account depends on a hierarchical notion of the will, and it understands moral responsibility as a matter of an agent's having a certain hierarchical structure in the will on which she acts. By contrast, the history of an agent's act is not pertinent to the assessment of her act, on Frankfurt's account; to determine whether or not her act is one for which she is morally responsible we do not need to look at events in her life antecedent to her act but only at the state of her will at the time at which she acts. An act's being causally determined does not therefore rule out its being an act for which someone is morally responsible as long as the agent has the right sort of hierarchical structure in her will, the right sort of mesh between her higher- and lower-order volitions.

Frankfurt's account of moral responsibility and of the will as hierarchical has raised many questions. One of the most troublesome has to do with whether or not the will on which an agent acts is her own. If all that is required for moral responsibility is a certain sort of harmony between hierarchically ordered volitions, then it seems that this harmony could be caused in a person by an external manipulator, who acts on his victim's first-order and higher-order volitions to bring them into accord. In that case, a person might meet Frankfurt's conditions for being morally responsible when she was completely manipulated by someone else.

Frankfurt himself has responded to this challenge with various attempts to specify what it is that makes a person's will her own, but his responses haven't been convincing to all of his critics. In their rich and impressive book, *Responsibility and Control: A Theory of Moral Responsibility*, John Martin Fischer and Mark Ravizza offer an account of moral responsibility that they present as an improvement on Frankfurt's. They mean their account, like Frankfurt's, to be compatible with the truth of causal determinism, but they think that their views can handle the objections that seem to trouble Frankfurt's account. In particular, they think that their account is able to show why a manipulated agent is not morally responsible for what she does under the influence of the manipulation. In this paper, I consider whether Fischer and Ravizza's account is in fact an improvement on Frankfurt's, and, in particular, whether their account succeeds better than they suppose Frankfurt's does in being a compatibilist account able to handle cases of manipulation.

Fischer and Ravizza define moral responsibility in terms of guidance control. They present their position as a historical account, and they contrast it explicitly with ahistorical "mesh" theories of moral responsibility, such as Frankfurt's. They say, "the mere *existence* of the mesh [between lower-order and higher-order volitions, for example] is *not* indeed sufficient for moral responsibility; the *history* behind the mesh is also relevant."[1] On Fischer and Ravizza's view, an agent has guidance control in virtue of acting on a reasons-responsive mechanism that is his own in consequence of his having taken responsibility in the past for the actions that issue from it. For guidance control, a mechanism has to be "moderately" reasons-responsive, where the conditions on moderate reasons-responsiveness specify a moderately strong connection between the reasons that there are for an agent, on the one hand, and the agent's recognition of such reasons and reactivity to them, on the other. On Fischer and Ravizza's account, guidance control is "the freedom-relevant condition necessary and sufficient for moral responsibility."[2] Finally, they contend that this account of moral responsibility is compatible with both the truth and the falsity of causal determinism.[3]

All of these claims, including the claim to be able to handle cases Frankfurt's account can't, raise questions that are worth pursuing. In this paper, I want to consider just one of them, namely, the question of whether Fischer and Ravizza are right in their claim that their account of moral responsibility is compatible with the truth of causal determinism. They say, "we wish to emphasize that one of the great virtues of our approach to moral responsibility is that, on our account, it is highly plausible that moral responsibility is compatible with causal determinism."[4] I will argue that they have not made a case for the compatibility of moral responsibility and causal determinism and that, on the contrary, their account of moral responsibility is unworkable if causal determinism is true. In particular, cases of manipulation that are problematic for Frankfurt's account are intractable for Fischer and Ravizza's.

I will look first at Fischer and Ravizza's argument for the compatibilism of their account of moral responsibility with causal determinism and then at their attempted refutation of an argument for incompatibilism, and I will argue that neither of these is successful. Then I will turn to their discussion of cases of manipulation; and I will argue that, contrary to their claim to have an advantage here over Frankfurt's account, their attempt not to rule out compatibilism has the result that a manipulated agent counts as responsible on their theory of moral responsibility.

Reasons and Causes

Fischer and Ravizza claim that "the account [of guidance control] sketched here leads to *compatibilism* about moral responsibility and the doctrine of causal determinism,"[5] and they offer an argument designed to support this claim. An agent is morally responsible for his act, they argue, if and only if his act is the product of his own reasons-responsive mechanism, and they maintain that the "reasons-responsiveness of [the mechanism operative in] the actual sequence leading to action is [itself] consistent with causal determination."[6] They try to defuse one possible objection to this view about the compatibility of causal determinism and the reasons-responsiveness of a mechanism by maintaining that two mechanisms—two ways of deciding how to act—can be the same even if they are not the same at the microlevel. But they fail to address a second, equally important concern.

Causal determinism is generally taken to be a theory about what happens at the microlevel,[7] and it appears that Fischer and Ravizza are taking it in this way also.[8] But why think that what is determined only by causes at the microlevel of physics can also track reasons or be responsive to reasons?

One might suppose that the answer is obvious. Our brains are reasons-responsive mechanisms, or so most philosophers believe; and many philosophers (but certainly not all)[9] believe that all material objects, including brains, are causally determined at the microlevel. Therefore, since (on this line of thought) in the actual world human brains are causally determined and reasons-responsive, causal determinism is compatible with the reasons-responsiveness of mechanisms leading to action. *Ab esse ad posse valet consequentia.*

But to have an *argument* for this conclusion, more is required than bare belief that in the actual world human brains have these features.

Someone might think that it is possible to give an argument to show that our brains are both causally determined at the microlevel and also reasons-responsive by pointing to the theory of evolution. The theory of evolution accounts for the reliability of our causally determined, materially based cognitive capacities, someone might suppose, because only those organisms whose causally determined brains did track reasons survived. But this is a highly controversial view of the theory of evolution; it is rejected by many philosophers.[10] For example, Patricia Churchland says,

Boiled down to essentials, a nervous system enables the organism to succeed in the four F's: feeding, fleeing, fighting, and reproducing. The principal chore of the nervous system is to get the body parts where they should be in order that the organism may survive.... Truth, whatever that is, definitely takes the hindmost.[11]

And Richard Rorty says,

The idea that one species of organism is, unlike all the others, oriented not just toward its own increased prosperity but toward Truth, is as un-Darwinian as the idea that every human being has a built-in moral compass....[12]

So, given the current state of the discussion, the theory of evolution cannot give uncontentious support for the claim that what happens at the microlevel in the brains of human beings tracks reasons.[13]

Alternatively, someone might suppose that contemporary neurobiology can provide strong and reasonably uncontroversial support for the claim that a cognitive mechanism causally determined at the microlevel can track reasons.[14] We now know enough about the way in which the brain works, someone might think, to be able to show that at least with respect to perception the brain is causally determined at the microlevel by extramental reality, and for that very reason gives reliable information about the external world. Similarly, the argument might run, if we understood higher cortical functions as well as we currently understand perception, we would see that those brain systems are also causally determined at the microlevel and yet track reasons as reliably as the brain's perceptual systems give information about the extramental world. Therefore, causal determination and reasons-responsiveness are compatible.

But this is a mistaken understanding of what contemporary neurobiology has so far shown even just about perception. It may be that incoming light reflected from extramental objects impinges on the retina in some relatively simple way that is causally determined at the microlevel, but things become immensely more complicated immediately after that. From a neurophysiological point of view, the causation exercised on the brain by extramental reality underdetermines perception. So, for example, a recent text puts the point this way:

the same information is treated in different ways in different parts of the brain.... Thus, although the kind of information sent to a [neural] network restricts what it can do, the input alone does not determine what a network computes.[15]

I share what I take to be Fischer and Ravizza's view, that the brain (or some neural system in the brain) is in fact a reasons-responsive mechanism, though it seems to me clear that I, and others, hold this view on faith in what neurobiology will show in the future, rather than on the current results of that science. But, apart from a general ideological commitment to the reliability of human cognitive faculties and the truth of causal determinism, there seems to be no reason—none based in biology at any rate—to maintain that the brain's cognitive functions are causally determined at the microlevel by extramental reality in a reasons-tracking way. And so claiming that our brains are determined by causes at the microlevel and yet are reasons-responsive isn't so much an argument for the compatibility of causal determinism and the reasons-responsiveness of some mechanisms as an expression of faith in it.

At any rate, to have an *argument* for the compatibility of causal determinism and the reasons-responsiveness of a mechanism that is based on the nature of human brains in the actual world, we would need considerably more than belief in the brain's being both reasons-responsive and causally determined. Without such an argument, or some other argument attempting to show that causal determinism is compatible with the reasons-responsiveness of human cognitive mechanisms, Fischer and Ravizza's claim that there can be a causally determined reasons-responsive mechanism is no more than an assertion on their part. This claim is, however, crucial to their case. Without some way of supporting it, Fischer and Ravizza do not have an *argument* for their compatibilism.

A Direct Argument for Incompatibilism: Transfer NR

As Fischer and Ravizza point out, there are two sorts of arguments that moral responsibility is *incompatible* with the truth of causal determinism. One is indirect; it maintains that moral responsibility requires alternative possibilities and argues that alternative possibilities are ruled out by causal determinism. The other is a direct argument that moral responsibility is ruled out by causal determinism. Fischer and Ravizza's contention that their own account of moral responsibility is compatible with the truth of causal determinism depends on their success in rebutting each sort of argument. Here I want to look just at their attempt to defuse the direct argument.[16]

The direct argument is based on a principle of the transfer of non-responsibility—"Transfer NR," as Fischer and Ravizza call it.[17] This principle says:

If

(T1) p obtains, and no one is even partly morally responsible for p;

and

(T2)   if p obtains, then q obtains, and no one is even partly morally responsible for the fact that if p obtains, then q obtains;

then

(T3) q obtains, and no one is even partly morally responsible for q.[18]

The direct argument for incompatibilism then goes, roughly, this way.

Let P be a proposition describing the state of the universe before there were any human beings, let L be a proposition describing the laws of nature, and let F be a truth about the way the world is today. Now assume that causal determinism is true. Then

(1) (P and L > F).

Clearly, no one is even partly morally responsible for this fact, and so this is also true (where N stands for *no one is even partly morally responsible*):

(2) N [(P and L) > F].

Since [(P and L) > F] is equivalent to [P > (L > F)], this is true as well:

(3) N [P > (L > F)].

Now

(4) N P,

and so by Transfer NR, from (3) and (4) we can conclude

(5) N (L > F).

Since

(6) N L,

by another application of Transfer NR, from (5) and (6) we reach the conclusion,

(7) N F.

Since F is any arbitrary truth, the incompatibilist conclusion follows.

Fischer and Ravizza attack the direct argument for incompatibilism by trying to show that although Transfer NR looks evidently true, there are cases in which it doesn't hold. Their counterexamples to the principle are all cases of preemptive or simultaneous overdetermination. Here is the counterexample they call "*Erosion*," which is a case of preemptive overdetermination.

[*Erosion*] Betty is on a mission to destroy a camp at the base of a mountain by starting an avalanche. She places her explosives accordingly and at t_1 pushes the plunger, detonating the explosives and starting an avalanche which destroys the camp at t_3. Had Betty not detonated the explosives, at t_2 an avalanche would have been started by natural erosion in a glacier, and it would have destroyed the camp at t_3.[19]

In this case, Transfer NR seems to be violated insofar as the following claims are true:

(1)   The glacier is eroding and no one is, or ever has been, even partly responsible for the fact that it is eroding; and

(2)   if the glacier is eroding, then there is an avalanche that crushes the enemy base at t_3, and no one is, or ever has been, even partly responsible for this fact;[20]

and yet it is apparently not true that

(3)   there is an avalanche that crushes the enemy base at t_3, and no one is, or ever has been, even partly responsible for this fact.[21]

That is, of course, because it seems that Betty is responsible for the destruction of the camp at t_3.

In this case there are two paths to the outcome of the camp's being destroyed. One of them, the path through natural forces involving the glacier's erosion, is such that no one is responsible for it. But the other path, Betty's detonating explosives, is different. It seems reasonable to suppose that in *Erosion* Betty is responsible for her detonating explosives. And if it is, then Transfer NR is not valid. In that case, the direct argument for incompatibilism is unsuccessful.

But is this apparently reasonable result correct?

What is at issue between Fischer and Ravizza and the incompatibilist is the question of whether causal determination is compatible with moral responsibility. But consider the way in which Fischer and Ravizza argue against the validity of Transfer NR in connection with *Erosion*. The case shows that the principle isn't valid, they say, because there are two paths to the effect, and in one of those paths a human agent, Betty, is responsible for the effect. Are we to suppose that in *Erosion* Betty's actions are causally determined or not? It is worth looking carefully at the case under either assumption.

Suppose we assume that

(1)   the world of *Erosion* is not causally determined and Betty acts indeterministically.

Then *Erosion* shows that in cases of overdetermined effects, one of whose causes is an agent acting indeterministically, Transfer NR fails. But this is not enough to show that Transfer NR should be rejected. Because Transfer NR is a highly plausible principle, we can take *Erosion* to show just that the principle needs to be restricted to exclude such un- usual cases as that in which an indeterministic agent is one of the causes of an overdetermined effect. Restricted in this way, Transfer NR still supports the direct argument for incompatibilism that relies on the prin- ciple. That argument assumes the truth of causal determinism, and so it needs no stronger version of Transfer NR than one restricted to exclude cases of an indeterministic cause of an overdetermined effect. There are no such causes in a causally determined world. So if we assume that Betty in *Erosion* acts indeterministically, *Erosion* will not undermine a direct argument for incompatibilism that relies on a suitably restricted version of Transfer NR.

Suppose, then, that we assume

(2) Betty's world is causally determined.

Does *Erosion* now constitute a challenge to the direct argument for incompatibilism? That depends, of course, on whether a causally deter- mined agent can be morally responsible. If the incompatibilist is right, then a causally determined agent cannot be responsible, and so Betty is not responsible for what she does in *Erosion* if she is causally determined to do it. But unless Betty is responsible for what she does, *Erosion* does not count as a counterexample to Transfer NR. So if we suppose that Betty is causally determined in *Erosion,* then in order for *Erosion* not simply to beg the question against the incompatibilist, Fischer and Rav- izza need to have some reason for calling the incompatibilist judgment into question.

They would have such a reason if they could show that causally de- termined decisions can be assimilated to the sort of case Fischer and Ravizza have tried to construct in *Erosion.* If they could do so, then morally determined decisions would themselves be exceptions to Trans- fer NR, and this result would certainly undermine the direct argument for incompatibilism.

But can causally determined decisions be assimilated to cases such as that which Fischer and Ravizza suppose they have provided in *Ero- sion?* I think the answer to this question is "no." And if that is right, then Fischer and Ravizza are not in a position to claim that causally determined decisions can themselves be exceptions to the principle of

Transfer NR. For that reason, if Betty is causally determined to do what she does in *Erosion*, Fischer and Ravizza's claim that Betty is responsible for her decision in *Erosion* simply begs the question against the incompatibilist.

To see why the Fischer and Ravizza strategy for devising apparent counterexamples to Transfer NR can't be applied to cases of causally determined decisions, consider the explanation they give of those counterexamples. As Fischer and Ravizza themselves point out, all their counterexamples to Transfer NR depend on there being more than one path to the same outcome. In arguing against Peter van Inwagen's support for Transfer NR, Fischer and Ravizza say,

Van Inwagen focuses exclusively on the one-path cases. But among the two-path cases there is a subclass of cases in which one of the paths to the outcome contains the appropriate sort of control. These cases provide counterexamples to Transfer NR. Van Inwagen's mistake is inappropriately to seek to generalize from a proper subclass (the one-path cases) to the totality of relevant cases.[22]

The question for Fischer and Ravizza, then, is whether causally determined decisions can be shown to belong to the relevant subclass of two-path cases.

Suppose that Cartesian dualism is false and that any mental act or state, such as making a decision, is correlated with some neural state, where by "correlation" we mean whatever the correct relation between the mental and the neural is, on the assumptions that causal determinism is true and that Cartesian dualism is false.[23] Let "D" stand for some mental act or state, such as recognizing a face or making a decision, and let "N" stand for the neural state correlated with it. For example, D might be the mental state of S's recognizing the face of his daughter. Then N would be the neural state in S in which a certain sequence of neural firings—from the retina, through the optic nerve to the lateral geniculate nucleus of the thalamus, into various layers of the visual cortex, to the inferior temporal cortex, and so on—is completed.

Now, on the assumption that causal determinism is true, we can construct an argument in this way to show that the case of a causally determined decision cannot be assimilated to cases such as *Erosion*. On the assumptions of the falsity of Cartesian dualism and the truth of causal determinism, the following claims are true:

(T1*)   The laws of nature and the conditions at the time of the Big

Bang causally determine that S is in neural state N at t_1; and no human being is or ever was morally responsible for this fact.

(T2*) If the laws of nature and the conditions at the time of the Big Bang causally determine that S is in neural state N at t_1, then S makes decision D at t_1; and no human being is or ever was morally responsible for the fact expressed in this conditional.

If causal determinism is true, then the states of neurons, like the states of any other material objects, are causally determined by initial conditions and the laws of nature. But no human being is responsible for the fact that the laws of nature and the conditions at the time of the Big Bang determine S's being in neural state N at t. So (T1*) is true, given the presupposition that causal determinism is true.

It is important to distinguish (T1*) from a related claim with which it might be confused, namely,

(T1**) S is in neural state N at t_1, and no human being is or ever was morally responsible for this fact.

A compatibilist might well want to argue that (T1**) is false. If mental and neural states are correlated, then an agent S who has a certain mental state ipso facto has the correlated neural state. Consequently, if moral responsibility is compatible with causal determinism, a compatibilist might suppose that S is responsible for his being in a particular neural state, even if that state is causally determined, just in virtue of the fact that S is responsible for his being in the correlated mental state.

Whatever one thinks of this strategy for defending the falsity of (T1**), it will not be effective against (T1*). That is because there is a difference in the two claims in the nature of the fact for which responsibility is being denied. (T1**) denies that an agent is responsible for the fact that he is in a certain neural state. But (T1*) denies that an agent is responsible for the fact that the laws of nature and conditions at the time of the Big Bang determine a particular neural state of his. Regardless of one's attitude toward compatibilism, it seems clearly true that no human agent is responsible for this cosmic connection between the laws of nature and initial conditions of the world, on the one hand, and a neural state, on the other.[24]

(T2*) seems unimpeachable as well, on the presupposition that Cartesian dualism is false. If there is no separate soul isolated in its acts from events in the nervous system, then mental acts are correlated with neural states. But that mental states and neural states are correlated in this way is clearly not something that any human being is or ever was responsible for.

From (T1*) and (T2*) it apparently follows by Transfer NR that

(T3*)   S makes decision D at t_1, and no human being is or ever was morally responsible for this fact.

To use the Fischer and Ravizza strategy against Transfer NR to show that this conclusion does not follow, we would have to show three things: (a) there is another path to the same result of S's making decision D, (b) this path is one for which someone is or was responsible, and (c) that someone is S himself. If there is no other path to the same result, if there is another path to the outcome of S's making decision D at t_1 but it is only one for which no one is responsible, or if there is another path to the outcome for which someone is responsible but it is only one in which the responsible person isn't S, then the Fischer and Ravizza strategy will not succeed in undermining the use of Transfer NR in this argument.

Given the plasticity of the brain, it is clearly possible that there be a different path to the outcome of S's making decision D. So, for example, it might be the case that, as things are, S's neural state N is in the left hemisphere of his cerebral cortex. But if some illness had destroyed S's left hemisphere in early childhood, then S's brain would have reorganized itself so that the neural state correlated with S's mental act of making decision D would have been not neural state N but rather some neural state R in S's right hemisphere. In that case, there would be a different path to the outcome of S's making decision D, namely, the path that goes through neural state R.

This alternative pathway is no help for Fischer and Ravizza's case, however, since a version of (T1*) and (T2*) could obviously be constructed for the alternative pathway as well.[25]

Now suppose that, although the world is causally determined in the normal course of things, there is a God who can override the laws of nature. Then God can bring it about directly, just by willing it, that S is in neural state N and therefore that S makes decision D. In this case, apart from miracles, causal determinism is true, and yet there is another path to the outcome of S's making decision D. Furthermore, in this case, it is not possible to construct a version of (T1*) and (T2*) for the alternative pathway. In addition, the alternative pathway is one for which someone—namely, God—is responsible. The problem with this case, of course, is that the alternative path isn't one for which S *himself* is responsible. On the contrary, since agents who can avail themselves of this alternative pathway have to be able to abrogate the laws of nature, this alternative pathway isn't open to human beings.

In fact, if causal determinism is true and if Cartesian dualism is false, then any path to the outcome of S's making decision D, which is a path involving *human* agency, will be a path for which some version of (T1*) and (T2*) can be constructed. Suppose, for example, that S arrives at decision D by considering different evidence, accepting different reasons, and basing his deliberations on different considerations from those he did in the original case. Any mental route S takes to reach his decision, no matter what it is, will be a route that is correlated with some neural state N*, on the presupposition that Cartesian dualism is false; and this neural state will be causally determined, on the presupposition that causal determinism is true. Consequently, some analogue of (T1*) and (T2*) will also always be true.

It is clear therefore that any alternative pathway to the outcome of S's making decision D will run into the same trouble. If causal determinism is true (and Cartesian dualism is false), then for any such alternative pathway to a decision, it will be true that

(T1*a)   the laws of nature and the conditions at the time of the Big Bang causally determine that S is in neural state N* at time t^*.

And to make this alternative pathway analogous to the putative counterexamples such as *Erosion*, one would have to go on to *deny* the truth of

(T1*b)   no human being is or ever was morally responsible for its being the case that the laws of nature and the conditions at the time of the Big Bang causally determine that S is in neural state N* at time t^*.

But, on the presupposition of causal determinism, (T1*b) is so clearly true that even the most ideologically committed compatibilist couldn't seriously deny it. To deny it would be to hold that in a causally determined world some human being S is responsible for the fact that natural laws and conditions at the time of the Big Bang causally determine S's neural states.

Consequently, insofar as any alternative path goes through material objects (as it must if human beings are not taken to be immaterial substances) and material objects are taken to be causally determined (as they must be if causal determinism is true), there is no alternative pathway to a decision for which any human being is or ever was responsible.

In that case, the Fischer and Ravizza strategy for devising counterexamples to Transfer NR doesn't apply to cases of causally determined decisions. Consequently, they are not in a position to claim without begging the question that Betty's act in *Erosion* is one for which she is morally responsible if she is also causally determined.

To sum up, then, the human agent in cases such as *Erosion* has to be taken as acting either (1) indeterministically or (2) deterministically. If indeterministically, then the case does not undermine the direct argument for incompatibilism, for the reasons given above in the discussion of (1). If deterministically, then Fischer and Ravizza have no basis for asserting that *Erosion* is a counterexample to Transfer NR. Consequently, their claim that it is begs the question against the incompatibilist.

So on neither alternative have Fischer and Ravizza succeeded in showing that the direct argument for incompatibilism fails. To that extent, their claim that their account of moral responsibility is compatible with causal determinism is undermined.

Manipulation and Moral Responsibility

Because Fischer and Ravizza want their account to be compatible with the truth of causal determinism, they cannot handle cases of manipulation in the simple way incompatibilists can, by rejecting as not morally responsible an agent whose act is causally determined.[26] Instead, Fischer and Ravizza have to find a way to distinguish those causally determined acts for which an agent is responsible from those for which he is not. In particular, Fischer and Ravizza need to rule out as not responsible agents who are manipulated by another person. Other accounts of moral responsibility or free will, such as Harry Frankfurt's account of free will in terms of a harmony between first-order and higher-order volitions, also are faced with this problem. But Fischer and Ravizza think such ahistorical accounts are unable to solve the problem, and they take it as an advantage of their account over theories such as Frankfurt's that their account can solve it.

They attempt to do so by stipulating that an agent is morally responsible only if he acts on a mechanism that is his own, and they give a detailed account of what it is for a mechanism to be an agent's own. They maintain that an agent is acting on a mechanism that is his own if and only if the agent's history includes his taking responsibility for that mechanism by taking responsibility for the actions that stem from it: "The process by which an agent takes responsibility for the springs of an action makes them *his own* in an important sense."[27]

Taking responsibility with regard to a mechanism, on their view, has three components. (i) An individual "must see himself as the source of his behavior.... That is, the individual must see himself as an agent...."[28] Then, in acting on the mechanism in question, (ii) the individual "must accept that he is a fair target of the reactive attitudes [of others] as a result of how he exercises this agency in certain contexts."[29] Finally, (iii) "the agent's view of himself as an agent and sometimes appropriately subject to the reactive attitudes [must] be grounded in his *evidence* for these beliefs."[30] An individual who has met these conditions with regard to the mechanism on which he acts is, on their view, acting on a mechanism that is his own.

On Fischer and Ravizza's view, a causally determined mechanism can still be an agent's own, but the mechanism on which a person acts when he is manipulated by someone else will not meet the conditions for being his own. I think, however, that Fischer and Ravizza are wrong in this view. A person who is being manipulated by someone else can meet their conditions for acting on a mechanism that is his own and also suitably reasons-responsive. Consequently, a manipulated person can count as morally responsible on their account of moral responsibility.

To see that this is so, consider Robert Heinlein's *The Puppetmasters*.[31] In the story, an alien race of intelligent creatures wants to conquer the Earth. Part of the alien plan for invasion includes a covert operation in which individual aliens take over particular human beings without being detected. When an alien "master" takes over a human being, the human being (say, Sam) has within himself not only his own consciousness but the master's as well. The master can control Sam's consciousness; he can make Sam's mind blank, he can suppress or even eradicate some affect of Sam's, or he can introduce thoughts and desires into Sam's consciousness. Most of the time, however, the master leaves Sam's consciousness alone but simply takes it off-line. That is, Sam's consciousness runs pretty much as always, but it has no effect on Sam's behavior; the master's consciousness causes Sam to do whatever he does. The master doesn't need to control Sam in this direct way, though; he sometimes controls Sam indirectly, by controlling Sam's thoughts and desires and then letting Sam's consciousness produce Sam's behavior.

Since it is crucial to the alien plan that their taking over human beings be undetected in the early stages of the invasion, they are careful to make the behavior of people like Sam correspond to the behavior Sam would normally have engaged in had he not been infected with the alien. So when, under the control of the alien, Sam does A, it is also true that if there had been reason sufficient for Sam in his uninfected state to do not-A, the alien would have brought it about that Sam in his infected state did not-A. In this case, then, Sam acts on a mechanism that meets Fischer and Ravizza's conditions for being strongly reasons-responsive: "if [a certain kind of mechanism] K were to operate and there were sufficient reason to do otherwise, the agent would recognize the sufficient reason to do otherwise and *thus* choose to do otherwise and *do* otherwise."[32]

Suppose that we now rewrite Heinlein's story a little, in order to take account of Fischer and Ravizza's conditions for a mechanism's being an agent's own. Let it be the case that, after the alien has infected Sam and before he starts to manipulate Sam's reason, the alien has what is, in effect, a conversation with Sam. The alien may have no purpose for this conversation other than to amuse himself. But suppose that, for amusement or some other purpose, the alien wants to convince Sam that when Sam acts under the control of the alien, Sam is as much an agent and as suitable a candidate for the reactive attitudes of others as he ever was in his uninfected state.

The alien might, for example, put forward arguments for determinism and compatibilism that Sam finds extremely plausible. In consequence, Sam might come to believe that all the states of his mind and will are causally determined by factors outside himself and that, nonetheless, when he acts, determined in this way, he is incontrovertibly an agent and that it is perfectly appropriate for others to maintain the reactive attitudes toward him. Next, the alien might argue to this effect: It can make no difference to our asssessment of a person S whether the external factors determining the states of S's mind and will are animate or inanimate, intelligent or blind. Our assessment of S himself should remain the same regardless of whether or not the causes determining S include something sentient among them. Suppose that Sam finds this argument, too, very plausible.[33]

By this means, Sam, in the revised story, is brought to believe that, in acting on his mind and will as they are controlled by the alien, he *is* an agent[34] and a suitable target for the reactive attitudes of others, just as he was in his uninfected state. These beliefs of Sam's will be false, but, of course, it is possible for human beings to reason themselves into very peculiar false beliefs. The history of philosophy is studded with examples, though, no doubt, we would not all agree on what those examples are.

Furthermore, these beliefs of Sam's will be founded on the evidence available to Sam, namely, what Sam knows and believes and the arguments of the alien which Sam accepts.

One might think that Sam would realize how false these beliefs of his are once he had some experience of being controlled by the alien, so that Sam would cease to take responsibility for the manipulated mechanism on which his behavior is based when he experiences the process of being controlled. But, given the way in which Sam came to these beliefs, in the grip of his alien-inspired philosophical theory, Sam might, even so, continue to hold his false beliefs, just as people under the sway of some ideology cling tenaciously to beliefs that seem to others around them to be perfectly incredible. Furthermore, since at least at the outset the alien takes care to ensure that Sam acts in character, people around Sam will react to him in his infected state just as they did before. And so they will only confirm Sam in his mistaken beliefs that in acting under the control of the alien, he is an agent and a fair target of reactive attitudes.

In this way, then, Sam takes responsibility for the mechanism on which he acts when he is controlled by the alien, and so this mechanism counts as his own, on Fischer and Ravizza's account. Since this mechanism is also reasons-responsive in the way I described, Sam meets the Fischer and Ravizza conditions for moral responsibility when he is controlled by the alien.

Fischer and Ravizza themselves consider a range of cases of manipulation and attempt to show that in each case their account of moral responsibility rules out attributing responsibility to the manipulated person. I think that the case of Sam and the puppetmaster is enough to show that Fischer and Ravizza's account has a serious problem in attempting to deal with manipulation, but I want also to consider two cases they discuss, in order to illuminate the relation of this problem to their compatibilism.

Here is the first case:

[*Judith I*] A scientist secretly implanted a mechanism in Judith's brain (let us say, a few days ago). Employing this mechanism, the scientist electronically stimulates Judith's brain in such a way as to create what will be a literally irresistible urge to punch her best friend, Jane, the next time she sees Jane. When Judith meets Jane at a local coffeehouse, Judith experiences this sort of urge, and does indeed punch Jane.[35]

Our intuitive response to this case is to think that Judith is not responsible for punching Jane. Fischer and Ravizza think that their account can support this intuition, in the following way:

First, the mechanism leading to the action is not moderately reasons-responsive; by hypothesis, given the kind of stimulation of the brain that actually takes place, Judith has an irresistible urge to strike Jane. Thus, Judith would strike Jane, no matter what kinds of reasons to refrain were present.... [Second,] it is *also* a necessary condition of moral responsibility for an action that the agent has taken responsibility for the kind of mechanism that issues in the action. And, whereas Judith can plausibly be thought to have taken responsibility for the mechanism of ordinary practical reason (uninfluenced by clandestine operations of scientists), it is *not* plausible to say that Judith has taken responsibility for the sort of mechanism that actually issues in her action: *this* sort of mechanism includes the manipulations of the scientist. Hence, Judith has *not* (on our view) taken responsibility for the kind of mechanism that actually issues in the action ...[36]

For these two reasons, Fischer and Ravizza think that their account explains and supports the intuition that Judith is not responsible.

But it is not difficult to flesh out *Judith I* in such a way that our intuition about the case remains the same, and yet Fischer and Ravizza's account no longer supports that intuition. We can easily assimilate *Judith I* to the sort of story in the revised version of Heinlein's *Puppetmasters*. In that case, the mechanism on which Judith acts in *Judith I* is the mind of the manipulator operating on her brain. As in the case of *Puppetmasters*, we can also suppose that that mechanism is suitably responsive to reasons that both Judith and the manipulator recognize as reasons for Judith, so that the mechanism is even strongly reasons-responsive. Finally, we can imagine that Judith comes to believe that she is an agent and the appropriate target of the reactive attitudes when she is controlled in this way by the manipulator. These beliefs on Judith's part will be false; but, as in the *Puppetmasters* case, they will be based on the evidence available to Judith. Judith then meets the conditions for acting on a mechanism that is her own when she is controlled by the manipulator.

Consequently, contrary to what Fischer and Ravizza suppose, a person such as Judith who acts on an irresistible desire produced in her by a manipulator can still meet the Fischer and Ravizza conditions for moral responsibility. She can act on a mechanism that is her own, in virtue of the fact that she has taken responsibility for it, and that mechanism can be suitably reasons-responsive, because the manipulator manipulates his victim in a way that tracks reasons for the victim.

The most complicated case of manipulation Fischer and Ravizza consider is one in which the process of taking responsibility is itself manipulated. For ease of reference, we can call this case "*Judith II.*"

[*Judith II*] It is conceivable that a different sort of manipulation takes place, in which the agent's taking responsibility itself is somehow electronically implanted. That is, it is conceivable that the individual's view of himself as an agent and an apt candidate for the reactive attitudes be electronically implanted.

Fischer and Ravizza are imagining that some agent—Judith—is controlled by a manipulator but that this time the manipulation not only includes the determination of an act of hers but also extends to her attitudes about herself. By electronic stimulation of her brain or in some other way, the manipulator causes Judith to see herself as an agent and as an apt target of reactive attitudes when she is being controlled by the manipulator. In this case, as in *Judith I*, we can stipulate that the manipulator controls Judith in such a way as to make her act on a mechanism that is not only moderately but even strongly reasons-responsive. So the question of whether Fischer and Ravizza's account can support and explain our intuition that Judith in *Judith II* is not morally responsible when she is manipulated into action turns on the answer to the question whether Judith in this case is acting on a mechanism that is her own.

Fischer and Ravizza think that the answer to this question is plainly "no," on the grounds that, in *Judith II*, Judith's beliefs that she is an agent and that she is an apt target of reactive attitudes are not based on the evidence available to her—Fischer and Ravizza's third condition for a mechanism's being an agent's own—but are instead produced in her electronically by the manipulator. So Fischer and Ravizza say,

We specified the third condition on taking responsibility as follows: the agent's view of himself must be based on his evidence in an appropriate way. Obviously, this is abstract and schematic. This condition is intended (in part) to imply that an individual who has been electronically induced to have the relevant view of himself (and thus satisfy the first two conditions on taking responsibility) has *not* formed his view of himself in the appropriate way. But the relevant notion of appropriateness must remain unanalyzed.... We would point out that the sorts of specifications of appropriateness required to rule out the direct electronic implantation of the relevant cluster of beliefs do *not* appear *also* to rule out causal determination.... most of us do not object to the idea that external circumstances causally determine our *beliefs*. It is presumably *less* problematic that our beliefs are causally determined by the external world than that our *motivational states* (such as desires, choices, and intentions) be so determined. Thus, it is at least plausible that the relevant sort of appropriateness could, in principle, be specified in a way that is consistent with determinism.[37]

It isn't clear, however, that Fischer and Ravizza can in fact construct a responsibility-preserving specification of the appropriateness at issue if that specification also has to be compatible with the truth of causal determinism.

To see the problem, suppose that we in fact have the right specification of appropriateness. That is, suppose that when a person, Judith, bases her beliefs on the evidence in the appropriate way (whatever that is), her basing of her beliefs on her evidence meets specifications S. Just for the sake of the example, suppose that these specifications are fairly simple. Just for the purposes of the argument, we can stipulate that Judith meets specifications S if and only if (Mi) she holds the relevant beliefs about herself (that she is an agent and that she is an apt target of the reactive attitudes), and (Mii) she holds these beliefs because (a) she has taken into consideration all the information available to her that she takes to be relevant to these beliefs about herself, (b) she has paid special attention to and deliberated about any claims which might plausibly be considered (by Judith herself) as defeaters of these beliefs about herself, and (c) she has concluded in some appropriate way that the cumulative evidence supports the relevant beliefs about herself. (This is much too simple, but it doesn't matter for the purposes of this example.)

Now let it be the case that causal determinism is true, and suppose also that Cartesian dualism is false, so that human beings too are causally determined material objects. In that case, mental acts and states are correlated with neural states (where by "correlated" I mean, as before, whatever the correct relation between the mental and the neural is, on the assumptions of the truth of causal determinism and the falsity of Cartesian dualism).[38] Then Judith has the mental states she is in when she meets conditions (Mi) and (Mii) if and only if she also has the correlated neural states. The mental state of holding the relevant beliefs about herself will be correlated in Judith with a (no doubt very complicated) neural state (or set of states) (Ni). The same point holds for each of the three conjuncts of (Mii). Judith's taking into consideration, deliberating, and concluding will all be correlated with neural states. To suppose otherwise is to suppose that Judith can engage in mental activity without there being in her any corresponding neural activity, and such a supposition is ruled out by the rejection of Cartesian dualism. So Judith will meet specifications S—the conditions (Mi) and (Mii)—if and only if she is in neural states (Ni) and (Nii).[39]

But these neural states are causally determined, on the assumption that causal determinism is true. They are produced in Judith by natural causes external to her.[40] Since this is so, however, they can also be produced in her by a manipulator. What is brought about by natural causes can be brought about as well by human means, given adequate science and technology. Any neural state can in principle be produced by a neuroscientist if the neuroscience is sufficiently advanced. Consequently, since mental states are correlated with neural states, they can also be produced by a neuroscientist, in virtue of his being able to produce the neural states with which they are correlated. And this will be just as true of the mental state of basing belief on evidence in an appropriate way as it is of any other, simpler mental state. If Cartesian dualism is false and causal determinism is true, then *everything* a person does—not just forming beliefs or having motivational states but even basing beliefs on evidence in a certain way[41]—is causally determined by natural forces acting on that person. But whatever natural forces can causally determine, a manipulator can causally determine as well, at least in theory.

So, on the assumptions that causal determinism is true and Cartesian dualism is false, no matter how we specify the way in which a person's beliefs about herself must be based on her evidence, a person can meet these very specifications in virtue of having electronically induced in her a certain (no doubt very complicated) neural state or set of states.

Consequently, Judith can meet the Fischer and Ravizza conditions for acting on a mechanism which is her own when she is so controlled by a manipulator that her very formation of her beliefs about her own agency on the basis of her evidence is electronically produced in her by the manipulator. Since, as was clear in the previous cases of *Judith I* and the revised *Puppetmasters*, the external controller can also manipulate his victim in such a way that the mechanism on which the victim acts is suitably reasons-responsive, it is possible for a person to meet the Fischer and Ravizza conditions for moral responsibility when she is controlled by another person even to the degree Judith is in *Judith II*.

It is plain, however, that a person who is controlled in this way is *not* morally responsible for what she does while she is being manipulated. Consequently, Fischer and Ravizza's contention that guidance control— acting on one's own moderately reasons-responsive mechanism—is "the freedom-relevant condition necessary and sufficient for moral responsibility"[42] is shown to be false.

It would be easy enough to ward off the objection regarding cases of manipulation that yields this infelicitous conclusion by stipulating that the mechanism on which an agent acts is her own only if it isn't causally determined by anything external to her; and so this part of Fischer and Ravizza's account would be workable if they abandoned their attempt to make their account compatible with causal determinism. As it stands, however, their account isn't workable, contrary to their claim to have improved over Frankfurt's work on this score.[43]

Conclusion

Fischer and Ravizza's claim to have provided an account of moral responsibility different from and superior to Frankfurt's that is nonetheless compatible with the truth of causal determinism appears to gain support from three things. The first is their attempt to provide some positive argument to show that their particular version of moral responsibility as guidance control is compatible with causal determinism. The second is their attempt to show that the arguments for the incompatibilism of responsibility and causal determinism do not work. And the third is their treatment of cases of manipulation, which requires their finding a principled explanation for why mechanisms causally determined only by nonintelligent causes don't undermine moral responsibility while mechanisms causally determined by a manipulator do.

I have argued that they are not successful in any of these three things.

The positive argument they give for the compatibility of the truth of causal determinism with their account of moral responsibility as guidance control rests on the claim that a mechanism that is causally determined at the microlevel can be reasons-responsive. They provide no support for this claim, however, and it is hard to see what could support it without begging the question at issue. Consequently, their case for compatibilism is not advanced by this argument.

Their attempted refutation of the direct argument for the incompatibility of moral responsibility and causal determinism shows that the principle in that argument, Transfer NR, is not valid in its most general form. But if Cartesian dualism is false, the cases in which Transfer NR fails do not include cases of decisions for which an agent is morally responsible. Consequently, a restricted version of the principle will still apply to cases involving human action. Therefore, Fischer and Ravizza's attack on Transfer NR does not invalidate the direct argument for incompatibilism.

Finally, their attempt to make guidance control compatible with causal determinism requires them to find some way of concluding that manipulated persons aren't morally responsible for their acts without also ruling out as not-responsible acts that are done as a result of nonhuman causal determination. The cases of *Judith I* and the revised *Puppetmaster* story show that they are unsuccessful in this attempt. And the problems with *Judith II* show that their strategy for solving the problem—their analysis of the conditions for a mechanism's being a person's own—is unworkable if causal determinism is true.

So for these reasons it seems to me that Fischer and Ravizza have not given an account of moral responsibility that is compatible with the truth of causal determinism, or provided a theory which is an improvement over Frankfurt's, whatever the other virtues of their powerful and interesting account of moral responsibility may be.

One of the main advantages of Frankfurt's account, in my view, lies in the rich, complicated moral psychology it provides. Rather than jettisoning it, as Fischer and Ravizza want to do, I think it's preferable to consider whether it can't be developed in ways that strengthen it without losing its insights. Elsewhere I have argued that Frankfurt's account resembles a certain strand of thought in medieval philosophy running at least from Augustine to Aquinas.[44] That medieval approach shares Frankfurt's views of freedom and moral responsibility as a matter of the structure of the will, without regard to the agent's history, but it supplements these views with a sophisticated theory about the connection between a person's volitions and her cognitive states. Supplemented in this way, Frankfurt's account, in my view, has the resources to handle the sorts of cases Fischer and Ravizza's position cannot.

Acknowledgments

I am grateful to William Alston, Sarah Buss, John Martin Fischer, Carl Ginet, Peter Graham, Scott MacDonald, Michael McKenna, Alfred Mele, Lee Overton, Mark Ravizza, David Robb, and Peter van Inwagen for helpful comments on an earlier draft. I am also grateful to the members of the Philosophy Department at the University of North Carolina, Chapel Hill, and to Richard Swinburne and the members of the Joseph Butler Society at Oxford for helpful discussion of an earlier draft. This essay was written at the National Humanities Center, where I was a Lilly Foundation Fellow for the academic year 1999–2000. It is hard to imagine a more pleasant environment in which to work, or one more conducive to research, than the National Humanities Center, and I am grateful to the Center and to the Lilly Foundation for my year there.

Notes

1. John Martin Fischer and Mark Ravizza, *Responsibility and Control: A Theory of Moral Responsibility* (Cambridge: Cambridge University Press, 1998), 196.

2. Ibid., 241, n. 2.

3. See, for example, Fischer and Ravizza, *Responsibility and Control*, 26.

4. Ibid., 253.

5. Ibid., 51.

6. Ibid., 51.

7. For a helpful discussion of this point, see John Dupre, *The Disorder of Things* (Cambridge, Mass.: Harvard University Press, 1993).

8. The threat to their account from causal determinism, as they see it, is that an agent S who acts differently in world W from the way in which he acts in the actual world will be causally determined by different causes in W from those that determine him in the actual world; consequently, it might seem to an objector that in W, S operates on a mechanism different from that on which he operates in the actual world. Since Fischer and Ravizza respond to this threat by arguing that the mechanism on which an agent operates can be the same even if there are differences on the microlevel, it seems not unreasonable to suppose that they are assuming causal determinism operates on the microlevel.

9. See, for example, Dupre, *The Disorder of Things*.

10. For a controversial examination of this contention, see Alvin Plantinga, "An Evolutionary Argument Against Naturalism," *Logos* 12 (1992): 27–49.

11. Patricia Churchland, "Epistemology in the Age of Neuroscience," *Journal of Philosophy* 84 (1987): 548–549.

12. Richard Rorty, "Untruth and Consequences," *New Republic* (July 31, 1995), 36. I am grateful to Bryan Cross for calling this passage to my attention.

13. Someone might worry about the connection between truth and the reasons at issue for Fischer and Ravizza. But whatever exactly Fischer and Ravizza's concept of reasons in this connection is, it explicitly includes beliefs, as well as preferences and values (see, e.g., 72), and these beliefs must be "at least minimally 'grounded in reality'" (73).

14. Perhaps (virtually) all philosophers assume that human beings are generally reasons-responsive, and perhaps most philosophers assume that when human beings respond to reasons, they do so by using brain mechanisms. The question at issue here, however, is not about these assumptions but rather about whether neurobiology is currently in a position to provide evidence for their truth. I am grateful to Sarah Buss and Lee Overton to calling my attention to the need for this footnote.

15. Stephen Kosslyn and Oliver Koenig, *Wet Mind: The New Cognitive Neuroscience* (New York: Macmillan, 1992), 33.

16. This section constitutes a significant revision of the argument in my "The Direct Argument for Incompatibilism," *Philosophy and Phenomenological Research* 1 (2000): 459–466. In their response in the same issue of the journal (467–480), Fischer and Ravizza concede the general conclusion of my argument but argue that it constitutes only a statement between the incompatibilist and their position. Fischer and Ravizza are not right in this view, as I hope to show in the revised version of the argument I give in this essay.

17. Fischer and Ravizza take the direct argument from Peter van Inwagen's work; see Peter van Inwagen, "The Incompatibility of Responsibility and Determinism," in Michael Bradie and Myles Brand, eds., *Bowling Green Studies in Applied Philosophy 2: Action and Responsibility* (Bowling Green, Ohio: Bowling Green State University Press, 1980), 30–37, reprinted in John Martin Fischer, ed., *Moral Responsibility* (Ithaca, NY: Cornell University Press, 1986); and Peter

van Inwagen, *An Essay on Free Will* (Oxford: Oxford University Press, 1983), 182–188. Van Inwagen calls the principle "Principle Beta."

18. I have given the formulation of the principle as Fischer and Ravizza present it when they first introduce it; see Fischer and Ravizza, *Responsibility and Control*, 152. When they discuss counterexamples to Transfer NR, Fischer and Ravizza sometimes formulate the principle slightly differently. So, for example, in connection with the counterexample *Erosion*, they formulate the relevant portion of the principle this way: "No one is, or ever has been, morally responsible." In general, I formulate the principle and the applications of the principle as Fischer and Ravizza do.

19. Fischer and Ravizza, *Responsibility and Control*, 157.

20. Ibid.

21. Ibid.

22. Ibid., 166–167.

23. "Correlation" and its related terms are becoming common in neurobiology as a means of referring to the connection between the mental and the neural without specifying very much about the nature of the connection. So, for example, in a recent article on visual perception in *Scientific American*, the author says, "Only a tiny fraction of neurons seem to be plausible candidates for what physiologists call the 'neural correlate' of conscious perception." Nikos Logothetis, "Vision: A Window on Consciousness," *Scientific American* (November 1999), 74.

For the purposes of this example, I am making two assumptions about the nature of this correlation.

The first is that (for human beings in this world) the mental is implemented in the neural, so that there is a given mental act or state if and only if the neurons in the neural sequence correlated with that mental act or state have fired. In the formulation of this assumption, the term "implemented," like the term "correlation," is vague; but, however exactly "implemented" is to be understood, the stipulation that the mind is implemented in the nervous system is intended to rule out the view that the mind and the nervous system are two distinct substances, each capable of action on its own without the other and each capable of causal interaction with the other.

The second assumption is that the correlation is a one-many relation; one mental act or state is correlated with the firings of many neurons in a neural sequence. The mental act or state doesn't occur or exist unless and until its entire correlated neural sequence is completed.

In my view, other than Cartesian dualism, most theories of the relation of mind and body (including Thomistic dualism) will be compatible with these two assumptions.

24. I am grateful to Scott MacDonald for calling my attention to the need to address this point.

25. As Carl Ginet has pointed out to me in correspondence, there is also an additional problem about whether such alternative pathways are actually available for most decisions.

26. For the point about incompatibilism to be put precisely, it would have to be modified to take account of those cases in which the agent himself is ultimately responsible for whatever causal determinism is operating on him. I have discussed such cases in detail in "Augustine on Free Will," *The Cambridge Companion to Augustine*, eds. Norman Kretzmann and Eleonore Stump (Cambridge: Cambridge University Press, 2001).

27. Ibid., 210.

28. Ibid., 210.

29. Ibid., 211.

30. Ibid., 213.

31. I discussed this story in connection with Fischer and Ravizza's theory of moral responsibility in "Persons: Identification and Freedom," *Philosophical Topics* 24 (1996): 183–214. Some parts of my discussion here are taken from that paper.

32. Fischer and Ravizza, *Responsibility and Control*, 41. I am supposing that the alien lets Sam's consciousness run at least to the recognition of reasons but that the alien himself in one way or another produces Sam's choice and behavior.

33. The reader who doesn't think much of these arguments is invited to invent his own or to imagine that Sam is philosophically inept and readily flummoxed.

34. In correspondence, David Robb has suggested that an account of moral responsibility should add as a necessary condition that a morally responsible person be an agent. If Fischer and Ravizza added such a stipulation to their account, on Robb's view, the Puppetmaster case would fail to be a counterexample to their account. But I think this response is not open to Fischer and Ravizza, because the Puppetmaster case can be thought of precisely as a counterexample to their construal of agency. On their view, moral responsibility is defined in terms of acting on a reasons-responsive mechanism that is a person's own, and a person who acts on such a mechanism is an agent. The Puppetmaster case is an objection to their account of what it is for a mechanism to be a person's own and so it is also an objection to agency understood in their way. It is therefore no response to the Puppetmaster case to object that in that case Sam is not an agent. Furthermore, Fischer and Ravizza are attempting to show that their account can support our intuition that a manipulated person is not morally responsible. If only agents are morally responsible, and if they stipulate that no manipulated person is an agent, then it would be trivially true that their account supports the intuition in question. It would support it in virtue of stipulating it.

35. Fischer and Ravizza, *Responsibility and Control*, 231.

36. Ibid., 232.

37. Ibid., 236. In a lengthy footnote, Fischer and Ravizza go on to suggest that reliabilist approaches in epistemology might be suggestive of ways in which to construct the analysis of the specifications, but they give little more than a promissory note on this score.

38. See note 23 on the nature of this correlation.

39. We can add, if we like, that the agent's beliefs about herself have to be causally produced by her evidence for them. This addition will make no difference to the case, since a manipulator can cause her evidence to cause these beliefs.

40. And if we add the stipulation in the preceding note, that the agent's evidence causes the agent's beliefs about herself, then the causing of her beliefs by her evidence is itself causally determined by natural forces, if causal determinism is true.

41. Someone might suppose that basing belief on evidence in the appropriate way is not just a matter of what a person S does but is also a matter of the world's being a certain way. For example, the appropriate way of basing belief on evidence might require that the evidence and the belief are really related in a certain way, no matter what S supposes. But in that case, we can simply stipulate that in *Judith II* these external conditions are met when the manipulator manipulates Judith. David Robb has suggested to me in correspondence that if the evidence together with the activity of a manipulator cause the belief, then the evidence hasn't caused the belief in the right way. But if *being caused in the right way* is stipulated to include *not being caused by the activity of a manipulator*, Fischer and Ravizza's third condition for a mechanism's being an agent's own is equivalent to the condition that the mechanism not be causally determined by a manipulator. In that case, their arguments to show that manipulated persons are not morally responsible on their account of moral responsibility are nugatory, because the conclusion will have been built into the conditions for a mechanism's being an agent's own.

42. Fischer and Ravizza, *Responsibility and Control*, 241, n. 2.

43. Or, more precisely, if causal determinism is true and if human beings are among the causally determined material objects in the world; that is, if causal determinism is true and Cartesian dualism is false.

44. See the following papers: "Intellect, Will, and the Principle of Alternate Possibilities," in *Christian Theism and the Problems of Philosophy*, ed. Michael Beaty (Notre Dame: University of Notre Dame Press, 1990), 254–285, reprinted in *Moral Responsibility*, ed. John Martin Fischer and Mark Ravizza, (Ithaca, NY: Cornell University Press, 1993), 237–262; "Persons: Identification and Freedom," *Philosophical Topics* 24 (1996): 183–214; "Aquinas's Account of Freedom: Intellect and Will," *The Monist* 80 (1997): 576–597; "Alternative Possibilities and Moral Responsibility: The Flicker of Freedom," *The Journal of Ethics* 3 (1999): 299–324; "Augustine on Free Will," *The Cambridge Companion to Augustine*, ed. Norman Kretzmann and Eleonore Stump (Cambridge: Cambridge University Press, 2001).

REPLY TO ELEONORE STUMP

Harry Frankfurt

1. Someone who manipulatively causes another to have certain thoughts or to act in certain ways may be morally responsible for causing those events. This does not entail that the person who is manipulated bears no moral responsibility for the thoughts and actions in which the manipulation results. The possibility that an individual's thoughts or conduct are being deliberately manipulated by another person is, as such, no more a threat to his moral responsibility than the possibility that his thoughts or behavior are being brought about by impersonal and indifferent natural causes. Certain sorts of manipulation threaten moral responsibility while others do not.

Fischer and Ravizza seek to insulate their account of moral responsibility against the possibility that someone who is manipulated by another person might be wrongly held to be morally responsible for what he does. It seems to me that Stump is correct in her claim that their attempt to accomplish this insulation is unsuccessful. Her discussions of the examples involving Sam and Judith show effectively that even an agent who is being manipulated in ways that undermine moral responsibility can, according to the criteria Fischer and Ravizza provide, act on a mechanism that is both suitably reasons-responsive and the agent's own. Thus she shows that their criteria do not satisfactorily identify the conditions upon which moral responsibility depends.

2. I agree with Stump that the evolutionary process of natural selection does not ensure an orientation toward truth but ensures only that the nervous system is oriented toward getting its body parts where they need to be in order to promote the organism's survival and reproduction. Contrary to what Stump evidently thinks, however, this is not tantamount to supposing that evolution fails to ensure an orientation toward reasons-responsiveness. Reasons-responsiveness does not, in fact, require an orientation toward true beliefs. Insects have reasons, to which they respond, for their defensive scurrying about, as they do when someone comes after them with manifestly deadly intent. Their movements are neither random nor tropistic, they have alternatives, and they make

mistakes. It is difficult to make sense of their behavior without understanding it as in some way rational. There is no need, however, to imagine that they believe anything.

Insects are very likely not conscious. In any event, they are almost certainly not sufficiently self-conscious to understand or to articulate for themselves what they are up to. Nonetheless, it seems to me that they do "track reasons" to the extent that their responses to stimuli are appropriate or intelligible in terms of the interest in survival that we naturally attribute to them. Stump may be correct in stating that Fischer and Ravizza's concept of reasons "explicitly includes beliefs" (though I do not find unequivocal confirmation of this at the location in their book that she cites). My own construals of the concepts of having reasons and of rational behavior do not include any essential reference to beliefs.

I am therefore inclined to reject Stump's claim that "apart from a general ideological commitment to the truth of causal determinism, there seems to be no reason—none based in biology at any rate—to maintain that the brain's cognitive functions are determined at the microlevel by extramental reality in a reasons-tracking way." In my view, there is indeed a reason for maintaining this—namely, that natural selection can be expected to see to it that many organisms (even some without brains) respond to reasons for getting their body parts where they need to be in order for those organisms to survive. I do not believe Stump has satisfactorily shown, accordingly, that Fischer and Ravizza's assumption that there can be a causally determined reasons-responsive mechanism "is no more than an assertion on their part ..."; nor do I believe she has established that, because they cannot support this assumption, they "do not have an argument for their compatibilism." This does not affect my judgment, expressed above, that she has nonetheless succeeded in undermining their criteria for moral responsibility.

3. Stump says that "Transfer NR is a highly plausible principle." This is not a very powerful reason for accepting it. After all, the Principle of Alternate Possibilities is now confidently rejected by many people to whom it once seemed highly plausible. In fact, however, Transfer NR does not strike me as plausible at all. The principle states that if no one has any moral responsibility for p, and if p necessitates q, and if no one has any moral responsibility for that connection between p and q, then q

and no one has any moral responsibility for q. I do not see why it should be thought that if p has a certain feature, and if the fact that p necessitates q has that feature too, it must follow that q also has it. One might just as well maintain the absurdity that if p has no cause, and if the fact that p causes q has no cause, then q has no cause.

Whatever plausibility Transfer NR might somehow appear to enjoy is in any case dissipated by the same considerations that dissipate the plausibility of the Principle of Alternate Possibilities. Insofar as those considerations are effective, as I believe they are, it is clear that Betty (the woman in Stump's example) may well be morally responsible for detonating the explosives; and insofar as that is clear, the example provides no support for Transfer NR. Thus the "direct argument" against compatibilism is not independent of the "indirect argument" against it. The direct argument (based on Transfer NR) is eviscerated when it is shown that the indirect argument (based on PAP) cannot be sustained.[1]

4.   In this connection, I will mention one quite minor further point. Stump says that since Fischer and Ravizza do not succeed in showing that the direct argument for incompatibilism fails, "their claim that the account of moral responsibility which they give is compatible with causal determinism is undermined." But why should their claim be undermined by their lack of success in showing that the direct argument for incompatibilism fails? This is surely not a matter of logic. If incompatibilism is true, it might follow that their account of moral responsibility must be false. But it would not follow that they are mistaken in claiming that it is compatible with determinism.

Note

1. It strikes me, incidentally, that Fischer and Ravizza take a wrong turn in the way they go about challenging the Transfer NR principle. They adduce putative counterexamples involving preemptive or simultaneous overdetermination. But how does it help their position if q has two causal determinants rather than just one? If Betty is morally responsible for detonating explosives, then this shows that the principle is false regardless of whether the avalanche would have occured anyhow.

3

Hierarchy, Circularity, and Double Reduction

Michael E. Bratman

I The First Reduction

A major element in Harry Frankfurt's ground-breaking work in the philosophy of action has been an emphasis on our capacity for "reflective self-evaluation"—in particular, our capacity to step back and reflectively assess our motivation.[1] Such reflective self-evaluation sometimes issues in "identification" with a form of motivation, sometimes in "withdrawal."[2] I might, on reflection, identify with my desire to help you. In contrast, a drug addict might reflectively reject and withdraw from his powerful desire for the drug,[3] and a person may despair of her extreme competitiveness and reject her powerful desire to win.[4] In this respect, we may suppose, our agency differs significantly from that of many nonhuman animals and of very young human children.

Frankfurt has been concerned to explain in what an agent's reflective identification with, or withdrawal from, such desires consists. Though the details have varied, Frankfurt's basic strategy has included an appeal to a hierarchy of higher-order pro or con attitudes. The project, I take it, has been to provide an account of the *agent's* identification with, or withdrawal from, a first-order desire in large part in terms of relations of support or rejection between higher-order pro or con *attitudes* and that first-order desire.[5] That is, concerning cases in which the agent has a first-order desire D, we seek to provide truth conditions for

(1) The agent identifies with first-order desire D

primarily in terms of certain higher-order attitudes of the agent in support of D. (We proceed in an analogous way in explaining the agent's withdrawal from a desire.) In this way we seek a reduction of the agent's identification with a desire, primarily to the support of that desire by relevant higher-order attitudes of that agent. For reasons that will become clear, I will call this effort to reduce agent identification to higher-order-attitude support an effort to achieve the *first* reduction.

Frankfurt once noted that a psychiatrist might desire to have a desire for a drug without desiring that that desire move her to act.[6] Frankfurt would not, I take it, suppose that such a psychiatrist identifies with that desire in the relevant sense. A lesson we can draw from this example is that identification, in the relevant sense, with a desire does not merely concern the presence of that desire. But, then, what does it concern?

Consider the following fascinating passage in "Identification and Wholeheartedness":

There are two quite different sorts of conflicts between desires. In conflicts of the one sort, desires compete for priority or position in a preferential order; the issue is which desire to satisfy *first*. In conflicts of the other sort, the issue is whether a desire should be given *any* place in the order of preference at all—that is, whether it is to be endorsed as a legitimate candidate for satisfaction or whether it is to be rejected as entitled to no priority whatsoever. When a conflict of the first kind is resolved, the competing desires are *integrated* into a single ordering,... Resolving a conflict of the second kind involves a radical *separation* of the competing desires, one of which is not merely assigned a relatively less favored position but extruded entirely as an outlaw. It is these acts of ordering and rejection—integration and separation—that create a self out of the raw materials of inner life.[7]

The suggestion, I take it, is that in identifying with a desire, one endorses it "as a legitimate candidate for satisfaction"; in withdrawing from a desire, one separates it from those desires that one endorses as such legitimate candidates.[8] The psychiatrist who just wants to know what it is like to experience a desire for the drug does not thereby endorse that desire "as a legitimate candidate for satisfaction."

But what is it for an agent to endorse a desire "as a legitimate candidate for satisfaction"? To answer we need to reflect on two potentially inter-related roles a desire may play in action. So that is what I will do in the next four paragraphs. I will then return to our question about endorsing a desire "as a legitimate candidate for satisfaction."

Begin by noting that a desire may function as an effective motive of intentional action. When a desire for *E* so functions, it is—at the least, and roughly speaking—part of a mechanism that cognitively tracks and thereby tends to promote (given true beliefs) bringing about or realizing *E*.[9] Now, Donald Davidson has supposed that when a desire functions in this way something else is also true, namely, the agent "sets a positive value on" E and in part because of that has "attitudes and beliefs from which, had he been aware of them and had the time, he *could* have reasoned that his action was desirable (or had some other positive attribute)."[10] When a desire functions in this latter way it provides, by way of its "natural propositional expression,"[11] a premise for "a piece of practical reasoning the conclusion of which is, or would be if the conclusion were drawn from the premises, that the action actually performed is desirable."[12]

Davidson's idea, I take it, is that when a desire for E motivates intentional action, the agent is at least disposed to engage in practical reasoning in which the desire motivates by way of her treating E as a *justifying* consideration or reason in favor of her action. It will be useful to have a label for the case in which this disposition is realized—the case in which the desire for E motivates by way of the agent's treatment of E as a justifying end in her deliberation or practical reasoning. Let us say that in this case the agent treats that desire as providing a justifying reason for action. I will below (in section VIII) try to say a bit more about this idea; but for now I think it clear enough to proceed.

In particular, we can reflect on Davidson's idea that these two roles of desire always go together; for one thing we have learned from the critical reaction to Davidson's philosophy of action is that it is not clear that they do.[13] That is, it is not clear that whenever

(i)   a desire functions as an effective motive of intentional action

it is also true that

(ii)   the agent is disposed to treat that desire as (in the indicated sense) providing a justifying reason for action.

One problem is that the existence of a motivational connection between desire and action is a general phenomenon, one that we see in both human and certain nonhuman animals. Once we grant this point it seems that the presence of such a motivational connection between desire and action may or may not involve a conception, on the part of the actor, of the desired end as justifying. After all, the desires of young children (and certain other Frankfurtian "wantons")[14] motivate intentional action; yet it is not plausible that these children (and other wantons) must have associated dispositions to treat those desires as providing a justifying reason.[15] It is a remarkable achievement of human agency that many cases of motivation really do involve some such disposition. But we should not be so impressed with this achievement that we lose track of the potential gap between (i) and (ii).

I think Frankfurt would agree. A distinction between (i) and (ii) seems implicit in his approach to motivation by first-order desire, as a phenomenon that is present in both wantons and persons. After all, in both cases first-order desires motivate, yet it is unlikely that all motivation in wantons involves (ii). The distinction also seems suggested by Frankfurt's discussion of the unwilling addict: it is natural to see such an agent as moved by a desire for a drug though he is not disposed to treat that desire as reason-providing.[16] And the idea that motivation by first-order desire is a general phenomenon present both in human and in nonhuman agents is in keeping with Frankfurt's advice that "[w]e are far from being unique either in the purposiveness of our behavior or in its intentionality."[17]

So let us distinguish these two related but different roles a desire might play in action: as a motive, and treated by the agent as reason-providing. Equipped with this distinction let us now return, as promised, to our question about what it is for an agent to endorse a desire "as a legitimate candidate for satisfaction." When an agent endorses a desire in this way (and so identifies with that desire), does she merely endorse that desire's functioning as an effective motive? Or must she as well endorse her treating that desire as providing, in deliberation and practical reasoning, a justifying reason for action?

I think that one natural reading of the cited passage from "Identification and Wholeheartedness" supports the latter reading. Talk of a *legitimate* candidate for satisfaction points to a connection with the practical reasoning and deliberation that frequently lies behind action. On this way of thinking about identification with a desire, what it involves is not merely taking sides in favor of a certain motivational pressure; it involves as well a commitment to associated forms of deliberation and practical reasoning. Deliberation and practical reasoning play fundamental roles in our agency. If identification is central to the constitution of the "self out of the raw materials of inner life," it is reasonable to expect it to involve a commitment not merely to forms of motivation but also to associated modes of practical reasoning.

However, though I think there is much to be said in its favor, Frankfurt has indicated that this is not his approach.[18] And we can see signs of this in other essays. In "Identification and Externality," for example, Frankfurt emphasizes that a "person may acknowledge to himself that passions of which he disapproves are undeniably and unequivocally his. . . ."[19] If this is a case of identification, then identification, so understood, may only involve a resigned and perhaps grudging willingness to be moved by a desire.[20]

But even if identification, as Frankfurt understands it, need not involve a commitment to associated forms of practical reasoning, it remains plausible that there is an important, related phenomenon that does. Given the importance of practical reasoning to our agency, we can expect that this related form of identification will be an important target for a theory of human action.

We can, that is, try to begin by interpreting

(1)   The agent identifies with first-order desire D

roughly along the lines of

(1a)   The agent endorses D's functioning as an effective motive.

But, given the kind of agents we are—agents whose actions are normally tied to practical deliberation and the like—at some point we will need also to turn to a version of (1) along the lines of

(1b)   The agent endorses her treating D as providing a justifying reason for action in motivationally effective practical reasoning.

The hierarchical model should at least be extendible to identification along the lines of (1b). We want to know, then, how to approach such identification within the framework of the hierarchical model. I want to sketch an answer. While my answer will be broadly in the spirit of aspects of Frankfurt's hierarchical model, it will also need to draw on further conceptual resources.

II A Threat of Circularity

We seek an account of agent identification in a sense that involves (1b). From now on when I speak of identification, it is this kind of identification I shall have in mind—though I will occasionally allude to (1b) as a friendly reminder. The first reduction, as I am understanding it, aims at an account of such identification primarily in terms of relevant higher-order attitudes of the agent.

What type of higher-order attitudes? I will later describe a view that takes the relevant higher-order attitudes to be certain higher-order policies or the like. But the issues I want to focus on at this point concern, instead, the precise *content* of these higher-order attitudes. And the questions about content that I want to raise do not depend on focusing in particular on higher-order policies. So let us for now simply say that the first reduction seeks an account of the agent's identification (in a sense that involves [1b]) with a desire, D, along the lines of

(2)   The agent has X-type higher-order attitudes in support of D.

Later we can consider in more detail what type X is. What I want now to note is a problem about the content of the higher-order attitudes to be cited in (2).

We have distinguished between a desire's functioning as an effective motive and a desire's being treated by the agent as providing a justifying reason. So we need to ask whether the higher-order attitudes to be cited in a fleshed-out version of (2) are simply to support the desire's functioning as an effective motive, or are to support the agent's treating that desire as providing a justifying reason in motivationally effective deliberation. That is, should we fill in (2) along the lines of

(2a)   The agent has X-type higher-order attitudes in support of D's functioning as an effective motive.

Or should we instead fill in (2) along the lines of

(2b)   The agent has X-type higher-order attitudes in support of her treating D as providing a justifying reason.

The first reduction—from, so to speak, the 1-level to the 2-level—is a reduction of agent identification to higher-order attitude support. In carrying out this first reduction, we seem to face a choice between a reduction to (2a) and a reduction to (2b). Consider an appeal to (2b). A problem here is that an agent's treating a desire as providing a justifying reason in deliberation seems to involve the agent's identification with, or endorsement of, that desire: when the agent treats what is desired as a justifying consideration in her practical reasoning, she seems to be identifying with that desire.[21] But then, in the absence of further analysis, it seems that the contents of the higher-order attitudes cited in (2b) will themselves involve the very idea of the agent's identification with the desire. So if we simply appeal to (2b) without further analysis of the relevant contents we are threatened by circularity.[22] We are seeking a reduction of agent identification to higher-order attitude support, but then seem to be invoking in the content of those higher-order attitudes the very idea of agent identification.

III Four Strategies and a Second Reduction

Consider four strategies of response. First, we could appeal directly to (2b) and just acknowledge that analysis stops here: a hierarchical theory needs also, at bottom, to appeal to a basic notion of one's treating a desire as reason-providing in deliberation. The problem here, however, is that an agent's treatment of a desire as reason-providing in deliberation seems itself to involve her identification with that desire. If this is right then the appeal to hierarchy is not doing the work it was supposed to do in an account of agent identification. Second, we could appeal to (2b) as part of a hierarchical theory of agent identification, but then go on to provide some sort of hierarchical account of an agent's treating a desire as reason-providing. Third, we could avoid direct appeal to (2b) and instead appeal directly to (2a) in our hierarchical theory of agent identification. Fourth, we could seek to appeal to a mode of functioning that is, in a sense to be discussed, in the space between that alluded to by (2a) and by (2b).

Which of these strategies is closest in spirit to Frankfurt's development of the hierarchical model? Well, a main idea of Frankfurt's essays has been that the higher-order attitudes central to agent identification concern whether or not a first-order desire is to be one's "will"—where to be one's "will" is to be an effective desire, a desire that "moves (or will or would move) a person all the way to action."[23] So one natural way to try to extend Frankfurt's theory would be to try to analyze identification, in a sense that involves (1b), along the lines of

(2a)   The agent has X-type higher-order attitudes in support of D's functioning as an effective motive.

This would be a version of the third strategy—the strategy of direct appeal to (2a). But there might also be available a version of the second strategy, one that allows initial appeal to

(2b)   The agent has X-type higher-order attitudes in support of her treating D as providing a justifying reason.

but then seeks to explain an agent's treating a desire as reason-providing in terms of the effectiveness of a hierarchy in favor of that desire's being one's "will." In either case, the suggested proposal would include a *second* reduction. The first reduction is a reduction (from the 1-level to the 2-level) of agent identification to attitude support. Frankfurt's use of his technical notion of "will," when extended in the envisaged ways, suggests a second reduction, a reduction from the b-level to the a-level—a reduction, roughly, of the agent's treating a desire as reason-providing to that desire's functioning as effective motive because of higher-order attitudes in favor of that functioning.

I am, however, skeptical about such a second reduction. A desire for E may motivate action without any thought that E is a justifying consideration. This is, for example, a plausible story about the motivation of the actions of young children or certain other wantons; and it may be a plausible story about certain unwilling addicts. But, then, it seems that merely desiring that such a motivational process occur may still not bring into the story any thought of E as a justifying consideration. Indeed, it seems that one might even desire that the motivational process involving the desire for E in no way involve a thought of E as justifying. So it is not clear how identification, in a sense that involves (1b), could consist solely of hierarchical structures of a sort characterized by (2a).

This problem raises the question whether the use of the hierarchical model in understanding such identification should be made to depend on the success of this second reduction. I think the answer is "no," and that we can instead give the hierarchical model something else to say.[24]

IV   A Way Between?

If we try to reduce the agent's identification with a desire all the way to (2a) we face objections along the lines just sketched. If we seek only a reduction to (2b) then—in the absence of further analysis—we face a threat of circularity. A response to this problem—and this is the fourth strategy mentioned earlier—is to try to locate a path between these two extremes.

An account of the agent's identification with a desire along the lines of (2a) is one version of a more general strategy. The general strategy is to characterize a mode of functioning of a desire such that, first, that mode of functioning does not itself entail that the agent identifies with the desire, and yet, second, we can understand the agent's identification with a desire in terms of higher-order attitude support of such functioning. We have described an extension of Frankfurt's work that involves a particular version of this strategy, one according to which the relevant mode of functioning is that of being an effective motive. I have argued that, when seen as an approach to (1b), this version of a double reduction runs into difficulties.[25] But perhaps we can find an alternative, and more successful, account of the relevant mode of functioning.

A more successful account would characterize a mode of functioning, F, of a desire—a mode of functioning that satisfies three desiderata. First, it goes beyond functioning merely as an effective motive. Second, by itself it does not entail the agent's identification with the desire. And third, it allows us to analyze the agent's identification with a desire—in a sense that involves (1b)—primarily along the lines of

(2-schema)   The agent has X-type higher-order attitudes in support of D's functioning in way F.

If we take "D's functioning in way F" in (2-schema) to be "D's functioning as an effective motive" we get (2a); if we take "D's functioning in way F" to be "D's being treated by the agent as providing a justifying reason" we get (2b). We have seen reason to be wary of either such version of this general strategy. So, as part of the fourth strategy, we are looking for a conception of F that locates a way between.[26]

Now, we should remain alive to the possibility that there is no such F. We may discover that an F that is sufficiently demanding to make a version of (2-schema) work will itself also entail the agent's identification. Such a result would show the limits of the hierarchical approach. But I think we can do better.

V Functioning as End-Setting for Practical Reasoning

What we need is a mode of functioning of a desire for E such that the thought of E as justifying plays a role in the motivational efficacy of that desire, but there remains the possibility that the agent does not endorse that functioning.

It is useful here to turn to Allan Gibbard's distinction between "accepting a norm" and "being in the grip of a norm."[27] As Gibbard understands these ideas, to accept a norm, or to accept that a certain norm "outweighs another in a given situation" is, roughly and in part, to be disposed explicitly to appeal to that norm (and/or its relative weight) in one's practical reasoning and in one's "normative discussion" with others, and to be, as a result, moved accordingly to action. Gibbard contrasts with this the case of merely being in the grip of a norm, one he explains in part by way of reflection on Stanley Milgram's famous experiment.[28] Many subjects in that experiment reluctantly go along with an experimenter's apparently authoritative orders to do that which appears to inflict suffering on a third party (though it in fact does not inflict suffering). Gibbard supposes that these subjects do not accept that norms of doing one's job override, in such a case, norms against the infliction of harm. Nevertheless, these subjects are in fact moved to act by their norms of doing their job. Gibbard says that these subjects are in the grip of (though they do not accept) that norm and/or its priority over harm avoidance.

Now, it seems likely that at least some obedient subjects in Milgram's experiment do not act without relevant thinking. Their actions are, instead, influenced by thoughts like: "Oh dear. He is the authority, and he told me to do this job, and I really should do my job I guess. . . ."[29] These are not cases of being motivated by a rule of which one is simply unaware, as in the case, cited by Gibbard, of the adjustment of conversational distance.[30] The actions of such subjects in Milgram's experiment are influenced by a kind of attenuated reasoning that tracks conformity to the norm of doing their job. For such subjects, thoughts like "I guess I should cooperate with such an authority" function as end-setting premises in a kind of attenuated reasoning.

This seems a not-uncommon phenomenon. Suppose that I have a strong desire for revenge. This may simply move me to act, perhaps without my even being aware that this is why I am doing what I am doing. But it also may move me by way of powerful thoughts like: "That creep! He harmed me and now he deserves to pay!" Such a thought about desert may exert a motivational influence by way of its role as end-setting in processes of reasoning. And it may do this even though, on reflection, I do not accept revenge as a justifying end. Again, my desire to procrastinate may involve wistful thoughts like "Wouldn't it be nice to wait until next week." This may lead to practical reasoning that appeals to procrastination as a justifying end. This may happen even though, on reflection, my higher-order attitudes reject such reasoning.

R. Jay Wallace explores a related phenomenon in his effort to describe certain kinds of irrational guilt. In some such cases, Wallace avers, agents are prone "to entertain evaluative thoughts of disfigurement that they need not accept, but that they tend to find natural." One is disposed "to entertain negative evaluative thoughts one does not necessarily endorse"—and this "does not require that one be fully committed to [those] evaluative thoughts, either in practical deliberation or as a basis for public discussion."[31] In these cases of irrational guilt the negative thoughts provide structure for the emotion. In the cases in which I am interested, thoughts of ends as justifying provide structure for processes of reasoning. In neither case, however, need there be full commitment, on the part of the agent, to these thoughts as elements in deliberation or public justification.[32]

Let us say that a desire for *E functions as end-setting for practical reasoning* when that desire motivates by way of a process of practical reasoning that appeals to *E* as a justifying end. For a desire to function as end-setting for practical reasoning is not merely for it to function as an effective motive: such functioning also involves thoughts of the desired end as justifying.[33] Nevertheless, a desire may function as end-setting for practical reasoning in the absence of a higher-order attitude in favor of that functioning. This is what is common to the Millgram case (as I have interpreted it) and the cited cases of revenge and procrastination. So a desire can function as end-setting for practical reasoning even though the agent does not endorse this functioning. It is then plausible to suppose that a desire can function as end-setting for practical reasoning even though the agent does not identify with that desire. And that is a possibility we wanted to keep open.

We have been trying to understand the agent's identification with a desire along the lines of

(2-schema)   The agent has X-type higher-order attitudes in support of D's functioning in way F.

We asked what F should be for this to work. The fourth strategy seeks a version of F in the space between (2a) and (2b). We now have the conceptual resources to articulate a version of this fourth strategy. We can say that for D to function in way F is for D to function as end-setting for practical reasoning. This leads us to the conjecture that we can understand the agent's identification with a desire along the lines of

(2c)   The agent has X-type higher-order attitudes in support of D's functioning as end-setting for practical reasoning.

Does this conjecture work?

VI   Self-Governing Policies and Identification

We need to return to the question: what is type X? In a recent essay I focus on higher-order policies concerning relevant functioning of one's desires.[34] I call such higher-order policies *self-governing policies*. I argue that self-governing policies can have authority to help constitute where the agent stands with respect to his desires. They can have this authority because of the central role of such policies in the constitution and support of the psychological continuities and connections highlighted by broadly Lockean approaches to the agent's identity over time.[35] Such policies support such cross-temporal connections, for example, when they concern future deliberation and action, and when one later carries out a prior policy; and the characteristic stability of such policies is an important kind of psychological continuity. Such policies have as a characteristic function the support of coordination and organization of action over time,[36] in part by way of support for such cross-temporal, Lockean continuities and connections. This characteristic role of such policies gives them a claim to speak for the agent, to help settle where the agent stands with respect to a particular form of motivation. This is because the agent is not a time-slice agent but, rather, is—and in practical reasoning and action understands herself to be—a temporally persisting agent whose agency is extended over time.

There is an important qualification. For a higher-order self-governing policy to have such authority it needs to be free from significant challenges from other relevant higher-order policies. Borrowing both an idea and a term from Frankfurt I have called this a condition of being "satisfied" with the policy.[37]

This suggests that the type of higher-order attitude needed in (2c) is, in the basic case, a higher-order self-governing policy with which the agent is satisfied. Here I will not try to add to the defense of this proposal.[38] Instead, my concern will be to bring this appeal to higher-order policies together with our reflections on the appropriate content of relevant higher-order attitudes.

Begin by considering a higher-order self-governing policy in support of one's treating D as providing a justifying reason.[39] We have seen that if we simply leave matters here in our account of agent identification we face a concern about circularity. Our reflections on the fourth strategy suggest that we consider instead a higher-order self-governing policy in support of D's functioning as end-setting for reasoning. Is this the kind of higher-order attitude to be cited in our version of (2-schema)?

Not quite. There are, I think, two further complexities. Let me indicate—albeit briefly and without a full defense—what I think they are. First, we will want the relevant policy to be in favor of such functioning *as a matter of policy*.[40] The relevant policy should include the idea that D so function in part because it is one's policy that it so function. A natural way to capture this idea is to suppose that the policy is reflexive: it is a policy that D so function by way of this very policy.[41]

Second, we will want the relevant higher-order policy to be noninstrumental: it is not to be held solely because such functioning of the desire is seen as a causal means to some further end distinct from the end specified by the desire itself.[42] This will allow us to preclude, for example, cases in which one has a policy in favor of such functioning of a desire solely because one believes that when the desire functions in this way it tends as a result to go away, thereby saving one from pain and frustration.[43]

These adjustments in hand,[44] we arrive at an account of agent identification with desire D along the lines of

(3)   The agent has a non-instrumental higher-order self-governing policy, with which she is satisfied, in support of D's functioning, by way of that very policy, as end-setting for practical reasoning.[45]

This is a double reduction, but it is one that is more modest than that sketched earlier. We analyze an agent's identification with a desire in terms of support by a relevant higher-order policy in favor of the functioning of that desire as end-setting for practical reasoning. This is a Frankfurtian reduction of agent identification to higher-order attitude support. But this account diverges from a second reduction that tries to appeal solely to the functioning of a desire as a motive. In (3) we explicitly appeal to processes of reasoning involving thoughts of ends as justifying, though to processes of reasoning that do not themselves ensure the agent's identification.

VII   Singular Commitments

An agent identifies with her desire only if she has a noninstrumental self-governing policy, with which she is satisfied, in favor of that desire's functioning, by way of that policy, as end-setting for practical reasoning. Suppose now that she has no such general policy. But suppose that on this particular occasion she does have a noninstrumental *singular* intention in favor of such functioning. That is:

($3_{singular}$)   The agent has a noninstrumental intention that D function this time, by way of that very intention, as end-setting for practical reasoning.

Suppose further that

(SC) D functions this time as end-setting for practical reasoning because of ($3_{singular}$).

(SC) goes beyond the mere fact that D functions this time as end-setting for practical reasoning. A desire for revenge, or to cooperate with an authority, may, it seems, function this time as end-setting for practical reasoning even in the absence of an intention that it so function this time. One may in this way be "in the grip" of certain thoughts about desert, or authority. The addition of an instance of ($3_{singular}$) and (SC) to such a case brings with it a way in which the agent is committed to this functioning of the desire.[46] After all, the intention in ($3_{singular}$), though singular, is still—by virtue of being an intention—subject to characteristic normative demands for consistency and coherence. These demands involve constraints that connect even a singular, present-directed intention with other intentions and plans. In that sense even such a singular intention involves a commitment, on the part of the agent, to such treatment of the desire.[47]

We have, then, three increasingly demanding cases in which higher-order noninstrumental, reflexive planlike attitudes support the functioning of a desire as end-setting for practical reasoning. One might intend this time that it so function; one might, further, have a policy in favor of its so functioning; and one might have such a policy and also be satisfied with that policy. These are three increasingly demanding ways in which higher-order intentions and policies, and their associated normative structures, can enter into our agency.

There is a tendency in the philosophy of action to limit attention to two main types of theories. There is, on the one hand, a broadly Humean theory that sees action as the output of the causal functioning of desires, and will as, at most, a mere spin-off. There is, on the other hand, a broadly Kantian theory that sees agency and will as essentially involving, and as embedded in, a system of universal principles. On the latter view, it is only when the role of one's desire has been "incorporated" into a system of universal principles that there is an agent and a will, and not merely a system of pushes and pulls.[48]

The present account of possible roles of higher-order planlike attitudes points toward a conception of agency and will in territory midway between these Humean and Kantian models.[49] This is another respect in which it is indebted to Frankfurt's work, for that work has, as I see it, mapped some of the "contours"[50] of this middle ground. On this middle view, agency and will can involve various kinds of higher-order commitments embedded in a system of intentions and plans. Such commitments can be singular and yet still bring to bear characteristic normative demands. But there are also substantial pressures—grounded in the temporal extension of our agency, and captured in the idea of the temporally persisting agent's identification with a desire—in the direction of higher-order policies.

VIII   Treating a Desire as Reason-Providing

We can now return to the idea of an agent's treating a desire as reason-providing. The conceptual resources we have introduced allow us to describe three increasingly strong cases that may merit the characterization "agent treats desire as reason-providing." The strongest case is one in which the general policy in (3) is effective: the desire functions as end-setting for practical reasoning because of the policy, in (3), in favor of that functioning of the desire.[51] The weakest case is one in which the singular intention in ($3_{singular}$) is effective. The intermediate case is one in which the relevant self-governing policy is effective this time (as in the strongest case), but it is not a policy with which the agent is satisfied. In all cases, treating as reason-providing involves a non-instrumental, reflexive intention or policy in favor of relevant functioning as end-setting for practical reasoning. So on all three views there is a gap between a desire's merely functioning as end-setting and its being treated by the agent as reason-providing. Further, these accounts of treating as reason-providing do not themselves explicitly appeal to the very idea of agent identification—though, on the theory, the strongest case does ensure such identification.[52]

IX   Conclusion

Frankfurt has emphasized hierarchical relations among desires of different orders. In earlier work I have emphasized planning structures—structures whose primary functions concern the coordination and organization of the temporally extended thought and action of a temporally persisting agent.[53] The present essay is part of an effort to bring together into a single theoretical conception both hierarchical and planning structures.[54] Here my primary concern has been to understand and to respond to a worry about circularity that appears to arise for hierarchical theories of identification in the sense of (1b). I have argued that one natural extension of Frankfurt's work to this phenomenon brings with it an overly ambitious double reduction. I have tried to replace this with a strategy for pursuing a less problematic, because more modest, double reduction. Finally, by bringing together both hierarchical and planning structures, we have been able to describe a complex range of ways in which higher-order intentions and policies can structure phenomena of agency and will.

Acknowledgments

Thanks to John Fischer, Harry Frankfurt, Thomas Hofweber, Keith Lehrer, Alfred Mele, Elijah Millgram, Peter Railton, Michael Ridge, Jennifer Rosner, J. David Velleman, Gideon Yaffe, members of my 1998 Fall Graduate Seminar in the Philosophy of Action, audiences at the University of Michigan and the "Contours of Agency" Conference, and, in particular, the editors of this volume, Sarah Buss and Lee Overton. Work on the issues discussed in this essay was begun while I was a Fellow at The Center for Advanced Study in the Behavioral Sciences. I am grateful for financial support provided by The Andrew W. Mellon Foundation.

Notes

1. The quote is from Harry Frankfurt, "Freedom of the Will and the Concept of a Person," in *The Importance of What We Care About* (Cambridge University Press, 1988), 12.

2. Frankfurt, "Freedom of the Will and the Concept of a Person," 18. Frankfurt remarks in "Three Concepts of Free Action" that "[t]his notion of identification is admittedly a bit mystifying.... In my opinion, however, it grasps something quite fundamental in our inner lives...." *The Importance of What We Care About*, 54.

3. Frankfurt, "Freedom of the Will and the Concept of a Person," 17.

4. I briefly discuss this example (which derives from an example of T. M. Scanlon) in my "Identification, Decision, and Treating as a Reason," in *Faces of Intention: Selected Essays on Intention and Agency* (New York: Cambridge University Press, 1999), 196–197.

5. See Frankfurt's reflections on "where (if anywhere) the person himself stands" in "Identification and Wholeheartedness," in *The Importance of What We Care About*, 166. And see J. David Velleman, "What Happens When Someone Acts?" *Mind* 101 (1992): 462–481. I discuss in more detail the sequence of views which Frankfurt has proffered in my "Identification, Decision, and Treating as a Reason." I also discuss views of my own that are closely related to the present paper in my "Reflection, Planning, and Temporally Extended Agency," *Philosophical Review* (2000): 35–61, and my "Valuing and the Will," *Philosophical Perspectives* 14 (2000): 249–265.

6. Frankfurt, "Freedom of the Will and the Concept of a Person," 14–15. Thanks to John Fischer for reminding me of this example.

7. Harry Frankfurt, "Identification and Wholeheartedness," in *The Importance of What We Care About*, 170. See also his "Identification and Externality," in *The Importance of What We Care About*, 67, though in this earlier discussion Frankfurt does not use the term "legitimate."

8. Though in the quoted passage Frankfurt does not explicitly say that this is a view about identification, I think it is clear from the context that this is his intent. See, e.g., the immediately preceding paragraph on p. 170.

9. I put to one side cases in which the desire motivates not by providing an end but in some other way, for example, by providing a side-constraint. The

terminology of "tracking" comes from Robert Nozick, *Philosophical Explanations* (Harvard University Press, 1981), chaps. 3 and 4. See also Harry Frankfurt, "The Problem of Action," in *The Importance of What We Care About*, 69–79, esp. 74–75.

10. Donald Davidson, "How is Weakness of the Will Possible?" and "Intending," in *Essays on Actions and Events* (New York: Oxford University Press, 1980), 31, 85. (Though compare "Actions, Reasons, and Causes," in *Essays on Actions and Events*, 4.)

11. Davidson, "How is Weakness of the Will Possible?" 31.

12. Davidson, "How is Weakness of the Will Possible?" 33. I take it that the desire may so function because the agent holds that E is desirable whether or not he desires E; indeed, that may be, at least in part, why he desires E. Alternatively, the agent may see the desirability of E as dependent on the presence of the desire. Finally, the desire need not be in the "foreground" of the practical reasoning, in the sense introduced by Pettit and Smith. See Philip Pettit and Michael Smith, "Backgrounding Desire," *Philosophical Review* 96 (1990): 565–592.

13. See Michael Smith, *The Moral Problem* (Cambridge, Mass.: Basil Blackwell, 1994), 137–141; J. David Velleman, "The Guise of the Good," *Nous* 26 (1992): 3–26; and J. David Velleman, introduction to *The Possibility of Practical Reason* (Oxford: Oxford University Press, 2000), 5–10.

14. "Freedom of the Will and the Concept of a Person," 16–18.

15. See Velleman, "The Guise of the Good," 7.

16. This is, pretty much, Smith's understanding of the example. See Smith, *The Moral Problem*, 134. For an alternative understanding of some versions of this case see Sarah Buss, "Autonomy Reconsidered," in Peter A. French, Theodore E. Uehling Jr., and Howard K Wettstein, eds., *Midwest Studies in Philosophy XIX: Philosophical Naturalism* (Notre Dame, Ind.: University of Notre Dame Press, 1994), 101. For a subtle and suggestive sketch of a general approach to addictive motivation, see Gary Watson, "Disordered Appetites: Addiction, Compulsion, and Dependence," in Jon Elster, ed., *Addiction: Entries and Exits* (Russell Sage Foundation, 1999), 3–28.

17. Frankfurt, "The Problem of Action," 78. Frankfurt also emphasized this advice in his comments at the "Contours of Agency" Conference.

18. In his comments on an earlier draft of this essay at the "Contours of Agency" Conference. In my earlier discussion of these matters in "Identification, Decision, and Treating as a Reason," I was unsure about how to interpret Frankfurt on this point. (See note 33 in the version in my *Faces of Intention*.)

19. Frankfurt, "Identification and Externality," in *The Importance of What We Care About*, 65.

20. It does seem to me, though, that seeing such cases as ones of identification is in tension with the idea that identification with a first-order desire always involves a higher-order desire in its favor.

21. I say only "seems" because my final view allows for some qualification. (See below, section VIII.) But for now we can work with the unqualified, but I think

intuitively plausible, idea that one's treatment of a desire as providing a justifying reason in one's deliberation itself involves one's identification with that desire. After all, it seems that in so treating that desire one is treating it as a "legitimate candidate for satisfaction."

22. I discussed an ancestor of this concern in "Identification, Decision, and Treating as a Reason," in *Faces of Intention*, 198.

23. Frankfurt, "Freedom of the Will and the Concept of a Person," 14. See also "Identification and Wholeheartedness," 164. Note though that in other discussions Frankfurt employs a considerably broader notion of the agent's will. See, e.g., Harry Frankfurt, "Autonomy, Necessity, and Love," in *Necessity, Volition, and Love* (New York: Cambridge University Press, 1999).

24. J. David Velleman also eschews this second reduction in his introduction to *The Possibility of Practical Reason*.

25. For a further difficulty see my "Identification, Decision, and Treating as a Reason," in *Faces of Intention*, 195–196.

26. The situation here to some extent parallels an analogous problem for the causal theory of action. See, e.g., H. A. Prichard, "Acting, Willing, Desiring," in his *Moral Obligation* (Clarendon Press, 1949), 187–198; and H. Grice, "Intention and Uncertainty," *Proceedings of the British Academy* 57 (1971): 263–279, at 275–278. The solution I go on to sketch, however, has a different structure than that proposed, in the action-theoretic cases, by Prichard and Grice.

27. Gibbard, *Wise Choices, Apt Feelings* (Harvard University Press, 1990), 60. The discussion throughout chapter 4 is relevant here.

28. Ibid., 58–60.

29. Or so it seems to me. At this point, though, I may be going beyond Gibbard's intended interpretation of the idea of being in the grip of such a norm.

30. Ibid., 69–70.

31. R. Jay Wallace, *Responsibility and the Moral Sentiments* (Harvard University Press, 1994), 46.

32. Lawrence Beyer has usefully explored related phenomena in theoretical reasoning. One of Beyer's many examples is the functioning of certain racist stereotypes. Beyer suggests that such stereotypes may in the absence of belief nevertheless shape actual thinking and reasoning. See Lawrence Beyer, *The Disintegration of Belief* (Ph.D. thesis, Stanford University, 1999).

33. Might Frankfurt say that, as he is understanding the idea of motivation, motivation by a first-order desire essentially involves that desire's functioning as end-setting for practical reasoning? I do not see that this move is available given his understanding of motivation in young children and certain other wanton agents.

34. "Reflection, Planning, and Temporally Extended Agency." I see policies as intentions that are appropriately general, and I understand intentions along the lines developed in my *Intention, Plans, and Practical Reason* (Cambridge: Harvard University Press, 1987; reissued by CSLI Publications, 1999).

35. Talk of continuities and connections comes from Derek Parfit, *Reasons and Persons* (New York: Oxford University Press, 1984), 204–209. I note differences in my use of these terms in "Reflection, Planning, and Temporally Extended Agency."

36. Frankfurt alludes to the coordinating roles of intentions in "Identification and Wholeheartedness," 175.

37. See Frankfurt, "The Faintest Passion," in *Necessity, Volition and Love*, (New York: Cambridge University Press, 1999). I develop the idea of satisfaction in a way that is slightly different from Frankfurt's in my "Identification, Decision, and Treating as a Reason," and in "Reflection, Planning, and Temporally Extended Agency."

A second qualification is that the relevant Lockean role can also be played by what I call higher-order "quasi-policies." Though important to the overall story I want to tell, we can safely put this qualification to one side here.

38. I see my discussion in "Reflection, Planning, and Temporally Extended Agency" as a partial defense, though more still needs to be said. Let me note here that, on my view, for a self-governing policy to have the relevant authority, it is not required that that policy be volitionally necessary or part of the person's "essential nature," in the senses recently developed by Frankfurt. (See his "On the Necessity of Ideals," in *Necessity, Volition, and Love*, 108–116, quotation at 113. And, for critical discussion, see J. David Velleman, "Identification and Identity" in this volume.) Self-governing policies have a special relation to the agent's identity over time, not because they are volitionally necessary or essential, but rather because of their roles in organizing thought and action by way of constituting and supporting relevant Lockean ties.

39. This is where I left matters in "Reflection, Planning, and Temporally Extended Agency," noting that I would return later to concerns about circularity. For somewhat related ideas about policies or principles concerning whether to treat a desire as reason-providing, see Rachel Cohon, "Internalism about Reasons for Action," *Pacific Philosophical Quarterly* 74 (1993): 265–288; Christine Korsgaard, *The Sources of Normativity* (Cambridge University Press, 1996); and T. M. Scanlon, *What We Owe to Each Other* (Harvard University Press, 1998), 41–55.

40. I owe this way of putting the point to Keith Lehrer.

41. See Gilbert Harman, "Practical Reasoning," *Review of Metaphysics* 29 (1979): 431–463, at 441–445.

42. Peter Railton, Michael Ridge, Michael Smith, and Gideon Yaffe have each helped convince me of the need for this second modification. The issue goes back to a challenge once posed to me by Alfred Mele.

43. Note, though, that a policy in favor of Y will be noninstrumental if one has it because one sees Y as partly constitutive of an ideal one embraces.

44. For reasons Gilbert Harman has discussed, we may also want the policy not to be held solely because it is thought that such functioning of the desire for E is evidence of (but not a cause of) some further desired end distinct from E. But

this is a complexity we can put to one side here. See Gilbert Harman, "Desired Desires," in R. G. Frey and C. W. Morris, eds., *Value, Welfare, and Morality* (Cambridge: Cambridge University Press, 1993), 149.

45. Such policies may go on to assign relevant weights to be given in practical reasoning to the end set by *D*. See Nozick, *Philosophical Explanations*, 297; and Gibbard, *Wise Choices, Apt Feelings*, 163. These policies might also see the desire as associated with a kind of side-constraint, though we do not need to examine this complexity here.

46. See G. A. Cohen's remarks about "singular edicts" in his "Reason, Humanity, and the Moral Law," included in Korsgaard, *The Sources of Normativity*, 176.

47. That intentions involve commitments is a theme of my *Intention, Plans, and Practical Reason*.

48. See Henry E. Allison's discussion of what he calls the "Incorporation Thesis" in *Kant's Theory of Freedom* (Cambridge University Press, 1990), 40. And consider Christine Korsgaard's remark that "it is the claim to universality that *gives* me a will, that makes my will distinguishable from the operation of desires and impulses in me." *The Sources of Normativity*, 232.

49. I discuss a related point in my "Review of Korsgaard's *The Sources of Normativity*," in my *Faces of Intention* at 276–277.

50. To borrow from the apt title of this volume.

51. If this is what it is for the agent to treat the desire as reason-providing, then by making the cited policy reflexive we ensure that it is, in effect, a policy in favor of one's treating the desire as reason-providing.

52. At this point we might try to use some such account of the agent's treating a desire as reason-providing in a version of the second strategy noted in section 3. However, this version of the second strategy, like the version of the fourth strategy I have sketched, would be modest with respect to the second reduction: it would not try to understand treating *D* as reason-providing solely in terms of higher-order support for *D*'s functioning as a motive. So such a version of the second strategy would still cohere with the central claim that such modesty is a better strategy for a hierarchical theory.

53. See esp. my *Intention, Plans, and Practical Reason*.

54. See also my "Identification, Decision, and Treating as a Reason," "Reflection, Planning, and Temporally Extended Agency," and "Valuing and the Will."

REPLY TO MICHAEL E. BRATMAN

Harry Frankfurt

1. I am not altogether confident that I have an entirely secure or perspicuous understanding of Bratman's views concerning the various issues with which his elaborately conceived and intricately articulated discussion deals. It is therefore unclear to me in just what ways (if, indeed, at all) his views and mine are truly in serious conflict. I suspect that when we appear to differ, that may sometimes be because we are actually discussing different things. He is focused primarily on the relationship between practical reasoning and the way in which individuals may be said, in a certain sense, to identify themselves. On the other hand, I am not mainly concerned—at least in those aspects of my work to which he refers—either with practical reasoning or with individual identification in the sense that particularly interests him.

Nonetheless, it cannot be assumed that therefore the differences in our views are likely always to be either illusory or innocuous. Even when it is quite clear that our attentions are indeed devoted to distinct topics, this divergence in our interests may itself rest upon judgments of relevance or of importance with respect to which we are genuinely at odds. In an effort to facilitate sorting these things out, I shall begin by explaining how I construe the relationship between identification in the sense that interests me most and the hierarchical structures upon which that sort of identification typically depends. Next, I shall try to dispel various misunderstandings of my views by clarifying certain unfortunate terminological usages by which I fear that I have encouraged them. Then I shall consider some issues concerning practical reasoning that Bratman's essay raises.

2. Reflective evaluation of a desire D may lead an agent to form a higher-order desire that supports (or rejects) D, and it may also lead the agent to identify himself with (or withdraw himself from) D. The fact that the agent is reflecting on D entails that he has already put his relationship to it in question. Considering or evaluating D precedes, and is not itself tantamount to, arriving at an evaluation of D or forming a higher-order desire or attitude concerning it. Finally, an agent who has

formed a higher-order desire supporting (or rejecting) D may not be willing to permit that desire to be fulfilled; he may fail or decline to accord the higher-order attitude effective authority. Accordingly, the agent identifies with D (or renders D alien to himself) only when a further psychic condition has been met. Thus, four elements or stages are conceptually distinguishable within the process, even though they may not be either separated or separable in fact. The agent (i) provisionally suspends or brackets his relationship to D, (ii) reflects on D, (iii) forms a higher-order desire or attitude toward D, and (iv) identifies himself with D or alienates himself from it.[1]

3. The higher-order attitudes that are formed in processes leading to identification involve "evaluations" only in a sense that is strictly value-neutral. In speaking of these matters, I have regrettably made use of terms—such as "endorse"—that naturally suggest a positive evaluation. However, what I have actually intended to convey by referring to "endorsement" is not that the agent *approves* of what he is said to endorse, or that he considers it to *merit* his support, but nothing more than that the agent *accepts* it as his own. The sense in which he accepts it as his own is quite rudimentary. It is free of any suggestion concerning his basis for accepting it and, in particular, it does not imply that he thinks well of it.

Bratman says that my views concerning identification have to do with "relations of support or rejection between higher-order pro- or con-attitudes" and first-order desires. It is true that the higher-order attitudes that I invoke must be either supportive or rejecting, but this is true only in a rather literal and limited sense. Higher-order attitudes provide backing for, or withhold backing from, first-order desires. That is, they draw the agent to get behind his first-order desires or they draw him to put himself against those desires. It is in this respect alone that they are *pro* or *con*. Their support or rejection of first-order desires need not include, or be based upon, any favorable or unfavorable attitude concerning how desirable or worthy of approval those desires may be.[2]

My suggestion that an agent who identifies with a desire endorses it "as a legitimate candidate for satisfaction" is similarly misleading. In characterizing a desire as a *legitimate* candidate for satisfaction, I did not intend to imply that the desire provides a justifying reason for actions that are designed to satisfy it. Rather, the legitimacy of a desire—in the sense I intended—means just that the desire is one with which the agent identifies. The point of my usage was that a desire with which an agent identifies is legitimately attributable to him as his own; it is not external to him or, in other words, an outlaw. It may happen that desires that are not legitimate candidates for satisfaction may nonetheless come to be satisfied; but their satisfaction is not among the agent's goals, and it is accomplished without his support. This is the sense in which such desires lack legitimacy.

A person who reflects on the desires by which he finds himself being moved has problems of two distinct types. On the one hand he must decide, with respect to each desire, whether to identify himself with it or whether to reject it as an outlaw and hence as not a legitimate candidate for satisfaction. On the other hand he must decide, with respect to the various desires with which he does identify, what relationships of priority to establish among them. The first type of problem has to do with psychic raw materials that a person may or may not accept for integration into himself. Problems of the second type concern psychic elements that are already fully attributable to the person but that must still be arranged in an order of precedence. Dealing with each of these problems requires a kind of "evaluation" of the desires at issue. In my discussions of identification, I have attended primarily to the variety of value-free and nonjustifying evaluation that is appropriate to problems of the first type.

4.   Bratman poses the following question: "When an agent endorses a desire [as a legitimate candidate for satisfaction] ... (and so identifies with that desire) does she merely endorse that desire's functioning as an effective motive? or must she as well endorse her treating that desire as providing, in deliberation and practical reasoning, a justifying reason for action?" It seems to me that a desire—even when the agent identifies with it as his own—never provides as such a reason for action. What a desire provides is a problem. The problem concerns what to do about the desire—whether to try to satisfy it, whether to suppress it entirely, or whether to put it provisionally aside in order to meet more urgent or more appropriate demands.

The fact that the agent identifies with a desire does mean, I suppose, that he is prepared to assign it some place in the order of his priorities.

Perhaps it might be said, then, that identifying with a desire gives an agent a reason to do *that*. However, this just means that identifying with a desire gives him a reason to take it seriously in a certain way. It does not mean that he is committed to treating the desire as having any specific role in deliberation as a justifying reason for action.

According to my account, as Bratman recognizes, people may identify with desires that they do not regard as meritorious and even with desires of which they disapprove. For someone to identify with a desire means merely that—for whatever reason, or for no reason whatever—he joins himself to the desire and accepts it as his own. Thus I do not believe that identifying with a desire entails considering that the desire justifies or provides a reason for a decision or for an action. In any case, I cannot see that reasons are required either by actions or by decisions. The supposition that people cannot make decisions or perform actions except for a reason strikes me as belonging to an excessively rationalistic conception of human life—a conception that is both theoretically gratuitous and false to the facts.

Now just as it is possible for people to decide and to act without reasons, so people may commit themselves to certain ends without supposing that those commitments are justified. It is certainly true, as Bratman points out, that someone who does not respect a certain norm may nonetheless be gripped by it in a way that leads him to think of it as justifying what he is doing. Someone in the grip of a strong desire for revenge may indeed be motivated by the thought that his enemy deserves to suffer, even though on reflection he does not accept revenge as a justifying end. On the other hand it is not true, as Bratman evidently supposes, that we cannot give a satisfactory account of practical reasoning unless we can identify "a mode of functioning of a desire for E [i.e., some end] such that the thought of E as justifying plays a role in the motivational efficacy of that desire." It is quite possible for a person to take revenge on someone without it ever crossing his mind that his conduct is justified. His desire for revenge may provide the "structures for processes of reasoning" with which Bratman is concerned simply because, without caring at all about what is or is not justified, he commits himself to the ends that his desire engenders.

5.   In Bratman's view, "deliberation and practical reasoning play fundamental roles in our agency." He therefore believes that "if identification

is central to the constitution of the self ..., it is reasonable to expect it to involve a commitment not merely to forms of motivation but also to associated modes of practical reasoning." I am not so sure that deliberation and practical reasoning do play fundamental roles in our agency, if this means that they are essential to our capacity to function as agents. No doubt they figure prominently in our selection of ends and in our design of plans for reaching our goals. It is far from clear, however, that they are indispensable conditions of action.

After all, agency is not unique to human beings or even to humans together with those various less evolved animals that may be regarded as also capable of some mode of practical reasoning. The difference between a creature that is actively in control of its own movements and a creature that is being moved passively by forces over which it has no control is familiarly instantiated even among species too primitive to engage in rational or deliberative thought. When they are active rather than passive, the members of those species function as agents even though processes of practical reasoning cannot plausibly be attributed to them.

Notes

1. Bratman says that I "provide truth-conditions for ... [the statement that an agent identifies with desire D] primarily in terms of certain higher-order attitudes of the agent in support of D." It is true that an agent is likely to identify with a desire only in virtue of a higher-order attitude that supports it (leaving aside here the delicate issue of whether identifying with a desire entails having a higher-order attitude towards it). Still, it is important to appreciate that identifying with a desire requires more than simply having a higher-order desire by which it is endorsed.

2. Bratman has the impression that my understanding of identification as value-neutral is "in tension" with the claim that identification with a desire necessarily involves a higher-order desire "in its favor." This impression should be dispelled once the phrase "in its favor" is correctly understood. A higher-order desire may be *in favor of accepting* a lower-order desire without manifesting a favorable opinion of that desire. An agent may in resignation or in exhaustion favor accepting a desire despite the fact that his opinion of the desire is quite unfavorable.

4

Identification and Identity

J. David Velleman

When Harry Frankfurt chose a title for the first volume of his essays, he must have been thinking of the direction in which his work was going rather than the direction from which it had come. Retrospect would have led him to the titles of the founding essays in his research program, such as "Freedom of the Will and the Concept of a Person" or "Identification and Externality." Instead he named the volume after the essay that set the theme for his future work, "The Importance of What We Care About."[1] In the years since the publication of that volume, Frankfurt has explored many topics suggested by its wonderfully resonant title: how our caring about things makes them important to us; how the process of caring about them is important to us; and how important a matter it is which things we care about.

What I most admire about Frankfurt's essays on these topics is their candor in reporting one man's efforts to understand life as he finds it. Reading this work, one has the sense of receiving dispatches from an examined life. Frankfurt's reflections on caring, in particular, are clearly an expression of what the author cares about, and as such they command a respect that transcends any disagreement.

Disagreement there is bound to be, however, when philosophy cuts so close to the bone. In this paper I am going to disagree with Frankfurt's view on the last of the topics mentioned above, the importance of which things we care about. Which things we care about is important, according to Frankfurt, because our cares and concerns define our individual essences as persons: what we care about determines who we are. I don't believe that we have motivational essences of this sort, though I agree that we sometimes seem to have them. I want to look for the source of this misleading appearance.

Frankfurt's New Conception of the Self

Ever since "Freedom of the Will and the Concept of a Person," Frankfurt has sought to draw a distinction among motives as internal or external to the self. The need for this distinction was first suggested to Frankfurt by cases in which an agent lacks autonomy because he is actuated by motives from which he is alienated. These motives seem to assail the agent from without and to compete with him for control of his behavior. Such cases suggest that being autonomous, or self-governed, is a matter of being governed from within—that is, by motives internal to the self. The question is what makes some motives internal in this sense.

Frankfurt's initial answer relied on the concept of identification. He suggested that motives are internal to the self when the subject identifies with them, by reflectively endorsing them as determinants of his behavior. An agent is autonomous, Frankfurt concluded, when he is actuated in ways that he reflectively endorses. This analysis of autonomy elicited a number of objections, which have been the subject of an extensive literature, leading to various revisions on Frankfurt's part.[2] More recently, however, Frankfurt has made a revision that is not obviously prompted by objections: it appears to express a further intuition about the boundaries of the self.

What Frankfurt now says about autonomy is this: "A person acts autonomously only when his volitions derive from the essential character of his will."[3] Frankfurt goes on to explain that inessential characteristics of a person's will are "separable" from it, and in that sense "external" to it, so that their governance of the person's behavior amounts to heteronomy rather than autonomy. Thus, Frankfurt still conceives of autonomy as governance by motives internal to the self, but he has adopted a new criterion of internality. Motives are internal to the self, according to the new criterion, when they are essential to the subject's volitional nature.

Frankfurt disavows what might be perceived as Kantian overtones in this statement. Kant would gladly join Frankfurt in saying that a person is autonomous when his behavior is determined by his essential nature. But what Kant would mean by this statement is that autonomy consists in being determined by practical reason, which places every agent under the same, universal laws.

Frankfurt explicitly rejects this Kantian reading of the relation between autonomy and personal essence. For he is loath to equate the self of self-governance with the anonymous faculty of practical reason:

[T]his *pure will* is a very peculiar and unlikely place in which to locate an indispensable condition of individual autonomy. After all, its purity consists precisely in the fact that it is wholly untouched by any of the contingent personal features that make people distinctive and that characterize their specific identities.... The pure will has no individuality whatsoever. It is identical in everyone, and its volitions are everywhere exactly the same. In other words, the pure will is thoroughly *impersonal*. The commands that it issues are issued by no one in particular.[4]

In Frankfurt's view, the self whose governance constitutes self-governance, or autonomy, must be a thoroughly *personal* self: it must be someone in particular. Frankfurt therefore conceives of personal essences as comprising features of the very sort that Kant purified out of the will—that is, "contingent personal features that make people distinctive and that characterize their specific identities."

Such features, which are contingent to the nature of personhood, can still be essential to an individual person, in Frankfurt's view. "Even though a person's interests are contingent," Frankfurt says, "they can belong to the essential nature of his will."[5] A person can thus have a volitional essence that consists in perfectly idiosyncratic concerns.

What makes contingent interests essential to the nature of a person's will? The answer to this question is best developed in stages, through which an initial intuition is gradually modified.

Frankfurt's initial intuition is that the essence of an agent comprises what is volitionally necessary for him, just as the essence of a triangle comprises what is conceptually necessary for a triangle. Volitional necessity differs from conceptual necessity, however, in that it doesn't constrain how the person can be classified or described: "Volitional necessity constrains the person himself, by limiting the choices he can make."[6] It thus involves the inability to choose some things or to refrain from choosing others.

As Frankfurt goes on to note, however, such an inability may be due to an overwhelming aversion or compulsion of the sort that is alien to the self, constraining the will from without. If an inability is to be constitutive of the self, it ought to constrain the will from within and hence autonomously. Volitional necessity must therefore be a voluntary or willing inability of the will. And Frankfurt believes that the will can indeed be subject to willing inabilities, such as the subject may express by calling an act unthinkable or saying that he cannot bring himself to perform it. To explain how an inability to will can be voluntary, Frankfurt modifies his initial intuition, by reintroducing the concept of identification. An inability becomes voluntary, Frankfurt explains, when it is due to a motive with which the subject identifies by means of a reflective endorsement.[7] If the motive's effectiveness in constraining his will is due in part to his reflective endorsement of it, then "the constraint is itself imposed by his will."[8]

Yet if the agent could potentially withhold his reflective endorsement from this constraint, then it isn't imposed by his will essentially. Hence more than reflective endorsement is required for the volitional necessities that define the subject's volitional essence. Frankfurt's initial intuition is therefore modified once again, to require not only that the agent endorse the motive constraining his will but that he be unable to help endorsing it. In such a case, the agent has a second-order inability: the inability to will any change in his inability to will. And for reasons already noted, this higher-order inability must itself be of the willing variety, by virtue of receiving a higher level endorsement, and so on. The subject's inability to alter his will thus appears to resound through higher and higher levels of the motivational hierarchy.[9] The subject finds that "it is not only unthinkable for him to perform the action in question; it is also unthinkable for him to form an effective intention to become willing to perform it."[10] Compound inabilities of this sort are what define the subject's essential nature, in Frankfurt's view.

Frankfurt describes these inabilities as "contingent volitional necessities by which the will of the person is as a matter of fact constrained."[11] They are contingent in the sense that they are not logically entailed by the subject's being a person or having a will. But they do have a quasi-conceptual consequence. By constraining the subject's will, they also define his essence as an individual, and so they give rise to a further constraint—namely, that he could not alter them while remaining the same person.

Frankfurt makes this point most clearly as follows:

Agamemnon at Aulis is destroyed by an inescapable conflict between two equally defining elements in his own nature: his love for his daughter and his love for the army he commands.... When he is forced to sacrifice one of these, he is thereby forced to betray himself. Rarely, if ever, do tragedies of this sort have sequels. Since the volitional unity of the tragic hero has been irreparably ruptured, there is a sense in which the person he had been no longer exists. Hence, there can be no continuation of *his* story.[12]

The necessitating concerns that make up Agamemnon's essence as a person, as Frankfurt conceives it, cannot be deduced from any of the generic concepts that apply to him, but they are necessary to his individual identity, to his being the particular person who he is. When Agamemnon sacrifices some of these concerns, he becomes a different person, and his former self ceases to exist.

Frankfurt makes the same point in several other ways. For example, he says that if someone is free of any volitional limits, then he has "no essential nature or identity,"[13] and he consequently suffers "a diminution, or even a dissolution, of the reality of the self."[14] A similar dissolution can be caused by boredom, which Frankfurt conceives as a lack of any compelling cares or interests. This state "threatens the extinction of the active self," and our dislike of it can be understood accordingly as an expression of our instinct for self-preservation—"in the sense of sustaining not the *life* of the organism but the *persistence of the self*."[15] Yet a third threat to the self, as conceived by Frankfurt, comes from ambivalence, which guarantees that one or another element of the self will have to be sacrificed when a choice is made.[16] If the self is to have a chance of remaining whole, it must be wholehearted, in the sense of being unequivocal in its essential concerns.

Because these concerns can be sacrificed only at the cost of the self, in Frankfurt's view, they "possess not simply power but authority,"[17] derived from the imperative of self-preservation. The subject has compelling reason not to oppose them, because of the "drastic psychic injuries" that such opposition would entail.[18] What someone cares about is thus important because, by defining who he is, it determines what he must do in order for that person to survive.

These recent developments in Frankfurt's conception of autonomy have, in effect, yoked it to a conception of personal identity, which also involves the boundaries of the self.[19] And Frankfurt's conception of personal identity agrees with the currently prevailing, neo-Lockean conception propounded by Derek Parfit. In particular, Frankfurt's conception of identity agrees with Parfit's in respects that, in turn, distinguish Parfit's conception from Locke's. Since the differences between Parfit and Locke have not been widely discussed, I want to pause a moment to review them.

Parfit follows Locke in thinking that what makes for the survival of a person is his psychological relation to past and future selves.[20] But Parfit differs from Locke on the nature of the relevant relation, and he thereby makes room for motivational essences of the sort that Frankfurt envisions.

Locke thinks that the psychological relation making for a person's survival is exclusively a relation of memory: one's past selves are those whose experiences one remembers first-personally, and one's future selves are those who will first-personally remember one's experiences. A natural extension of Locke's theory applies this definition recursively, so that one's past and future selves include not only those who are linked to one by memory but also anyone similarly linked to them, and so on. In either version, Locke's theory implies that one may share virtually no motivational characteristics with one's past or future selves. One may in the past have possessed vastly different attitudes and traits of character, so long as one remembers being the person who possessed them (or being someone who remembers being that person, and so on); and one may yet have vastly different attitudes and traits in the future, so long as the person possessing them remembers being oneself (or being someone who remembers being oneself, and so on). Not only can a prince and a cobbler end up inhabiting one another's bodies, according to Locke's theory; they can also end up possessing one another's beliefs, desires, ideals, loves, projects, and so on.

Parfit thinks that some of the latter characteristics are in fact relevant to survival.[21] Part of what makes for one's survival, in Parfit's view, is the persistence of attitudes and traits of character.[22] And for this purpose, some attitudes and traits are more important than others. Characteristics that differentiate one from other people tend to be more important to one's survival, as Parfit conceives it, than those that one shares with everyone else;[23] characteristics that one values in oneself may also be more important than those that one wishes to shed.[24] Parfit's theory thus allows for the possibility that some cluster of desires and intentions might be so distinctive of a person, and so valued by him, that he would be as good as dead without them. Sacrificing these attitudes would be the end of him, and so they would derive authority from the imperative of self-preservation, just as Frankfurt believes.[25]

The recent developments in Frankfurt's conception of autonomy have thus brought it into harmony with the distinctively un-Lockean strain in Parfit's otherwise Lockean conception of personal identity. Like Parfit, but unlike Locke, Frankfurt believes that one may have to retain particular motives in order to remain oneself. And he believes that motives essential to the self in this sense are the motives whose governance of one's behavior constitutes one's self-governance, or autonomy.

A Critique of Frankfurt's New Conception

Even if I believed that a person had a motivational essence of this kind, I would not infer that his being governed by this essence was what made him autonomous. Being governed by such an essence might amount to authenticity, perhaps, but not autonomy.

To see the difference, consider the paradigm case of inauthenticity, the person who manifests what D. W. Winnicott called a "False Self."[26] This person laughs at what he thinks he is supposed to find amusing, shows concern for what he thinks he is supposed to care about, and in general conforms himself to the demands and expectations of others. The motives that his behavior is designed to simulate are motives that he doesn't genuinely have. And the overriding motive that he does have— namely, to satisfy the expectations of others—is hardly a motive that he cannot help endorsing; on the contrary, he doesn't even acknowledge this motive, much less endorse it. Hence neither the motives that he simulates nor the motive on which he thereby acts belong to his essential nature, as Frankfurt conceives it.

But is this person lacking in self-control, self-governance, or autonomy? To be sure, he has a problem with autonomy, but his problem is one of excess: he is overly self-controlled, overly deliberate; his grip on the reins of his behavior is too tight, not too loose. His failure to be motivated from within his true self makes him inauthentic, but it seems to result from his being all too autonomous.[27]

So if I believed in a person's motivational essence, I still wouldn't identify it as the source of autonomy; but I don't believe in a motivational essence. I am inclined to say of the essential self posited by

Frankfurt what the psychoanalyst Jeffrey Rubin has recently said of the True Self posited by Winnicott:[28]

The process of searching for one's True Self, regarded as a singular entity waiting to be found, is a quixotic enterprise that may promote self-restriction and self-alienation.... [S]ingular notions like the True Self subjugate selfhood's possibilities by obscuring and limiting its multidimensionality. Facets of self-experience that do not fit into preexisting images of who one *really* is are neglected or not assimilated into one's sense of identity.... Not only is a monolithic sense of self limiting, but psychological health may involve access to, and comfort with, our multidimensionality. From this perspective, a sense of the complexity, multidimensionality, and polyvalency of the self is a developmental milestone and achievement.

With these words in mind, I turn to a critique of Frankfurt's new conception of the self.

I have argued elsewhere against the notion that there must be motivational constancy between a person and his past or future selves. Specifically, I've argued that a person has past and future selves in virtue of psychological connections that give him first-personal access to past and future points-of-view—connections that can be forged by memory and anticipation but not by the retention of motives or traits of character.[29]

I don't deny that some of our concerns are authoritative for us because they are somehow central to our personalities; nor do I deny the temptation to describe these concerns as essential to who we are, integral to ourselves, definitive of our identities, and so on. At the end of this paper, I'll explain how I think we should understand these descriptions. For now, I want to argue only that we shouldn't take them literally by claiming that the defense of our central concerns is a matter of self-preservation, a matter of life or death for the self. Such literalism can easily lead to absurdity.

Consider this passage, which is sometimes cited with approval by critics of impartial morality:

I am not a person who just happens accidentally and irrelevantly, to be a man, forty years old, the husband of a professor of English literature, the son of two aging and sick parents, the father of two small boys six and four, a comfortably well-off member of the upper middle class, American-Jewish, born and raised in New York. I am *essentially* such a man.[30]

Can a man be essentially forty years old, essentially the father of young children, or essentially the son of elderly parents? One cannot read this statement without wondering whether the author still believes it, now that he is in his sixties, his parents have passed away, and his children are grown.

Of course, Frankfurt would not include most of these attributes in a person's essential nature. But if we read this enumeration of attributes as an expression of the associated concerns—of the author's love for his wife and children; pity for his ailing parents; pride in his masculinity, his American-Jewish heritage, or his hometown of New York—then we arrive at a personal essence that Frankfurt might recognize. And we can still wonder whether the author would be a different person simply because of having become estranged from his parents or having fallen for someone other than his wife.

According to Frankfurt, such crises may have no sequels, because their protagonist ceases to exist. But surely estrangements and betrayals are precisely what set the stage for a sequel. The Agamemnon legend would lose much of its power if the man who sacrificed his daughter at the beginning didn't survive to be murdered by his wife in the end. If a crisis like the one at Aulis necessarily put an end to its protagonist, we wouldn't just be lacking sequels to particular stories: we wouldn't have the concept of a sequel at all.

In light of how implausible the notion of personal essences can be when applied to particular cases, we have to wonder why it remains so attractive. Frankfurt never offers us a convincing example of someone who ceases to be the same person because of abandoning a project, betraying a commitment, or undergoing some other change of heart; nor does he offer any argument for thinking that motivational changes can have such momentous results. He simply asserts that our projects and commitments are sometimes essential to who we are. We welcome his assertion, but not as something of which he has convinced us; we welcome it as something that we, too, want to say about ourselves. The question is why we want to say it. In the absence of examples or arguments to show that we have motivational essences, what moves us to apply this self-description?

My worry is that believing ourselves to have motivational essences is a case of wishful thinking on our part. We'd like to have motivational essences, and so we're happy to agree when someone says that we do.

Now, a conception of the self cannot be faulted simply for being associated with wishes. Any conception of how we are constituted will yield implications about what it is for us to be well constituted. A conception of the self will thus entail an ideal of the self, to which holders of the conception will naturally aspire. What's crucial, however, is the logical order between conception and aspiration. We are justified in wishing to embody an ideal implicit in our self-conception; but our self-conception should not be tailored to suit our antecedent wishes. My worry is that Frankfurt's conception of the self appeals to us only because its implicit ideal represents us as we wish we could be.

The ideal implicit in Frankfurt's conception of the self is the ideal of wholeheartedness. Frankfurt reasons that if the self is constituted out of irresistible motives, then it had better be constituted out of motives that are in concert rather than conflict, so that it will not be divided against itself. He therefore concludes the well-constituted self is wholehearted rather than ambivalent.

Frankfurt's term "wholeheartedness" does not denote the complete absence of conflicting motives. A person can be wholehearted in Frankfurt's sense while retaining desires that conflict, so long as he has decisively identified with one of the desires and dissociated himself from the other. This process "involves a radical *separation* of the competing desires, one of which is not merely assigned a relatively less favored position but extruded entirely as an outlaw."[31] The motivational conflict is not thereby eliminated. Rather, "the conflict between the *desires* is in this way transformed into a conflict between *one* of them and the *person* who has identified himself with its rival."[32]

Frankfurt compares and contrasts this process with "the self-reparative activities of the body":

When the body heals itself, it *eliminates* conflicts in which one physical process (say, infection) interferes with others and undermines the homeostasis, or equilibrium, in which health consists. A person who makes up his mind also seeks thereby to overcome or to supersede a condition of inner division and to make himself into an integrated whole. But he may accomplish this without actually eliminating the desires that conflict with those on which he has decided, as long as he dissociates himself from them.[33]

Thus, ambivalence is a disease of the self, to which wholeheartedness stands as the contrasting state of health. What cures the disease, and restores us to health, is the process of dissociating ourselves from unwelcome desires, a process that expels them from the self without necessarily eliminating them entirely.

This prescription for self-health is undeniably attractive. The question is whether it attracts us by articulating what would in fact be ideal for us, given how we are constituted. I suspect that it attracts us for other reasons.

Frankfurt is not alone in thinking of ambivalence as a disease of the self. One of the most famous discussions of ambivalence casts it literally as an agent of disease—specifically, the mental illness suffered by the patient of Freud's who has come to be known as the Rat Man.[34]

Freud diagnoses the Rat Man's problem as "a splitting of the personality"[35] resulting from "a battle between love and hate [that] was raging in [his] breast"[36] with respect to one and the same person. The Rat Man desperately loved and violently hated his father, and his personality was consequently divided, according to Freud, into distinct loving and hating selves.[37] Freud cites this division to explain the Rat Man's symptoms, which often involved repeatedly doing and undoing an action, or thinking and contradicting a thought.

At first glance, then, Freud seems to agree that ambivalence is a disease of the self, a disease whose cure requires the attainment of wholeheartedness. A second look reveals, however, that the Rat Man's problem was not so much ambivalence as his response to it. What caused the Rat Man's neurosis, according to Freud, was the means by which he sought to cope with the battle between love and hatred within him—namely, by repressing his hatred and acknowledging only his love. This repression is what allowed the two emotions to survive unmixed and hence to continue pulling the patient so violently in opposite directions. Freud concludes, "We may regard the repression of his infantile hatred of his father as the event which brought his whole subsequent career under the dominion of the neurosis."[38]

The Rat Man's strategies of repression were not the ones with which we are familiar from Freud's more accessible writings. Most of the Rat Man's thoughts and feelings, both loving and hostile, were available to his consciousness; he simply disconnected them and reconnected them in such a way as to conceal their true significance.[39] Thus, for example, he frequently had thoughts of harm befalling his father, but he had disconnected those thoughts from their wishful affect. He insisted that they were merely "trains of thought" rather than hostile wishes.[40] Conversely, his hostile feelings were displaced from their true objects onto others, including his psychoanalyst[41] and himself.[42]

The Rat Man's repression thus consisted in a concerted practice of self-misinterpretation. And what motivated this misinterpretation was precisely the desire to dissociate himself from his own hatred and hostility. Thus, Freud tells us that on the occasion when the Rat Man first divulged the hostile thought that became the centerpiece of his case history (and the source of his analytic moniker), "He broke off his story in order to assure me that these thoughts were entirely foreign and repugnant to him."[43] On another occasion, the Rat Man said "that he would like to speak of a criminal act, whose author he did not recognize as himself, though he quite clearly recollected committing it."[44] His hatred was thus something that he had alienated from himself, so that he no longer regarded its resultant thoughts and actions as his.

We might even say that the Rat Man's hatred had been repressed by being "extruded as an outlaw"—but then we would be quoting Frankfurt rather than Freud.[45] Conversely, Freud's discussion of this case begins with a statement that might easily have been written by Frankfurt. Referring to an erotic wish felt by the Rat Man in childhood, Freud says: "This wish corresponds to the later obsessional or compulsive idea; and if the quality of compulsion was not yet present in the wish, this was because the ego had not yet placed itself in complete opposition to it and did not yet regard it as something foreign to itself."[46] The theory expressed in this statement is that a wish becomes a compulsion when the ego comes to regard it as foreign—which is close to what Frankfurt believes as well.

Unfortunately, this point of agreement between Freud and Frankfurt suggests that the Rat Man suffered, not from the disease of ambivalence, but from something like Frankfurt's cure. What made him ill was his effort to dissociate himself from one of his emotions, which is just what Frankfurt prescribes for cases of ambivalence. The "radical separation of ... competing desires" recommended by Frankfurt ultimately led to the "splitting of the personality" diagnosed by Freud.[47]

Of course, Frankfurt does not recommend separating desires by repressing some of them. Although Frankfurt's view implies that the Rat Man was right to expel his hatred, it also implies that he was wrong about where to expel it from. He expelled it from his self-awareness or self-understanding; whereas Frankfurt's view implies that he should have consciously rejected it and thereby expelled it from the self.[48]

Yet the suspicion remains that this prescription, though different from what caused the Rat Man's illness, would hardly have been more healthy. Surely, what the Rat Man should have done was to accept his filial hostility as part of himself, to accept *himself* as ambivalent toward his father.[49] The Rat Man's mistake was indeed his attempt to separate competing desires by expelling one of them, not the specific form of expulsion by which he tried to separate them.

We can draw this moral from the Rat Man's story without relying on any distinctively Freudian hypotheses—childhood sexuality, the Oedipus complex, or even repression. Beneath these overlays of psychoanalytic theory is a story intelligible to pure common sense.

To begin with, the species of ambivalence attributed to the Rat Man is familiar to all of us. Almost all of us love our parents, but most of us also retain sources of deep hostility toward them—sore spots that can be inflamed into powerful anger or even hate. Other elements of the Rat Man's history may seem weird or incredible, but the element of filial ambivalence is not extraordinary in the least.

Second, beneath the theoretical apparatus of Freud's account lies a piece of folk wisdom about dealing with mixed emotions. When we are angry with someone we love, the first step toward dealing with our anger is to let it mingle with, and be modified by, our other emotions toward the same person. Isolating our hostility from our other feelings is a way of not dealing with it, of allowing it to remain undigested, a lasting source of inner strife and outer impulsiveness. Of course, new-age common sense about the importance of "processing" problematic emotions is derivative of Freudian theory; but Freudian theory about the return of the repressed is, in turn, derivative of a common sense that is ageless, as Freud himself was the first to point out. When Freud explains why repression brought the Rat Man "under the dominion of the neurosis," his explanation strongly implies, on commonsensical grounds, that any attempt by the Rat Man to segregate his emotions would have been equally harmful.

A third piece of common sense in this case history is that allowing our emotions to mingle with their opposites is difficult, daunting, even terrifying. The Rat Man chose to regard his hatred as foreign because he was afraid of letting it into his emotional life, even though doing so was his only chance of domesticating it. All of us are like the Rat Man at least to this extent, that we feel threatened by various emotions that would introduce conflict into our lives. We consequently wish that our commitments were not tinged with regret, that our projects were not fraught with doubts, that our loves were not complicated by hate. We wish, in short, that we could be wholehearted.

What has now emerged is that wholeheartedness is an object of wishes that do not necessarily represent a healthy trend in our thought. Our attraction to the idea of being wholehearted is one manifestation of the fears that move us to defend ourselves against our own emotions. Hence our affinity for Frankfurt's ideal may not indicate that he's right about the constitution of the self; it may indicate no more than our own defensiveness.

Conceiving of ourselves to have motivational essences can serve the same defensive purpose. What's threatening about our hostility toward loved ones is that it might efface our love for them and move us to do things that love would never allow us to do.[50] Our love therefore entails a fear of its own obliteration. How comforting it would be to think that our love was indelibly written into our nature, so that we didn't have to protect it from exposure to contrary feelings. Are we attracted to this thought because it is true or because it is comforting?

A similar question can be asked about the very notion of an inner self. When we defend ourselves against unwelcome emotions, we would like to think that we are expelling, excluding, or (in Frankfurt's term) "extruding" them from ourselves. We are trying to neutralize troublesome elements of our psyches, and one way to neutralize troublemakers is to banish them beyond some enforceable boundary. When we picture the inner sanctuary of the self, we are picturing a defensible territory— which is precisely what's needed for successful defenses. Given our wish for this safe haven, however, our belief in its existence may be another case of wishful thinking.

Indeed, there is also a defensive way of applying Frankfurt's term "identification." I'm sure that Frankfurt didn't intend the term to be applied in this way, but I wonder whether we as readers haven't departed from his intentions. The term "identification" has an ordinary meaning, different from Frankfurt's, whose substitution into our interpretation of Frankfurt's theory would further suit our defensive purposes.

A Digression on Identification

Frankfurt is responsible for bringing the term "identification" into widespread use among contemporary philosophers and for shaping their intuitions about it. Following Frankfurt, philosophers have come to speak of identification as primarily reflective and evaluative—as a process of endorsing some parts or aspects of ourselves.[51] But the term "identification" ordinarily stands for a process that is not, in the first instance, either reflective or evaluative.[52] I want to examine what we ordinarily mean by "identification" and then to consider the possibility that we can be misled by that meaning in our reading of Frankfurt.

In ordinary parlance we are more likely to speak of identifying with other people than with parts of ourselves. The remark "I can identify with that" is a way of saying that we have experienced what someone else is going through and that we empathize with his reaction to it. We speak of identifying with fictional characters or with their actions and reactions in particular scenes.[53] We also describe ourselves as identifying with authority figures and role models in our lives. Identifying is thus something that we do, in the first instance, with people other than ourselves.

In the case of role models, identification involves a positive evaluation: identifying with these people goes hand-in-hand with admiring them and wanting to emulate them. But in other cases identification can be evaluatively neutral or even negative. "I can identify with that" may be our response to someone's self-depreciating tale of ineptitude or weakness. What elicits our identification may be another person's rendition of that which we find most disappointing or embarrassing in ourselves. Fiction would lack much of its educative force if it couldn't induce us to identify with characters whom we don't admire or wish to emulate. Our identification with these characters may soften our judgment of them, but only because it makes us empathize with them, not because it involves any judgment in their favor.

Perhaps the most extreme example of identification without positive evaluation is the phenomenon that Anna Freud called "identification with the aggressor."[54] When a child plays at being a hungry lion or an angry teacher, he may be identifying with what he most fears, so as to escape from being the target of its aggression. The same mechanism may be at work when an adult directs at others the very sort of criticism to which he feels most vulnerable himself. This person doesn't necessarily admire his critics or want to be like them; he would just prefer being the critic to being the object of criticism.

If identification doesn't necessarily involve a favorable evaluation, then what do instances of identification have in common? The nature of identification can only be obscured, I think, by a moral psychology confined to the categories of belief and desire, or belief and pro-attitude. If identification must sit with either the beliefs or the pro-attitudes, it will sit more comfortably with the latter, in the form of an endorsement or a desire to emulate. Yet to insist on placing identification in the matrix of belief and pro-attitude is to miss the fact that it involves, above all, an exercise of the imagination.[55]

To identify with someone, you have to imagine that you are he, or that he is you. Such an exercise of imagination isn't sufficient for identification: you can imagine that you are Caligula or Lady Macbeth even though you can't identify with them. But identifying with someone can be characterized, I think, as a particular way of imagining that you are he, with particular psychological consequences.

One respect in which identification exceeds merely imagining that you are someone else is that it must be spontaneous. You can deliberately conjure up the thought of being Lady Macbeth, but unless you were spontaneously affected by that thought, you wouldn't be said to identify with her. Another difference is that when you deliberately conjure up the thought of being Lady Macbeth, it occupies the focus of your awareness, while knowledge of your real identity is pushed into the background.

When you identify with someone, the position is reversed: the thought of being that person is in the background—perhaps so far in the background as to be unconscious—while actual identities remain salient.

Finally, deliberately imagining that you are someone else doesn't necessarily affect your realistic attitudes—that is, your attitudes toward the world as you believe it to be rather than as you have imagined it. The activity of imagining that you are Caligula may leave no traces on your thoughts and feelings about the real world, including yourself and the historical figure of Caligula. But when you identify with someone, the thought of being that person, though outside the focus of awareness, somehow colors your attitudes toward yourself or him, toward your individual situations or shared relationship. Your attitudes toward the actual world are modified by your having spontaneously though perhaps unconsciously imagined a world in which you are he.

The most common way to imagine that you are someone else is to imagine being that person, by imagining the world as experienced by him—as seen through his eyes and traveled in his shoes.[56] This sort of imagining is also the most common means of identification. Identifying with someone is usually a matter of having your view of reality colored by a spontaneous image of how things are for him.

This image is of necessity incomplete, in that it doesn't represent every facet of the other person's perspective. Sometimes it can be so incomplete as to represent no more than a single sensation. Watching a sweaty jogger lift a drink to his lips, you may suddenly imagine a cool draught in your own throat; watching a couple pause to embrace on the street, you may spontaneously imagine a warm breath against your own face; seeing someone catch his finger in a car door, you may imagine a shooting pain in your own finger. These brief and fragmentary identifications have only an ephemeral impact on your view of the world, but they exemplify the same psychological process as identifications that are more consequential.[57]

One consequence of imagining things from someone else's perspective is a tendency to empathize with him. Picturing the world as seen through his eyes or heard through his ears, you feel first-personal emotions on his behalf.[58] A further consequence of identification is insight into the other person's thinking and behavior. You are better able to anticipate the thoughts and actions of someone with whom you identify, because you have imaginatively simulated his situation, either consciously or unconsciously.

Another consequence of identifying with someone is a tendency to behave like him, partly because of empathizing with him but also because of the direct motivational force of the imagination. On the one hand, you tend to do what the other person does or would do because you feel the way he does or would feel. Loving his friends, you tend to favor them; hating his enemies, you tend to oppose them; and so on. On the other hand, you tend to pick up the person's behavioral style—his accent, his idiom, and his body-language as well—as if you were impersonating him.

The latter mechanism is similar to that of deliberate pretending or make-believe. When you played make-believe as a child, you did not just copy the behavior of the character or creature you were pretending to be; you imagined being that character or creature, and your imagination moved you to behave accordingly.[59] Similarly, when you identify with someone, the image of being that person leads to move as if inside his body, to speak as if with his voice, even to think and feel as if with his sensibilities. Your identification with him may thereby become recognizable to observers, if they can detect these echoes of his behavior in yours.

What would happen if we interpreted Frankfurt's term "identification" as referring to this phenomenon, identification as ordinarily understood? Frankfurt's claim that we identify with some of our attitudes would then seem to describe us as imagining ourselves to *be* those attitudes. To identify with a desire or emotion would be to imagine being the desire or emotion. But how could we imagine being one of our own mental states, a proper part of ourselves?[60] How could we identify, in this sense, with something that isn't a whole person?

Come to think of it, there is a famous description of just this process. It goes like this:

Let us consider this waiter in the café. His movement is quick and forward, a little too precise, a little too rapid. He comes toward the patrons with a step a little too quick. He bends forward a little too eagerly; his voice, his eyes express an interest a little too solicitous for the order of the customer.... All his behavior seems to us a game. He applies himself to chaining his movements as if they were mechanisms, the one regulating the other; his gestures and even his voice seem to be mechanisms; he gives himself the quickness and pitiless rapidity of things. He is playing, he is amusing himself. But what is he playing? We need not watch long before we can explain it: he is playing *at being* a waiter in a café.[61]

When Sartre says that this waiter is playing at being a waiter, he means that the waiter is playing at being less than a whole person—a waiter-on-tables and nothing more. The waiter imagines that he is nothing but the nexus of motives and skills exercised in his waiting on tables; that he is, not a person choosing to exercise those motives and skills, but a mechanism wholly composed of them; that he is, so to speak, a waiting machine. The waiter thus identifies with a proper part of himself.

This waiter is Sartre's prime specimen of bad faith, which is a mode of defensive thinking. Of course, the defenses diagnosed by Sartre are fueled by a different anxiety from the defenses diagnosed by Freud: they are fueled by a fear of our radical freedom rather than our threatening emotions. But the strategy of defense described by Sartre is available to the latter anxiety as well. If we are afraid of hating our parents, we can imagine being identical with our love for them—parent-lovers and nothing more. We can imagine shrinking to occupy the loving aspect of our personalities, just as the waiter imagines shrinking to occupy his waiterly motives and skills. Once we have imaginatively retreated to within the boundaries of our love, we can hope to keep our hatred at bay.

When Frankfurt describes us as identifying with some of our motives and alienating others, his description rings true, I suspect, because it accurately describes this common defensive fantasy. We do indeed identify with some of our motives, but we thereby engage not in self-definition but self-deception. We identify with some of our motives by imagining ourselves as *being* those motives, to the exclusion of whatever might complicate or conflict with them.

To repeat, I do not believe that Frankfurt uses the term "identification" in this ordinary sense. I think that he initially introduced the term by stipulation, with the intention that it would carry a new, philosophical meaning. "Identification" was meant to describe the psychological process by which a person empowers some of his motives to implicate him in causing behavior, so that whatever they motivate will be attributable to him, as his doing. The attention that Frankfurt has drawn to the process of identification, so defined, has greatly advanced the philosophy of action over the past twenty years. But I think that Frankfurt's own notion of identification has turned out to involve some assumptions that ought to be reexamined, in light of the conclusions at which he has now arrived.

Frankfurt assumed from the outset that identification works by incorporating motives into something called the self, so that behavior governed by those motives qualifies as self-governed, or autonomous. This assumption is harmless, I think, so long as it leaves open the sense in which the term "self" is being used. The reason some behavior counts as autonomous action, attributable to the subject as his doing, is that it is governed by motives constitutive of something deserving to be called the self in some sense of the word. What has emerged in Frankfurt's recent work, however, is the further assumption that the sense of the word "self" used in an account of autonomy will be the same one that is used in accounts of other phenomena that merit philosophical attention.

Thus, Frankfurt conceives of the self as an inner core or kernel comprising that *in* the person which really *is* the person and whose impact on the world is therefore his. The self so conceived underlies not just autonomy but personal identity as well. It is not just that part of a person whose participation in causing behavior is necessary and sufficient for his participating; it's that part of a person whose existence is necessary and sufficient for his existing. Indeed, it is the former precisely because it is the latter—the source of the person's autonomy because it is the basis of his identity, causing what he can be said to cause by virtue of being what he is.

Similarly, Frankfurt conceives of the self as that to which a person must be true in order to be true to himself, or that which he must not betray lest he be guilty of self-betrayal. Motives constitutive of the self therefore carry a special authority in the subject's practical reasoning. They exercise not only the force of his autonomy but also the claim of his self-worth, and for the same reason—namely, that they constitute what he is.

An Alternative Conception of the Self

I don't believe in the self, so conceived. That is, I don't believe that a person has a proper part that is both the source of his autonomy and the target of his self-regard because of being the basis of his identity. Expounding my own views is not the purpose of this paper, but I want to state them briefly in order to illustrate that believing in the self is optional.[62]

In my view, "self" is just a word used to express reflexivity—that is, the coincidence of object and subject, either of a verb or of the activity that it represents. ("She accidentally cut herself.") In many philosophical contexts, "self" expresses the reflexivity of representations, especially their notional reflexivity, the property they possess when they represent their object *as* their subject. ("He's always talking about himself.") In this sense, "self" is used to report indirectly a thought or utterance that originally contained a first-person pronoun. We use "self" to report a thought or utterance containing "I" just as we use "present" to report a thought or utterance containing "now."

As a word expressing reflexivity, "self" has various uses in various contexts, including several contexts that are of interest to philosophy. "Self" can express the reflexivity of the control that an autonomous agent exerts over his own behavior; the reflexivity of the memories and anticipations that link a temporally extended person to his past and future; or the reflexivity of any first-personal attitudes that he may hold. Although "self" expresses reflexivity in each of these contexts, there is no single entity to which it refers in all of them. We shouldn't assume, in other words, that there is something called The Self that governs a person's behavior when it is self-governed, persists so long as the person remains himself, and is the object of his self-concept or self-image.

I want to explain briefly how I understand the term "self" in these philosophical contexts. I begin with the context of personal identity.

I think that a person's past or future selves are just the past or future persons whom he can pick out with thoughts that are notionally reflexive, or first-personal.[63] There is no kernel or core whose presence in past or future persons makes them selves of his; there are only the psychological connections that mediate his reflexive references to them, thus enabling him to think of them first-personally. Locke was right to name experiential memory as the psychological medium connecting a person to his past selves, because replaying past experiences is how the person naturally and without contrivance thinks of past individuals as "me." I would merely add that there are experiential forms of anticipation that can mediate first-personal reference to future persons as "me," thus linking the subject to his future selves.

This conception of selfhood implies that a philosophical theory of the self should have as little substance as a philosophical theory of the present. We can theorize about the reflexive aspect of things, just as we can theorize about their present aspect, but we must avoid reifying the present or the self.[64]

If a person's relation to past and future selves doesn't depend on a shared subset of attributes and attitudes, then it doesn't depend on anything that might be the object of his self-regard. The self for whom the person may have esteem, and with whom he can keep or break faith, is not an inner core of traits and states that he must retain in order to remain himself.

In this latter usage, I think, the term "self" refers—not to the person, or a part of the person, represented reflexively—but to the person's own reflexive representations, which make up his self-image or self-conception.[65] This sense of the word "self" crops up frequently in the field known as self-psychology, where it is often paired with a corresponding sense of the word "identity." When someone suffers an identity crisis, as we call it, what is threatened is not his identity as a person but his conception of himself as a person, which might also be called his sense of identity or his sense of who he is.

In this context, I am happy to say that particular cares and concerns can be definitive of a person's identity or essential to the self.[66] That he has these motives may be a fundamental, organizing principle of a person's self-understanding, without which the rest of his self-image would no longer cohere. If he had to stop thinking of himself as having these motives, he would temporarily lack any coherent conception of himself as a person, and so he might be described as no longer knowing who he was. But the fact that jettisoning the representation of these motives from his current self-image would result, temporarily, in his no longer knowing who he was—this fact doesn't mean that jettisoning the motives themselves would result in his never again being who he is. These motives are essential to his self, or identity, in the sense that refers to his self-conception, which can in time be revised or replaced if his actual motives should change.[67]

This abstract distinction may be clarified by an example. A philosopher recently told me that when he discusses same-sex marriage in his Introduction to Political Philosophy, the fundamentalist Christians in the class find the subject threatening to their identities.[68] Frankfurt might explain this phenomenon by pointing out that the doctrinal commitments of these students involve various volitional necessities, such as an inability to condone homosexuality or even to wish that they could condone it, or a similarly structured inability to question the dictates of scripture. If the students allow these essential aspects of their natures to change, they would bring their current selves to an end—a "drastic psychic injury," in Frankfurt's view.[69] Frankfurt's view thus seems to imply that these students are justified to resist any change of mind on the issue, on grounds of self-preservation.

I would say that a commitment to religious doctrines is essential to these students' identities only in the sense that it is central to their self-conceptions. They think of themselves as Christians first and foremost, and much else that they believe about themselves is based on this premise. If they had to question their faith in the doctrines that they regard as essential to Christianity, they would have to question most of what they currently believe about themselves. Changing their minds on doctrinal matters is therefore threatening to their identities because it threatens to enforce a major revision in their self-conceptions. They would still be themselves after changing their minds, but they would have temporarily lost their grasp of who they are. Some resistance to such radical change may well be justified, but not as much as would be justified for the sake of literal self-preservation.

I have now explained what an aspectual interpretation of "self" implies for discourse about personal identity and self-regard. In discourse about personal identity, "self" refers to those past or future persons whom the subject can denote reflexively, as "me"; in discourse about self-regard, it denotes the subject's reflexive representation, his self-concept or self-image. I turn, finally, to discourse about autonomy, or self-governance. My aspectual interpretation of "self" doesn't require me to deny that a person has a source of autonomy that might be called his essential self: the source of a person's autonomy can be his essential self in an aspectual sense.[70]

Suppose that a person has a part that he is unable to regard non-reflexively, a part on which he cannot attain a truly detached, third-personal perspective. That part of him will be essentially "self" to him, in the sense that it is inalienably "me" from his perspective. Its being his essential self won't mean that it is essential to his identity; only that it always presents a reflexive aspect to his thinking.

Maybe an analogy would help. Consider that spot, right between your eyes, which is at the origin of your visual perspective—the vertex of all the angles that your visual images subtend. That spot is your visual location, or visual standpoint, in the sense that you always see things as projected onto that point. Of course, you can look at yourself in the mirror and refer to the relevant point in space as "over there," in the mirror. But even when you look at it "over there," you are still looking at it *from* that point, and so it remains "back here" as well.

Now, is your visual standpoint an essential part of your visual apparatus? No. Indeed, it isn't a part of your visual apparatus at all. It's just a part of you that always presents a particular aspect to you—the aspect of being visually "here," at the geometric origin of your visual perspective.[71] Surely, we would be making a mistake to regard this point as the origin of your vision in any other sense.

If there is a part of your personality with which you necessarily think about things, then it will be your mental standpoint, always presenting a reflexive aspect to your thought. You will be able to think about this part of your personality as "it," but only from a perspective in which it continues to function as the thinking "I"—just as you can find a reflection of your visual location "over there" only from a perspective in which it is also "back here."

I believe that this phenomenon is what Aristotle had in mind when he said that "each person seems to be his understanding."[72] A person can never conceive of his own conceptual capacity from a purely third-personal perspective, because he can conceive of it only *with* that capacity, and hence from a perspective in which it continues to occupy first-person position. Just as the person cannot attain a visual perspective from which the point between his eyes isn't "here," so he cannot attain a cognitive perspective from which his understanding isn't "I." That's why the person seems to be his understanding.

This Aristotelian observation does not imply that a person's understanding is his essence or the basis of his identity through time. On the contrary, it comports best with the view that his past and future selves are determined aspectually, too, as the past and future persons whom he can think of first-personally, as "me." Their being his past and future selves need have nothing to do with whether they preserve some component of his psyche.

I believe that a person's understanding makes a distinctive contribution to just those behaviors which count as his autonomous actions. Roughly speaking, my view is that autonomous action is behavior motivated in part by the understanding. How the understanding motivates is a question beyond the scope of this paper. What's relevant here is that this part of a person can be the locus of his autonomy, by virtue of being his essential self, but without necessarily constituting his essence or identity as a person. Autonomy can be an aspectual matter, a matter of whether behavior originates in a part of the person that inevitably presents a reflexive aspect to him.[73]

This conception of autonomy remains deeply indebted to Frankfurt. The guiding insight of Frankfurt's work is that a person's capacity to act autonomously rests on his capacity to reflect on aspects of his personality and to feel a special relation to some of them. My aspectual conception of autonomy is little more than a reinterpretation of this insight.

In fact, my aspectual conception of autonomy is just a reinterpretation of a statement from Frankfurt's most recent work on the subject. What Frankfurt now says, in part, is that autonomous behavior is motivated by parts of the subject with which he cannot help identifying.[74] If "identification" is read as a term for first-personal thinking—for thinking of something as "me" or "mine"—then Frankfurt's statement simply becomes the aspectual thesis.

Like much philosophy of action over the past twenty years, then, my view can be expressed as a commentary on Frankfurt—specifically, on what Frankfurt meant, or should have meant, by "identification." I agree with Frankfurt that autonomous action is guided by a part of us with which we cannot help identifying; I disagree mainly with his claim that our identifying with a part of ourselves incorporates it into something called the self.

Acknowledgments

For comments on earlier drafts of this essay, I am grateful to Nomy Arpaly, Linda Wimer Brakel, Michael Bratman, Sarah Buss, Jennifer Church, and Connie Rosati. The essay was presented to a conference on autonomy organized by Joel Anderson and Sigurdur Kristinsson, to the Philosophy Department of Kansas State University, and to the Contemporary Philosophy Workshop at the University of Chicago. Work on the essay was supported by a fellowship from the John Simon Guggenheim Memorial Foundation, together with matching grants from the Department of Philosophy and the College of Literature, Science, and the Arts, University of Michigan.

Notes

1. *The Importance of What We Care About* (Cambridge: Cambridge University Press, 1987).

2. I discuss some of the relevant literature in "What Happens When Someone Acts?" in *The Possibility of Practical Reason* (Oxford: Oxford University Press, 2000). For a more recent discussion, and a promising alternative to Frankfurt's view, see Michael Bratman, "Identification, Decision, and Treating as a Reason," in *Faces of Intention* (Cambridge: Cambridge University Press, 1999), 185–206.

3. Harry Frankfurt, "Autonomy, Necessity, and Love," in *Necessity, Volition, and Love* (Cambridge, Cambridge University Press, 1999), 132. Frankfurt first made this claim, though less explicitly, in the paper "Rationality and the Unthinkable," in *The Importance of What We Care About*, 178: "With respect to a person whose will has no fixed determinate character, it seems that the notion of autonomy or self-direction cannot find a grip."

4. Frankfurt, "Autonomy, Necessity, and Love," 132. This remark about Kant's conception of the person as a subject of autonomy bears a striking resemblance to remarks often made about Kant's conception of the person as an object of moral concern. In Kant's view, a person is worthy of moral concern insofar as he is an instance of rational nature, which is the proper object of respect. Many critics reply that concern for someone as an instance of rational nature is concern for no one in particular, since the same generic nature is instantiated in everyone alike. As Robin Dillon puts it: "In Kantian-respecting someone, there is a real sense in which we are not paying attention to *her*, for it makes no difference to how we respect her that she is who she is and not some other individual. Kantian respect is thus not a 'respecter of persons,' in the sense that it does not discriminate or distinguish among persons." Robin Dillon, "Respect and Care: Toward Moral Integration," *Canadian Journal of Philosophy* 22 (1992): 105–132, at 121. See also Elizabeth Spelman, "On Treating Persons as Persons," *Ethics* 88

(1977): 150–161; Robert Paul Wolff, "There's Nobody Here but Us Persons," in *Women and Philosophy; Toward a Theory of Liberation*, eds. Carol C. Gould and Marx W. Wartofsky (New York: G. P. Putnam's Sons, 1976), 128–144; Seyla Benhabib, "The Generalized and the Concrete Other: The Kohlberg-Gilligan Controversy and Moral Theory," in *Women and Moral Theory*, eds. Eva Feder Kitty and Diana T. Meyers (Totowa, NJ: Rowman and Littlefield, 1987), 154–177; Edward Johnson, "Ignoring Persons," in *Respect for Persons*, ed. O. H. Green, *Tulane Studies in Philosophy* 31 (1982): 91–105. I discuss Dillon's statement in "Love as a Moral Emotion," *Ethics* 109 (1999): 338–374.

5. Frankfurt, "Autonomy, Necessity, and Love," 135.

6. Frankfurt, "On the Necessity of Ideals," in *Necessity, Volition, and Love*, 113; see also "Autonomy, Necessity, and Love," 138.

7. Frankfurt, "On the Necessity of Ideals," 111–112; see also "Autonomy, Necessity, and Love," 136–138; and "Rationality and the Unthinkable," 182–183.

8. Frankfurt, "On the Necessity of Ideals," 112.

9. The image is Frankfurt's. See, e.g., "Freedom of the Will and the Concept of a Person," in *The Importance of What We Care About*, 21; "Identification and Wholeheartedness," in *The Importance of What We Care About*, 168.

10. Ibid. See also "Rationality and the Unthinkable," 187. Presumably then, the person must endorse his inability to will any change in his inability to will. Here the threat of a regress reappears.

11. Frankfurt, "Autonomy, Necessity, and Love," 138.

12. Ibid., 139, n. 8.

13. Frankfurt, preface to *The Importance of What We Care About*, vii–ix, at ix. See also "Rationality and the Unthinkable," 188; and "On the Necessity of Ideals."

14. Frankfurt, "Rationality and the Unthinkable," 179.

15. Frankfurt, "On the Usefulness of Final Ends," in *Necessity, Volition, and Love*, 89.

16. Frankfurt, "Autonomy, Necessity, and Love," 139, n. 9.

17. Ibid., 138.

18. Ibid., 139.

19. In "The Necessity of Ideals," 113, Frankfurt says: "The idea that the identity of a thing is to be understood in terms of conditions that are essential for its existence is one of the oldest and most compelling of the philosophical principles that guide our efforts to clarify our thought. To grasp what a thing is, we must grasp its essence—viz., those characteristics without which it is not possible for it to be what it is. Thus, the notions of necessity and identity are intimately related."

20. Parfit denies that the relevant connections constitute a relation of identity, because they can branch in such a way as to connect a person to two distinct selves existing at one time. I will use the term "selves" to denote those person-

stages to whom one bears the survival-relation that matters, whether or not they are stages of a single person.

21. In this discussion I gloss over many other differences between Locke and Parfit. Most important, perhaps, is that Parfit distinguishes survival from strict identity through time. Parfit thinks that survival, unlike identity, admits of degrees and intransitivities.

22. Derek Parfit, *Reasons and Persons* (Oxford: Oxford University Press, 1984), 205–206; see also 301–302.

23. Ibid., 300–301. See also 515, n. 6.

24. Ibid., 299.

25. This consequence of Parfit's view is confirmed by his discussion of "The Nineteenth Century Russian" in *Reasons and Persons*, 327–328. This idealistic nobleman bequeaths his land to the peasants, in a document that can be revoked only by his wife. He then makes his wife promise that she won't revoke the document, even if he later asks her to. Parfit comments, "The young Russian socialist regards his ideals as essential to his present self. He asks his wife to promise to this present self not to act against these ideals. And, on this way of thinking, she can never be released from her commitment. The self to whom she is committed would, in trying to release her, cease to exist."

26. "Ego Distortion in Terms of True and False Self," in *Collected Papers: Through Paediatrics to Psycho-analysis* (London: Tavistock Publications, 1958).

27. One might be tempted to say that the exaggerated self-control of such a person is only an imitation of real self-control, amounting only to pseudo-autonomy. See David Shapiro, *Autonomy and Rigid Character* (New York: Basic Books, 1981), 74–75. But even if this person has only pseudo-autonomy, the reason is not that he is only pretending to be autonomous; it's rather that he's somehow misapplying the self-control that would otherwise count as very real autonomy. His pseudo-autonomy consists in the misdirected self-control by which he holds himself to a pretense; but the pretense is one of authenticity. Autonomy is not what the agent simulates but what he misuses in mounting the simulation.

28. "Does the True Self Really Exist? A Critique of Winnicott's True Self Concept," in *A Psychoanalysis for our Time: Exploring the Blindness of the Seeing "I"* (New York: New York University Press, 1998), 109. Also relevant here is Erikson's discussion of the difference between "wholeness" and "totalism," in *Identity, Youth, and Crisis* (New York: W. W. Norton, 1968), 74–90. Erikson concludes: "To have the courage of one's diversity is a sign of wholeness in individuals and in civilizations" (90). See also John D. W. Andrews, *The Active Self in Psychotherapy: An Integration of Therapeutic Styles* (Boston: Allyn and Bacon, 1991), 7–8, 35; Roderick Anscombe, "The Myth of the True Self," 52 *Psychiatry* 209–217 (1989); Mark Epstein, *Thoughts Without a Thinker: Psychotherapy From a Buddhist Perspective* (New York: Basic Books, 1995), 71–73.

29. "Self to Self," *Philosophical Review* 105 (1996): 39–76, esp. 42, n. 5. I do include long-range intentions among the mental states that connect the self to

itself through time. Hence a person's plans and policies are part of what make him (in Locke's phrase) "self to himself" from one time to another, in my view. But I do not believe that particular plans and policies can play a privileged role simply because of their distinctiveness or importance to the subject.

30. Robert Paul Wolff, "There's Nobody Here But Us Persons," 136–137. This passage is quoted by Johnson, "Ignoring Persons," 97. Another author who thinks that the authority of our concerns can be traced to their place in our identity, and hence to the imperative of self-preservation, is Christine Korsgaard. See *The Sources of Normativity* (Cambridge: Cambridge University Press, 1996). For a critique of Korsgaard on this point, see David Copp, "Korsgaard on Normativity, Identity, and the Ground of Obligation," in *Rationality, Realism, Revision: Proceedings of the Third International Congress of the Society for Analytical Philosophy,* vol. 23 of *Perspektiven der Analytiscen Philosophe,* ed. Julian Nida-Rümelin (Berlin: de Gruyter, 1999), 572–581. I discuss Korsgaard's version of this view in "Willing the Law," to appear in *Practical Conflicts,* ed. Monika Betzler and Peter Baumann (Cambridge: Cambridge University Press).

31. Frankfurt, "Identification and Wholeheartedness," in *The Importance of What We Care About,* 170.

32. Ibid., 172. See also Frankfurt, "The Faintest Passion" in *Necessity, Volition, and Love,* 100: "Wholeheartedness does not require that a person be altogether untroubled by inner opposition to his will. It just requires that, with respect to any such conflict, he himself be fully resolved. This means that he must be resolutely on the side of one of the forces struggling within him and not on the side of any other."

33. Frankfurt, "Identification and Wholeheartedness," 173–174. In "The Faintest Passion," Frankfurt quotes Saint Augustine as calling ambivalence "'a disease of the mind' from which we suffer in punishment for Original Sin" (100). Frankfurt himself calls it here "a disease of the will."

34. Sigmund Freud, "Notes Upon a Case of Obsessional Neurosis," in *The Standard Edition of the Complete Psychological Works of Sigmund Freud,* ed. James Strachey et al. (London: Hogarth Press and the Institute of Psycho-Analysis, 1953–1974), Vol. X, 153–249.

35. Ibid., 177.

36. Ibid., 191; see also 180–183; 237–241.

37. For the image of two selves, see Freud, "Notes Upon a Case," 177.

38. Ibid., 238.

39. Ibid., 196–197; see also 175–176; 231–232.

40. Ibid., 178–180, 222;

41. Ibid., 209.

42. Ibid., 188–189.

43. Ibid., 167.

44. Ibid., 184.

45. Quoted at note 31, above.

46. Ibid., 162–163.

47. These expressions are quoted above at notes 31 and 35, respectively. See Andrews, *The Active Self*, 29.

48. Morris Eagle has argued that expulsion from the self is the ultimate aim of repression, and that expulsion from consciousness is adopted as a means to that aim. "Psychoanalytic Conceptions of the Self," in *The Self: Interdisciplinary Approaches* (New York: Springer-Verlag, 1991), 49–65. Eagle writes: "[T]he logic of Freudian theory, particularly the clinical logic, points to the expulsion of mental contents from *self-organization* as the significant aspect of repression. Or, to put it more fully, it is the *disowning or disavowal* of mental contents, the rejection of these contents as one's own, that is the clinically (and theoretically) significant aspect of repression. According to the view I am suggesting, expulsion from conscious awareness is mainly *a means*, albeit the most frequently employed means, toward the end of rendering certain mental contents as an impersonal 'it,' as not mine, as ego alien. But it is the disowned ego-alien status that is the critical element in dealing with mental contents incompatible with one's self-structure" (55). See note 66, below. See also Morris Eagle, "Psychoanalysis and the Personal," in *Mind, Psychoanalysis, and Science,* ed. P. Clark and C. Wright (Oxford: Blackwell, 1988), 91–111.

49. In other words, the Rat Man needed to attain the "developmental milestone" that Rubin describes as "access to, and comfort with, [his] multidimensionality," or "a sense of the complexity, multidimensionality, and polyvalency of the self" (quoted at note 28, above). Compare here Eagle's interpretation of psychotherapeutic change, as expressed in Freud's formula "where id was, there should ego be": "Freud is defining psychotherapeutic change, not in terms of consciousness and understanding, but in terms of alterations in self-structure. That is, he is saying that real change is marked by an enlargement of the self." Eagle, "Psychoanalytic Conceptions of the Self," 61.

50. See Freud, "Notes Upon a Case," 226–227, 233–236. Freud's view was that we fear the magical fulfillment of our hostile wishes, via the "omnipotence of thoughts."

51. There is at least one passage in which Frankfurt uses the term in a different sense: "A person who cares about something is, as it were, invested in it. By caring about it, he makes himself susceptible to benefits and vulnerable to losses depending upon whether what he cares about flourishes or is diminished. We may say that in this sense he *identifies* himself with what he cares about." Frankfurt, "On the Necessity of Ideals," 111. Here the target of identification is, not one of the subject's own motives, but the external object of those motives.

52. For a related argument, see Nomy Arpaly and Timothy Schroeder, "Alienation and Externality," *Canadian Journal of Philosophy* 29 (1999): 371–387.

53. We also use the term "identification" to describe a person's sense of affiliation with a social group or movement; but this context usually calls for a different construction. What a person usually does with respect to a group or movement is, not simply to identify with it, but rather to identify *himself* with

it—which is a slightly different maneuver. Frankfurt tends to use the constructions "to identify with" and "to identify oneself with" interchangeably.

54. Anna Freud, *The Ego and the Mechanisms of Defense* (London: Hogarth Press, 1937), 109–121; reprinted in *Pivotal Papers on Identification*, ed. George H. Pollock (Madison, CT: International Universities Press, 1993), 105–114. On the variety of motives for identification, see Roy Schafer, *Aspects of Internalization* (New York: International Unversities Press, 1968), chap. 1.

55. See Richard Wollheim, "Imagination and Identification," in *On Art and the Mind* (Cambridge, MA: Harvard University Press, 1974), 73ff.

56. I discuss this claim at length in "Self to Self."

57. In addition to imagining that you are someone else, you can also imagine that he is you, by regarding him externally and thinking "That's me," as you might think in reference to a photograph or a reflection of yourself in a shop window. Can you identify with someone by means of this external sort of imagining?

Imagining an external figure to be oneself may not seem like a compelling way of identifying with him. But consider the universal phenomenon of dreaming about oneself from a perspective outside one's own body, a perspective from which one sees oneself as an external figure. This phenomenon suggests that representing an external figure as oneself is deeply entrenched in the representational idiom of the imagination. And imaginatively representing another person as one represents oneself in dreams ought to be a compelling way of identifying with him.

But how exactly does a dream represent which figure is oneself? As the dream unfolds, one doesn't suddenly focus on one of the characters and think "That's me," as one does when recognizing oneself in a home movie. It's implicit from the outset of the dream that a particular figure is oneself, and so it never gets formulated explicitly in thought. The question is how one's identity among externally represented figures can be implicit in the dream.

Maybe one's identity is implicit in the emotional structure of the dream. Although one sees and hears all of the characters from the outside, one reacts emotionally to the dreamed events from the perspective of one character in particular, fearing whatever threatens him in the dream, resenting whoever insults him, and so on. Indeed, one doesn't so much react emotionally to dreamed events as one dreams them emotionally, to begin with: one fearfully dreams threats to a character and resentfully dreams insults to him. One thus dreams the dream from the emotional perspective of a particular character, and this structural feature of the dream may be what implicitly casts him in the role of one's dream-self.

If so, then dreaming of an external figure as oneself is not very different, after all, from dreaming of being that person. Although the dream doesn't represent things as seen or heard by him, it does represent them as emotionally felt by him, and its so representing them is what casts him in the first-personal role. The emotions experienced in the dream are a partial image of being that person, just as a feeling imagined in the throat can be a partial image of being someone who is seen taking a drink. Thus all identification may involve imagining from within the other's perspective in some respect.

58. On the effects of first-personal imagining, see Wollheim, "Imagination and Identification"; and *The Thread of Life* (Cambridge, MA: Harvard University Press, 1984), chap. 3. I think that empathy itself may be a mode of identification, in which we imagine the world as experienced by someone else emotionally rather than perceptually. My thought here is that the emotions we feel on behalf of the other person play the same role as the sensations that we feel on behalf of the drinking jogger described above. To develop this thought, however, I would need to offer a theory of the emotional imagination, explaining how we can feel imaginary emotions in the way that we can taste an imaginary drink. For some remarks in this direction, see my "On the Aim of Belief," in *The Possibility of Practical Reason* (Oxford: Clarendon Press, 2000), 270, n. 51.

59. I defend this claim at length in "On the Aim of Belief."

60. This question is also raised by Arpaly and Schroeder.

61. Jean-Paul Sartre, *Being and Nothingness; An Essay on Phenomenological Ontology*, trans. by Hazel E. Barnes (New York: Philosophical Library, 1956), 59.

62. The views stated in this section are developed more fully in my "What Happens When Someone Acts?"

63. This paragraph summarizes the thesis of my "Self to Self." Also relevant here is Rom Harré's contrast between the self as a point-of-view and the self as a bundle of personal qualities. *The Singular Self: An Introduction to the Psychology of Personhood* (London: Sage Publications, 1998).

64. Here again see Rubin's critique of Winnicott's "True Self Concept."

65. See, e.g., Frederic J. Levine and Robert Kravis, "Psychoanalytic Theories of the Self: Contrasting Clinical Approaches to the New Narcissism," in *The Book of the Self: Person, Pretext, and Process*, ed. Polly Youaang-Eisendrath and James A. Hall (New York: New York University Press, 1987), 306–330; J. F. Kihlstrom and N. Cantor, "Mental Representations of the Self," in *Advances in Experimental Social Psychology*, ed. L. Berkowitz (New York: Academic Press, 1984), vol. 17, 2–40.

66. This sense of the word also allows us to say that the Rat Man's strategies of repression were strategies of expelling unwelcome emotions from the self. For as I explained above, the Rat Man repressed his hatred by writing it out of his self-conception. (See 194, "Notes Upon a Case," and n. 48, above.)

67. Frankfurt sometimes speaks of a person's "sense" or "grasp" of his identity, or "the clarity with which he comprehends who he is" ("On the Necessity of Ideals," 108–109; see also "Rationality and the Unthinkable," 177). But he doesn't adequately distinguish the person's grasp of his identity from the identity so grasped. He thus slides from the statement that "extensive proliferation of [a person's] options may weaken his grasp of his own identity" ("Rationality and the Unthinkable," 177; see also "On the Necessity of Ideals," 109: "extensive growth in the variety of a person's options may weaken his sense of his identity") to the statement that "an excess of freedom gives rise to a diminution, or even to a dissolution, of the reality of the self" ("Rationality and the Unthinkable," 179;

see also "On the Necessity of Ideals," 110: "With total freedom, there can be no individual identity").

68. Thanks to John Exdell for this useful example.

69. Quoted at note 18, above.

70. I discuss this claim in the introduction to *The Possibility of Practical Reason*.

71. As Dan Dennett demonstrates in his paper "Where Am I?" your visual standpoint can migrate out of your body with the help of prosthetic sense-organs. In *Brainstorms: Philosophical Essays on Mind and Psychology* (Cambridge, Mass.: MIT Press, 1981), 310–323. I take myself to be making the same point as Dennett—namely, that your visual location is a merely aspectual matter.

72., *Nicomachean Ethics*, 1178a.

73. My claim that selfhood is an aspectual matter does not apply to personhood. What makes someone a person is not merely that he presents a particular aspect to himself; what makes him a person includes various other facts about him, including the fact that he is autonomous. Of course, his autonomy consists in the fact that his behavior is governed partly by his understanding, which inevitably presents a reflexive aspect to him, thus qualifying as his essential self; and being governed by such a self is part of what makes him a person; but the self by which he is governed must not be conflated or confused with the person he thus becomes.

In "Self to Self," I argue for a similar distinction between selfhood and personhood in the discussion of personal identity. A person's past and future selves are those past and future persons who present a particular aspect to him, but they need not be the same person.

74. See the quotations at note 10, above.

REPLY TO J. DAVID VELLEMAN

Harry Frankfurt

1. Some of the apparent conflict between Velleman's ideas and mine is due more, I think, to relatively superficial rhetorical differences than to important philosophical disagreement. This is especially so with regard to his objections to my account of "the self." I shall begin by commenting on those, and then consider certain other issues.

Velleman attributes to me the view that the self is "a singular entity waiting to be found." What I believe awaits being found is not the self. It is the *limits* of the self—the volitional necessities that make it impossible for a person to bring himself to behave in certain ways. I have sometimes referred to these limiting necessities as boundaries of the self, which define its shape. Perhaps this language suggested that, since I said the self has boundaries, I must have been thinking of it as "a singular entity." My figure of speech was not intended, however, to have any ontological implications. The truth is that I am not inclined to construe the self as an "entity" at all.

2. Is it improper for me, then, to speak of "the essential nature" of the self? Velleman chides me for asserting that Agamemnon no longer existed after he ruptured a defining feature of his nature by sacrificing his daughter. He wonders how I can account for the fact that Agamemnon was still around later on when Clytemnestra killed him. What I said about Agamemnon's essential nature, and about his being destroyed, certainly does lead quickly to absurdity if it is taken as Velleman takes it. However, it is not necessary to take it in that way. There is a familiar and respectable usage in which it makes perfectly good sense to speak of the essence of a person, and to say that the continued existence of a person—though not the person's life—depends upon the continuity of his essential nature.

Velleman alleges that I have never offered a convincing example of someone who ceased to be the same person, or who ceased to exist, because of some change of heart. Be that as it may, suitable examples are not so hard to find. Suppose that a hateful bully undergoes a moral conversion, with the result that he genuinely renounces his aggressively vicious ways. It might correctly be said of him that he is not the same person that he was, meaning (among other things) that he is no longer inclined, and would no longer be able even to bring himself, to do the dreadful things for which everyone once feared and despised him. In virtue of his having reformed, the shape of his will has altered; his volitional limits are different than they were. As we might quite commonly say, he has become a different person. Perhaps there are some people who do not know how he has changed, and who are therefore still wary of him. If so, we might naturally tell them that their anxiety when he is around is misguided because the dangerous brute about whom they are worried no longer exists.

There is of course another sense in which, despite the alteration of his volitional character, the reformed man is identical with who he was prior to his change of heart. He is numerically the same person before and after that transformation. Our customary usage of "the same person" is, however, less univocal than Velleman allows. There is a sense, on which I relied when speaking of Agamemnon, in which people may be defined by their volitional limits and in which the survival of the self therefore requires a certain motivational constancy or continuity. In this sense, of course, survival is not a matter of life and death.[1]

3.   In commenting on what I say about ambivalence and wholeheartedness, Velleman discusses the Rat Man, whose repression of his hostility toward his father generated some famous pathology. On my account, as Velleman says, the Rat Man would have been better off if, instead of repressing his hostility and thus secreting it in his unconscious, he had rejected it at the conscious level and had identified himself wholeheartedly with his more benign attitudes. Velleman disagrees; and he suspects that my prescription, "though different from what caused the Rat Man's illness, would hardly have been more healthy." In his view, it would have been better for the Rat Man to be ambivalent than to be wholehearted. "Surely," he says, "what the Rat Man should have done was to accept his filial hostility as part of himself, to accept *himself* as ambivalent toward his father."

The Rat Man should certainly have accepted, rather than hidden from himself, the fact that he had hostile as well as loving feelings toward his father. To say this is hardly the same, however, as saying that he should have accepted himself as being ambivalent. Ambivalence is not a matter simply of having conflicting feelings. It consists essentially in having a divided will—that is, of being unresolved as to which side of the conflict among one's feelings one is on. Thus it cannot be eliminated by repression, for that only renders the unresolved conflict unconscious.

In order for the Rat Man to be wholeheartedly on the side of his benign attitudes, it would not have been necessary for him to conceal his hostile feelings from himself. Nor would he have had to refrain from making a conscious effort to deal with those feelings in whatever ways might be effective and helpful. It would have required only that, in the struggle between his hatred and his love for his father, he himself come to stand decisively against the hatred and behind the love.

4.   Velleman reports Freud's belief that "a wish becomes a compulsion when the ego comes to regard it as foreign," and he says that this "is close to what Frankfurt believes as well." Actually, it is not close to what I believe. When Freud speaks of the ego coming to regard a wish as foreign, he has in mind a situation in which the wish is repressed. When I speak of the self rendering a wish external and regarding it as alien, what I have in mind is a quite different maneuver. This maneuver does not entail repressing the wish or making it unconscious, and it is in no way pathogenic.

After asserting that what made the Rat Man ill was "his effort to dissociate himself from one of his emotions," Velleman adds that this is "just what Frankfurt prescribes for cases of ambivalence." But the Rat Man did not become ill because he tried to achieve dissociation. He became ill because he tried to achieve dissociation *through repression*. Repression is quite unlike the mode of dissociation that I prescribe as an antidote to ambivalence. Resolving ambivalence by taking a decisive stand against certain feelings does not require (or even permit) that a person misrepresent those feelings or that he conceal them from himself.

Velleman acknowledges that I do not recommend repression. But it was repression that caused the Rat Man so much trouble. I am therefore puzzled by his claim that the Rat Man would hardly have been better off if he had unified his will in the way that I do recommend—that is, by identifying with his love for his father, without repressing anything and without neglecting conscious ways of coping with feelings of hatred by which he did not wish to be driven. I agree that defensive and self-deceptive wishes, which Velleman says may play a role in the desire for wholeheartedness, are inimical to health. However, I see no reason to think that the desire for wholeheartedness naturally depends upon such wishes.

5. Surely it is ambivalence, and not wholeheartedness, that is a disease of the will. Velleman himself makes it clear why this is so. Thus he reports that the Rat Man's symptoms "often involved repeatedly doing and undoing an action, or thinking and contradicting a thought." That sort of self-defeating behavior and thought violates the elementary requirements of rationality. It is not a consequence of repression as such, but of ambivalence. It is a manifestation of the incoherence in which, precisely, the divided will of ambivalence consists. The desire for wholeheartedness is nothing other than a desire to be free of this crippling irrationality.

6. In his discussion of identification, Velleman says that his paradigms are cases in which a person imagines that he is someone else. These, he claims, are instances of "identification as ordinarily understood" (27). The examples he provides, however, are not actually of that kind; they are not cases in which a person imagines that he is someone else. Instead, they are cases in which someone imagines having an experience like the experience another person is having.

What does it mean to identify with another person? When I say that I can (or that I do) identify with someone, I do not mean that I can (or that I do) imagine being that person. I mean just that I can (or do) imagine myself actually responding as that person does to a situation of a certain kind. Suppose that in the aftermath of Waterloo, I tell Napoleon that I can identify with him since I too have suffered catastrophic defeats. I do not mean that I can imagine myself being Napoleon (whatever that might mean) but, at most, that I can imagine what it is like to be in Napoleon's shoes. That is, I know what it is like to suffer a catastrophic defeat.

It also seems to me inaccurate to suppose, as Velleman evidently does, that when I identify with a desire or with an emotion, I "imagine being the desire or emotion." Identifying with something is, in the relevant sense, not a matter of becoming identical with it. It is, as Velleman himself puts it, "a psychological process by which a person empowers [authorizes?] some of his motives to implicate him in causing behavior." Velleman believes that this is not what the term ordinarily means, but the usage seems commonplace enough. After all, we do say things like: "You've got me wrong, you don't understand who [what sort of person] I am." In other words, we complain about being identified with desires and motives with which we do not truly identify.

Note

1. This usage, more than the other, lends itself to (perhaps it even encourages) an undesirable mushiness. Although it is well enough established in common speech, perhaps it would after all be better to keep it out of philosophical discourse. I confess that some of the statements in which I have resorted to it do now strike me as a bit overblown.

5

Volitional Necessities

Gary Watson

I Introduction

My aim, ultimately, is to investigate what Harry Frankfurt calls *volitional necessity*:

> If a person who is constrained by volitional necessity is for that reason unable to pursue a certain course of action, the explanation is not that he is in any straightforward way too weak to overcome the constraint. That sort of explanation can account for the experience of an addict, who dissociates himself from the addiction constraining him but who is unsuccessful in his attempt to oppose his own energies to the impetus of his habit. A person who is constrained by volitional necessity, however, is in a situation that differs significantly from that one. Unlike the addict, he does not accede to the constraining force because he lacks sufficient strength of will to defeat it. He accedes to it because he is *unwilling* to oppose it and because, furthermore, his unwillingness is *itself* something which he is unwilling to alter.[1]

The topic Frankfurt opens up here is profoundly difficult. One difficulty has to do with "necessity." What does it mean to speak of volition being *necessitated* in this way? Another hard question concerns "volition." How are we to understand that which is necessitated? These questions, and especially the second, take us to the heart of Frankfurt's philosophy of agency.

Any satisfactory constructive (that is, nonskeptical) treatment of volitional necessity must distinguish it both from inability to act and from other ways in which the "will" might be constrained. As a preliminary, then, I begin by contrasting the sorts of impairment involved in addictions and phobias with a more basic notion of inability to act. Then I turn to the task of distinguishing such impairments from volitional necessity. In the end, I find that Frankfurt's discussion of this phenomenon exposes a theoretical tension between two conceptions of volition.

II Inability to Act

Donald Davidson's characterization of this concept is a useful starting point. He suggests the following analysis of "what a man can do":

A can do x intentionally (under the description d) means that if A has desires and beliefs that rationalize x (under d), then A does x.[2]

Davidson's point, I take it, is that the basic concept of what someone can do is given by a certain kind of dependency relation between the individual's concerns or reasons and his or her behavior. Roughly, I can do what I will succeed in doing if I want to do that, rather than another thing. As Davidson puts it, "... what an agent does do intentionally is what he is free to [that is, can] do *and* has adequate reasons for doing."[3] If I did something intentionally, it follows that my doing what I did depended on my "desires" and beliefs, and hence, in the sense just defined, that I could at that time do (in his language "was free to do") what I did.[4]

Almost everyone agrees by now that this basic concept, in all its variants, leaves untouched many important issues about freedom and incapacity. Davidson himself hastens to add: "I do not want to suggest that the nature of an agent's beliefs and desires, and the question how he acquired them, are irrelevant to how free he, or his actions, are. But these questions are on a different and more sophisticated level from that of our present discussion."[5] These more "sophisticated" questions arise, among other sources, from reflections on ways in which an individual's capacity to choose (or form intentions, or try) might be impaired. We can signal this need for refinement by amending the basic notion accordingly: what we can do is what depends on the exercise of our unimpaired capacity for choice.

Before we consider some of these refinements, I want to underscore the centrality of this basic concept to the way we think about human action. One fundamental contrast marked by this basic concept is a distinction between will and power; it is one thing to be unwilling to do something, quite another to be unable. Consider Clara, who lies cozily in bed. Though she has no reason or inclination to arise, she is perfectly able to do so. In attributing abilities in this way, we bracket questions about the agent's actual desires and reasons, focusing instead on what is open to her, whatever those reasons might be.

For many purposes—for instance, prediction or control—this distinction seems irrelevant. We might as effectively ensure that Clara remains in her room by making her comfortable as by chaining her to the bedposts. Either way, we've removed a necessary condition of her exit; in this sense it is not possible that she will in these circumstances arise.

But from the (overlapping) standpoints of responsibility and agency, the distinction is vital. If Clara doesn't turn up at the office, her colleagues and students will be inconvenienced anyway. Yet it might well matter to them whether she stayed at home for her own (good or bad) reasons, or whether she was prevented from coming. Furthermore, this distinction frames each individual's view of his or her prospective behavior. In thinking about what to do (for example, as I consider whether to arise), I am of course not trying to predict my future but determine it; I am trying to determine which of what I take to be my (feasible) options I shall take. To discover that I am paralyzed is to realize that certain options do not in fact exist. It is crucial to this standpoint of deliberation, then, to distinguish what I am able to do (what my options are) from what I shall do. The point is to determine the latter in view of the former. And the relevant notion of an "option" from this standpoint is roughly this: my options are those courses of action whose realization depends on what I determine to do, as the case may be, on my decision, choice, or intention. To learn that something is not an option, not within my capacity in this sense, is to learn that it does not stand in this relation to my choice.

Thus the distinction between what does and does not depend on my will is central both to interpersonal concerns of responsibility and to first-personal concerns about agency and deliberation.[6] What others might want to know is whether Clara's absence is due to factors independent of her will, or whether she would have come if she had chosen. They want to know whether the absence was her choice. This distinction is salient as well in her question about whether to get out of bed, which presupposes that whether she arises depends on what she decides—that is, that getting up is among her options. When this dependency relation obtains, it follows that certain things are in one important sense under her control; they are, as we say, up to her.

We can sum up the point so far in this way. Our conception of human ability relies on a distinction between the *performance conditions* and the *enabling conditions* of an action. Roughly put, the latter are a proper subset of the former. From the standpoint of theoretical explanation and prediction, the fact that Clara has no intention of getting up this morning is on a par with any other *sine qua non* concerning the conditions of her limbs and muscles and central nervous system. From that point of view, the ordinary notion of ability to act seems arbitrary and uninteresting, as though one were to insist that the coffee in my cup can boil here and now, in the cool environment of my study, because it *would* boil if it were heated up. A possible way of speaking, I suppose, but pointless.

In contrast, it is crucial to our practical lives to distinguish some necessary conditions from others. Intending to get up is a condition of the performance but not of the ability. We can ask sensibly whether it is possible for certain behavior to occur in the absence of certain conditions—whether it is possible that Clara arises here and now, given that her legs have been removed or immobilized, or given that she doesn't intend to do so. Presumably not. Again, in the same sense, it is not possible that my coffee will boil in the present atmosphere of my study. But it would show confusion about the meaning and role of the ordinary notion of ability to say of lounging Clara that she can't get out of bed just because one of the conditions of her doing so is absent— namely, her intending to get up.[7] The will to get out of bed is a performance condition, not an enabling condition.

III Disabilities of the Will

The limits of this concept for understanding human freedom come to the fore when something goes wrong with the will. Suppose Clara were instead afflicted with the pathological depression or anxiety depicted in the following autobiographical report by Andrew Solomon:

> I ran home shaking and went to bed, but I did not sleep, and *could not get up* the following day. I wanted to call people to cancel birthday plans, but I *couldn't*.... I knew that for years I had taken a shower every day. Hoping that someone else could open the bathroom door, I would, with all the force in my body, sit up; turn and put my feet on the floor, and then feel so incapacitated and frightened that I would roll over and lie face down. I would cry again, weeping because the fact that I *could not do it* seemed so idiotic to me.[8]

This passage describes what it is natural to call a *volitional disability* or *impairment*, in this case, an incapacity to will to get out of bed (as distinct from an incapacity to get out of bed as and when one wills). I won't undertake a systematic discussion of phobias and similar phenomena here. But I must make a few observations in preparation for the discussion of what Frankfurt has in mind by volitional necessity.

To begin with, it is perhaps not obvious that we need to invoke a notion of volitional incapacity at all to understand a case like Solomon's. After all, Solomon struggles hard to sit up in an effort to get out of bed; he sees and responds to reasons to arise. But his fear overcomes him. His fear is an obstacle to his efforts to carry out his intentions. It prevents him from carrying out his will. So this is just incapacity in the basic sense, it seems. The problem is not with his will but with the relation between his will and his actions. He is as effectively disabled by his fear as he would be by literal paralysis of the limbs. Nothing in the basic concept requires the obstacle to be physical.

This analysis seems wrong. It doesn't deal with cases in which the individual is too terrified even to try. But even where the agent does struggle, as in this case, the phobia works not by conquering his fullest, wholehearted efforts, but by leading him to abandon his intentions. This marks an important contrast with a case of literal paralysis. Suppose that Clara attempts to arise, only to discover that she has been paralyzed by a stroke. She struggles mightily but to no avail. Although Paralyzed Clara's agency is ineffective in this respect, her basic agency remains intact. In contrast, Solomon (to say the least) is in serious conflict. He is ineffective in carrying out his intentions because his agency is undermined by his melancholy. In contrast to Paralyzed Clara, his problem is not that he can't get out of bed *simpliciter* but that he can't get himself to do so. Part of what makes his plight so horrible is that his integrity as an agent is compromised.

It might be thought that phobias impair judgment, rather than will. No doubt this kind of impairment is common. But that doesn't seem to be all that's going on in the scene Solomon describes, or in numerous others. Quite apart from being unable to see clearly what is to be done, or to do as he wills, he is sometimes unable to commit himself to implementing his judgments or prior intentions. Of course, it is not easy always to distinguish impairments of judgment from impairments of will; they are often combined and are equally vexing to practical reason. Furthermore, phobias can "handicap" without fully incapacitating. Disabilities come in degrees. If I have a phobia of dogs, I might walk far out of my way to avoid certain neighborhoods. This choice might reflect the perfectly reasonable judgment that exposing myself to the objects of my dread is just not worth it, given my fear. I might even form the intention and make an effort to walk that way, as exposure therapy,[9] and then decide, in the end, perfectly rationally (and non*akratically*) that my efforts are not worth the agony.

It is worth noting two distinct kinds of reasons that I might express by saying "I fear the dogs." The first is simply the consideration that I might get bitten; (nonphobic) fear, like (well-functioning) emotions in general, registers an independently existing (at least apparent) reason. But, independent of its content, anxiety as such can also give rise to a reason. To be apprehensive of dog bites in this way means that I will be able to go into that neighborhood only at the cost of extreme distress, which may make it reasonable for me to avoid the area, quite apart from the probability of my sustaining the dreaded injury. The prospect of unfriendly dogs and my fear of dogs both work as obstacles or constraints by threatening the costs, respectively, of dog bite or dread of dog bite. The latter is a distinctive consideration, which can figure as a reason in the formation of one's intentions. This can be so, even though one takes one's fear to be unreasonable, and experiences it as a constraint.

What is crucial to our topic is fear's effect as a volitional impediment, not just as a rational constraint of either of these kinds. This effect emerges when one decides that the costs are worth it. Here one has counted and overruled whatever reasons the anxiety itself (as distinct from the considerations expressed by its content) provided. The dread remains, and must be dealt with, not just as a potential cost of the action but as something that might defeat one's agency by leading one to abandon the intention to pay the price.

There appears to be a difference between being unable to bring oneself to act and simply giving up in the face of great difficulty, but the distinction is obscure. To fail in one's wholehearted and persistent efforts might seem to be as decisive a test of inability to act, there and then, as we ever have.[10] But this criterion doesn't apply very clearly in cases of volitional incapacity, in which the individual is torn by conflict. In these cases, it will almost always be true that the individual is led to give up his attempts. This point of course does not demonstrate that the person is not incapacitated; but it makes the concept of volitional ability rather more obscure than the basic concept of ability to act.[11] Perhaps "necessity" here is really a matter of degree; we speak of incapacity to emphasize the magnitude of the difficulty. The distinction seems to be in part normative, to mark the point at which we think it is unreasonable to expect someone to hold out.[12]

One point is reasonably clear, however: the fact that one might in different circumstances be brought to do the thing to which one is averse is not sufficient to show that one is after all capable of doing it. Otherwise, there would be few if any volitional incapacities of the kind in question. For as Isaac Marks notes, when the house is burning down, agoraphobics always find the wherewithal to "temporarily overcome their phobias and venture forth. Once the emergency subsides, the phobia reappears in pristine form."[13] As Marks also notes, the observation that the phobic is virtually always susceptible to counterincentives underlies a good deal of skepticism about such assertions. Family and friends are inclined to see the individual's inactivity as "the result of mere laziness, lack of willpower, or a way of getting out of awkward situations ..." (344–345).

Marks rejects this skepticism: "It is very hard for agoraphobics to muster their energies in such a way that every minor shopping trip is treated like a house on fire. Not only agoraphobics but everybody performs unexpected feats in an acute crisis, but it would be unrealistic to demand such feats of everybody as a routine..." (345).[14] The skeptical reaction is based, I think, on the thought that the counterincentives to which the phobic is susceptible work solely by changing the structure of her reasons. Since she would get out of bed in these other circumstances, her failure to leave the house in the actual situation is a function of her relative judgment about what is worthwhile under the circumstances. But, as we've insisted, the presence or absence of perceived reasons for action is part of the performance conditions, not the enabling conditions, of an action. So the skeptic sees the case of the so-called phobic as more like that of Cozy Clara—a reflection of the individual's peculiar priorities, not capacities.[15]

This reasoning fails to attend sufficiently to the distinction between incentives and reasons.[16] Implicit in our discussion of psychological obstacles is the point that the motivational force of a consideration is not necessarily in proportion to its rational force. This is a familiar point from the experience of everyday aversions—say, to eating a plate of maggots, or to use Bernard Williams's example, roast rat.[17] You might not be able to overcome your repugnance even in response to a credible offer that in your judgment made doing so well worth it—say for a rather large sum of money which you badly need. But you might manage to do so with a gun at your (or your child's) head. It is not just that the threat to your child presents you with a stronger reason (though it does); its capacity to counter the aversion, I suggest, depends on the nature of the incentive it creates. It gives you the strength to overcome the initial aversion.[18]

The strength of a consideration *qua* inducement is thus distinguishable from its strength *qua* reason. This distinction comes out more clearly in the case of the phobic in the house afire. It might well be that the reasons he has to leave the house in general, namely to pursue his career, or support his children, or have a self-respecting life, are in his view as strong, or stronger, *qua* reasons, than those created by the immediate danger of the fire; he may see his housebound existence as scarcely worth preserving.[19] But only the latter is sufficient to move him. It does so, I think, not (just, if at all) by giving rise to weightier reasons but by in effect creating counteraversions. In contrast to Cozy Clara, the presence of these incentives is not only part of the performance conditions but *enables* him to get out of bed, either by overcoming or even entirely eliminating (albeit temporarily) his dread.

To sum up, I have contrasted three cases. The fact that there is no chance that Cozy Clara will get up, given her present incentives, is no reason to say she can't. It is not as though she is rendered impotent by an overwhelming lack of interest in leaving her comfortable environment. In contrast, Paralyzed Clara is incapable of getting out of bed; her behavior is not dependent on her will. The third case is Agoraphobic Clara, who, like Solomon, displays a volitional impairment; she is incapable of willing in certain ways.

IV   Volitional Necessity: Some Interpretations

So far I have been discussing a basic sense of ability according to which one's options are identified by what depends upon one's unimpaired will.

A central feature of this notion is that ability is identified independently of the presence or absence of an agent's reasons or concerns. Both Frankfurt and Bernard Williams argue that Martin Luther's "I can do no other" asserts a kind of necessity that is importantly different from what we have considered so far: it is at once a genuine incapacity and yet in no way compromises one's agency or self-control. How are we to understand this kind of necessity?

As we will see, Frankfurt's and Williams's views differ subtly and significantly. But their initial characterizations of the phenomenon are similar. "A moral incapacity," Williams says, is an incapacity "with which the agent is identified."[20] Similarly, Frankfurt remarks that volitional necessity is not "the same thing as simply being overwhelmingly averse.... In addition, the aversion has his endorsement; and it constrains his conduct so effectively precisely because of this."[21] Or as he puts it in a later essay, "the effectiveness of the person's incapacity derives from the fact that the person considers that incapacity to be important to him."[22] For both philosophers, then, the necessity is somehow dependent on the agent's identifications or sense of what is important.

How are we to understand this? I begin by considering some alternative proposals regarding Luther cases. I will then return to Williams's and Frankfurt's remarks.

Kane's Proposal

Robert Kane suggests one way to reconcile necessity, responsibility and agency in Luther cases. "If we have no hesitation in saying that he was responsible for the final affirmation ['Here I stand']," Kane proposes, "it is because we believe that [Luther] was responsible through many past choices and actions for making himself into the kind of man he then was."[23] However, this proposal fails to capture the way in which Luther cases appear to involve a form of necessitation that is in itself fully voluntary. In describing the relationship as one for which the agent is only ancestrally responsible, Kane would assimilate Luther cases to those in which we treat addicts as responsible for having become addicted. This derivative relationship fails to bring out the sense in which acting under volitional necessity is supposed to be in itself an instance of free and responsible agency.

Normative Necessity

A natural alternative is to take cases like Luther's to be instances of practical or normative necessity.[24] We say the following sort of thing everyday: "I can't come to the meeting; I must look after the baby," or "I can't sleep with you; I'm engaged." The necessity in question is just the requirement of practical reasons. It is impossible for me to come to the meeting (sleep with you) and also take care of my child (remain faithful to my engagement). This kind of necessity is also asserted in first-person, retrospective judgments. "I couldn't turn in the paper on time; my car broke down." In practice the statement would be meant elliptically: "I couldn't turn the paper in on time without ...," where the ellipsis is filled in by specifying alternatives (stealing a car, hiring a helicopter) that would be prohibitively costly or immoral, but not physically out of reach. Of course, such talk is often insincere, or hyperbolic.[25] But it is sometimes entirely apt.

Is this a plausible understanding of Luther cases? Here Williams makes an important observation. Assertions of genuine incapacities should answer to the principle that "can't" implies "doesn't," and this appears to distinguish them from normative necessity as construed so far. Consider the bank official who "simply can't" let one into the bank because it has just closed. This assertion of normative necessity is not refuted by his subsequently being browbeaten or bribed into doing so.

This point is related to another. According to Williams and Frankfurt, the "I can't" in Luther cases is not merely a judgment about normative priorities, as it seems to be on the normative interpretation, but a conclusion about *oneself*, a personal judgment. As Williams puts it (somewhat elusively), such a judgment "can present itself to the agent at once as a decision, and as a discovery."[26] Normative necessity asserts not a real incapacity but a relation among norms or reasons. This leaves out what is most interesting in Luther cases.[27]

There is more to be said on behalf of the normative interpretation. Assertions of normative impossibility are not equivalent to some statement, N, say, that my going to the meeting is inconsistent with my parental duties. By itself, N doesn't preclude the inference: "Therefore, I'll have to neglect the baby." N fails to capture the fact that I, like Luther, was *taking a stand*. Statements of normative necessity not only assert an inconsistency between certain courses of action and certain considerations, but also express a commitment to certain normative priorities. These two features can be seen in the two ways in which statements of normative necessity are open to challenge. One might challenge N ("Why don't you bring the child?") or dispute the commitment of normative priority ("The meeting is just too important for you to miss"). In either of these cases, one would be challenging my stand. Furthermore, the second feature brings statements of normative necessity into conformity with the principle, *"can't" implies "doesn't,"* after all. "I can't but I will" suffers from the same kind of performative infelicity as "I hereby commit myself to X-ing but I won't X." Taking a stand forecloses certain options, and in this sense rules out acting otherwise.

Still, on this reading, talk of necessity could be dropped without loss of meaning. One might have thought "I can do no other" purported to give a kind of backing to or elaboration of "Here I stand." On the normative interpretation, "I can do no other" adds nothing that was not already implicit in the latter. This brings out a crucial difference between (mere) normative necessity and what Williams and Frankfurt have in mind. The necessity they mean to identify attaches to the stand taken by the agent. Perhaps the officious security guard is quite correct to say that allowing customers into the building after closing hours exceeds his rightful authority—that he can't, consistently with the commitments of his office, permit us to enter the building. The question of moral or volitional necessity is the further question of whether or not he can abandon his commitments or endorse his exceeding his authority in this way.

Dennett's Proposal

Both of the proposals we have considered so far fail to bring out what strikes Frankfurt and Williams as philosophically interesting in Luther's stand: the way in which agency and necessity are combined. However, they fail in converse ways. Kane's proposal gives agency too derivative a position, whereas normative necessity by itself is not a personal incapacity.

Daniel Dennett's remarks on Luther cases seem more promising. "[W]hen I say I cannot do otherwise I mean I cannot because I see so clearly what the situation is and because my rational control faculty is *not* impaired. It is too obvious what to do; reason dictates it; I would have to be mad to do otherwise, and since I happen not to be mad, I cannot do otherwise."[28] This remark seems closer to combining agency and incapacity in just the right way, since it attaches necessity precisely to the deliberative faculties in which agency is exercised. Nonetheless, it falls short of providing what Williams and Frankfurt are after. For the incapacity Dennett identifies is not the necessity that is expressed in deliberative conclusions. This proposal interprets judgments of moral impossibility from a nondeliberative point of view. The "cannot do otherwise" here is a judgment *about* someone's (perhaps one's own) deliberative faculties, rather than a first-personal deliverance of them. This interpretation therefore fails to make sense of Williams's idea that the "I cannot" at once reports an incapacity and expresses a "decision."

Once judgments of necessity are read in this external way, it is hard to avoid a slippery slope leading to the general conclusion that we are unable to do anything for which we lack a reason or incentive.[29] Thus, by parallel reasoning:

1. To do otherwise, I would have to have a reason or incentive to do otherwise.
2. I don't happen to have such a reason or incentive.
3. Therefore, I can't do otherwise.

Here again, (3), the conclusion asserting necessity, is not the deliberative judgment; premise (2) is. Perhaps there is some useful sense in which the absence of reasons implies that a reasonable person can't do (or believe) otherwise in circumstances in which she is faced with no counterreasons. But that is not the sense under investigation here. Our enterprise is to understand the notion of impossibility that agents invoke in cases like Luther's but not in Cozy Clara's. To construe moral or volitional incapacity in the forgoing terms is to collapse the difference. From the comfort of her covers, Clara might now appropriately declare: "Here I lie: I can do no other."

Dennett's interpretation, then, shifts the necessity from a deliberative to an explanatory perspective.[30] It is from the deliberative perspective that the situations of Luther and of Clara are different. From the explanatory perspective, they are arguably in the same position. Neither will act otherwise unless a certain kind of reason is available. In the circumstances, there is no such reason, nor is it up to them whether such a reason obtains, or whether they are reasons-sensitive beings. (Compare belief.) This gives an intelligible sense in which neither could in the circumstances do otherwise. But this is not quite what Frankfurt and Williams have in mind.

V   Unthinkability and Deliberative Necessity

I want to try to clarify some of these points by means of an example from Jane Austen's *Pride and Prejudice*. In this novel, Mr. Collins makes a proposal of marriage to Elizabeth Bennett. Elizabeth replies as follows: "I am very sensible of the honour of your proposals, but it is impossible for me to do otherwise than decline them."[31] The necessity here is not, as it were, blind or brute; it is grounded in Elizabeth's ideals of marriage. Miss Bennett is a woman for whom a precondition of marriage is mutual love and respect, which could not be satisfied in a relation to the ridiculously self-satisfied Mr. Collins. "You could not make *me* happy," she bluntly informs him, "and I am convinced that I am the last woman in the world who would make *you* so."[32] Hence, she reiterates, marriage in this situation "is absolutely impossible. My feelings in every respect forbid it."[33]

By contrast, Elizabeth's friend and neighbor, Charlotte Lucas, has less romantic notions. While "marriage had always been her object," Charlotte conceives of this state less as a union of mutual love than as "an honourable provision for well educated young women of small fortune," a "preservative from want."[34] When Charlotte finds herself next in line for Mr. Collins's attentions, she accepts his proposal "solely from the pure and disinterested desire of an establishment." This development seems to her, "at the age of twenty-seven, without having ever been handsome," a piece of good fortune.

This example brings out a number of points. First, Elizabeth's case (like Luther's, we may suppose) involves a certain kind of *unthinkability*. Unthinkability here is not of course a kind of cognitive deficit. Elizabeth is indeed forced by Collins's proposal to have thoughts about a certain proposition. The unthinkability of accepting the proposal consists in its being "out of the question," in its being altogether off the deliberative screen. To have ideals and principles is to be committed to not taking certain considerations seriously as reasons in certain contexts.[35] The structure of reasons that excludes certain considerations from practical force can itself have evolved from deliberation. At an earlier stage, the deliberative conclusion that such and such was impossible might have decisively placed certain considerations beyond the pale. In some cases, though, it might be less deliberate than that. One might discover that one just can't take certain proposals seriously—not just that one cannot give a lot of weight to a certain consideration but that one cannot take them as counting at all.[36]

So judgments of impossibility of this kind are often deliberative starting points rather than conclusions; they indicate the boundaries of the space of reasons in which deliberation takes place. In either case, such judgments involve normative reflection about the structure of reasons and what is eligible for deliberation. To say a proposal is impossible is to give it a certain status: it means that it is not eligible for consideration. This defines a narrower sense of option from that given by the basic concept of what a person can do—only some among the courses of action whose realization depend on the agent's choice are what we might call *deliberative* options. Accepting Collins's offer is an option in the broader, nonnormative sense, but not in the narrower sense.[37] Let us call this deliberative necessity.

Deliberative necessity is distinct from both mere normative necessity and from the necessity identified by Dennett—that is, the impossibility of acting contrary to the weightiest reasons, given that one is a rational agent. Given her feelings, Elizabeth cannot be attracted to Collins. Given her ideals, she cannot see marrying Collins as in any way worthwhile. So she is just as incapable of marrying Collins as she is of believing it to be raining while she stands open-eyed in the bright sunshine. But the assertion of moral or volitional necessity is not just the assertion of a constraint on one's deliberative judgments (due, say, to the limits imposed by one's nature as a rational being) but part of the content of those judgments. Elizabeth's "feelings forbid it"; that is part of what they *say*, not just what they do. The recognition of the impossibility of giving practical force to certain considerations and hence as taking them as grounds for action is itself a discrimination of ethical sensibility. In this way, we can understand how moral incapacity can combine the features alleged by Williams: "I can't" can be at once a decision and a report of an incapacity.

Contrast Elizabeth with Cozy Clara. For Clara, getting out of bed is an option in both senses. It is not out of the question; it just doesn't come up. She may judge, "I have no reason to arise, and plenty of reasons to remain in bed." If her reason-recognitional faculties are intact, she can't, in the sense identified by Dennett, rouse herself. But if so, they do not constrain her by rendering the proposal to get up deliberatively impossible.[38]

Notice, as well, that deliberative necessity seems fully compatible with agency and responsibility. According to Elizabeth, to be unable to accept Collins's proposal is a mark of good character. She is astonished by, and disapproving of, her friend's capacity to set aside her "better feeling":

> She had always felt that Charlotte's opinion of matrimony was not exactly like her own, but she could not have supposed it possible that when called into action, she would have sacrificed every better feeling to worldly advantage. Charlotte the wife of Mr. Collins, was a most humiliating picture!—And to the pang of a friend disgracing herself and sunk in her esteem, was added the distressing conviction that it was impossible for that friend to be tolerably happy in the lot she had chosen.[39]

Finally, we can see the difference between deliberative necessity and "overwhelming aversion" by imagining a variation on Charlotte's case. Being fully aware of "the stupidity with which [Collins] is favored by nature,"[40] Charlotte might well have found herself so repelled in the end that she was unable, regretfully, to take advantage of her best opportunity for security. That would have been a case of psychological, not deliberative, necessity. In contrast to Elizabeth's, her aversion would not have been constituted by her sense of what was most appropriate, important, or best; rather, it would have prevented her from enacting that sense.

VI   Williams and Frankfurt: A Comparison

This account of deliberative necessity seems a plausible answer to the first question we posed at the beginning: how should we distinguish the kind of necessity involved in what Frankfurt and Williams (respectively) call volitional or moral impossibility? So far, however, I have been ignoring important differences in their positions. These differences bear on the second question: how should we understand that which is necessitated? In Frankfurt's case, this is the question: how should we understand the relevant notion of volition?

Moral Incapacity and Volitional Necessity

Despite Williams's title, neither philosopher is concerned with an agent's relation to *moral* considerations specifically. Clearly Williams has in mind at least the broader category he elsewhere calls "ethical." Even so, the phrase "ethical incapacity" describes a narrower range of cases than Frankfurt is concerned with. The contrast here is subtle and complex, but significant.

For Williams, the "I can't" of Luther cases expresses a deliberative conclusion, where deliberation is concerned with considerations of "the good, the useful, the obligatory, and so on.... "[41] A deliberative conclusion is thus a conclusion about what it is best to do (however broadly construed). On Frankfurt's view, however, such conclusions may not express a judgment about what is best at all. They may express a determination of one's *will*, from which Frankfurt takes pains to distinguish not only the appetitive, the emotional, and the cognitive, but also the evaluative or choiceworthy.[42] In particular, the first-person recognition of volitional necessity does not imply the judgment that doing otherwise would be a worse thing to do. A person might be "unable to bring himself to pursue a certain course of action even if he were to recognize it as best."[43] For instance, Frankfurt imagines a mother who believes it would be best to give up her child for adoption, but who finds that she cannot will or endorse what is required by her sincere evaluation. (I'll return to this case later.)

Evaluation and Volition

At the same time, throughout his writings on the subject, Frankfurt links the volitional attitudes essential to human agency to what he calls an evaluative capacity. A distinguishing feature of a wanton, we are told, is that "he is not concerned with the *desirability* of his desires themselves."[44] Personhood is said to involve "the capacity for reflective evaluation that is manifested in the formation of second-order desires."[45]

To be a person entails *evaluative* attitudes (not necessarily based on moral considerations) toward oneself. A person is a creature prepared to endorse or repudiate the motives from which he acts and to organize the preferences and priorities by which his choices are ordered. He is disposed to consider whether what attracts him is actually important to him.[46]

The issue of what to endorse is, then, an evaluative issue.[47] It is an issue about what is important or matters to one, or what one cares about. But this is not the same question as what is most choice-worthy. The former is an essentially volitional and personal question; the latter is not.

Perhaps this blunts the contrast with Williams a bit. Since the task of deliberation is to decide what to do, to make up one's mind, to determine what's important to one, the "I can't" of volitional necessity is indeed a deliberative conclusion for Frankfurt as well.[48] That task is not necessarily completed when one arrives at a firm belief about what is best to do. Nonetheless, an important difference remains. For Williams, moral incapacities depend on, and express, the agent's ethical conception of the alternatives. Frankfurt's volitional necessities would take this ethical form, if an individual's volitional nature were bound up with the ethical; but they need not be, he thinks. For a conclusion about what is important to one is not for Frankfurt equivalent to a judgment about what is choiceworthy.[49]

This difference can be put in terms of the notion of reasons. "To understand moral incapacity," Williams says, "we have to consider ... the way in which the incapacity is connected with the agent's reasons" (50): "'I can't' recognizes an incapacity in the light of deliberative reasons" (53). One cannot do otherwise because one cannot take certain considerations as reasons to do otherwise. In contrast, the possible disconnection between identification and judgments of what is best means that, for Frankfurt, volitional necessity might involve the discovery that one's identifications are less than rational.[50] So the attitude in which such an incapacity consists need not be reasons-sensitive.[51]

Identification

This last contrast reflects a crucial difference about the nature of identification. Williams tells us that an individual cannot coherently set out to remove or overcome his moral incapacity

because a fundamental way in which a moral incapacity expresses itself is in the refusal to undertake any such project. A moral incapacity in the sense under discussion is one with which the agent is identified. Of course an agent may come to see a moral incapacity of his as something with which he is no longer identified, and try to overcome it. But so soon as this is his state of mind ... then he has lost the moral incapacity.... [I]t is no longer a moral incapacity, but rather one that is merely psychological.[52]

For Williams, to oppose one's own identifications is to cease to have them. Frankfurt thinks otherwise:

[I]t is surely open to someone for whom an action is unthinkable to alter his own will in such a way that the action becomes thinkable for him. The fact that a person cannot bring himself to perform an action does not entail that he cannot bring himself to act with the intention of changing that fact.[53]

To "take steps to alter one's volitional capacities"[54] is to take steps to alter what one identifies with.

This last difference, especially, raises important questions about Frankfurt's notion of the volitional. What is the nature of the opposition that is exhibited in struggles to bring oneself to act otherwise? What does it teach us about identification and agency?

VII Identification, Endorsement, and Caring

If volitional activity consisted in the formation of highest-order volitions, as Frankfurt preferred to say in his earlier work, then volitional necessity would be the inability to form one's highest-order volitions in any other way.[55] But to characterize the motivational standpoint of those who struggle against their own volitional capacities requires a more complex picture of what volitional activity consists in. And it is not clear how the more complex account is to be filled in, for the idea brings out some tensions in Frankfurt's treatment of the subject.

At one point, for example, Frankfurt argues that volitional necessity delineates the province of one's will.

To the extent that a person is constrained by volitional necessities, there are certain things that he can't help willing or that he cannot bring himself to do.... [T]he essential nature of a person consists in what he must will. The boundaries of his will define his shape as a person.[56]

This remark would make sense if Frankfurt were in agreement with Williams about identification, or if volitional necessity were confined to unthinkability in the strict sense. In view of his remarks on cases of volitional struggles, as we might call them, the passage is in fact very puzzling. If the effort to overcome what turns out to be volitional necessity is an effort to work against the limits of one's will, one's opposition to that necessity exhibits a source of agency that is independent of those confines. On what ground can the struggle be mounted?

Take Frankfurt's case of the woman who believes that giving up her child would be best overall. By her unsuccessful attempt to overcome her deep attachment,[57] she discovers the limits of what she can, in one sense, will. Yet in this endeavor she is not a witness, but active on behalf of her sense of what is best. Now a "person is active when it is by his own will that he does what he does, even when his will is not itself within the scope of his voluntary control."[58] So her will must be engaged in volitional opposition, too, and the necessity exhibited in her failure to bring herself to give up the child cannot completely define the bounds of the mother's volitional capacities—nor, a fortiori, what Frankfurt calls her "shape as a person."[59]

The source of these tensions lies, I think, in the divergent ways in which Frankfurt characterizes the distinction between volitional necessity and other kinds of incapacity. As we've seen, one criterion is that "the aversion has [one's] endorsement ... and ... constrains [one's] conduct so effectively precisely because of this."[60] Here what one can will is shown by what one can *endorse*. Frankfurt also tells us that in volitional necessity, "the effectiveness of the person's incapacity derives from the fact that the person considers that incapacity to be important to him."[61] On this second criterion, a mere aversion is one whose motivational force does not depend on one's sense of what's important. These criteria, which we may call the endorsement and the caring criteria, respectively, can and do come apart in many struggles of the kind that Frankfurt discusses.

This divergence is especially conspicuous in cases in which one not only attempts to overcome what one cares about in a particular situation, but also undertakes the longer-term project of modifying or eliminating one's identifications. Frankfurt imagines someone who cannot bring himself to consume human flesh but finds himself regularly in circumstances in which this inability proves to be "inimical to his interests."[62] Such a person "might take steps to alter his volitional capacities so as to be capable of doing what he now finds unthinkable."[63] How is this example to be distinguished from a case of mere revulsion? On the endorsement criterion, the cases seem indistinguishable. In view of his sustained campaign against it, it makes no sense to say that the aversion any longer has the man's endorsement. What one endorses is a matter of what one stands behind, what one commits oneself to. To take on the project of extinguishing the aversion *is* to repudiate it, and to repudiate the aversion is to withdraw one's endorsement. Higher-order endorsement logically constrains lower-order endorsement.

The logic of caring is different. What one cares about is measured by how much one is "invested" in or bound up with something, by one's sense of loss or diminishment upon not realizing or achieving the object of one's care. The man's endorsement of the transformation does not negate the fact that it continues to matter to him not to be "cannibalistic." The foregoing characterizations of volitional necessity, then, are not equivalent; one might not endorse everything that means something to one. Contrary simultaneous endorsements by the same individual cancel out one another, but not so with what one cares about. A person under volitional necessity "may care about something even though he wishes that he didn't, and despite strenuous efforts to stop."[64] The man's aversion to eating human flesh is distinguishable from an overwhelming aversion only on the caring criterion.

There are, correspondingly, two distinct notions of identification: identification as endorsement and identification as what one cares about.[65] Both notions pick out something naturally called "identification." On both conceptions, furthermore, volitional necessity contrasts with "mere overwhelming aversion." In struggling against what one cares about, one is indeed in a contest with (part of) oneself, not just with what appears as an alien force.[66] Nevertheless, the difference between these conceptions explains the contrast we noted above between Williams's and Frankfurt's positions. Williams's position follows the logic of endorsement rather than caring.[67] A plausible explanation of why undertaking to alter one's concerns precludes identification with them is that it rescinds, or presupposes the withdrawal of, one's endorsement. In contrast, what Frankfurt has in mind in cases of volitional struggles is the endeavor to go against what one cares about.[68]

When an agent opposes her own sense of what is important in this way, must that opposition be prompted by something else she cares about? Or can endorsement, and hence agency, have another provenance? Now, Frankfurt does not in fact think that we are active only on behalf of what we care about:

We often devote our time and effort and other resources to the pursuit of goals that we desire to attain because we are convinced of their intrinsic value but that we do not really consider to be of any importance to us.... There is no incoherence in appraising something as intrinsically valuable, and pursuing it actively as a final end that is worth having in itself, and yet not caring about it.[69]

So one can be prompted to pursue something valuable even though the value in question is of no importance to one. But Frankfurt's own illustration is the enjoyment of inconsequential pleasures, where nothing much is at stake; enjoying oneself here neither realizes nor conflicts with anything one takes to be important. This passage leaves it open whether one can actively counter something of great significance to one just because of the perception of the "intrinsic value" of doing so.

Consider again the case of the unfortunate mother. How are we to characterize the motivational standpoint of someone who struggles against her own concerns in this way? This question is quite independent of the issue of necessity; it arises equally in cases that fall short of that, cases of severe volitional difficulty in which the individual succeeds in her struggle.[70] Imagine that the woman manages, despite her attachment, to give up her child for adoption. Her effort manifests an identification with the standpoint of what is best. Must this mean that she *cares*, in the end, more about conforming to that standpoint than about maintaining her relationship? If we insist that it must, then we are clearly not *grounding* identification, and hence agency, in caring, but rather using identification in the sense of endorsement as a criterion of what is most important to her. Her agency is exercised in the privileging of some of her concerns over others. Perhaps this stance entails that doing what's best overall is more important to her than following her heart. But if we say that, we are taking her volitional activity to be fundamentally a matter of what she stands for or endorses, rather than what she cares about in some independent sense.

To be sure, a crucial feature of this case is that the woman's love is at war with itself. It comprises both her need for the relationship and her desire for the well-being of her child. She will in a way be betraying her love in any case. So it would be misleading to portray the case as one in which she makes a personal sacrifice for merely impersonal considerations. She is after all acting out of concern for *her* child. Just the same, there is something to that portrayal, as we can see by comparing the original case to the scenario in which she succeeds in her struggle. It is unlikely, for example, that the outcome of her failure to give up the child, as in the original example, would be as personally devastating as the outcome in the modified case. What she has to live with differs significantly in the two scenarios. She might or might not feel guilty in the original case, but she will not feel alienated or broken in the way it would be natural for her to feel in the second case. In that scenario, she is likely to feel empty, just "going through the motions." For a source of meaning will have been removed from her everyday experience. Just the same, she may do all this tearfully but in a sense resolutely and without regret, not because that would be too mild a description of her reaction but because that would be the wrong description. For she is doing, we may suppose, what she sees clearly to be the right thing, in a way unequivocally, though perhaps, since her heart's not in it, not exactly wholeheartedly.

The divergence between endorsement and caring raises the question: how important, in the end, *is* what we care about? Or, better, how important is the notion of what we care about to understanding human agency? Whatever the answer to this question may be, the divergence also suggests to me an important difference in the two cases with respect to the issue of agency. Although the outcome in the first scenario might be easier for her to live with, there is an important sense in which it involves a failure—one to which she might resign herself, but a failure just the same. In deliberately violating her attachment, as in the second case, she indeed does injury to herself. But in an important sense, her agency has not been damaged or defeated, since the outcome is an upshot of her endorsement. This means that she authorizes the outcome in a way in which she would not have in the first case. So the idea of endorsement seems more central to agency than is the idea of what we care about.[71]

To invoke another elusive notion, we might say that the woman's "integrity" is compromised in either case. But the difference between endorsement and caring brings out two dimensions of integrity. When caring comes apart from endorsement in this way, it still remains integral to what one's life is about, but its reason-giving status is altered. As shattering as the triumph of her efforts might be, the second outcome leaves her with a kind of volitional or authorial integrity that is not achieved in the other case. Her privileging of her conviction about what is best for

the child over her needs for the relationship imposes a coherent deliberative structure among her ends and concerns. This kind of order is
unavailable to her in the other scenario.

Whether this achievement is enough to help her to carry on is another
question entirely. The mother loses in either case, and I am not making
any claims about the relative value of volitional integrity in comparison to preserving her attachments. My claim is just that the losses are
significantly different. One loss involves a defeat of agency in a way in
which the other does not.

VIII   Conclusion

A satisfactory description of volitional struggle requires a distinction
among three motivational structures. First, there are the sources of motivation whose force is independent of one's endorsement, or of what one
cares about.[72] Second, there is what one cares about, is attached to, and
finds meaningful, the loss of which tends to be felt acutely. Third, there is
what one endorses as an end, project, or principle—what one commits
oneself to, stands for and behind. The relations among these structures
are complex; they are largely overlapping but distinct. Even if we only
endorsed projects that independently mattered to us, we would have to
take a position (make a deliberative commitment) regarding the ordering
of our various concerns.

Each of these structures is a possible source of necessity. The first
structure raises questions about irresistible desires and overwhelming
aversions. Frankfurt's discussion of volitional struggle brings to light two
further locations for motivational necessity. Perhaps I am unable to bring
myself to do something because of what that would mean to me; that is
one thing that Frankfurt calls volitional necessity. In such a case, I might
or might not undertake to bypass or transform what I care about. That
further undertaking would be an exercise of agency, an authorization of
the project of overcoming. The stances that I take with respect to my
sense of what matters might themselves be subject to necessity. Perhaps
I am unable to do anything but undertake to oppose my own concerns in
certain ways. That could be the situation of the mother who cannot
bring herself to give up her child because that relationship is too important to her. At the same time, it may be, she cannot do otherwise than

attempt to bring herself to give it up—because, for instance, she thinks it is best to do so. In that case, on Frankfurt's criteria, she is subject to two levels of volitional necessity at once.

Acknowledgments

I want to express my gratitude to Sarah Buss and Lee Overton for organizing the conference for which this essay was first prepared, and to the conference participants for the extraordinarily high level of philosophical intelligence and good spirits they brought to the occasion. I am also grateful to Sarah and Lee for their painstaking editorial work on this volume; in preparing the final draft, I have profited enormously from their comments. The comments of Michael Bratman, John Fischer, Paul Hoffman, and Jennifer Rosner have also helped me a great deal. Finally, I want to thank Harry Frankfurt for opening up and shaping this philosophical territory in the first place; without him, we are unlikely to have gone there at all.

Notes

1. Harry Frankfurt, "The Importance of What We Care About," in *The Importance of What We Care About: Philosophical Essays* (New York: Cambridge University Press, 1988), 87. As far as I know, Frankfurt is the first to take up this topic. Bernard Williams singles out a similar range of phenomena. See his "Moral Incapacity," in *Making Sense of Humanity* (Cambridge, England: Cambridge University Press, 1995). I compare Williams's treatment of the topic with Frankfurt's later in this essay.

2. Donald Davidson, "Freedom to Act," in *Essays on Actions and Events* (New York: Oxford University Press, 1980), 73.

3. Davidson, "Freedom to Act," 74.

4. There are importantly different variants on this type of conditional account. In place of the notion of a desire/belief pair, for example, one could speak instead of the formation of intentions so to act (as I would prefer). For the purposes of this discussion, these questions won't matter much. Notice two points about this notion. It satisfies standard modal principles by preserving inferences of the form "if S Xs, then S can X" (where "X" is a description under which the agent acts intentionally). Notice also that since Davidson identifies reasons with desire/belief pairs, to act intentionally is on his account to act on a reason. It follows, in this minimal sense, that if someone can do otherwise, she is "responsive to reasons." This idea figures in the discussion later.

5. Davidson, "Freedom to Act," 73.

6. In her book, *Freedom and Responsibility* (Princeton: Princeton University Press, 1999), Hilary Bok shows the importance of distinguishing the kind of possibility that is central to many theoretical contexts (which she calls possibility *tout court*) from that which is important to deliberative concerns. Philosophers who are inclined to look at the notion of ability to act from a theoretical point of view will say that the idea of what an individual would do if she intended or tried yields at most a notion of what an individual *could* do under certain conditions, which is of course not at all the same as what an individual can do under actual conditions. This is, again, a possible way of speaking, but for understandable reasons not of much use in deliberative contexts.

7. This is a major theme of Stuart Hampshire's *Freedom of the Individual* (New York: Harper and Row, 1965).

8. Andrew Solomon, "Anatomy of Melancholy," *The New Yorker* (January 12, 1998), 46–58 (my emphasis). The sentence before the ellipsis is from p. 46; the rest of the quotation comes from p. 49.

9. Exposure therapy can backfire. Isaac Marks tells the sad story of a woman with a dread of flying who "was put on her test flight from Tel Aviv to Paris only to find that it was hijacked to Entebbe." *Fears, Phobias, and Rituals* (New York: Oxford University Press, 1987), 391.

10. As Hampshire puts it: "When we definitely, and without qualification or conflict, want to do something at a particular moment, sincerely make the attempt in normal conditions, and yet fail, we know as surely as we can ever know, that at that moment we could not do it." Hampshire, *Freedom of the Individual*, 3. It is often hard to know, of course, whether the antecedent conditions have been fulfilled. But even when we think they have been, we do not infer inability from single failures. Paul Hoffman has reminded me that failures of execution in complicated performances often do not lead us to conclude that we were unable to do the thing then and there, especially if we have succeeded (or go on to succeed) in similar circumstances. Athletes frequently say, "We could have won that game," without implying that their effort or concentration was insufficient. This judgment seems to rest on the assessment that they had the opportunity and the requisite skill to win. So the issue is more complicated than Hampshire's criterion would have it.

11. The contrast should not be drawn too starkly. To persist in physically demanding tasks takes not only muscular strength and coordinational skills but the capacity to deal with pain, tedium, discomfort, discouragement and hence with the desire to quit. Tests of physical strength are typically, in part, tests of will. (Much of the drama of athletics turns on this.) So obstacles to physical feats almost always include motivational resistance as well.

12. In his article, Solomon moves easily from talk of inability/incapacity to the language of "difficulty." He compares his efforts here to an earlier experience as a skydiver, noting that it had been "easier to climb along a strut toward the tip of a plane's wing against an eighty-mile-an hour wind at five thousand feet than it was to get out of bed those days." Solomon, "The Anatomy of Melancholy," 49. This move is natural because there is no precise line between "that would be too

difficult to do" and "that would be beyond my capacity." We distinguish them only for practical purposes.

13. Isaac Marks, *Fears, Phobias, and Rituals* (New York: Oxford University Press, 1987), 344.

14. Note the normative criterion to which Marks appeals here.

15. The skepticism about the phobic is bolstered by the strangeness of the fear, in contrast to the more familiar and "natural" aversion to eating what is conceived as filthy or putrid.

16. For a development of the idea that the lack of control exhibited in phobias and compulsions can be understood in terms of the lack of reasons-responsiveness, see John Fischer and Mark Ravizza, *Responsibility and Control* (New York: Cambridge University Press, 1997): "When an agent acts from a literally irresistible urge, he is undergoing a kind of physical process that is not reasons-responsive, and it is this lack of reasons-responsiveness of the actual physical process that rules out guidance control and moral responsibility" (48). Insofar as reasons-responsiveness is understood just in terms of susceptibility to counterincentives, this criterion is inadequate, as the examples above show. Fischer and Ravizza do not explicitly discuss the kinds of examples I have raised, but they do consider in general terms cases in which an "agent somehow gets considerably more energy or focus if he is presented with a *strong* reason to do otherwise ..." (74). They would say, presumably, that the susceptibility to certain counterincentives changes the mechanism in the kinds of cases I have in mind. The theory is that the "actual mechanism" that motivates the action must be reasons-responsive. In our example, the "mechanism" that operates to keep the man inside the house before the alarm goes off (the phobia) is not the same mechanism as that which is operating in the emergency (the fear of fire). My worry is that this claim is either ad hoc, or trivializes the thesis by distinguishing mechanisms according to the types of reasons to which they are responsive—a worry that the authors themselves acknowledge.

17. These examples remind us that volitional incapacities are not necessarily *dis*abilities, but part of the equipment of a healthy creature.

18. The fact that a phobic could get on the plane with a companion doesn't show that she can get on without one—any more than the fact that she could move the boulder with the aid of another implies that she could move it by herself. Of course there are interesting differences. Her companion comforts her, giving her confidence that she can make it without calamity; her companion's help supports her agency.

19. We shouldn't forget how ruinous agoraphobia can be. The following cases are not untypical of the malady. "Finding myself in the midst of a large gathering would inspire a feeling of terror [which] ... could be relieved in but one way—by getting away from the spot as soon as possible. Acting on this impulse ... I have left churches, theatres, even funerals, simply because of an utter inability to control myself to stay.... This malady ... has throttled all ambition, and killed all personal pride, spoiled every pleasure.... [O]ver this the will seems to have

no control." Marks, *Fears, Phobias, and Rituals*, 325–326. Joy Melville tells of an American woman who "hid for two days at Heathrow Airport, rather than catch her flight to New York. When she was questioned by a police officer, she confessed to being too afraid to fly. She was allowed to stay another night at Heathrow and, next day, got as far as boarding a plane—but officials decided she was unfit to travel and she was taken to hospital." Joy Mellville, *Phobias and Obsessions* (London: George Allen and Unwin, 1977), 53.

20. Bernard Williams, "Moral Incapacity," 54. All parenthetical page references to Williams in the text will be to this essay.

21. Harry Frankfurt, "Rationality and the Unthinkable," in *The Importance of What We Care About* (New York: Cambridge University Press, 1988), 182.

22. Harry Frankfurt, "On the Necessity of Ideals," in *Necessity, Volition, and Love* (New York: Cambridge University Press, 1999), 111–112. Of course, we should not understand this to mean that moral incapacities or volitional necessities are just welcome aversions or compulsions. (Otherwise, Frankfurt's example of the happy addict ["Freedom of the Will and the Concept of a Person," in *The Importance of What We Care About*] would perforce be a case of volitional necessity.) Most of us unequivocally affirm our deep revulsion to eating maggots, even if we can imagine circumstances in which we would see good reason to counter it. The crucial difference is that the incapacity or necessity is not here mediated by an ethical conception (in Williams's terms) or, as Frankfurt wants to say, by a conception of what matters to one. I say more about this below.

23. Robert Kane, *The Significance of Free Will* (New York: Oxford University Press, 1996), 39–40.

24. Rogers Albritton understands these cases in this way in "Freedom of Will, and Freedom of Action," Presidential address delivered in 1985 to the Pacific Division of the APA, in *Proceedings and Addresses of the American Philosophical Association* (1985).

25. A familiar kind of "bullshit," on Frankfurt's analysis; see Harry Frankfurt, "On Bullshit," in *The Importance of What We Care About*.

26. Williams, "Moral Incapacity," 52.

27. For all we've said, of course, either this interpretation or Kane's proposal might be just the right thing to say about the historical example of Luther, in which case Luther's case might not be what I am calling a Luther case.

28. Daniel Dennett, *Elbow Room* (Cambridge, Mass.: MIT Press, 1984), 133.

29. Peter van Inwagen willingly makes this slide; he argues that an "agent cannot do anything other than the thing that seems to him to be clearly the only sensible thing." Peter van Inwagen, "When is the Will Free?" in *Agents, Causes, and Events*, ed. Timothy O'Connor (New York: Oxford University Press, 1995), 232. By the same reasoning: ". . . if a person has done A, and if he wanted very much to do A, and if he had no desires whatever that inclined him toward not doing A, then he was unable not to do A; not doing A was simply not within his power" (230). For a critical discussion, see "When the Will Is Free," John Martin Fischer and Mark Ravizza, in *Agents, Causes, and Events*.

30. The distinction here is in an important sense different from the one stressed in the first section of the essay. In contrast to the explanatory perspective I had in mind there, Dennett's explanation here is normative, in that it involves judgments on the part of the *observer* about what it is rational for the agent to do under the circumstances. That, together with the proposition that the agent *is* rational, yields the conclusion in question.

31. *The Oxford Illustrated Jane Austen*, third ed., ed. R. W. Chapman (Oxford: Oxford University Press, 1932–1954), vol. 2, 107.

32. *The Oxford Illustrated Jane Austen*, 107.

33. *The Oxford Illustrated Jane Austen*, 109.

34. *The Oxford Illustrated Jane Austen*, 122–123.

35. For helpful remarks on the ways in which reasons are structured and silenced by principles and intentions, see T. M. Scanlon, *What We Owe to One Another* (Cambridge, Mass.: Harvard University Press, 1998), 50–55.

36. Here I have profited from comments by Sarah Buss.

37. That marrying Collins is, as Elizabeth says, "absolutely impossible" doesn't entail that there are no conceivable circumstances in which she would marry Collins without changing her ideals. We may imagine that if her family depended on it to remain out of the poor house, or if it were necessary to save the life of her sister, Jane, then she could have resigned herself to such a dismal union. The impossibility in question here depends on the structure of reasons in which Elizabeth finds herself. What she cannot do is to "sacrifice every better feeling to worldly advantage." That's what the marriage to Collins would mean in the actual circumstances. In the imagined circumstances, she would have faced a different choice. Marrying Collins would then have meant something else: devotion to her family, say.

38. Conceivably, Clara's ideals might be such that to force herself out of bed whimsically or capriciously would violate her sense of who she is; her "feelings" might forbid it. But I am supposing that, as for most of us, this matter is of no real importance to her.

39. Austen, *Pride and Prejudice*, 125.

40. *The Oxford Illustrated Jane Austen*, 122.

41. Williams, "Moral Incapacity," 48. Of course, they express more than this, as we saw in the discussion of so-called normative necessity; they are also conclusions about oneself. Significantly, for Williams, all deliberation is in some sense about oneself, not, trivially, in that it concerns what it is best for one to do, but in that such questions are always somehow about one's "underlying dispositions" (52). This difficult idea is central to the account in Bernard Williams, "Internal and External Reasons," in *Moral Luck* (Cambridge: Cambridge University Press, 1981).

42. See, among other places, Frankfurt, "On the Necessity of Ideals," 110. Perhaps the present difference reflects Frankfurt's rejection of the kind of internalism referred to in the previous note.

43. Frankfurt, "Rationality and the Unthinkable," 184.

44. Frankfurt, "Freedom of the Will and the Concept of a Person," 17 (my emphasis).

45. Ibid., 12.

46. Frankfurt, "On the Necessity of Ideals," 113–144 (my emphasis). Personhood involves "the capacity for reflective evaluation that is manifested in the formation of second-order desires." Frankfurt, "Freedom of the Will and the Concept of a Person," 12. See also Frankfurt, "The Faintest Passion," in *Necessity, Volition, and Love*, 103, n. 14. "To be a person, as distinct from simply a human organism, requires a complex volitional structure involving reflective self-evaluation."

47. Early on, it is true, Frankfurt's notion of evaluation was extremely thin; higher-order volitions "express evaluations only in the sense that they are preferences." Frankfurt, "Freedom of the Person and the Concept of a Person," 19, n. 6. But the talk of evaluation assumes more substance in later work, once the notion of caring is in the foreground.

48. See Harry Frankfurt, "Identification and Wholeheartedness," in *The Importance of What We Care About*, 174–175.

49. Frankfurt, "On the Necessity of Ideals," 112.

50. Frankfurt, "Rationality and the Unthinkable," 184.

51. If, following Michael Bratman, "Identification, Decision, and Treating as a Reason," *Philosophical Topics* 24 (1996): 1–18, we link deliberation or decision with reasons by construing the upshot of deliberation as a commitment to take or exclude certain considerations as reason giving, then volitional necessity can be described as a condition in which one finds that one cannot take *R* as a reason even though one might judge that *R* supports the best course of action—that is, that *R* is a conclusive reason.

52. Williams, "Moral Incapacity," 54.

53. Frankfurt, "Rationality and the Unthinkable," 187.

54. Ibid.

55. The mere absence of alternative possibilities is not sufficient for volitional necessity, however. The thesis that higher-order necessity is compatible with agency and responsibility is defended in the early essays by appealing to cases of "overdetermination." These are not cases of volitional necessity, I take it, because the source of the impossibility is exogenous.

56. Frankfurt, "On the Necessity of Ideals," 114.

57. In contrast to the man who undertook to transform his attitudes toward eating flesh, what the woman opposes here is not the love itself but that to which the love inclines her.

58. Frankfurt, "The Importance of What We Care About," 88. Although Frankfurt does not say "only when," this follows if we read the remark as a definition rather than as a statement of sufficient conditions.

59. Frankfurt, "On the Necessity of Ideals," 114. Note that the case of the woman does not fit Frankfurt's characterization of volitional necessity in the passage we quoted at the beginning of this essay. Unlike the addict, the person under volitional necessity is said not to "accede to the constraining force because he lacks sufficient strength of will to defeat it. He accedes to it because he is *unwilling* to oppose it and because, furthermore, his unwillingness is *itself* something which he is unwilling to alter." Frankfurt, "The Importance of What We Care about," 87. This is a plausible description of unthinkability, perhaps, but not of cases of volitional struggle. The woman *is* in a plain sense willing to oppose her attachment, and does so because she is willing.

60. Frankfurt, "Rationality and the Unthinkable," 182.

61. Frankfurt, "On the Necessity of Ideals," 111–112.

62. Frankfurt, "Rationality and the Unthinkable," 187.

63. Ibid.

64. Frankfurt, "On Caring," in *Necessity, Volition, and Love*, 161–162.

65. Bratman's notion of identification as committing oneself to take certain considerations as reasons fits (and can perhaps be seen as an analysis of) the endorsement, rather than the caring, conception.

66. As addictive desire can sometimes do. That is not to say that people don't commonly care about their addictions. If I am unable to resist the addictive desires I affirm, as in Frankfurt's case of the happy addict, that is not necessarily a case of volitional necessity, for the force of the desire might be independent of my endorsement or of my sense of what is important to do or be. Yet being addicted might be incorporated into my sense of importance in such a way that it is that sense, and not just the chemically rooted motivational dependency, against which I am struggling. If I am an unhappy addict, I might deplore not only my addictive tendencies, but also my attachment to my addiction. Then I would be struggling against myself in a different sense. (I discuss the idea of attachment to one's addictions in "Disordered Appetites: Addiction, Compulsion, and Dependence," in *Addiction: Entries and Exits*, ed. Jon Elster [Russell Sage Foundation, 1999], 3–28.)

67. So does the notion of identification that Frankfurt tended to employ in his earlier essays: "It makes no sense to ask whether someone identifies himself with his identification of himself, unless this is intended simply as asking whether his identification is wholehearted or complete." Frankfurt, "Three Concepts of Free Action," in *The Importance of What We Care About*, 54. Note that this is not true on the caring conception. Endorsement "resounds throughout the potentially endless array of higher orders," as Frankfurt famously puts it in his first formulation of these issues ("Freedom of the Will and the Concept of a Person," 21) because endorsement implies commitment all the way up. Perhaps caring has a hierarchical structure as well. If friendship with you really means anything to me (in contrast to my taste for spicy foods), I cannot be entirely unconcerned about ceasing to care about you. But the hierarchical structure of endorsement is importantly different, it seems to me, in virtue of its connection with commit-

ments and reasons. (Here I am indebted to a discussion with the participants of the Stanford Workshop on Moral Responsibility, especially Michael Bratman and Jennifer Rosner.) I return to this point briefly at the end.

68. The idea of volitional struggle as opposition to one's own identifications appears to be ruled out by the doctrine of "The Faintest Passion," according to which identification "is constituted ... by an endorsing higher-order desire with which the person is satisfied" (105), where "satisfaction" entails "an absence of restlessness or resistance" (103). On the satisfaction criterion, neither that against which one struggles, nor that on behalf of which one struggles could be said to reveal what one identifies with. Perhaps we should take "The Faintest Passion" to be defining *complete* or *full* identification. Elsewhere, Frankfurt speaks of ambivalent agents as "*in part* opposed to a motivational tendency with which they are also *in part* identified" (my emphases). Frankfurt, "Autonomy, Necessity, and Love," in *Necessity, Volition, and Love*, 137–138. Thus cases of volitional struggle would be instances of conflicting partial identifications. And this in turn could be a matter either of contrary caring, or of a divergence between caring and endorsement.

69. Frankfurt, "On Caring," 159.

70. To see the distance between Frankfurt's early treatment of freedom of the will and his later account of volitional necessity, it is instructive to notice that the earlier hierarchical treatment would imply that the mother did not act with freedom of the will. For her endorsement of the project of giving up her child is a higher-order desire to which her first-order will does not conform. Frankfurt does not want to say that volitional necessity is a violation of free will, however. Perhaps he thinks that there is an even higher-order volition in support of her keeping the child, but that seems strained in this case. Instead, he may think that this highest level endorsement does not amount to a volition.

71. It doesn't follow that the idea of what we care about is less important to one's identity; for one's identity is not merely a matter of one's agency.

72. These are part of the self, so to speak, only so long as they behave in ways that are harmonious with the others. Insofar as they don't, they are estranged in an important sense. See Harry Frankfurt, "Identification and Externality," in *The Importance of What We Care About*.

REPLY TO GARY WATSON

Harry Frankfurt

1. As Watson recognizes, I do not regard determinations of the will as necessarily based on determinations of what is choice-worthy or best to do. On the other hand, he observes that often "Frankfurt links the volitional attitudes essential to human agency to what he calls an evaluative capacity." There is a problem of communication here, for which I fear I am responsible.[1]

In various places, I have said such things as that the concept of a person is to be understood in terms of the capacity for "reflective evaluation," that human beings and other animals are wantons insofar as they are indifferent to the "desirability" of their desires, and that inner freedom is a matter of whether or not a person "endorses" the desires by which he is moved in what he does. It was a mistake on my part to use those locutions. My doing so has naturally created a strong impression that "an evaluative capacity" of some kind figures essentially in my understanding of human agency, but this impression is misleading.

What is essential to persons is not, in my view, a capacity to measure the value of their desires or to assess the desirability of their impulses. Rather, it is a capacity to identify themselves with (or to refrain from identifying themselves with) their tendencies to be moved in one way or another. These reflective attitudes of identification or of withholding are often based on or grounded in evaluations of desirability. However, they need not be. A person may identify himself with (or withhold himself from) a certain desire or motivation for reasons that are unrelated to any such assessment, or for no reason at all. What I have had in mind when I have employed the notion of endorsement is something that makes no claim or judgment whatever, and that is more accurately specified as the altogether neutral attitude of acceptance. A person may be led to accept something about himself in resignation, as well as in approval or in recognition of its merit. The fact that he accepts it entails nothing, in other words, concerning what he thinks of it.

2. This naturally has a bearing on Watson's suggestion that there are, in my writings, "two distinct notions of identification: identification as

endorsement and identification as what one cares about." In fact, the notion of identification that I do care about, and which I both accept and endorse, is neither of the two that Watson mentions. It is the notion of identification as acceptance, which I adumbrated first in "The Faintest Passion." Since I may identify with desires of which I do not approve, identification does not entail endorsement. Since I may identify with desires that I consider to be quite trivial, such as a desire to have some ice cream, identifying does not entail caring. Perhaps it is more or less true, as Watson observes, that "what Frankfurt has in mind in cases of volitional struggle is the endeavor to go against what one cares about." To the extent that this is true, however, it is not because there is some essential linkage between identification and caring. It is just because a person ordinarily has no reason or motive to struggle except in cases where there is something at stake that he cares about.

3.   Watson acknowledges that "early on ... Frankfurt's notion of evaluation was extremely thin," and that volitions were said to express evaluations "only in the sense that they are preferences." He supposes, though, that "the talk of evaluation assumes more substance in [Frankfurt's] later work, once the notion of caring is in the foreground." In supporting this supposition, he refers to my observation that it is characteristic of a person to reflect upon "whether what attracts him is actually important to him."

Now the fact that a person cares about something, or that something is important to him, means just that the person is disposed to behave in certain ways. This fact need not derive from or depend on any evaluations or judgments that the person makes or accepts. The fact that something is important to someone is a circumstance that naturally has its causes, but it may neither originate in, nor be at all supported by, reasons. It may be simply a brute fact, which is not derived from any assessment or appreciation whatever. I am therefore reluctant to accept Watson's suggestion that the "I can't" of volitional necessity is, on my account, "a deliberative conclusion." On my account, such necessities are not necessarily grounded in any cognitive process.

4.   Watson thinks there is something puzzling in my notion that volitional necessity "delineates the province of one's will," especially when this notion is taken together with my discussion of instances of

volitional struggle. He explains what puzzles him as follows: "If the effort to overcome what turns out to be volitional necessity is an effort to work against the limits of one's will, one's opposition to that necessity exhibits a source of agency that is independent of those confines. On what ground can the struggle be mounted?" Volitional necessities dominate the will and, indeed, define its limits. Since there is no will outside those limits, Watson wonders where an agent can find the will to undermine or to oppose them.

There is really no difficulty, it seems to me, in accounting for the possibility that a person may resist the grip of a volitional necessity, or that he may endeavor to free himself from it entirely. The fact that someone would be unable to bring himself to perform a certain action does not entail that he cannot try to bring himself to perform it. It means only that no matter what attempt of such a kind he makes, it is bound to be unsuccessful. It is even clearer that a person who is subject to some volitional necessity is not thereby precluded from trying to eliminate it altogether by taking steps that are designed to alter the causally relevant circumstances from which the necessity derives.

In discussing the case of the mother who believes that it would be best to give up her child for adoption, but who cannot bring herself to do so, Watson says that "her will must be engaged in volitional opposition ... and the necessity exhibited in her failure to bring herself to give up the child cannot completely define the bounds of ... [her] volitional capacities." The volitional necessity to which the mother is subject means that her desire to give up her child is a desire that she cannot permit to be effective. Her opposition to that necessity requires only that she permit a quite different desire to be effective—namely, the desire to try to give up the child. The volitional necessity that is exhibited in her failure to bring herself to give up the child does not completely define the bounds of her volitional capacities. It only defines the bounds of her capacity to perform the act of giving up her child. It naturally does not limit her capacities to perform innumerable other actions, such as those involved in going to the adoption agency and completing all the work of giving up the child until the final act by which the adoption would have been decisively accomplished.

5.   Watson's intuitions concerning problems of integrity and agency in the case of the mother and adoption are plausible, but I do not find them

entirely convincing. If the mother succeeds in doing what she thinks best—that is, she gives up the child—then, Watson believes, she retains:

a kind of volitional or authorial integrity that is not achieved in the other case. Her privileging of her conviction about what is best for the child over her needs for the relationship imposes a coherent deliberative structure among her ends and concerns. This kind of order is unavailable to her in the other scenario [in which she keeps the child]. . . . The mother loses in either case . . . [but] one loss involves a defeat of agency in a way in which the other does not.

It seems to me that how the two scenarios are to be assessed is actually rather indeterminate. It depends a great deal, I believe, on circumstances that simply are not specified in the example as it has been presented.

Suppose the mother discovers that she cannot bring herself to give up the child. The question then posed by Watson is whether she experiences this as a defeat or as a liberation. There are two possibilities, each of which provides this question with a different answer. On the one hand, the mother may continue to wish that she could give the child away; and she may regret, and even chastise herself for, her inability to do so. On the other hand, she may recognize her discovery as a revelation not just of the fact that keeping the child is what is most important to her, but also of the deeper fact that it is what she truly wants to be most important to her. In the latter case, she is glad to be putting her need for the relationship above what is best by a measure that she now refuses to regard as decisive. In the former case, she also places her need above what is best, but she wishes that she did not find herself constrained by volitional necessity to do so.

In my earlier discussion of this example, I had always taken it for granted that the mother is liberated when she is overcome by the force of the volitional necessity that makes it impossible for her to give up her child. I had assumed, in other words, that she experiences her inability to give the child up as revealing what she most deeply and genuinely wants. It does seem clear, however, that some mothers might experience it instead as a surrender to forces with which they cannot help identifying, but from which they nonetheless wish they could separate themselves. For some mothers, in other words, it might be only in resignation and in disappointment with themselves that they accept as their own the will by which they are constrained. They would try to change this will if they believed it would be possible for them to succeed in changing it. Whether the mother experiences her submission to volitional necessity as a defeat, or whether she experiences it as a liberating release of her previously stifled or misunderstood real desires, is critically pertinent to deciding whether her volitional integrity is sustained or whether her agency is defeated. But how the mother experiences her submission to necessity is an additional feature of the situation, which cannot be inferred merely from the fact that she is unable to bring herself to give up her child. We cannot know, on that basis alone, what she makes of what is happening to her. It seems to me, accordingly, that Watson's assessment of the matter is unwarranted.

Note

1. I have already addressed this problem, especially in my response above to the essay by Michael Bratman. What I shall say about it here inevitably recapitulates much of what I said about it there.

6

Reasons and Passions

T. M. Scanlon

I

The pleasure and excitement of first reading "Freedom of the Will and the Concept of a Person" are unforgettable. It is one of those rare articles that immediately strikes one as at the same time quite novel and yet clearly to be uncovering something that is obviously true, something that, without realizing it, we had been thinking all along. That article stimulated renewed attention to the question of when an action or mental state "belongs" to a person, and Frankfurt himself went on to pursue this question in a series of fine articles. He puts the problem very clearly in "Identification and Externality."

> We think it correct to attribute to a person, in the strict sense, only some of the events in the history of his body. The others—those with respect to which he is passive—have their moving principles outside him, and we do not identify him with these events. Certain events in the history of a person's mind, likewise, have their moving principles outside of him. He is passive with respect to them, and they are likewise not to be attributed to him. A person is no more to be identified with everything that goes on in his mind, in other words, than he is to be identified with everything that goes on in his body. Of course, every movement of a person's body is an event in his history; in this sense it is his movement, and no one else's. In this same sense, all the events in the history of a person's mind are his too. If this is all that is meant, then it is undeniably true that a passion can no more occur without belonging to someone than a movement of a human body can occur without being someone's movement. But this is only a gross literal truth, which masks distinctions that are as valuable in the one case as they are in the other.[1]

Frankfurt is here criticizing a view put forward by Terence Penelhum, which emphasized the idea of "ownership" of one's mental states according to which everything in a person's mental life "belongs to him." In this passage Frankfurt is suggesting that there is a "strict sense" of attributability, narrower than the one Penelhum emphasizes, on which we should concentrate. This sense of attributability, or internality, is the quarry in many of Frankfurt's articles, and it has proved to be an elusive one. In this paper I want to explore, in a tentative fashion, the question of why we should be interested in finding this quarry. It seems to me that there are at least two quite distinct kinds of reason for this concern, and that when they are distinguished the problem may look less difficult than it has seemed.

When we are trying to characterize this narrower sense in which an action or attitude may or may not "belong to" an agent, we may be doing so with either, or both, of two aims in view. The first of these aims is to arrive at an understanding of the conditions under which an action or attitude is properly attributed to an agent as part of the basis for some assessment, moral or otherwise. When is an action or attitude something for which an agent is properly given credit or criticism? This is, of course, a question that can arise for the agent him or herself, since we can appraise our own conduct and character. But the second aim that I have in mind is one that is rooted more particularly in concerns of the agent. The question here is what makes a desire or other attitude fully a person's own—his own in the sense that makes it constitutive of who he is?

Each of these questions can be put in terms of freedom, or of an agent's control over his actions and attitudes. The first is: what kind of control does an agent have to exercise over an action or attitude in order for the agent to be morally responsible for it (in order for it to figure in the proper grounds for moral, or other, appraisal of that agent)? The second question might be *answered* in terms of freedom: it may be said that what makes our actions, desires and attitudes truly ours is that we have the right kind of control over them. But this is not the only possible answer: desires may be said to be truly part of us in virtue of their role in our lives, or their relation to our other desires, rather than because they are freely adopted, or freely held.

In the case of Frankfurt's famous unwilling addict, the two questions I have distinguished coincide: the addict is not morally responsible for taking the drug, and he suffers from a kind of internal unfreedom that is bad from his own point of view. Frankfurt gives us terminology to mark this distinction: the addict both acts unfreely and lacks free will, understood as the ability to have the will he wants. In the case of the willing addict the two come apart. The willing addict is morally responsible for taking the drug because he acts freely in doing so. But he lacks free will, since it is only a coincidence that the desire he acts from is one he wants to act on. In these cases the kind of conflict or control that is at issue in having "free will" is a matter of the relation between the addicts' first-order desires and their higher-order volitions. In his later articles, however, Frankfurt raises a similar question about an agent's relation to these higher-order elements: an agent's having the will he wants is a matter of his identifying wholeheartedly with some of these elements rather than others.

It has struck me in rereading Frankfurt's articles that over the twenty-five years that they cover there has been a shift of emphasis from the first of these questions to the second—from concern with an agent's "ownership" of his or her desires as a precondition of moral appraisal to a concern with an ideal of psychic health. In his early articles, a certain relation between first- and second-order desires is seen as a criterion of freedom. In his later work, a certain attitude toward our various desires—wholeheartedness—is investigated as something desirable in itself, quite independent of questions of freedom and of moral responsibility. What unites these works, however, is the question of when a desire or other attitude "belongs to" a person, and this is the question I want to examine.

II

I will begin by trying to distinguish various senses in which a state or action might "belong to me" and will then consider the kind of significance that is to be attached to belonging or not belonging in these different senses. To discuss the senses in which something may belong to me, however, I have to begin with a few thoughts about who or what I am.

I am, I take it, a conscious, rational, embodied creature. As a conscious creature, I have a stream of conscious thoughts and experiences. This stream is not continuous—it is interrupted by deep sleep and other periods of unconsciousness—but it is united by a degree of constancy in its elements, by the intentional content of these elements, and by its supposed causal basis. By the first of these, "constancy," I mean such things as the high degree of continuity in my cognitive and affective reactions: in what I like and dislike, in what I believe and reject. By the second, I have in mind the way in which elements of my conscious life refer to each other, as when it seems to me that I am remembering a past experience or decision or carrying out a previously formed intention. It is a controversial question in discussions of personal identity whether the third element—the continuity of the causal basis of my mental life—has independent significance as a determinant of my identity. I will not take a stand on this general issue. But some particular ways in which the causal basis of one's experiences may be relevant to their significance will figure in what I have to say later on.

As Frankfurt points out at the beginning of "Identification and Whole-heartedness," my mental life is not limited to my conscious life. Beliefs and aversions, for example, may be correctly attributed to me—may "belong to me" in the sense or senses we are concerned with here—even though I am never aware of them. Despite this lack of awareness, they can be correctly attributed to me because they are the best explanation of my overall behavior—not only of what I do and think, but also of what I fail to think of.

As rational creatures, we are capable of making judgments about reasons and hence of having judgment-sensitive attitudes such as belief and intention.[2] In calling these attitudes judgment-sensitive, I do not mean to suggest that they always arise from conscious judgment. My point is, rather, that it is part of the nature of such attitudes that, insofar as we are rational, we come to have them when we judge ourselves to have compelling reason of the relevant kind to do so, and cease to have them when we judge there to be compelling reason against them.

Three features of our mental lives as rational creatures are particularly relevant for my purposes. First, it can seem to us that a certain consideration is a reason for some action or attitude. It may seem to me, for example, that the way a chocolate dessert would taste is a reason for having one tonight, or it can seem to me, when I am feeling annoyed with my colleague, that the fact that a certain incident presents him in a bad light is a reason for mentioning it in the department meeting. Second, as rational creatures we are capable of judging whether considerations that seem to us to be reasons actually are good reasons. I may decide, for example, that I do have good reason to have the chocolate dessert and that presenting my colleague in a bad light is not a good reason for referring to that incident in the department meeting. Third, it is often the case that we have what we judge to be sufficient reason for adopting any one of several attitudes or actions, and we are capable of choosing one of these over the others, for example, by adopting a certain aim, or forming an intention to pursue an aim in one way rather than another. For example, I may take myself to have good reason for pursuing any one of several careers. Given these reasons, I can adopt one of them rather than the others, and the fact that I have done this affects the reasons I have in the future to do what is required in order to pursue it. I will refer to these familiar elements in our mental lives as, respectively, seemings, assessings, and optings.

These familiar elements in a rational creature's mental life are what they are not only in virtue of their phenomenal content when considered in isolation, but also in virtue of their normative and descriptive relations with other elements. If I have adopted the intention of doing something at a certain time, and have not reconsidered this, then insofar as I am rational I do that thing at that time. If I have judged a certain consideration to count in favor of a certain intention or belief, then insofar as I am rational this consideration generally occurs to me as relevant when I am considering whether to adopt that attitude, and if I judge a consideration to be irrelevant to a certain attitude, then if I am rational I do not count it in favor of adopting that attitude. If I opt for a certain goal or intention, then insofar as I am rational this will seem to me to be a reason for acting in ways required to carry it out.

These connections are not only a matter of consistency in conscious judgment but also a matter of what might be called the relation between my conscious and unconscious life. My taking something to be a reason is not just a matter of its seeming to me to be a reason when I present the question to myself and consciously reflect on it. The fact that I take or do not take something to be a reason—the fact that I think my wife's feelings are important, for example—will also show up in what occurs to me or fails to occur to me, in what I notice and fail to notice, and in what I feel and do "without thinking."

These connections have both a descriptive and a normative aspect. Descriptively, if I did not exhibit these connections and others like them to a significant degree, then I would not be a rational creature, and attitudes of the kind I have described would not be attributable to me. But, considered normatively, these connections constitute a standard of perfect rationality that I often fall short of. I am only very imperfectly rational. I often fail to do what I judge myself to have compelling reason to do, and, more frequently than I would like, I count as reasons for action, or for other attitudes, considerations that I actually believe do not, under the circumstances, count in favor of those attitudes. Considerations can seem to me to be reasons even when I have judged that they are not.

Much more would need to be said to flesh out and defend this view of rationality. With these rather hasty observations as background, however, I want to return to the various ways in which an attitude might or might not be attributable to me, and to the kinds of significance these attributions can have. I will start with the broadest contrast between two ways in which some action or attitude might be said to "belong to me." The first is the sense involved in what Frankfurt called the "gross literal truth" that every passion and every action belongs to someone. This is the sense in which everything is attributable to me that occurs in my conscious life or figures in the best overall explanation of my conscious life and behavior. The class of things attributable to me in this broad sense includes conscious states such as judgments and decisions, visual perceptions, itches and pains, and also unconscious desires and beliefs that move me to do what I do. As I am understanding it, this sense of attributability is neutral as to the causes of these states. If any thoughts or desires have been produced in me by neuroscientists stimulating my brain, these are mine in the sense I am now describing, along with thoughts, itches, and pains produced in "normal" ways.

In contrast to this broad sense of attributability, at the opposite extreme, is an idea of attributability according to which what is attributable to me are just my conscious choices, decisions, and the actions I am aware of performing. These, it might be said, are the things that I *do*, as opposed to others that merely occur in my mental life.

It is easy to see why this class should seem particularly important if what we are interested in is the class of things that are attributable to a person for purposes of *moral* assessment. Since moral appraisal is appraisal of the way a person has governed him or herself—appraisal that, for example, asks the person to explain his or her reasons for acting a certain way and to justify or make amends for that action—an agent's conscious decisions are obviously of *particular* relevance for such appraisal. They are things for which he or she most obviously cannot escape responsibility. It is, however, a further question whether these are the *only* things that are attributable to a person in the sense that is a precondition for moral appraisal (let alone for other important purposes). In fact, it is clear that this class is too narrow even for moral purposes. Negligence is a trivial example: we can be open to moral criticism for failing to take due care even when this reflects no conscious decision on our part. What negligence often consists in is just this: failure even to consider whether we were in a situation in which care needed to be taken. But the cases that are most likely to come to mind here are ones in which the negligence for which we are open to criticism involves action. We are criticized for what we do, or fail to do. It is a more controversial question whether we are open to moral criticism for attitudes that arise in us spontaneously, without any decision on our part, when these are contrary to the judgment we make when we consider the matter reflectively, and when this attitude has no influence on our action, perhaps because it is our reflective judgment rather than our immediate and unreflective reaction which governs our behavior.

As Thomas Nagel says, "A person may be greedy, envious, cowardly, cold, ungenerous, unkind, vain, or conceited, but *behave* perfectly by a monumental act of will."[3] I believe that states such as these are attributable to a person in the sense we are presently concerned with. They are relevant to a moral assessment even if he disapproves of, rejects, and controls them, and would eliminate them if he could. (It remains, of course, a further question in *what way* they should affect this assessment—how serious a fault this is, and how it compares with other failings.)[4]

Described in the terms I introduced above, Nagel's examples involve people to whom certain considerations regularly seem to be reasons for action even though they consistently judge on reflection that these are not good reasons. Even if it is conceded that such seemings "belong to the person" in the sense required for moral appraisal, there is the further question why this is so. Two related but distinguishable explanations occur to one. The first emphasizes the fact that even though these particular attitudes are, ex hypothesi, not under this particular agent's control, they are the kind of thing that should, ideally, be responsive to his or her considered judgment—would be responsive to it if he or she were fully rational. As states that fall within the rational authority of the person's judgment, they are things he or she is answerable for.

The second explanation ignores (or at least does not directly appeal to) ideas of authority or control. It appeals rather to two other kinds of facts. The first is that the state in question is, we are assuming, one that does occur to the agent and occurs to him or her with some regularity. The second is that this state is of a kind that we have reason to care about—whether these things seem to a person to be reasons or not is significant in some way for our relations with him or her. These two explanations are closely related. States of the kind I have in mind have the significance just alluded to because they involve taking something to be a reason. Insofar as they are such states, they are the *kind* of thing that is in principle subject to control by the agent's judgment. But they retain their significance even when this control is, in fact, absent. The fact that a person rejects a certain attitude—hatred or greed, for example—when it occurs to him makes a difference to our moral assessment of him. But the fact that it regularly occurs still makes a difference as well, whether or not it has any effect on his actions.

This is more obvious if we shift from moral appraisal to the appraisal of someone as a friend or lover. We might imagine, for example, a man who is in no doubt as to whether his wife's feelings and interests are important to him. Nevertheless these considerations do not present themselves to him spontaneously as reasons. When he is making plans with others, he does not automatically consider how his wife would be affected and what she would prefer. But he is aware of this weakness, and carefully monitors himself—reminding himself to go back and consider how his wife would feel before making a final commitment. No doubt his wife would appreciate this if she knew about it, but I do not think she would be overly demanding if she regretted that it was necessary, and thought this a fault in her otherwise admirable spouse. What she would like best, not unreasonably, would be a husband to whom her interests occurred immediately and instinctively as important considerations.

In moral assessment, as in this example of spousal loyalty and concern, both reflective and unreflective attitudes matter. Their relative significance may, however, be different in the two cases. The morality that applies between strangers, we might say, is in an important sense *about* self-regulation, and we expect it to involve checking one's immediate responses. Certain kinds of negative attitudes toward others are moral faults, but controlling such feelings is an important and expected function of moral awareness. We do not expect purity from everyone. Relations of love and friendship are another matter. It is not just that we owe those we love a kind of concern that others cannot expect. It is also important (not just an ideal) that this kind of concern should be, to a large degree, a matter of immediate and spontaneous feeling.

So the relative significance of spontaneous response and reflective judgment is different in the two cases. Given the importance of spontaneous reactions in the case of friendship, however, it would be odd to say that these reactions do not fully belong to the person. If, in the moral case, these reactions are less significant than reflective judgments, this must be for some other reason.

This leads me to conclude that the elements of a person's mental life that are atrributable to him or her in the sense required for them to be potential grounds of moral assessment include, at least, all of a person's judgment-sensitive attitudes. (Indeed, the argument I have just concluded may suggest that more than this is included. The attitudes we have reason to care about in those whom we love may include some that are not judgment-sensitive. If so, then if these are not morally significant it cannot be because they do not *belong* to the person.)

So let's turn to the other extreme—the broadest sense in which every element of a person's mental life "belongs to him." Are there things that are part of a person's mental life in this broadest sense but that we should say do not "belong to the person"—are not properly attributable to him—in the sense that is relevant to moral criticism or to other related forms of assessment, such as assessment as a friend?

What about itches and pains, for example? That a person feels an itch or a pain is clearly not a morally significant fact about him. But why is this so? Such sensations are not morally significant because they do not have the right content—they do not indicate anything about the person's attitudes towards others. It is also true that they are not the kind of things that, even in an ideally rational agent, would be under the control of reflective judgment. So we cannot draw any conclusions from their occurrence about judgments that the person holds. But what is primary here—the lack of significant content or lack of control?

To answer this question, it may help to consider our reactions to science-fiction examples in which mental states are produced by neural stimulation, since these are, it is imagined, states with potentially significant content but without the right kind of control. Suppose a neuroscientist were, by stimulating a person's brain in the right way, to cause him, momentarily, to feel deep hatred for certain people and to see harm to them as something to be promoted. I think we would all agree that the occurrence of these feelings is not morally significant. Why not? One reason is that the fact that he responds to neural stimulation in this way does not tell us anything interesting about this person. Anyone would react in the same way. Moreover, what we are told about the causal origin of this response means that the fact that he responds in this way gives us no basis for inference about what the person was "really like" at other times, hence no reason to reexamine or reinterpret his past behavior.

But now suppose that the effect of what the neuroscientist does is more than momentary. She changes the person so that in the future he becomes upset and angry whenever he sees the people in question and angry when he hears that things are going well for them. Perhaps he still believes, on reflection, that these feelings are unjustified and morally disreputable, but he has them nonetheless. This would, I believe, constitute a morally significant change in what the person is like. He has become a worse person, morally speaking, just as much as he would have if the change had occurred "naturally"—that is to say, without the neuroscientist's intervention, perhaps as an overreaction to some bitter disappointment combined with some unpleasant interactions with members of the group in question. What matters is the content of the attitudes, not their origin or susceptibility to rational control.

III

I want now to consider how the framework I have described for discussing these matters compares with that employed by Frankfurt in various papers in the series I have mentioned.

In "Freedom of the Will and the Concept of a Person," he operates mainly with the notion of desires of different orders. Desires of the first order seem to be understood, as far as I can see, simply as motivationally efficacious states. Higher-order desires differ from first-order ones simply in having a different kind of object. The object of a first-order desire is some state of affairs that one might bring about through action. The object of a second-order desire is also a state of affairs, but in this case a state that involves one's having or not having some first-order desire. A second-order volition is a particular kind of second-order desire, namely a desire that a particular first-order desire be the one that moves us to action. But while second-order desires and volitions are distinguished in this way by their objects, they remain, it seems, desires—that is to say, simply motivationally efficacious states. So a second-order volition that I act out of loyalty is a state that moves me to bring it about that I act in this way.

First-order desires can conflict with each other when their objects are incompatible. Second-order desires can conflict in this way with first-order desires (my desire to act out of loyalty may conflict with my desire to avoid danger, if what loyalty prompts me to do is to take a risk). But second-order desires, or at least second-order volitions, can conflict with first-order desires in a further way, namely the way in which a first-order desire can conflict with a force in the world that works to prevent its fulfillment. Just as, for example, a shift in the tide can conflict with my desire to sail to the harbor quickly, by making this desire more difficult to satisfy, so my desire for safety can conflict with my second-order volition to act out of loyalty, by making it more difficult for me to do this.

Neither of these forms of conflict is the same as the kind of conflict that can occur between what I called above a seeming and an assessment—that is to say, the kind of conflict that occurs when it seems to me that showing my colleague in a bad light is a reason for mentioning a certain incident in a department meeting, but I judge this not in fact to be a good reason for doing so. For this kind of conflict to be possible, the conflicting elements must involve conflicting claims, not just incompatible motivational tendencies or ways the world might be. Desires can enter into such conflicts if, as I suggested above, they involve "seemings"—if having a desire that X involves X's seeming to have some feature that makes it worth pursuing—but I do not see how they can do so otherwise.

Frankfurt's terminology in later work is somewhat different from what I have described above. In "Identification and Wholeheartedness," for example, he responds to Watson's charge that decisive identification with a desire seems arbitrary by emphasizing that what he calls "decisive commitment" should be understood as a decision, and one that the agent makes for a reason.[5] It is noteworthy, I think, that Frankfurt then goes on to distinguish two kinds of conflict between desires. Conflict of the first kind occurs when two desires compete for priority. Each is trying to prevail in the struggle to determine the agent's course of action, and the resolution of this conflict requires the establishment of an order between them. One of them must take precedence in the determination of action, but even when this is established both remain, in the fullest sense, the agent's desires. Conflict of the second kind is deeper. Its resolution, he says, "involves a radical *separation* of the competing desires, one of which is not merely assigned a relatively less favored position but excluded entirely as an outlaw."[6]

Frankfurt does not say exactly what he has in mind here, but the examples that come to my mind are conflicts of the deeper sort described above, which I called conflicts between seemings and assessments. If I judge that what seemed to me at first to be a reason for a certain attitude is not in fact such a reason, then my initial tendency to see it as a reason is overruled, and in this sense rendered an "outlaw." Conflict may remain, however, if the "outlaw" attitude does not surrender but remains, within the person's psychic territory, defiant. This kind of conflict is certainly a common feature of our mental lives. The question is how it is best described.

Frankfurt is clear that this kind of conflict can occur only between higher-order desires. He says, in "The Faintest Passion" that "conflicts involving first-order psychic elements alone—for example, between an attraction and an aversion to the same object—do not pertain to the will at all. They are not volitional but merely impulsive or sentimental. Conflicts that pertain to the will arise out of a person's higher-order, reflective attitudes."[7] But if first-order desires count as such "first-order psychic elements" and are thus merely impulses or sentiments, it seems to follow not only that they cannot conflict with each other in a deeper sense, but that they cannot *conflict with* higher-order volitions either. If first-order desires are only competing impulses and do not involve "seemings" then they cannot be overruled and hence cannot be declared to be "outlaws," except in the sense in which my fatigue is an outlaw if it interferes with my ability to do what I take myself to have reason to do.

This suggests to me the possibility that I may have, for years, been misreading Frankfurt's talk of first- and second-order desires. As I have said, I understand a desire, in the most familiar and ordinary sense, as involving a tendency to see some consideration as a reason. This seems to me to fit with my experience of "conflict situations": even when I declare some desire, such as the desire for another drink, to be an "outlaw," the kind of force that it continues to have involves not just an unruly impulse but a tendency to see something as a reason. So I have always understood Frankfurt's example of the unwilling addict on this same model. I assumed that this addict is moved to take the drug by the thought of how good it would feel to do so, and that the pleasure, and relief from his pain, that taking the drug would bring keep presenting themselves to him as reasons to shoot up, even though he judges, without reservation, that these are not, under the circumstances, good reasons. But of course there is a more radical understanding of the case, according to which the addict feels a strong urge to take the drug but sees no reason to do so. When he takes the drug, he is thus not acting on a reason at all, but only being overpowered by an impulse. I would not deny that there could be such a case, but it seems much more unusual than the phenomenon I have (mistakenly, I now think) understood the example to describe. Moreover, if desires are understood in the way this reading of the example suggests—as mere impulses—this seems to deprive them of the normative force we are accustomed to attribute to them in both conflict and nonconflict cases.

But this view of first-order desires does seem to be the one that Frankfurt takes in other work as well. In "Autonomy, Necessity, and Love," for example, he says that passions such as jealousy and craving "do not include any affirmative or negative volitional attitudes toward the motivational tendencies in which they consist." He then continues,

> However imposing or intense the motivational *power* that the passions mobilize may be, they have no inherent motivational *authority*. In fact, the passions do not really make any *claims* upon us at all. Considered strictly in themselves, apart from whatever additional impetus or facilitation we ourselves may provide by acceding to them, their effectiveness in moving us is entirely a matter of *sheer brute force*. There is nothing in them other than the magnitude of this force that requires us, or that even encourages us, to act as they command.[8]

It seems, then, that for Frankfurt, although first- and second-order desires are both called *desires*, they are really quite different sorts of things—different in the kind of authority they claim and in the ways they can conflict. My view of desires (*sans phrase*) is akin to Frankfurt's view of higher-order desires. I believe that it is essential to what we most commonly call a desire that having a desire involves something's seeming to us to be a reason. So, for example, when I feel a desire for a piece (or a second piece) of rich chocolate cake, its delicious taste and the pleasure it would give me seem to me to be reasons for eating it. When I feel a desire for revenge against my rival, the fact that something I could do would cause him embarrassment strikes me as a reason to do it. Not every case of something seeming to me to be a reason is a case of desire, however. I can see that the fact that exercise would improve my health is a reason to engage in it. But I have no desire to exercise. My wife, on the other hand, exercises for the reason just mentioned—to improve her health—and she has a strong desire to do so. The difference between us, at least in part, is that the prospect of improving her health in this way presents itself to her insistently and effectively as a reason. She has what I call a desire in the directed-attention sense. But while this fact of directed-attention explains the motivational difference between us, it is not itself a source of motivation. What moves her is a consideration she takes to be a reason—the prospect of improving her health.

Given that I hold this view, Frankfurt's characterization of what is absent from these passions as he understands them strikes me as peculiar. He says that passions "do not include any affirmative or negative volitional attitude toward the motivational tendencies in which they consist." This suggests that what is missing from a passion itself, and could be added by a higher-order attitude, is something like approval of the passion, or a desire to be moved by its motivational power. But neither of these gets at what I see as crucial. Suppose I am a teacher in a school and I feel a strong desire that a certain pupil not get a leading role in the school play. Her father is my hated rival, and I can't stand the thought of the pleasure that it would give him to see her in this role. I may judge that this is not in fact a good reason to deny the child the part. I may feel only "disapproval" of the "motivational tendency" of this vengeful thought, and no desire to be moved by it. Yet it is crucial to the "motivational tendency" that it retains that when I think of the play, the pleasure the father would derive from seeing his daughter in the limelight, keeps presenting itself to me as a reason to prevent this from happening. The *claim* that this desire has on me is not a matter of my approval or endorsement, but of the fact that it consists in something *seeming* to me to be a reason, even though I judge that it is not.

I disagree with Frankfurt, then, at least in holding that most of what we commonly call desires are not first-order desires as he characterizes them. Perhaps this just means that desires as I understand them, and what I have called seemings, are already higher-order phenomena. It is less clear, given the passage discussed in my previous paragraph, how far Frankfurt and I agree about what is essential to these higher-order attitudes. I would not put this in terms of approval and disapproval, but in terms of judgments about what is a good reason and which good reasons to act on. Whether there is disagreement here or not, what I want to do in the remainder of this paper is to show how, using the language of reasons, I would account for some of the things Frankfurt says about necessity, freedom and love.

IV

At the beginning of the paragraph that contains the remarks about jealousy and cravings that I quoted above, Frankfurt contrasts these passions with an agent's higher-order attitudes. He writes, "The volitional attitudes that a person maintains toward his own elementary motivational tendencies are entirely up to him." It is certainly common, and natural, to say that the things that belong most clearly to a person are the things that are "up to him." But it is also correct to say, as Frankfurt does repeatedly, that it is essential to being a person that certain things— the things one cares most deeply about—strike one with necessity, as things one *must* care about. This may sound paradoxical, but it becomes clear that there is in fact no paradox when we ask what is involved in something's being "up to us."

Consider what I have called seemings, assessings, and optings. In what sense are these "up to us," and in what way are they, on the contrary, forced on us? One sense (a morally important sense, I believe) in which something can be up to us is if it depends on and hence reflects our judgment. Assessings—our reflective judgments about whether certain considerations do or do not count in favor of certain attitudes—are certainly up to us in this sense. They *are* our judgments and hence, trivially, they would be different if our judgments were different. But from the fact that it is up to me in this sense to decide whether something is a reason for a certain action or not, it does not follow that I am free to choose either answer. It is up to me to decide whether the fact that I would break many bones if I were to jump from a moving car counts against opening the door and leaping out at the next turn, but I do not, in another sense, enjoy much freedom in forming this decision. Under the circumstances the answer is so clear that I couldn't decide differently. I am constrained by my perception of the relevant reasons.

Seemings—desires and other states in which considerations appear to me to constitute reasons—are a slightly different case. In one sense, they are not up to me since they do not always arise from my judgment. But since they involve tendencies to see things as reasons, they implicate my judgment. If I were fully rational, then when I judge something not to be a good reason it would cease to seem to me to be one. Alas, we do not invariably have this kind of control. Not only can we not command the "vasty deep" of our (first-order) passions as Frankfurt understands them,[9] we cannot always command our instinctive judgments. But they are ours, nonetheless, and can reflect something significant about us even when we reject them.

With respect to optings we have an additional degree of freedom. If there are good reasons for me to choose either of two careers, it is "up to me" in a further sense which of them I take up. I can choose either way, and whichever way I choose will be supported by reasons, but neither choice is compelled by them. The important point, which Frankfurt emphasizes, is that this extra degree of freedom does not bring with it an added degree of responsibility. Nor does its absence in the other cases—the fact that these judgments are more constrained by reasons, and hence less "up to us" in the further sense we are now discussing—make these judgments less fully attributable to us. It is inviting to think that the self is more fully revealed in choices that are less constrained. That this is not always so is due to the fact that what we and others regard as particularly significant about us is the considerations we regard as reasons and how we respond to them. (Here I return to a point made earlier about significance.) Statements such as "He couldn't help it" or "He couldn't have done anything else" serve to mitigate attributability when the necessities alluded to are ones that prevented the agent's assessment of certain reasons from determining his action. So the action does not show that he failed to care about these things. In other cases, such as Martin Luther's, the same words serve to underscore the degree to which the action was the agent's, because it reflected what he took to be compelling reasons.

It thus seems to me that the framework I have described can give an entirely adequate account of the phenomena of volitional necessity that Frankfurt discusses. He describes, for example, the case of Lord Fawn, in *The Eustace Diamonds*, who "had thought that it would be a good idea" to interrogate Andy Gowran, a lower-class estate-steward, about the behavior of Fawn's fiancée on a certain occasion.[10] But when he tries to do this "every feeling of his nature" revolts against it, and he finds that he cannot continue the conversation. What happens in this case, as I would describe it, is that the fact that his intended plan of action would involve discussing such an intimate matter with a coarse person of low class strikes Lord Fawn as an absolutely compelling reason against it. As a conclusion about the reasons he has, this judgment is "up to him" in the first of the senses I distinguished. (As Frankfurt says, "It is not against his *will* that Fawn's feelings revolt.") But he is nonetheless not free to reach an opposite conclusion, and this "necessity" is, as I pointed out above, a common feature of our judgments about reasons.

Let me turn, in closing, to say something about love, which Frankfurt discusses in several of his most recent articles. He is concerned here with love in a broad sense, including not only emotional love for another person but also other deep commitments such as to a place, a cause, or an ideal. Just as I said above about desire, I believe that love in this sense essentially involves seeing certain considerations as reasons. To love something, as Frankfurt says, is to be guided in a certain way by what is good for, or required by, it. Explaining love in terms of reasons may seem hyperrationalistic. But it seems this way, I believe, only if we fail to distinguish between what love involves (which is what I have been discussing) and the grounds of that love. At least in the case of emotional love, there is often something inappropriate about giving reasons for loving or to think that one needs to give reasons for doing so. (It would not, in a similar way, be inappropriate to offer a justification for valuing. There is generally a reason why something is valuable.)[11]

As Frankfurt observes, although love is a contingent matter, it involves a kind of volitional necessity—the lover feels that he or she must do certain things.[12] "The claims of love ... possess not simply power but authority."[13] He contrasts this authority with the necessities of reason and duty. I agree that these are different in content. In particular, the requirements of love are not properly understood as a special case of moral obligation. But I would not say, with Frankfurt, that the authority of the demands of love can be traced to the claims of one's identity as a person. He writes that in betraying the object of one's love, one therefore betrays oneself as well.[14] This is correct, however, only if particular stress is put on *as well*. Otherwise, it seems to misdescribe the (no doubt somewhat elusive) division of normative labor between elements that are contingent or in some cases voluntaristic and those that are neither. On the one hand, it is quite true that I can betray an ideal or beloved only if it is *my* ideal, or my beloved. (This is the contingent part.) But when it comes to the crunch, it seems to me that the authority of an ideal comes from my sense of its value, and the thought of betraying my beloved is devastating because it is *she* whom I would betray. Thoughts about *my commitment* to either, or my integrity as a person, seem secondary, and a little too self-referential. This relative emphasis seems, if anything, clearer when the object of love is a person than when it is an ideal. In the latter case, appealing to my commitment as a source of authority seems less out of place. This is surprising, since love of a person need not be justified, and the adoption of an ideal is more likely to be based on reasons. One might therefore expect these reasons to play a larger role in explaining authority in the latter case. I don't have an explanation for this puzzle.

The view I have been advocating, which finds the motivating force of desires, and now even that of the claims of love, in reasons, may seem to extend the authority of Reason over other aspects of life in a way that is very implausible. But I have said nothing about Reason as a faculty. I have spoken only of *reasons*. I have claimed that desires are best understood as involving taking something to be a reason, but I do not mean by this to suggest that there is some calculative process of reasoning through which we should decide what to desire. What I am offering should not, then, be seen as a defense of the claims of Reason against passion. I am suggesting, rather, that the idea of an opposition between Reason and passion is misconceived. If desires are not to be mere urges, as most of them are not, they must involve seeing something as a reason. So if Reason is involved in every attitude concerning reasons, passion and Reason cannot be two separate capacities.

Acknowledgment

I am indebted to the participants in the conference at Wake Forest for very helpful discussion and to the editors for their detailed comments on an earlier version of this essay.

Notes

1. Harry Frankfurt, "Identification and Externality," in *The Importance of What We Care About* (Cambridge: Cambridge University Press, 1988), 61.

2. I present more fully the view of rationality that is summarized in this and the following four paragraphs in *What We Owe to Each Other* (Cambridge: Harvard University Press, 1998), chap. 1, esp. 18–25.

3. Thomas Nagel, "Moral Luck," in *Mortal Questions* (Cambridge: Cambridge University Press, 1979), 32.

4. This is argued very effectively by Angela Smith in *Attitudes, Agency, and Responsibility* (Ph.D. dissertation, Harvard University, 1999). I am much indebted to her for discussion of this topic.

5. Harry Frankfurt, "Identification and Wholeheartedness," in *The Importance of What We Care About*, 168.

6. Ibid., 170.

7. Harry Frankfurt, "The Faintest Passion," *Necessity, Volition, and Love* (Cambridge: Cambridge University Press, 1999), 99.

8. Ibid., 137.

9. Frankfurt's remark about passions occurs in "The Faintest Passion," in *Necessity, Volition, and Love*, 101.

10. Harry Frankfurt, "Rationality and the Unthinkable," in *The Importance of What We Care About*, 183.

11. In this respect Frankfurt's inclusion of ideals as instances of love may push the boundaries of the concept.

12. Harry Frankfurt, "Autonomy, Necessity, and Love," in *Necessity, Volition, and Love*, 136.

13. Ibid., 138.

14. Ibid.

REPLY TO T. M. SCANLON

Harry Frankfurt

1. Scanlon relies heavily on an account of desire that I regard as excessively intellectualized or rationalistic. He maintains that a desire involves "a tendency to see some consideration as a reason." It is true that desires are often associated with such tendencies. In my judgment, however, Scanlon misconstrues the relationship between desires and reasons.

Animals of many species have desires, but only animals of our species—or, perhaps, of a few others—are capable of seeing anything as a reason. Our most elementary desires come to us as urges or impulses; we are moved by them, but they do not as such affect our thinking at all. They are merely psychic raw material. A desire provides us not with a reason but with a problem—the problem of how to respond to it.

Impulses and urges have power, but in themselves they have no authority. They move us more or less strongly, but they make no claims on us. One of the thematic preoccupations of my work in this area has been a concern with trying to understand just how to account for the authority—as distinct from the mere impulsive force—that certain desires appear to have. Scanlon supposes that, on my account, the authority comes from higher-order desires; and he suggests that his claim that a certain rational normativity is built into many desires from the start may actually be tantamount to a claim that those desires themselves involve higher-order phenomena. However, it is not my view that desires acquire authority by virtue of desires of a higher order.

A person's elementary urges and impulses do not become authoritative for that person because he has favorable second-order attitudes toward them, or even because he has second-order volitions manifesting his desires that those desires and impulses move him effectively to act. What gives a desire authority is, rather, that the person identifies with it or commits himself to it. It is only with this identification or commitment that the desire becomes the person's own in a sense more meaningful than the gross literal sense in which it is attributable to him simply because it occurs in the course of his psychic history. Thus I do not accept Scanlon's suggestion that "although first- and second-order desires are both called desires, they are really quite different sorts of things—

different in the kind of authority they claim and in the ways they can conflict."

We have relatively few desires with which we do not—either wholeheartedly or ambivalently—identify ourselves. This is partly because many of our desires, far from being urges or impulses to which we are passively subject, are actually created by us: we *decide* that this or that appeals to us; we *make up our minds* that we want it. In such cases, our identification with the desire is built into the very creation of the desire. If the desire tends to provide us with a reason, that is because the decision by which the desire is created is precisely a decision concerning what is to count with us as a reason.

When I decide that it might be a good idea to go to the movies, I often describe myself as having a desire—of greater or of lesser strength—to go to the movies; and when I make up my mind that I will go to the movies, I often describe myself as then wanting to do that. These ways of describing such situations, albeit utterly familiar and for ordinary purposes clear enough in meaning, are in truth somewhat misleading. The upshot of deciding, or of making up one's mind, is not really that one begins to desire something—in a sense that would imply some feeling or some experience of being moved—but that one begins to take something as a reason for acting. Thus a person who decides that it might be a good idea for him to go to the movies considers that he has a reason to go to the movies.

It is not the desire, of course, that provides or that constitutes the reason. The reason is given by whatever consideration it was that led to the decision. In cases of this kind, the truth of the matter is not that having a desire gives us a reason. It is that once we have decided on what is to count with us as a reason, we then have given ourselves what is commonly (albeit, as I suggested above, somewhat misleadingly) thought of as a desire. The reason is not derived from the desire, but creates it.[1]

2. In his discussion of the conditions for moral appraisal, Scanlon argues that a number of attitudes that arise in us spontaneously—for instance, greed, envy, cowardice, vanity, lack of kindness or generosity— "are relevant to a moral assessment" even of people who disapprove of them and would eliminate them if they could. These are people, he says, "to whom certain considerations regularly seem to be reasons for action

even though they consistently judge on reflection that these are not good reasons." It seems to me that Scanlon's characterization of the people to whom he refers is incorrect.

A person who finds himself moved against his will by vanity or by greed does not see the fact that a certain action would serve his vanity or his greed as a reason for performing that action. Scanlon suggests that the person sees the fact as *a* reason but not as a *good* reason. However, the judgment that is made by a person who wishes to rid himself of a certain attitude, and who is altogether unwilling to be moved by it, is actually a judgment that the attitude provides him with no reason for action at all. That is what his unwillingness to be moved by it means.

To see something as a reason for performing a certain action is to see it as in some degree supporting or warranting the performance of that action. It adds a certain weight to considerations in favor of the action. The reason may not be a very good one. It may be a weak reason, which provides very little support; there may be far weightier considerations against performing the action. But nothing is seen as a reason for performing an action unless it is seen as providing *some* support in favor of the alternative of performing that action. Now the people whom Scanlon describes as spontaneously but unwillingly greedy, or vain, or cowardly, or whatever, are—by his own account—people who do not see these attitudes as providing *any* support for the actions to which they would naturally lead. They resist any inclination to be effectively moved by them. They do not weigh up the interests of vanity, or greed, or cowardice on one side of the balance, and find them outweighed by interests on the other side of it.

To judge that a reason is not a good reason is to assess the reason as relatively weak—too weak, given the considerations that oppose it, to warrant acting on it. Weak reasons are nonetheless far from entirely lacking in positive significance. Even if they do not count for enough, they do count for something. On the other hand, the envious, or greedy, or vain person whom Scanlon has in mind refuses to assign those attitudes (or the considerations that appeal to them) any weight whatever. That is what it means to say of such a person, as Scanlon does, that he "rejects" the attitudes in question. His rejection of them is not a matter simply of concluding that they are weak reasons. It is a rejection of them as reasons altogether.

3.   At one point, Scanlon suggests that "we owe those we love a kind of concern that others cannot expect." The point is only incidental to the main concerns and theses of his essay. Nonetheless, I wish to call attention briefly to its falsity. It is easy to see that love imposes on lovers no obligations whatsoever to those whom they love. After all, it is possible to love someone who is completely unaware of being loved and who may even be ignorant that the lover exists. Surely, under such conditions, it makes little sense to suppose that the lover owes something to the person whom he loves.

If we have obligations to those whom we love it is not because we love them but because of other aspects of our relationship to them, in virtue of which we have acquired some responsibility for their well-being. Love does, to be sure, entail a concern that consists in seeing the interests of the beloved as reasons for acting to protect them; but it does not entail this as a matter of obligation. It entails it simply because loving *is* essentially, among other things, a matter of taking the interests of the beloved as reasons for acting in behalf of them. This concern for the beloved goes necessarily with loving, not as a matter of obligation but simply in the nature of the case.

4.   Scanlon is quite correct in wishing to avoid an excessively self-referential way of understanding the authority of our ideals or the way in which betraying those we love is unthinkable to us. He makes his point as follows: "the authority of an ideal comes from my sense of its value, and the thought of betraying my beloved is devastating because it is she whom I would betray. Thoughts about my commitment to either, or my integrity as a person, seem secondary, and a little too self-referential." I certainly do not believe that my reason for living up to my ideals, or for refusing to betray those whom I love, is that otherwise I would somehow be injuring myself. It is not a desire to avoid harming myself, of course, that warrants and motivates my loyalty.

On the other hand, the fact that the claims of my ideals and of my beloved count for me as reasons in the way they do does seem to me to derive from the fact that I have certain attitudes toward them. If I did not love her, the interests of my beloved would not provide me with reasons for acting that possess such commanding authority. Indeed, the very possibility of "betraying" her, and of being devastated by recognizing that I had done so, would hardly arise. Similarly, the peculiar authority over me of my ideals does not come simply from my recognition that they are, like many things that are not among my ideals, worthy or valuable. It comes from my sense of the particular way in which my ideals are valuable to me. In cases of neither kind is my loyalty nothing more than a response to a perception of the inherent merit or appeal of the object, which leaves aside any sense of my own investment of myself in it. In both cases, the stringent and intimate necessity to which I feel subject derives from the fact that my personal integrity is at stake.

Note

1. Scanlon acknowledges that people may sometimes be driven by the sheer power of desire, apart from any influence of reason, but he thinks that this is unusual. In my opinion, he underestimates its prevalence. Of the behavior of Trollope's Lord Fawn, for instance, he says: "What happens in this case, as I would describe it, is that the fact that his intended plan of action would involve discussing such an intimate matter with a coarse person of low class strikes Lord Fawn as an absolutely compelling reason against it." It is worth noting that this is not how Trollope describes it. According to Trollope, what happens is not that Lord Fawn finds compelling reasons against carrying out his original plan. Rather, Lord Fawn finds that "every feeling of his nature" revolts against it.

7

Frankfurt on Identification: Ambiguities of Activity in Mental Life

Richard Moran

Identification and Agency

In the preface to his collection *The Importance of What We Care About*,[1] Harry Frankfurt remarks how the dominance of mechanism in our philosophical and scientific culture, along with the "evisceration" of the notion of cause itself in the eighteenth century, "have made it difficult to give a good account of the difference between being active and being passive." It is, of course, not easy to imagine how we could do without some such distinction and still think of ourselves as persons at all, for the "difference between passivity and activity is at the heart of the fact that we exist as selves and agents and not merely as locales in which certain events happen to occur" (ix). The distinction between what happens to us and what we *do* is, of course, central to our specifically *moral* self-consciousness, and the ability to draw this distinction in practice is part of thinking of ourselves as agents at all, creatures who are peculiarly *accountable* for certain events that occur and not others. And later developments in moral philosophy have placed this distinction at the center of the understanding of autonomy, including under this head the question of what it is to stand toward elements of one's own psychic life as an agent rather than as a "passive bystander."

But our concern with autonomy, both inside and outside of the study of philosophy, is not restricted to a concern with what we can be held responsible for, or how we may be proper subjects of praise and blame. The importance of *this* source of interest in autonomy doesn't need to be argued for, but the value of autonomy is broader than the requirements of moral evaluation, and is intimately connected with seeing oneself as a person living a life at all, rather than simply as a thing with a particular career through time. And the idea of being a particular person brings with it the distinction between what is "one's own" and what is experienced as other or alien. It is only with respect to something with a quite particular kind of unity that we can speak of either identification or alienation.

In various papers Frankfurt has investigated the sense in which a person may fail to identify with some part of his mental life, an element of his thought or desire which, in another sense, is undeniably *his* and no one else's. In "Identification and Externality," he explicates this strong sense of identification by, among other things, comparing obsessional thoughts or desires with involuntary bodily movements that the person may not think of as *his*.

It is not incoherent, despite the air of paradox, to say that a thought that occurs in my mind may or may not be something *I think*. This can be understood in much the same way as the less jarring statement that an event occurring in my body may or may not be something that *I do*.[2]

As with various bodily reflexes that just "happen" to the person, a person may be more or less the passive witness of certain mental events which he experiences as "external" to him. He may feel he has no more to do with them than being the scene of their occurrence. As Frankfurt notes, there is a distinction to be made here between two ways we may speak of an aspect of psychological life "belonging" to some person. An obsessional thought that a person feels alienated from is nonetheless an episode in the psychological history of *that* person and no other. In this respect it may be like a reflex-movement or internal bodily process that, while not an action of the person, is nonetheless *his* reflex and no one else's. We may call this the weak or "empirical" sense in which the thought or movement is his. But the fact that we can describe such a person as *alienated* from his obsessional thought, as if coming to him from without, shows that there is also a stronger sense in which such a thought may or may not be experienced as "his own." The failure of this stronger sense of identification is expressed in various different ways in Frankfurt's writing. For example, the person may feel that the source of the thought or desire is *outside* of him, or that he is the *passive* scene of its occurrence, or that its occurrence is inexplicable to him, that he cannot link it up with the rest of his mental life, or that he does not endorse its promptings. Thus the failure to identify in the stronger sense with some part of one's mental life is described in terms of several different oppositions: between internality and externality, activity and passivity, explicability and inexplicability, and the attitude of endorsement and rejection or disavowal.

I want to understand which, if any, of these oppositions may be thought of as primary, and how some of the other features associated with this notion of "identification" may be understood in terms of it. In addition, I hope to say something about the point of having such a concept as "identification" or "alienation" in the first place. That is, once it is agreed that even a "disowned" thought or desire nonetheless empirically belongs to the psychological life of *that* person, we will want to know what the point could be of insisting on some "stronger" sense of identification that may nonetheless fail to obtain in such a case. If the language of "identity" is appropriate here at all then this idea must express more than the person's disapproval of some part of himself; and making this out will require getting clearer about just what concept of the person, what sense of "agency," is being invoked here, such that a failure of the normal "active" relation to some aspect of psychic life can be described as a failure to "identify with" it.

Endorsement, Control, and Choice

As mentioned, Frankfurt begins the discussion of "Identification and Externality" with a parallel between two contrasts. Among physical events concerning my body, only some of these count as things that I *do*, and among mental events only some of these count as thoughts that *I think*. And much of what he says both in that paper and later in "Identification and Wholeheartedness" and elsewhere suggests that he believes the distinction between activity and passivity is central to the distinction between internality and externality with respect to states of mind. The interplay between these two sets of distinctions is subject to important qualification in the later work, but one of the more explicit presentations of it is in his 1975 paper, "Three Concepts of Free Action."

Now a person is active with respect to his own desires when he identifies himself with them, and he is active with respect to what he does when what he does is the outcome of his identification of himself with the desire that moves him in doing it. Without such identification the person is a passive bystander to his desires and to what he does, regardless of whether the causes of his desires and of what he does are the work of another agent or of impersonal external forces or of processes internal to his own body. As for a person's second-order volitions themselves, it is impossible for him to be a passive bystander to them. They *constitute* his activity—i.e., his being active rather than passive—and the question of whether or not he identifies himself with them cannot arise. It makes no sense to ask whether someone identifies himself with his identification of himself, unless this is intended simply as asking whether his identification is wholehearted or complete.[3]

If it is the concept of the person as *agent* that enables us to speak of "identification" in the case of bodily movements, does a similar sense of agency have application in the case of mental life? It is not immediately clear how it could, since we do not appear to produce our desires and other attitudes in anything like the way we produce our immediate physical movements. A simple physical movement can be performed "at will," for an arbitrary reason, or for practically no reason at all. But a person's beliefs, desires, fears or cares are not simply chosen by him, and especially not when we would see his identification with them as most complete. Here it would seem not only that full identification with an attitude does not involve the sort of simple control we have over our immediate movements, but that the very considerations that are suggestive of "identification" with a desire run *contrary* to the requirements of simple control. Indeed, it is essential to the will itself, according to Frankfurt, that it is not subject to our immediate arbitrary control: "A person's will is real only if its character is not absolutely up to him. It must be unresponsive to his sheer fiat."[4] At the very least, then, we are going to have to pursue an understanding of what it is to be "active" beyond the picture of arbitrary acts of will, beyond the idea of free choice, if the idiom of "activity" is to help us to explicate the notion of what it is to "identify" with an element of one's psychic life.

The unwilling addict, or the akratic person who is aware of his condition, feels alienated from his desire. That is, although the attractiveness of what he craves may be all too familiar and comprehensible to him, he feels controlled by his desire, rather than the other way around. And the force of his desire in a given case may be wholly unhinged from his own conclusions about what's desirable or even worth bothering with. It grows and persists independently of his more classically active exercises of reflecting, evaluating, and endorsing. In a different way, the schizophrenic also suffers a "passivization" of the person's normal, directed relation to his thinking.[5] He is alienated from the content and experience of his thinking because its arrivals and departures are split off from the rest of his activity and the reasons that are part of it. The thought he experiences does not appear in the course of thinking about a particular thing, but seems to come of its own, and the desire is one that is similarly isolated from (and contrary to) the person's wider values and practical *projects*.

In these cases, however, it seems to be something more like the absence of rational endorsement of the state in question that makes the person feel passive in the face of it, not the fact that the belief or desire itself is not subject to direct control or adopted at will. Or if the difference does not lie in rational endorsement of the state itself, then it may lie in seeing that state (e.g., as thought or as willing) as responsive to and expressive of one's engagement in the world, rather than something with sources and a direction wholly independent of that engagement. But in neither case does the happier state which these cases are alienated *from* appear to involve any direct role for decisions or acts of will with respect to the thoughts and desires themselves. And in other contexts we may feel that the sense of identification is incompatible with the feeling that the state in question is, or even could be, directly under the control of one's will. Many of a person's deepest emotional commitments, that is, the ones he identifies with *most* strongly, are precisely the ones that do not appear to him to arise from any *decision* of his, but rather to express the limits of what it is possible for him to will, and thus to define the shape of his will. This, of course, is an idea that Frankfurt has explored in several of his more recent papers.[6]

If an experience of choosing seems absent from both the feelings and desires we feel are most deeply ours, as well as those we disown and struggle against, then the existence of an act of choice or volition cannot be what distinguishes them. And further, if the idea of rational endorsement still has some role to play in capturing the sense of "identification" we're pursuing, this notion will have to include more than the fact that one *approves* of the state or disposition in question. For a person may approve of, and even follow the guidance of, some state of mind which he nonetheless experiences as "other" to him, and coming to him from without. Socrates said that from childhood he had a divine guide [*daimon*], a kind of voice that would prevent him from continuing in something he was about to do.[7] He certainly approved of its promptings, for he always followed them and believed them to have saved him from many evils and mistakes. But nonetheless he did experience the voice as something "other" to him; much as he endorsed it, he did not identify with it as he did with his other thoughts and intentions. What was most apparently missing from his relation to the voice was that he would have no access to the *reasons* for the prohibition in question. The *daimon* would simply halt him and issue an injunction, and it was usually only some time after following it that he would figure out what the rationale was. He would follow it both because it had a certain independent power over him, and because he had a belief which was justified by repeated experience that the advice it gave would turn out to be good. Thus his relation to it was like that toward some wise but inscrutable advisor (or parental superego), and this is very much *not* the relation a person has to the ordinary beliefs and desires he identifies with and acts on. Thus in addition to simple endorsement, the ordinary way in which a person identifies with his desires and other states of mind would appear to require a kind of involvement in and accessibility to the reasons in question.

Yet even endorsement combined with accessibility to reasons (of the sort absent from Socrates' relation to his *daimon*) does not give us what we want, does not capture the ordinary case of unquestioned identification with one's thought or desire. For it is not enough for a person to approve of his desire, or even to appreciate its reasonableness, for him to identify with it wholeheartedly. The person is, after all, not just the *appraiser* of his own mental life. At the least, identification would seem to require that he takes his thought or desire to be an expression of *him* and not simply some force inside him, and that its direction and development is in some sense "up to him," even though we've seen reason to reject the picture of the agent directing his thought just in the same way that he directs his bodily movements. What is wanted is an explication of the idea of identifying with one's thought in terms of assuming some kind of active stance toward it, but which doesn't involve a voluntaristic picture of the formation of desires and other attitudes. Further, certain familiar senses of "activity" not only fail to capture the stance a person takes toward those attitudes of his he identifies with, but are actually incompatible with such identification. For instance, the thoughts I take steps to drive from my mind, as well as the desires I have to work myself up to, are certainly ones I may be said to take some kind of active stance toward, but they are partly for that very reason *not* states I identify with in the sense that concerns us here.

Activity and the Attitudes

As a way of gaining some perspective on the part played by the active-passive contrast, and its relation to the contrast between internality and externality, it will be helpful to compare this pair of contrasts with a certain traditional picture of the distinction between sensations and intentional states such as beliefs, desires and other attitudes. (Elements of this picture can be found in such diverse figures as Plato, Descartes and Kant, but I am not ascribing the picture to Frankfurt.) What this distinction within mental life will show is a distinction between two senses of the person's responsibility for his thought or feeling, and the proper sense of responsibility will, I suggest, be what shows us the sense of "activity" that is relevant to the notion of "identification."

There is a natural sense in which a sensation like a headache *is* something one is passive with respect to. It is a happening to which the person is passively subject, something that befalls him, and he is the scene of its occurrence. A person's beliefs and intentions, on the other hand, are not like this. Because they are attitudes, concerning some state of affairs, they are subject to justification. My beliefs don't just happen to me; rather I am responsible for the reasons which I take to support them. This is part of what makes them mine. Thus I am active with respect to my beliefs and intentions in a way that I am not with respect to my sensations. The fact that I am active with respect to them goes with the fact that they belong to me as a *person* in a way that does not apply to my various bodily sensations. The line here need not be sharply drawn, and not all of a person's mental life will fall neatly on one side or the other. But we should notice that even when Descartes, for instance, speaks of "mixed states" such as the passions, he is indicating both their passive nature and their kinship with sensational states, something which complicates the sense of them as attitudes.[8] Pure feelings and sensations belong to our bodily nature and as such are manifestations of mere passive matter.

This is mere reactivity. By contrast, the *person* as such is something essentially active, autonomous and self-moving. All the more reason within this tradition to identify the person as such with the thinking part of his nature, where he is active without external impediment or dependency on the cooperation of the physical world, and master of his own house. And hence the tendency to explicate the notion of "identifying" with some aspect of one's mental life with the adopting of some kind of *active* stance toward it.

Naturally, the opposition as set forth here is fairly crude. Nonetheless I think we can see that neither identification nor alienation of the sort that is relevant to our attitudes (e.g., fear or desire) has any application to a purely sensational state like a headache. Within mental life, the categorical difference between the intentional and the nonintentional runs across the two senses of identification we have distinguished. With respect to sensations, it is *only* the weaker, empirical sense of identification that has any application. A person's headache is simply a part of his psychological history, and there is no deeper sense of identifying with it, or seeing it as truly his own, which might apply or fail to apply to his relation to it. Nor does the possibility of his being *active* with respect to it seem relevant to this point. His headache does not become in any deeper sense *his* if it is somehow produced by the person himself. This is another limitation of the comparison with the distinction between bodily events that I cause and those that happen by themselves. For, as we will see, that distinction does not capture the difference between those physical movements that are actions and those that simply happen on their own. For example, I might *cause* my heartrate to increase, or my digestive processes to resume, without that making either of these into actions of mine.

Instead, the stronger sense of identification at issue here concerns only attitudes and appetites that are directed on some object or state of affairs. The directedness on an object means that the ideas of reasons and justification have application to these states, and these are the same ones for which identification in the strong sense can even be an issue for the person. Hence whatever the sense of activity and passivity is that may help to explicate this notion of identification, it must not only apply to attitudes as such, but must be the *specific* sort of activity that is characteristic of our relation to our attitudes in the normal case, and not simply the sense in which we may be active with respect to our sensations.

It will help in identifying this characteristic sort of activity to begin by distinguishing different kinds of desire. Some desires, such as those associated with hunger or sheer fatigue, may be experienced by the person as feelings that simply come over him. They simply happen, without the person as such playing any role. On some occasions their occurrence may be inexplicable to him, but their inexplicability in such cases need not diminish their force. Like an alien intruder they must simply be responded to, even if one doesn't understand what they're doing there or the sense of their demands. The person's stance toward such desires, and how he deals with them, may be little different from his stance toward any other empirical phenomenon he confronts. From this angle, a brute desire is a bit of reality for the agent to accommodate, like a sensation, or a broken leg, or an obstacle in one's path.

Other desires, however, may be states of great conceptual complexity, attitudes we articulate, revise, argue about, and only arrive at after long thought. Thomas Nagel, for instance, distinguishes between "motivated" and "unmotivated" desires, and by now the general distinction is familiar from various contexts.[9] When someone wants to change jobs, or learn French, or avoid being seen, these desires are "motivated" or "judgment sensitive" in that they depend on certain beliefs about what makes these various things desirable. This dependence is twofold. The desire to change jobs depends for its justification on various beliefs (e.g., about oneself, about one's present job and prospects elsewhere). Were the person to lose these beliefs he would lose justification for the desire. And second, losing *justification* for this desire is supposed to make some difference to whether he continues to *have* this desire. The actual existence of the desire may well not survive the discovery that the new job prospect involves even more heavy lifting or a more toxic environment than one's present situation. This connection can fail, of course, and when it does the person may be open to familiar forms of criticism. It is the normal expectation of the person, as well as a rational demand made on him, that the question of what he actually does desire should be dependent in this way on his assessment of the desire and the grounds he has for it. For the person himself, then, his thought-dependent desire is not a brute empirical phenomenon he must simply deal with, like any other bit of reality he confronts. For this sort of desire, as a "judgment-sensitive" attitude, owes its existence (as an empirical psychological fact) to his own deliberations and overall assessment of his situation.

In fact, by far, most of our desires are of this sort, and not of the sort that simply assail us with their force (despite the nearly exclusive concentration by philosophers since Plato on the "brute" desires of hunger and lust). For a desire to belong to the thought-dependent category, it is not necessary that it be *formed* as the result of deliberation. Very few of our desires come into existence as the conclusion of an exercise of practical reasoning. Equally, however, very few of our beliefs arrive as the conclusion of any *theoretical* reasoning that we undertake. It is nonetheless essential to the category of belief that a belief is a *possible* conclusion of some theoretical reasoning. That possibility defines the kind of state belief is. Similarly, what is essential for a desire to belong to the thought-dependent category is for it to be the possible conclusion of some practical reasoning. This already indicates a categorical difference between such desires and mere feelings, including such things as the sensation of thirst. With respect to the sensation of thirst, neither identification nor externality has any application. The only sense in which such a state is *mine* is as an empirical episode in my psychological history.

Two Kinds of Responsibility

This brings us a bit closer to the particular sense of "activity" that should be characteristic of our relation to our attitudes, if this notion is to shed light on the idea of "identification." There's more than one way of being active with respect to an attitude or other mental state of one's own. Consider again one's relation to one's feelings and sensations. On the picture sketched out earlier, sensations and the like are typically mere "happenings" to which the person is passively subject. But in what sense do we understand sensations or "brute" desires as mere happenings to which the person is passively subject? After all, a person *can*, of course, inflict various sensations on himself, and can do this quite actively and freely. He pinches himself, and produces the very sensation he intended to. But naturally this possibility does not contradict what is meant by the passivity of sensation. True, as the person doing the pinching, he is active, but the sensation itself is the passive effect of his action. It has no *telos* of its own; it is *merely* an effect, much as if he has produced a scratch on himself. By contrast, a person's thinking that it's getting too late to take the train, or his hoping for rain, are not *effects* he produces, even when they result from a process of thinking on his part. Instead, such attitudes are constituents of his thinking, and are thus more analogous to the act of pinching than to the sensation produced by that act.

So there is a sense in which a person can be active with respect to his sensations when he manipulates himself in one way or another to produce some feeling. And a similar stance is possible with respect to one's attitudes. In various cases a person may work to produce in himself various desires, beliefs or emotional responses, either by training, mental discipline, the cooperation of friends, or by hurling himself into a situation that will force a certain response on him. But exercising this sort of control over one's attitudes is not the expression of autonomy or identification. In such cases of producing a desire in oneself the attitude itself is still one I am essentially passive with respect to. It is inflicted on me, even if I am the one inflicting it.

There is, of course, another way in which a person may assume responsibility for some aspect of his psychological life, one that does not apply to sensations but *only* to his relation to his "judgment-sensitive" attitudes of one sort or another. Consider the distinctive kind of responsibility a person assumes for his desire when it is the conclusion of his practical reasoning. In such cases, he is not only prepared to justify it, but the presence or absence of justification makes a difference to the presence or absence of the desire itself, and the direction of his desire is in fact guided by the direction of his thought about what is desirable. He is active with respect to his desire not because he has *produced* it in himself, but because he takes the general question of what he wants here to be the expression of his sense of what he has best reason to pursue in this context. Were those considerations to be undermined, the desire itself would be undermined. And that means there is a kind of control he does *not* take himself to have here, in that he won't take himself to be in a position to *retain* the desire, or to reproduce it at will, were he to lose or abandon the considerations that supported it, so that the object in question now seems worthless to him. Or rather, perhaps he could find some way to retain it, if we think of this now as a purely causal question, a choice of effective means to somehow maintain the presence of this desire. But if his "activity" with respect to this desire were confined to this sort of external control, this would be the very expression of his alienation from it, even though he managed to produce it in himself.

By contrast, the kind of responsibility for my desire that is the expression of my identification with it is the responsibility for its internal justification. In considering what we might call "internal" responsibility, compare two of Frankfurt's addicts, whose addictive desires are fully independent of their practical reasoning. Given their condition, the sort of "internal" rational responsibility sketched out above is not available to them. For the desire arises on its own, and will persist and move them, regardless of how they conceive or evaluate it. Nonetheless, there is still a possible difference between two such addicts, with respect to what we might call "external" responsibility. The way the cases are described, neither addict *identifies* with his desire, but one of them may still take responsibility for it in the "external" way that he might take responsibility for any other condition of his which he cannot control. He tries to anticipate its onset, he makes allowances for it in his planning, and tries to minimize its harmful effects, and so on. But the fact that he is alienated from it precludes his taking responsibility for it in the "internal" sense, the sense that is relevant to identification. Being alienated from it *means* that he does not take his desire to be subject to his thinking about what is good to be pursued.[10] The desire itself, as an empirical fact about what drives him, does not adjust itself in the light of his own considerations of what's worth pursuing. It is not an expression of his thinking or his other attitudes, but is rather experienced by him as a facticity that his thinking and other attitudes must somehow accommodate.

This second "external" sort of responsibility is not essentially first-person at all. It is the sort of responsibility I might take toward the actions or attitudes of another person, for instance a child under my care. I do not produce those actions, they are not an expression of *my* will, but nonetheless I can exert some influence over them.[11] And in similar ways one may take some responsibility not only for the actions but also for the thoughts and attitudes of another person. And here, perhaps, the differences between the two kinds of responsibility show up most clearly. I can take responsibility for the beliefs of another person when I believe I can exert some influence over them, redirecting them in one way or another. But I do not thereby see the other person's beliefs as the expression of *my* sense of the balance of reasons. In seeking to redirect them, I need not myself share the reasons I offer to the person to change his mind. My concern is with what will appeal to *him*. This stance toward changing his mind need not be crudely instrumental, but it can develop in that direction. By contrast, the specifically first-person responsibility that a person has for his own desire is essentially not instrumental, and approaches incoherence insofar as it takes that direction. The person's responsibility here is to make his desire answerable to and adjustable in the light of his sense of some good to pursue. It is not a responsibility that reduces to the ability to exert influence over one's desires, and that is why the idiom of "control" is misleading in this context.[12] At the beginning of his practical reasoning he was not aiming to produce a particular desire in himself (as he might with respect to another person), but rather holding open his desire to how the balance of reasons falls out.

This is the same sense of activity and responsibility we rely on in ordinary reasoning with others where the operating assumption must be that the person is in a position to *respond* to the considerations offered, to see the point of some criticism, and thereby determine whether such considerations shall count here and now as a reason for changing his mind. Otherwise the whole activity of offering certain reasons and countering others would be quite senseless. Without the understanding that the person you're speaking to is in a position to exercise some effective agency here, there would be no point in criticizing his reasoning on some point since otherwise what would *he*, the person you're talking to, have to do with either the process or the outcome? He might be in a superior position to view the results of your intervention ("from the inside," as it were), but both of you would have to simply await the outcome.[13] Instead, it seems clear that the very possibility of ordinary argument (and other discourse) presumes that the reasons he accepts and the conclusions he draws are "up to him" in the relevant sense. Acknowledging this sort of agency and responsibility does not involve us in any sort of voluntarism about the formation of beliefs or desires, any more than we need to see ordinary argument with others as aiming at getting one's interlocutor to somehow adopt a new belief by sheer act of arbitrary will.

This "internal" responsibility is also different from the responsibility I may have for a desire of mine that is by its very nature not subject to (because not the expression of) my sense of what is good. Something like hunger or fatigue, for instance, may be a judgement-*in*sensitive desire, something just given, in which case it is not the possible conclusion of any practical reason. And yet, of course, a person may be responsible for getting tired or hungry at an inconvenient time. In certain circumstances he may even be *blamed* for being hungry (more precisely, he may be blamed for letting himself get hungry: the passive voice is appropriate here). Perhaps he should have eaten earlier, when there was time. This is a different kind of responsibility from that which attaches to an essentially "judgement-sensitive" desire. Here one's responsibility would attach to the considerations internal to the desirability of the object, seeing it as the expression of one's sense of what is worth wanting in some way.[14]

Further, as mentioned, the specifically first-person responsibility relevant to "identification" goes beyond the mere *appraisal* of one's state. The person is not only responsible for rethinking his reasons favoring wanting this thing, but it is also up to him for the rethinking he does to *make a difference* to what his desire actually is. If the actual course of his desire or other attitude were not in any way sensitive to his thinking about what supports it or undermines it, then he would indeed be alienated from it. At the least he must take his *other* attitudes (including other desires) as having some voice in determining the course of *this* desire. That is, he may not be able to offer reasons in the sense of considerations that would *produce* the desire in someone, but he must see what he wants in the light of considerations that make it attractive to him. Were he unable to see the course of his desire as answerable to such considerations, then the only influence he could have over it would be the sort of "external" control he may exert over his judgement-*in*sensitive desires, or indeed over the desires of another person.

So, when a person does reach a (thought-dependent) desire through a process of practical reasoning he assumes a kind of responsibility for it, and he identifies with it. When he identifies with a thought-dependent desire in such a case he sees it as the expression of his reasons. But it would be misleading to say that he is active with respect to it in the sense of controlling or producing it. Since it is (already) the expression of his reasons, he doesn't *need* to exert any control over it. As in the case of ordinary theoretical reasoning, which issues in a belief, there is no further thing the person needs to *do* in order to acquire the relevant belief once his reasoning has led him to it. The need for such a further exercise of control would be the indication of his failure to identify with his thought or desire. At the beginning of his practical reasoning he was not aiming to produce a particular desire in himself (as he might do with respect to another person). Instead, he was thinking about what's good to pursue, and holding himself *passive* in a sense, to how the balance of reasons would fall out in the end. The person's responsibility or "activity" here is twofold: to be clear and undistorted in his thinking about the matter, and to allow the desire he arrives at to be the result of the conclusion of this thinking. This latter aspect of his responsibility is not the sort of responsibility for which he may have to produce or suppress a particular desire in himself.

The Activities of Love, Care, and Pleasure

All this may seem excessively rationalistic to capture the sense of "activity" Frankfurt has in mind in explicating the notion of "identification." And it may also seem that this story pictures the agent as too purely active with respect to what reasons count for him, and does too little justice to the sense in which we are hostage to the contingencies of the empirical which we do not control, even in our most resolute declarations of will and desire. As Frankfurt reminds us, after the person has done all his "resolving" and "deciding," there always remains the empirical question of whether he has indeed succeeded in making his will what he wants it to be.

Indeterminacy in the life of a real person cannot be overcome by preemptive decree. To be sure, a person may attempt to resolve his ambivalence by deciding to adhere unequivocally to one of his alternatives rather than to the other; and he may believe that in thus making up his mind he has eliminated the division in his will and become wholehearted. Whether such changes have actually occurred, however, is another matter. When the chips are down he may discover that he is not, after all, decisively moved by the preference or motive he supposed he had adopted. Remember Hotspur's reply when Owen Glendower boasted, "I can call spirits from the vasty deep." He said: "Why, so can I, or so can any man; but will they come when you do call for them?" The same goes for us. We do not control, by voluntary command, the spirits within our own vasty deeps. We cannot have, simply for the asking, whatever will we want.[15]

In this and in other passages, particularly in his more recent writing, Frankfurt is rightly critical of the philosopher's occupational tendency to "intellectualize" anything he can bring himself to take seriously in human life, to treat all internal conflicts as conflicts of judgments. And this same tendency to intellectualize is normally also an expression of an exaggerated sense of the authority and control of reason over the self. Nonetheless, I would like to argue that the picture of our "active" relation to our attitudes developed so far remains appropriate both in itself and as an explication of the sense of "identification" we've been tracking, and that this sense of "activity" is in danger of being lost in comparisons such as the one made by Frankfurt above. Let me begin by noting that, if the sort of case under consideration in this passage is to be seen as a case of *ambivalence*, we will have to assume a particular understanding of its description, and I will suggest that unpacking this understanding will bring us back to the sense of "activity" that is the one that was relevant all along.

When the person finds that he is moved by something *other* than the will he previously identified with, seeing this specifically as a case of ambivalence means distinguishing it from all the other ways in which the carrying through of a decision can be interrupted or interfered with (e.g., seizure, fainting, a new threat from without, another person's intervention). For the example to serve this purpose, this must be a different kind of case from the one where the person finds himself moved in a contrary direction by something that is not his will at all, either a purely external force or something within himself that is alien to any will of his. We need, therefore, to see the way in which he *is* moved, contrary to his resolution, as being nonetheless an expression of his divided *will*. Not every interference with the will is something to which the language of identification and alienation has any possible application. And at the same time, *being moved* by some force is not sufficient to make it (part of) the person's will, not even a will that he disapproves of or is alienated from. When he recoils from some manifestation of his will and seeks to defeat it, his recoil or shame expresses the fact that he recognizes this will as his own. In both cases the alienation itself is a response to an expression of one's agency, and not simply disappointment at some failure of transmission.

So even when the chips *are* down, we are not to imagine this person as simply waiting and watching to see how he will end up being moved. And then further, to understand this as a case of divided *will* we will need to know what reason we have to describe the situation as his "discovery that he is not decisively moved" as he resolved, rather than seeing it either as his refusal to follow through on his previous decision or his having changed his mind about it. (The expectation being that under-standing *those* features of the case as determining it as specifically one of *ambivalence* will take us back to the complex of the person's own con-flicting *reasons*, which he has an active relation to.) True, as Frankfurt says, in the clutch I may *find* that I can't go through with what I have decided on, or that, when the time for action arrives, I don't in fact care about the thing I had decided in favor of. A person can be confused or willfully blind to himself in these ways. But to speak of alienation or ambivalence here requires reference not simply to some forces within (or without) the person, but to his cares and concerns, which are active attitudes, even when the person is confused about them.

The image of Glendower's impotent summons is certainly compelling, but in thinking about the kind of "activity" I am claiming is proper to the attitudes generally, there is the danger that this image most naturally represents the situation of an *already* alienated will, one subject to ex-ternal manipulation at best, and hence directs our attention to the wrong kind of "activity," the wrong kind of control. That is, the image of call-ing up spirits from the deep suggests not only the exercise of some extraordinary causal power, but in particular the situation of the person *aiming at* the securing of some particular will (and then either succeeding or failing). But in that case the only activity in question would be the "external" sort, merely a matter of causal control, and not relevant to the explication of "identification." The agent's relation to his ordinary willing, wanting, believing does not involve the exercise of either magic powers or a voluntaristic ability to pick the will, desire, or belief that one would most prefer to have.

What the relevant sort of "activity" does mean in this context will be different according to the type of orientation in question. In outlining the two different senses of being active with respect to one's attitude, the "internal" sense was illustrated with respect to the case of belief, where the internal sense of activity is given by the internal demands of belief itself (e.g., the relations of evidence and justification). In this sense of "activity," being active with respect to my belief means such things as a responsiveness to reasons and evidence, and a responsibility for justifi-cation and revision. It does *not* mean selecting a belief for acquisition and then setting about doing whatever it takes to make that happen. Rather, the primary sense of "activity" with respect to attitudes like belief has its own passive aspect, because the person takes his belief to be answerable to standards and demands that are independent of his other aims and interests.

The possibility of this activity and this passivity is part of what defines the same difference between attitudes and sensations. It is because sensations and the like are *not* defined by internal normative demands that the possibilities of alienation and failure to identify that are characteristic of desires and beliefs simply don't apply to them. And it is for similar reasons that aiming at the direct production of some sensation is not fraught with the same paradox and self-defeat that we find with respect to the various projects of the external manipulation of one's attitudes. Someone in Glendower's position with respect to his will or desire is already alienated from it; that is to say, already in a position where the primary agent's relation to his will or desire has failed him. Hence, even if we were to imagine him as in this case *successfully* calling up this spirit, such a special causal relation to it would not capture the sense of activity that is relevant to identification.

The normative dimension of the attitudes, which differentiates them from mere happenings, and which I am tying to the sense of activity that is relevant to identification, is probably most familiar in the case of belief, in part because the understanding of its basic terms has been such a long-standing concern of epistemology. But, while being a central case for thinking about attitudes and their normative structure, belief is also a rather special case, with a much greater and more explicit role for reasoning and justification than belongs to other attitudes which nonetheless are defined by their own specific requirements. The thought to be developed further is that when we speak of identification or alienation, we are talking about the possibility of distortions with respect to this wider normative dimension of the attitudes generally—a dimension that will constitute one sort of issue with respect to belief, another one with respect to desire, and something else with respect to love, anger, or pleasure. And I want to suggest that this wider sense is the key to understanding the person's relation to these states as an essentially "active" one, active in a way that does not apply to states like sensations. In this way, I believe, we gain a better understanding of failures of "identification" as compromises of the person's agency. I think we can see this active dimension at work in some of the less classically "cognitive" relations that have concerned Frankfurt lately, including love, caring about something, and even ordinary pleasure. Sketching out how this looks should help allay fears that in aligning the possibilities for identification and alienation with a sense of activity illustrated at first by the case of belief, I have constructed an overly rationalistic or voluntaristic picture of our relations to our wills, desires, and concerns.

Presumably even the most "intellectualizing" of philosophers would not wish to reduce pleasure to a form of judgment. Hence it is certainly natural (though I will argue misleading) to think of pleasure as itself a feeling, a state of the person like some sensation that either obtains or fails to obtain. In favor of this is the fact that it is clearly something which is subject to Glendower-like successes and failures. Pleasure can be the expected or hoped-for attendant of one's activity, and yet not arrive. (Or, of course, it can arrive unbidden, even unwanted.) And that can make the pursuit of pleasure seem like seeking to produce a certain state in oneself. And if so, then like the work of other productions, you keep the end in view while you try to approach it, acknowledging that the outcome is not entirely up to you, but is subject to all the stubborn and unpredictable contingencies of the empirical world. But ordinarily pleasure is not an outcome aimed at in this way. For instance, when a person takes pleasure in dancing, he is not aiming at the production of a particular feeling, which he believes dancing will secure for him. And normally when someone does take pleasure in dancing, this proceeds not by his aiming at a particular feeling, but by his letting himself become absorbed in the activity itself, giving himself over to it. Of course, with pleasure as with caring, one's expectation can be disappointed, and the response fail to come when called upon. The person may find, after "trying" in some way, that he just can't enjoy this, or that he just can't come to care about it as before. The truth is, you can't take pleasure in something or come to care about it just because you want to, or make this true "by fiat." But at the same time, when someone does derive pleasure from dancing, his relation to this activity and what he hopes for from it is not like the wait-and-see attitude he takes to the effect of a sleeping pill either. The result of pleasure requires the involvement of the person in some way that the action of the pill does not. And hence, neither "fiat" nor passive self-inducement seem the proper models for the person's relation to his pleasure.

An activity may be pursued for pleasure, but the arrival of its pleasure is normally dependent on allowing it to follow in the train of engaging in the activity "for its own sake." Taking the production of pleasure as one's direct aim, being "active" with respect to it in *that* sense, is normally self-defeating, since such an aim brings one into an instrumental relation to the activity, which (for many of the most pleasing ones) is incompatible with taking the kind of pleasure in them that proceeds from pursuing them for their own sakes. This is an aspect of the familiar "paradox of hedonism." In such a case, the person is neither active nor passive in the right way, trying to harness the activity to some independent end, rather than allowing the dancing to seize and direct his attention on its own terms, leading him to respond with pleasure to what is there in the dancing to be enjoyed. In this context, the phrase "for its own sake" connotes directedness toward an object or an activity with its own internal demands, its own *telos*, a structure independent of the person's other aims. To say that the person pursues this activity "for its own sake" is to say that doing this stands as a reason for him *by itself*, and does not require (and may not admit of) any support from some further end. In pursuing it for its own sake, he gives himself over to it; and it is then at least as true to say the activity makes demands on him as it is to say that he makes demands on it.

As with belief, to say that pleasure is not to be summoned "at will" is not to say that we are passive to it in the sense that applies to sensations, or that it is a state somehow effectively beyond our reach, but rather specifically to indicate the particular kind of responsibility that belongs to *that* mode of response. Because there is what we could call a characteristic internal normative structure to these types of response, they are at once insusceptible to arbitrary adoption (and in *that* special sense something one is passive with respect to), and also expressive of the agent's norm-guided activity. For what is meant by "at will" in these locutions is the idea that some actions I can perform for any number of reasons, or for practically no reason at all, on a whim. If I can raise my arm at all, then it is the sort of thing I can do simply because I feel like it, or just because someone asked me to. The execution of my will here does not require determination by any particular *kind* of reasons, or any *particular* ends; that part is pretty much up to me. But, by contrast, believing some proposition requires a very particular set of reasons, epistemic ones; and within that set only a particular range will be even relevant to securing belief in a particular proposition. To believe that p just is to take the internal norms determinative of the justification of that belief to be satisfied. Those norms are not up to me, and instead I must take my belief to be answerable to *them*. What is up to me, what I am active with respect to, is the responsiveness to epistemic reasons relevant to the truth or falsity of this belief.[16]

As Frankfurt insists, caring about something is also a relation that cannot be adopted arbitrarily, or "at will." And I am suggesting that this is so for reasons of what is *shared* by belief and pleasure or love and care, and not for reasons of any similarity between love and care, on the one hand, and sensations to which we are passive in *their* sense. Loving or caring about something are unresponsive to sheer fiat *because* they are essentially active responses to something else, and answerable to the specific norms of that something else. I can take pleasure in something when I learn to enjoy it, and learning to enjoy it is a matter of coming to see what there is in this thing or this activity that could be enjoyed either as delicious, or mildly diverting, or an intense turn-on, or a surprising resolution, or a guilty pleasure, and so on. If I can't see it in any of those ways then I am not taking pleasure here, however much I may otherwise want to. That open-ended variety of ways in which something can be pleasurable maps out the norms of pleasure for me. These norms are not up to me. Only certain modes of attending to something can constitute being diverted, soothed, turned-on, or gratified. And for any instance of pleasure there must be answers to questions like, "Is this a pleasure in, say, touch and warmth, or is it more like the pleasure in besting one's opponent in chess?" "Is this pleasure something savored and repeated, or something fleeting and barely experiential?" "Is it a pleasure for which repetition even makes sense (as it arguably does *not* for the pleasure of some unexpected good news, or in being a favorite son, or in the recovery of health)?" "Is taking pleasure here a matter of sustained, diffuse attention, or is it absorbed and intense, eclipsing awareness of everything else?" "Is it more like the pleasure in drinking when thirsty, or the pleasure of living in Manhattan, or more like the pleasure which supervenes on the exercise of some complex skill or knowledge?" These categories define the particularities of what it is to take pleasure in some thing, fact, or activity, and not everything we encounter will be so much as a candidate for every conceptual variety of pleasure. The norms of the pleasures of either solving some problem or idly stroking some surface will determine that only some activities and some surfaces can be possible providers of just those pleasures. To be conducive to the specific pleasures of idle stroking or problem-solving, the thing or activity in question has to be seen as answering to certain quite particular and demanding requirements. These are independent of me and not determinable by my fiat.

It is also not a matter of my fiat whether I *do* in fact take some specific pleasure in such an object or activity. But here there is room for norm-guided activity on my part. As with believing or caring, to say that I do not "accomplish" these things "arbitrarily" is hardly to say that I do not exercise my agency with respect to them. I can make myself open to caring about something, and take steps to realize this, just as I may refuse to care about something. And I am active with respect to my belief when I hold myself responsible to the norms of justification for that belief, either tacitly or explicitly in the course of reasoning to some conclusion. Again, it is *because* the person is active with respect to the norms governing his belief that he is *not* active in the sense of being able "arbitrarily" to adopt some belief. It is because his belief is responsive and responsible to those particular norms (hence "active" in that sense) that he cannot foist some belief on himself that he does not take to respect those specific norms.

None of this is to say that all these different types of response should be seen as simply forms of *judgment,* or that we either reason our way to them; or abandon them, or are obliged to abandon them, when they turn out to lose some rational foundation. This much I take to be plain about the case of pleasures, and that is why they are such an important case to consider in this context. It is because their normative structures are so manifestly different from a judgment's requirement of justification, more manifestly even than the case of caring, that it is worth exploring how they can nonetheless be seen as normative *responses* of this person, in a way that explains why pleasure (like love and caring, and unlike a sensation) is subject to identification and failure to identify, and are thus the expression of the active nature of the person. We can, I am claiming, preserve this crucial aspect in which pleasures, like loves and cares, are aspects of the whole person's engagement with the world, without "rationalizing" or "intellectualizing" them in the familiar ways that Frankfurt wants us to avoid.

Although we do not arrive at what we love or care about by anything like reasoning, that is not because these are less active modes of engagement than belief is, but because the *kind* of activity they represent does not express itself through reasoning and inferring. That is a central form of norm-governed activity, but hardly the only sort. Even in the extremely stripped-down and atypical case of taking pleasure purely in some feeling, one's relation to enjoyment here is unlike waiting for a pill to take effect since one will still need to know *how* to take pleasure here, and make or allow one's consciousness to be active with respect to the aspects of pleasure in that particular feeling. In my consciousness of this feeling I like, I have to know my way around, I have to know what there is to enjoy in it, which aspects are central to its pleasure and which are incidental to it, which to attend to and seek more of, and which are indifferent to the pleasure. I have to know how to orient myself toward this feeling in order to enjoy it. That is, it might be a constituent of my pleasure in this sensation that it comes from a certain source, or that it recurs, or that I can control the appearance of the feeling or that it is quite beyond my control, or that it is faint or that it is sharp, and so on. And just as easily, any of these noticeable aspects of the feeling might be entirely irrelevant to the pleasure I take in it. The point is that *taking* pleasure in it means knowing which is which, whether tacitly or explicitly.

It is sometimes said that certain drugs "produce" pleasure, but this is true only in the same sense that either string quartets or ripe cheeses "produce" pleasure. In both cases we can provide the cause without producing the effect, because the person exposed to either the drug or the music doesn't like it, doesn't see what there is to enjoy in it. What was the very form of hazy, druggy pleasure for someone else is to this person merely some unpleasant dizziness and disorientation. Even here, when we speak of drugs "doing" this or that, finding pleasure in the experience is a matter of being inclined to take pleasure in what is given. And the fact that such "know-how" may simply come naturally or spontaneously to the person does not make his engagement any the less active, anymore than it does for ordinary physical skills or habits of inference.

Not being based on reasons, the pleasure or the caring can certainly (and legitimately) survive the realization that the thing in question does not fully satisfy the conditions which would make it *worth* caring about, or the realization that it is a cheaper, or nastier, or otherwise less reputable pleasure than one wishes it were (or presents it as being). But the point to notice is that these terms of evaluation don't even begin to apply to genuinely passive states like sensations, whereas it is internal to pleasures that such terms do apply. When we insist that such terms of criticism have application to pleasures or cares, this still leaves open what the *consequences* of such application are, or ought to be, in a given case. The very fact that a person can indeed experience some pleasure "in spite of himself" testifies to the relation to agency here, since a person does not experience a sensation like heat or a headache "in spite of himself." The idea simply doesn't apply. Here the comparison with laughter can be instructive, as well as the possibility of laughing "in spite of oneself." For laughter is also not exactly an *action*, in that it is not something deliberately performed for some reason (not when the laughter is genuine, anyway). It is neither produced "at will," for some independent end, nor is it the conclusion of any reasoning. And yet it is of course an overt *response* of the person, an expression of him, in a way that something like a shooting pain is not. It is because the laughter is such a response that it can clash with the rest of a person's attitudes, and hence is something for which a failure of identification is a possibility, testifying to the presence on the scene of a self to laugh in spite of.

Frankfurt himself, of course, is far from assimilating care or even pleasure to anything like a mere feeling, and one can see some of the consequences of this categorical difference being worked out in his more recent writing exploring the theme of "volitional necessity" and its relation to psychic unity.[17] The kind of mutual implication of activity and passivity that I have been claiming is distinctive of the states or attitudes which are subject to either identification or alienation is under investigation throughout several papers on the structure of care and its relation to love, and also in essays on final ends, and the necessity of ideals. And indeed the deep relation in this regard between love or care on the one hand and logic or rationality on the other is thematic in the initiating discussion of "volitional necessity" in "The Importance of What We Care About." Toward the end of that essay he remarks that "The idea that being rational and loving are ways of achieving freedom ought to puzzle us more than it does, given that both require a person *to submit* to something which is beyond his voluntary control and which may be indifferent to his desires."[18] One central aspect of this commonality lies in the fact that, with respect to the commitments of love and care, the person not only sees himself as unable to release himself from this necessity, but (more importantly) unable so much as to *choose* to do so, not without risk to psychic unity. And indeed, in the very language for the transitions of thought most paradigmatically "rational," we describe ourselves in such terms as "swayed by the force of argument," "logically compelled" to accept the conclusion, something that is experienced as "irresistible." And yet, somehow, the very point of such language is to capture something of our most centrally *active* nature, something the very opposite of either inertia or coercion. So there is a familiar, if still mysterious, paradigm of our freedom and activity that expresses itself in the language of necessitation. And in the case of both love and the conclusions of rational thought, the necessitation is aligned not only with some central aspect of activity, but also with the most complete identification of the person with what moves him. It is in such activities as the drawing of a conclusion or the commitment to what one loves that the person is furthest from being a "passive bystander" to his thought or desire.

Love and care are not the conclusions of reasoning, but they are productive of reasons for the person, and express themselves actively in commitment, desire, and concern. A person's love may be beyond his control, and it may not depend either on his approval of *it* or his "good judgment" about the loved object. But for all that it is an active mode of engagement of the person rather than a mere happening. And it is still a matter of reason in the end. For without either love or pleasure being themselves the products of reason, it remains true that either loving or taking pleasure in something *provides one* with reasons, makes something count as a reason that otherwise was not one. Loving someone makes that person a reason for the lover, necessary for him, something to be pursued for its own sake. And similarly, further down the scale to our pleasures, including the less exalted or more purely sensuous among them: the person taking pleasure in some quality of feeling thereby makes it a reason for him. It now counts as something to be pursued, whereas apart from his pleasure it was just a particular quality of texture, no reason for anything. So, to adapt a current phrase, we might say that taking pleasure in something is an expression of our active natures because we thereby place that feeling "in the space of (our) reasons," and it is precisely the elements that are within this space of reasons that can be "identified with" or experienced as either "internal" or "external" to the person.

As I understand it, in the activity of "identification" someone determines what shall be part of him as a *person*. If so, then this prompts the question of how it is that he has any particular *say* over this; that is, beyond a hopeful recommendation. It is not like the influence he might exert in determining his empirical desires (as in training oneself into certain desires, or suppressing other ones). And it is not a matter of picking and choosing from possible desires. When he determines what shall be part of him as a person, he is deciding, among other things, what kinds of considerations shall count for him at all in deciding what to do. And this is a very different matter from the psychological question of what desires or other motives may in fact be operative in him. There may be no reason a person should have any particular say in determining the facts of his empirical psychological make-up. He may simply do what he can. But if it were not "up to him" in some sense to determine what sorts of considerations shall count for him as reasons, then it would be unclear at best how any reasons could count as *his* reasons, or any actions could count as his actions.

Acknowledgments

This essay is dedicated to Harry Frankfurt, in gratitude for his friendship and example. I would also like to thank the editors of this volume, Sarah Buss and Lee Overton. An earlier and quite different version was delivered at a conference on Frankfurt's work organized by Rudiger Bittner at the ZIF in Bielefeld, Germany in 1996. Later, Angie Smith provided some very helpful written comments, which prompted a good bit of rethinking. In writing the final version I have felt the influence of conversations with Pamela Hieronymi, Adam Leite, and Sean Greenberg. Most of this essay, especially the second half of it, was written out of response to the general discussion of Frankfurt's thinking at the memorable conference on his work hosted by Wake Forest University in October 1999. Some of Frankfurt's responses on that occasion, as well as the direction of his most recent writing, raised the question for me of just how far he was willing to distance himself from a concern with reason in thought and action as part of the account of identification and whole-heartedness. In this essay I have tried to suggest that the problems of identification and alienation are inextricably related to those responses of the person for which reason is an issue, so that the rejection of the appeal to reasons would mean the abandonment of the very problems of iden-tification or alienation themselves. Further, I hope to have begun to show that this appeal is at the heart of the distinction between the activity and passivity that concerns us in this context, and that doing justice to it does not force us into a hyper-intellectual picture of our cares, commitments, or pleasures.

Notes

1. Harry Frankfurt, *The Importance of What We Care About* (Cambridge: Cambridge University Press, 1988).

2. Harry Frankfurt, "Identification and Externality," in *The Importance of What We Care About*, 59–60.

3. Harry Frankfurt, "Three Concepts of Free Action," in *The Importance of What We Care About*, 54.

4. Harry Frankfurt, "The Faintest Passion," in *Necessity, Volition, and Love* (Cambridge: Cambridge University Press, 1999), 101. The context of this passage is a discussion of the conditions for overcoming ambivalence and hence achieving full identification. On the previous page he says, "A person cannot make himself volitionally determinate and thereby create a truth where there was none before, merely by an 'act of will.' In other words, he cannot make himself wholehearted just by a psychic movement that is fully under his immediate voluntary control" (100).

5. See, for example, Louis Sass, "Introspection, Schizophrenia, and the Frag-mentation of the Self," in *Representations* 19 (1987): "All these symptoms are quite specific, and all involve passivization or other fundamental distortions of the normal self-world relationship. The patient feels, for example, that his thoughts, actions, feelings or perceptions are imposed on him, or are under the control of some external being or force. He may hear his thoughts aloud, as if spoken outside him, or may feel that his thoughts are broadcast throughout the world" (4).

6. I'm thinking in particular of "Rationality and the Unthinkable," in *The Im-portance of What We Care About*, and "On the Necessity of Ideals," in *Neces-sity, Volition, and Love* (Cambridge: Cambridge University Press, 1999). The title essay of *The Importance of What We Care About* also criticizes the "exag-gerated importance [that] is sometimes given to decisions, as well as to choices and to other similar 'acts of will'"(84).

7. *Apology*, 31c–d, 40a–b.

8. Cf. in particular *The Passions of the Soul*, in *The Philosophical Works of Descartes*, volume I, trans. Elizabeth S. Haldane and G. R. T. Ross (Cambridge University Press, 1911–1912 and 1931).

9. Thomas Nagel, *The Possibility of Altruism* (Princeton: Princeton University Press, 1970). In *Freedom of the Individual* (Princeton: Princeton University Press, 1975), Stuart Hampshire distinguishes between "thought-dependent" and "thought-independent" desires, and more recently T. M. Scanlon employs a concept of "judgment-sensitive" attitudes, with specific reference to desires in *What We Owe To Each Other* (Cambridge: Harvard University Press, 1998), chap. 1.

10. For a helpful exploration of the internal relation Aquinas claims between desire and the thought of a "good to be pursued," see Eleanore Stump's paper "Sanctification, Hardening of the Heart, and Frankfurt's Concept of Free Will," in *Perspectives On Moral Responsibility*, eds. John Martin Fischer and Mark Ravizza (Ithaca: Cornell University Press, 1993).

11. My being responsible for this person's actions is not just a matter of my having some influence over his actions, but also of my standing in a certain relation to him, one that would make sense of my *assuming* some responsibility for his actions. After all, I may have *some* potential influence over the actions of any arbitrary person, and in many cases this may be *more* influence than I have over the actions of my own child.

12. For these reasons I think Daniel Dennett is mistaken in claiming that "one changes one's own mind the way one changes somebody else's." Daniel Dennett, "How to Change Your Mind," in *Brainstorms* (Cambridge: MIT, 1981), 308. This claim is elaborated in another paper with regard to altering one's desires: "Acting on a second-order desire, doing something to bring it about that one acquires a first-order desire, is acting upon oneself just as one would act upon another person: one *schools* oneself, one offers oneself persuasions, arguments, threats, bribes, in the hopes of inducing in oneself the first-order desire. One's stance toward oneself *and access to oneself* in these cases is essentially the same as one's stance toward and access to another." Daniel Dennett, "Conditions of Personhood," in *Brainstorms*, 284–285. In a sense, there would be nothing to argue with here once it was understood that these scenarios do not describe the ordinary situation of the formation of desires (or other attitudes) through deliberation, explicit or otherwise. We *can*, but we typically do not, arrive at a new desire by first identifying *it* and then acting on the second-order desire to adopt it.

13. Cf. Philippa Foot's remark that reasons are not like medicine you take in the hopes that it will work. Philippa Foot, "Moral Arguments," in *Virtues and Vices* (University of California, 1978).

14. The line between these two classes of desire can be a porous one, and the most basic, intractable of instincts become woven into the most elaborate dependencies of judgment, symbolization, and fantasy. And the transformation of desire from the brute to the judgment-sensitive can itself be pursued deliberately.

This process is explored by William Gass in his essay "The Stylization of Desire," *Fiction and the Figures of Life* (Boston: David Godine, 1980), 191–205.

15. Frankfurt, "The Faintest Passion," 101.

16. There is by now an extensive literature on the question of the relation of believing to the will. For an initiating discussion see Bernard Williams, "Deciding to Believe," in *Problems of the Self* (Cambridge University Press, 1973). A particularly subtle, more recent discussion is David Velleman, "On the Aim of Belief," in *The Possibility of Practical Reason* (Oxford University Press, 2000).

17. I have in mind particularly p. 139 of "Autonomy, Necessity, and Love," and elsewhere throughout the examination of ambivalence in that paper, and in other writings.

18. Frankfurt, "The Importance of What We Care About," 89.

REPLY TO RICHARD MORAN

Harry Frankfurt

1. Moran seeks to explain "what it is to 'identify' with an element of one's psychic life." In his view, identifying with something like a thought or a desire consists in "assuming some kind of active stance toward it." The relevant sort of activity plainly does not consist in producing the psychic element in question; it is not a matter of being causally efficacious in bringing about some mental state of affairs. Rather, Moran maintains, the nature of the activity is connected essentially to the exercise of reason.[1]

As Moran says, what makes desires and attitudes ours is certainly not that we cause them to occur. In my judgment, indeed, the nature of identification cannot be understood as dependent in its origin on our engaging in action of any sort whatever. Perhaps it is true that we become active with respect to our desires and attitudes insofar as we identify with them. It is not by virtue of any act on our part, however, that such identification comes about.

2. In his final footnote, Moran says that he has been interested in understanding "just how far ... [Frankfurt is] willing to distance himself from a concern with reason in thought and action as part of the account of identification and wholeheartedness." Briefly, my position regarding this matter is as follows. Identification and wholeheartedness are volitional states that necessarily create reasons but that do not otherwise depend upon them. We can identify with various psychic elements, and we can be wholehearted in various thoughts and attitudes, without having any reasons for doing so. On the other hand, it is in virtue of these states of our wills that certain things count for us as reasons.

In a way, then, I can agree with Moran's claim that "the problems of identification and alienation are inextricably related to those responses of the person for which reason is an issue, so that the rejection of the appeal to reasons would mean the abandonment of the very problems of identification and alienation themselves." The appeal to reasons is an appeal that identification and wholeheartedness make possible. Moreover, a responsiveness to reasons is a necessity that they inescapably impose. Thus it is true that identification and reasons are essentially related. This is not, however, because the former depend essentially on the latter as their indispensable ground.

The relationship of dependency goes the other way around. It is identification that indispensably constitutes the source and the ground of reasons. The creation of reasons is, indeed, close to being the whole meaning of it. Someone to whom reasons meant nothing would necessarily be someone for whom the distinction between identification and alienation could not mean anything either.

It is unclear to me how far Moran would recognize this way of construing the relationship between reason and identification as coinciding with his own. With regard to the main points, it is possible that we may actually be in more or less substantial agreement. Nonetheless, there are a number of significant matters concerning which we do appear to differ. Perhaps I can at least clarify what my own position is by calling attention to a few of the points at which it seems to conflict with his.

3.   Moran suggests that what makes an unwilling narcotics addict "feel passive in the face of" his desire for the drug is "the absence of rational endorsement of" that desire. In my opinion, the fact that the unwilling addict feels passive has nothing much to do with the absence of rational endorsement of his desire by him. In fact, it has nothing much to do with the absence of what is most naturally understood as "endorsement" at all.

First of all, insofar as endorsing a desire could contribute to enabling a person to feel or to be active with respect to it, it would do so whether the endorsement were "rational" or not. Whatever attitude or relationship to a desire someone must have in order to feel or to be active with respect to it, reason need play no role whatever in accounting for the fact that he has that attitude or that he is in that relationship. Endorsing a desire would be no less effective in making a person feel or be active, in my view, if the person endorsed the desire altogether willfully and without even considering the possibility that there might be good reasons for endorsing it.

Second, although in the past I myself have invoked the notion of "endorsement" in contexts such as the one in which Moran employs it, I now think that this employment of the notion is a mistake. The statement that a person endorses something is most naturally understood as implying that the person approves of it. In order to feel or to be active with respect to his desire for the drug to which he is addicted, however, an addict need not approve of that desire. He may be active with respect to the desire even though he disapproves of it and even, indeed, without having any evaluative attitude towards it at all.

Third, there is in any case a fundamental and ineradicable error in the very attempt to explicate being active either in terms of endorsement or in terms of any other kind of activity. Such attempts are manifestly bound to be circular. Clearly, a psychic event or condition that might be presumed to constitute a person's endorsement cannot be regarded as truly doing so if it is an event or condition with which the person does not identify himself and with respect to which he is passive. Let us say that someone experiences, as running through his mind, thoughts whose content is an endorsement of some state of affairs. The mere fact that those thoughts occur in his mind does not establish that he actually endorses the state of affairs in question. Their occurrence constitutes his endorsement of it *only* if they are fully attributable to him as what he himself really thinks.

Suppose that they are instead thoughts—for example, obsessional thoughts—from which he is alienated. In that case, they are thoughts by which he is beset and with which he does not identify. They are external to him, and they do not constitute what he himself thinks. Their occurrence does not mean that he actually endorses anything. The attempt to explicate being active in terms of endorsement is inevitably circular, accordingly, since asserting that a person endorses something necsssarily presupposes that he is active.

The same point plainly holds for other varieties of mental activity as well. Thus it decisively undermines Moran's proposal to illuminate the nature of identification by relating it to "the distinctive kind of responsibility a person assumes for his desire when it is the conclusion of his practical reasoning." We cannot tell whether some thought that occurs to a person is a conclusion of his practical reasoning unless we can tell when the person is identified with his thoughts.

Nothing can count as his practical reasoning unless he identifies himself with the thoughts of which the reasoning is comprised. The fact that a sequence of logically related thoughts occurs in a person's mind entails that the person is engaged in practical reasoning *only if* they are thoughts that he himself actively thinks rather than merely thoughts that are external to him and with respect to which he is passive. The very supposition that a person has deliberated or reasoned cannot be warranted, in other words, unless it is already possible to distinguish between thoughts with which he identifies and those from which he is alienated.

4.   In commenting on the passivity of Socrates with respect to the prohibitions issued to him by his *daimon*, Moran says that "what was most apparently missing from his relation to the voice was that he would have no access to the reasons for the prohibition in question." Moran offers this comment in support of his claim that "the ordinary way in which a person identifies with his desires and other states of mind would appear to require a kind of involvement in and accessibility to the reasons in question." Now it is clear that mere access to the reasons is insufficient, and that some sort of "involvement in" them is indeed essential. After all, Socrates might well have regarded the voice as no less "something 'other' to him" even if the *daimon* had given him the reasons for its prohibitions. It was not on account of the sheer content of the *daimon*'s messages that Socrates regarded them as coming to him from outside himself.

Suppose, then, that Socrates not only knew what the *daimon*'s reasons were but that he had become "involved in" them by making them his own. Presumably, he would have accomplished this by thinking them through and coming to understand and to accept them as warranting the *daimon*'s prohibitions. That would significantly have altered his relationship *to the reasons*, for it would have meant that he had come to identify with them and to incorporate them into his thinking as reasons of his own. It does not seem to me, however, that his relationship *to the daimon* or *to its voice* would thereby have changed at all.

That he had come to adopt the reasoning of the *daimon*, and thus to have reasons of his own for accepting its prohibitions, does not imply that he had ceased regarding the *daimon* as "something 'other' to him." Nor does it imply that he had come to identify the voice of the *daimon* as his own voice. Whatever accounted for his sense that the *daimon* was something other than himself would have been totally unaffected by his coming to understand and to accept the rational basis for what the *daimon* told him. Appreciating the rationality of a command does nothing to eliminate the distinctness between the source of the command and the recipient of it.

Furthermore, identifying with a thought or a desire does not really require any access to reasons for it. Suppose that Socrates had construed the voice he heard to be the voice of his own conscience or superego rather than the voice of some being other than himself. In that case he might well have identified the voice and the thoughts it conveyed as his own, without considering any reasons that could be adduced to support those thoughts and without even assuming that any sort of rational justification for them could in fact be given. A person can surely believe that he is hearing himself talk without making any assumptions concerning the rationality or the reasonableness of what he hears being said.

5.   Moran calls attention to certain desires—for example, to change jobs, or to learn French—that derive from beliefs about what makes their objects desirable. As he explains, a desire of that sort "owes its existence (as an empirical psychological fact) to ... [the person's] own deliberations and overall assessment of his situation." It is by coming to believe that changing jobs or learning French would be valuable that the person comes to have the desires in question, and he would cease to have them if he ceased regarding their objects as valuable.

People do certainly have desires that result from and depend on practical reasoning showing that the desires are justified. In my opinion, however, Moran exaggerates the nature and the significance of this dependency. Although a person's desire to change jobs or to learn French may be quite directly linked to his deliberations and to his beliefs concerning the desirability of doing those things, it is possible that a person may desire to change jobs or to learn French without there being any such linkage.

The desire might somehow just be caused to arise in him by noncognitive circumstances of one sort or another, and he might feel comfortably at home with it. He might have no inclination to distance himself from the desire, or to resist it, and thus he might allow it to play a certain role in guiding his choices and his conduct. Without thinking at all of any question concerning desirability, then, the person might accept the desire as his own and include its object among the things that he really wants.

Moran insists that it is in many instances essential to the character of a desire that "it be the possible conclusion of some practical reasoning." However, the fact that a person's desires are *susceptible* to rational justification does not entail that the person must actually *have* those desires on the basis of rational considerations. Nor does it entail that a person can identify with his desires only insofar as he supports them with reasons or believes that it is possible to do so. A person who has no reasons for his desires may perhaps be open to criticism for his mindlessness. The desires with which he mindlessly identifies may nevertheless be fully his own.

6.   Moran maintains that for a person to be "alienated from ... [a desire] *means* that he does not take his desire to be subject to his thinking about what is good to be pursued." It seems to me, however, that some of the desires with which a person is most deeply and significantly identified, and from which it is nearly impossible for him to become alienated, are not based on any thought about what is good to be pursued. My love for my children, for example, entails a desire for their well-being that is not subject in any sense to thinking on my part concerning whether it is good for their well-being to be pursued. The desire does not arise out of thoughts about that, nor would such thoughts affect it.

Suppose I were to conclude for some reason that it is not desirable for me to seek the well-being of my children. I suspect that I would continue to love them and to care about their well-being anyhow. This discrepancy between my judgment and my desire would not show that I had become alienated from the desire. On the contrary, it would show at most that my love for my children is nonrational and that it is "stronger than I am." What this latter characterization would mean is, precisely, that I *cannot* alienate myself from the desires that my love for my children entails.

Certain of the desires with which we are most unequivocally identified are in this sense stronger than we are. We are not only unable to resist being effectively moved by them. We are unable to reject them, and hence to render them external to ourselves. Our identification with these desires is not subject in any way to judgments concerning what is good to be pursued. On the contrary, our judgments concerning what is good to be pursued tend to be subject to these desires. Some of our deepest desires, which express our natures most fully and most authentically, do not accommodate themselves to our thinking. Rather, our thinking accommodates itself to them.

Like parental love, the desire to live is notably resistant (though not always, of course, impervious) to being affected by evaluative judgments. Even when a person regards his life as terrible, he ordinarily desires not that it end but that it improve. On the other hand, the fact that something threatens our life is usually conceded without argument to be a good reason for avoiding it. Thus the desire to live is generally accepted as providing an especially solid and legitimate grounding for much of our practical reasoning. It is a source of justification, and not a desire for which justification is normally thought to be required.

7. A final small point. My reference to Glendower and Hotspur was not meant to be taken as Moran takes it. It may well be true, as he points out, that the power to call forth spirits, of which Glendower boasts, would be paralleled most closely by "a voluntaristic ability to pick the will, desire, or belief that one would most prefer to have." However, that was not the parallel I had in mind.

The particular relevance of Glendower for me was not as a person who attempts to call forth spirits. What I had in mind was only that he is someone who believes he has accomplished something when, in fact, he has merely tried to accomplish it and has failed to do so. Thus I was thinking of him as analogous to a person who thinks that he has made up his mind about something, but who finds that his mind has not actually been made up about it at all.

My point was just this: the fact that someone concludes a process of practical reasoning does not entail that his conclusion constitutes his will or his desire. His subsequent conduct may reveal that he does not really want the object that he has shown by his reasoning to be desirable and that he thought he wanted. His will may not have the character with which he thought he had endowed it.

Note

1. I am uncertain of the extent to which the idioms of *being active* rather than passive with respect to some mental element, and of *identifying* with some psychic state or processs, do actually go together as closely as Moran supposes. A person who is suffused with a feeling of sadness may identify himself unequivocally with that feeling, and recognize without qualification that it expresses what he truly feels. The sadness by which he is overcome may not be at all external to him. Yet in such an experience, there appears plainly to be an inescapable aspect of passivity. For the sake of convenience in responding to Moran's essay, I shall ignore this point and the issues that it raises.

8

The True, the Good, and the Lovable: Frankfurt's Avoidance of Objectivity

Susan Wolf

In the title essay of Harry Frankfurt's first collection of essays,[1] Frankfurt makes a plea for the importance of a topic rarely addressed by philosophers: what to care about. It is curious that the question of what is *worth* caring about comes up quite late in the essay and is treated as relatively peripheral. Even more curious is Frankfurt's answer: Some things, Frankfurt writes, may be important to a person independently of whether she cares about them.[2] But we care about many things that would not be important to us if we did not care about them—our individual friends, for example, and such activities as philosophy, basketball, or music. With respect to this category, Frankfurt's answer to the question of what to care about is striking: it is "suitable," he says, to care about what it is *possible* for you to care about.[3] Care, in other words, about what you can. In "Duty and Love"[4] he writes in a similar vein about love.[5]

My main purpose in this paper will be to take issue with this provocative claim, or at least with the suggestion lurking behind it that the question of whether something is *worthy* of our love and concern is out of place. Though philosophers, perhaps especially moral philosophers, may tend to place too much importance on the worthiness of possible objects of love, the proper, albeit unexciting, response is to take a more moderate position rather than to reject the relevance of worth entirely. The bulk of this paper, then, is aimed at making this unexciting point and at exploring the way in which worthiness does or should fit in to our considerations of what to love and care about.

The degree to which my position on this matter is opposed to Frankfurt's is not easy to pin down, for Frankfurt does not explicitly reject the relevance of worth entirely. He rather avoids the subject. But it is curious that Frankfurt's silence, or near silence, on the relevance of objective value to the questions of what to care about and love resonates with Frankfurt's discussion of other topics, where I also think inattention to (or silent denial of) the relevance of objective value leads Frankfurt to flawed conclusions. One such topic is wholeheartedness, a virtue for which Frankfurt has unbounded enthusiasm. Another is free will, which Frankfurt famously analyzes as the freedom to have the will you wholeheartedly want to have. I shall discuss these briefly at the end of this essay. On these issues, as well as on the question of what to care about, Frankfurt avoids an acknowledgment of the relevance of worth. Because of this—at least so I shall argue—his positions are ultimately unsatisfactory.

Frankfurt's View and Its Opposite

In both "The Importance of What We Care About" and "Duty and Love," Frankfurt's primary concern is not to address the question of *what* to care about but to stress the importance to us of caring about *something*. As Frankfurt emphasizes, caring about or loving things (activities, persons) other than ourselves makes an enormous difference to our ability to live fulfilling lives. Moreover, Frankfurt believes that "it is not so easy for most of us to find things that we are capable of loving."[6] These points together, presumably, lead him to conclude that we should care about what we can.

"What makes it more suitable," Frankfurt asks, "for a person to make one object rather than another important to himself?" He answers:

> It seems that it must be the fact that it is *possible* for him to care about the one and not about the other, or to care about the one in a way which is more important to him than the way in which it is possible for him to care about the other. When a person makes something important to himself, accordingly, the situation resembles an instance of divine *agape* at least in a certain respect. The person does not care about the object because its worthiness commands that he do so. On the other hand, the worthiness of the activity of caring commands that he choose an object which he will be able to care about.[7]

What Frankfurt is recommending, however, is not completely clear. What does it take to license the claim that a particular person *is able* to care about a thing (that is, that it is possible for him to care about it)? Although we cannot care (or cease to care) about things at will, with effort over time we can come to care about things that we do not care about naturally. Perhaps, and especially if we allow the use of nefarious or misguided psychological techniques, we can come to care about some very odd or very creepy things. One might come to develop a passion for making dishes that include marshmallow fluff as an ingredient—or more seriously, one might develop a love of torture.

Now Frankfurt nowhere suggests that we should care about everything we possibly can. So the fact that one *can* care, say, about torture, does not imply that one positively *should*. On the other hand, if we look to the passage above for advice about *whether* we should (or, for that matter, for advice about whether we should care about recipes with marshmallow fluff), the kinds of questions on which it urges us to focus seem to leave some salient considerations out (at least, it leaves them out as considerations having direct unmediated importance). Frankfurt seems to advocate that we care about what we can—and that, if we have a choice about what to care about, we care about whatever will be most fulfilling, rewarding, and satisfying to us to care about. If our make-up and circumstances are such that we will be more rewarded by caring about helping people rather than hurting them, then we should cultivate our sympathies. If, however, we would be more fulfilled by taking up the call of sadism, nothing in Frankfurt's remarks seems to discourage it.

These concerns should make us wary about Frankfurt's position—or at least cautious about stating it precisely. If the view that love need not reflect any judgments of worth in the beloved seems problematic, however, the opposite view—that love *should* reflect worth—may seem even worse. Indeed, I suspect that antagonism toward that view lies behind the extreme statement of Frankfurt's own position.

The view I have in mind as the opposite view, that love should reflect worth, may be stated more precisely as the view that one's love of a person or object or activity should be proportional to its value or worthiness to be loved. One should love most that which is most deserving. One might put this by saying one should love the Good. Such a view seems more or less taken for granted by both Plato and Aristotle, and is at least implicitly suggested by some high-minded styles of Christianity and some versions of consequentialist thinking. Despite the venerable figures and traditions that have explicitly or implicitly embraced it, however, we have strong reason to reject it.

That there is *something* wrong with the view seems evident from the very thought of the conclusions it seems to imply: that we should love or care about one person more than another because she is a more worthy candidate of love (more intelligent, stronger, wittier, perhaps) is highly offensive. Even the view that one should care about activities or objects in proportion to their worth—classical music more than rock, for example, or philosophy more than fashion or food—seems absurd. A person who holds such a view and tries to pattern her cares after it seems alternately pompous, stiff, and self-righteous, or naive, foolish, and pathetic. I can think of at least two ways of trying to articulate what is so objectionable about these suggestions. Both seem to me to have something right about them.

First, one might think that the idea that some things are more worthy candidates of love and concern than others reflects a mistaken view about the existence or nature of objective value. The view that one should love what is good in proportion to its goodness evidently presupposes that some things are better than others. But, so the objection goes, this is simply false. Though people differ in intelligence, attractiveness, and virtue, they do not (it is said) differ in worth, so the idea that one should love according to worth is out of place here. Similarly, it may be argued, the idea that some activities and interests are worthier than others is misguided. One activity is as good as another if one can get equally enthusiastic about it. Pauline Kael's writing about movies is as good—for her and for the world—as Quine's writing about the indeterminacy of translation. My aerobics instructor lives as worthwhile a life as my doctor. The idea that one's loves should proportionally reflect the value of the objects of love thus may seem to reveal a false picture of the evaluative facts of the world. If we reject the false presuppositions about value on which the view is thought to rely, the position may seem literally unintelligible.

Alternatively, one might regard the view in question as intelligible but horrible. The problem is not that there are no evaluative facts that could be a basis for channeling one's affections. It is rather that a world in which people did so direct their loves would be the worse for it. Perhaps, so this objection goes, some people and things are better than others. Mozart's body of work is presumably better than Salieri's. People like Mother Theresa are presumably better than drug-dealing slumlords. But the idea that one should love according to what's worth loving nonetheless seems seriously misguided. Just imagine the parent who loves one child more than another because the one is better (smarter, perhaps, or less selfish).

The view that one should love what is worth loving and in proportion to its worthiness, then, seems horribly wrong. Yet the view that Frankfurt's work seems to suggest—that worthiness and love have nothing to do with each other—seems, for reasons already hinted at, problematic as well. This suggests that the truth lies somewhere in between—that worth figures in, somehow, to what it is desirable to care about, but not exclusively or perhaps decisively. In the next section, I shall explore what role worth might play in answer to the question of what ideally to care about. Following that, I shall take up the question of what, beyond or behind our intuitive responses, might justify the view that worth plays a role.

The Role of Worth in What to Care About

Our intuitive responses may appear to support the view that the role worth plays in determining what to care about is to set a minimal condition. For it is not until we consider extreme examples—examples, we might say, of utterly worthless activities or objects—that the judgment that these are unsuitable objects of care wins general approval. When it comes to people, the dominant view is that all people are appropriate objects of love. Even regarding the question of what activities or interests to have, we are tolerant, even encouraging, about a very wide range— sports and science, food and philosophy, cars, movies, antiques, jazz— all seem fine as objects of interest, even passion. Never mind whether and which things are better or "most important."

It is a common view of parents and teachers that it doesn't matter what a child cares about, as long as he or she cares about *something*. This thought seems to support the Frankfurtian view, until we force the issue by looking at extreme cases. When parents say they just want their children to care about *something*, they mean they don't care whether it is soccer or ballet, mathematics or piano. But they start to get worried if their children spend all their time and money following the career of The Backstreet Boys, or playing bingo on the internet, or working at breaking the world record for long-distance spitting. Even worse if their interests veer to the morally objectionable—to hate groups or Satanic cults or sexual sadism, for example.

A plausible hypothesis is that there is a condition of worthiness lurking in the background of our views about suitable, desirable caring, but that it is a minimal condition. We want what people care about to have some worth, to go above some bottom line of goodness, but there is no need to try to match one's cares proportionately to relative amounts of goodness. As long as the things you care about are good enough (and most things people tend to care about are), you're fine. You don't need to worry about whether they are as good as other possible objects of care.

Successful as this view seems to be in matching most of our intuitive judgments, I don't think it is strictly right. The phrase "You can do better," offered in advising a friend about her love life or her job, is at least sometimes in order. As the use of the comparative suggests, its point is not to insist that the man or the job at issue is utterly worthless or even falls below some minimal line—it is rather that as long as one has or is in a position to cultivate having more options, there is something to be said for aiming higher for a more interesting or virtuous or appealing partner, or a more challenging or responsible or socially useful job.

Furthermore, interests we might approve of, even delight in, as hobbies on the side, may worry us if they take over too much of a person's attention and energy. Being a fan of a sports team, a bridge player, a lover of musical comedies, adds interest and variety to life, and helps make one person different from another, giving us distinct identities. Interests like these are good and healthy—but they can take more time, and demand more sacrifice of other things than they are worth. These reactions suggest that some kind of proportionality requirement, rather than a simple minimal condition, is operating in shaping our judgments about what it is suitable to care about. People should care about only what is at least somewhat worth caring about; and how much people should care about things, both in themselves and relative to other things they care about, depends somewhat on *how* much worth caring about the objects in question are.

But how can we accept such a requirement without committing ourselves to the view that we have already criticized—the view that you should love what is good and only insofar as it is good? A few further considerations may temper the requirement in ways that make it more acceptable.

The first is that in accepting the view that worthiness of an object is a factor in the suitability of that object to be an object of care, we are not committed to the view that it is the sole or dominant factor. Just as, to use a mundane example, expense and comfort are both factors in the suitability of a pair of shoes for purchase, worth may be one factor among others in the suitability of an object for our affection. Indeed Frankfurt's own discussions of what to care about and what to love provide us with another factor. I shall call it affinity.

As Frankfurt notes, loving, caring deeply about some things, is itself of enormous importance to living a good and satisfying life. To go through life not loving anyone, not caring about anything, is a horrible fate—far worse, most of us would say, than living with cares that bring with them considerable grief and frustration. Friendship and love bring with them the risk of pain at the beloved's misfortunes and sorrow; aspirations and ideals cannot be reached without difficulty, striving, and often stress. Few, however, would trade a life of love and commitment with its concomitant sorrows for a life free of risk and pain that lacked any real cares.

Caring, then, and loving, are goods in themselves—especially if the caring is deep and passionate. This—and the fact that one cannot make oneself care deeply and passionately about something at will—is what supports Frankfurt's judgment that one should care about what it is possible for one to care about. This is what is sensible in the parents' desire that their children just care about something.

Imagining a parent trying to find a suitable spouse for her child highlights the difficulties with the idea that a person can and should love according to some impersonal list of good qualities. It seems pointless even to try to love a person, career, or project that one cannot get excited about even if one recognizes that he, she, or it is tremendously worthwhile. When it comes to choosing (insofar as one *can* choose) what to love or care about, then, the fact that one activity, object, or person is not objectively as good or better than any number of others may pale in importance before one's enthusiasm for that particular one. Affinity, then, in addition to worth, is relevant to the question of what to care about.

Even this position—that worth and affinity are both factors that weigh in to the question of what to care about, factors that interact and possibly compete—would be dry and wrongheaded if taken in a certain way against the background of certain assumptions about value. If, for example, one believes or even takes seriously the possibility that people can be rated and ranked rather precisely on some scale of merit—if one thinks, perhaps, that the traits our society standardly values in people, like intelligence, physical attractiveness, kindness, and talent, make one person more valuable, and so more worthy of love than another—the view that worth and affinity are both factors determining the suitability of an object of love may remain as offensive as the original view that worth alone matters. For it suggests that it would be preferable if one's loves did match this ranking (would that I had a more objectively worthy child!), even if that consideration might be outweighed or compensated by affinity. This seems as repugnant as the "purer" view that one should love what is good just insofar as it is good.

The fact is, however, that the realm of value is both complex and pocketed with indeterminacies. Though total skepticism about value seems to me unwarranted, the idea that each person or object can be assigned a precise quantity of value on a scale by which it can be compared with others seems deeply mistaken.

In the domain of persons, the dominant view is that no person is more valuable than any other—not because there is no such thing as value, but because each person has a value beyond price. It would follow from this that the chilling idea that we should try to train our affections so as to love people in proportion to their value is out of place not because of any objection to the idea that value is an appropriate consideration in connection with what to love, but rather because, when it comes to people, any person qualifies as maximally satisfying this consideration.[8] By contrast, there is less consensus on the appropriateness of showering comparable affection on a pet, a disagreement plausibly explained by doubts about whether lower animals *merit* the same kind and degree of devotion.

In evaluating possible objects of interest and love other than people—activities, projects, and inanimate objects, for example—we can expect to find similar indeterminacies and incommensurabilities. There may be no answer to questions like, "Is it more worthwhile to pursue sculpture, basketball, or chess?" or it may be that, particularly when one breaks free of some traditional, elitist, or otherwise narrow-minded assumptions, the answer to such questions is, more often than might be expected, that each is in its own way more or less equally worthwhile.

Perhaps even more important than the considerations mentioned so far is a further point—namely, that affinity for an object, activity or person encourages or makes possible kinds of worth or value that would not exist without it, value that lies not in the object considered in itself, but in the lover of that object or the relationship between them. Some people bring out the best in each other; they allow or encourage each other to fulfill their potentials. Similarly, a person's affinity for a genre or for a more particular type of entity can inspire and stimulate him in ways no other thing can. One thinks of Glenn Gould's relation to Bach, of Merchant and Ivory's relation to post-Victorian fiction.

In asking what it would be best or "most suitable" for a person to care about or love, then, we are apt to take into account at least three sorts of consideration: whether (and how much) the object in question is itself worth caring about, whether (and how much) the person has an affinity for the object in question, and whether (and how much) the relation between the person and the object has the potential to create or bring forth experiences, acts, or objects of further value.

I conclude, then, that, when held in conjunction with the qualifications discussed above, the view that considerations of worth are relevant to the question of what to care about and what to love accords better with our considered untheoretical judgments than the view I have attributed to Frankfurt, that one should care simply about what one can, never mind how worthwhile what one cares about is.

Reasons Why Worth Should Play a Role

That a view matches our untheoretical judgments (our intuitions, as they are often called, even though they are meant to embrace reflective and considered judgments and not just gut reactions) gives some support to the view. Still, we can look for reasons supporting or explaining the view we find ourselves pretheoretically to have. *Ought* we to care that the things we care about are worth caring about—that they meet some standard of objective value? What difference does it make whether what we care about is objectively valuable or not? I can think of two reasons for wanting our cares to be attentive to what is worth caring about—two reasons, that is, for thinking that worth should be a consideration for what to care about. One has to do with an interest in truth, the other with an interest in meaning.

We have, I believe, an interest in truth—or, more precisely, an interest in living in the real world. We do not want to be living in a fantasy world, to be deluded, particularly about aspects of the world with which we interact and on the basis of which we make decisions and orient our lives. This interest may not be universal—that there are some who are untroubled by the thought of a life plugged into Nozick's pleasure machine suggests that it is not. Nor need it be overriding—some truths may be so painful and disruptive that we would be better off not knowing them. Nor am I sure that the question of whether one *should* care fundamentally about the truth admits of any argument. Still, the interest is natural enough, prevalent enough, and sensible enough to allow us to say that, other things being equal, we are better off not being deluded, especially about things that play a significant role in our lives.

Among other things, this implies that we do not want to be deluded about the things that we love and care about. But if you love something, or seriously care about it, it is hard not to think of it as good. If you love something, you probably will think of it as good—though not necessarily better than things that you do not love. Often, love develops out of our finding or seeing something good about the things we come to love; our loving something also tends to make us look for and attend to the good that is in it. To love a thing that one doesn't regard as good or worthy of love is, at the least, uncomfortable. As Michael Stocker notes, it is a mark of a good life that there be a harmony between what one cares about and what one thinks good.[9] This provides one reason why it is preferable to love what is worth loving: loving what is worth loving allows us to love happily, wholeheartedly, and unashamedly[10] with our eyes wide open.

The second reason for wanting to love what is worth loving is related to the first. It is that, in addition to wanting to live in the real world, we want to be connected to it—that is, we want our lives to have some positive relation to things or people or ideas that are valuable independently of us. This, I believe, is at the core of the desire to live a meaningful life.[11] More specifically, I think meaning in life arises when affinity and worth meet. In other words, meaning in life arises when subjective attraction meets objective attractiveness, when one finds oneself able to love what is worth loving, and able, further, to do something with or about it—to contribute to or promote or preserve or give honor and appreciation to what one loves.

Again, the interest in living a meaningful life may be neither universal nor overriding. Again, the question of whether one should care about living a meaningful life may not admit of argument.[12] Still the interest is natural enough, prevalent enough, and sensible enough to allow us to say that, other things being equal, it is better to live a meaningful life. If there is nothing we love or are able to love, a meaningful life is not open to us. But if what we love, and so what we devote ourselves to, is worthless, our lives will lack meaning as well.

In case these remarks seem harsh or overly judgmental, let me remind you that they are offered against the background assumption that the facts about value are likely to be highly pluralistic and complex and that in consequence our approach to questions of objective value should be tolerant and open-minded. The values recognized by somber moralists hardly exhaust the sorts of values that make things and people worth caring about and loving.

I assume, indeed, that most of what people love and care about—nature, culture, religious community, knowledge, sports, and of course family and friends—are well worth loving and caring about. And most of the time, people care to an appropriate degree about the various things they care about. If this is so, one might wonder whether it is necessary to bother mentioning, much less harping on, the need for the objects of our love and care to be worth loving and caring about. Why bother mentioning a condition that is almost always satisfied without even thinking about it?

One reason to mention it is that it is part of a complete answer to the question of what to love and care about, even if a part that is easily satisfied in a wide variety of ways. Another is that even if most of what people love and care about is suitably worth caring about, not all of it is, nor is there a guarantee that, without attending to considerations of value, people's patterns of caring will forever meet this condition. If we forget that worthiness is a consideration relevant to the question of what to care about, we may become confused about whether and why we should encourage our children, for example, to develop some of their interests rather than others. Moreover, in a world in which people's tastes and passions are increasingly determined by market forces that do not have the good of their subjects or of the world at heart, the possibility that people will increasingly come to care about what is not worth caring about may be a growing danger.

Thus it seems to me we should accept the unexciting thesis I announced at the beginning of the paper—that relevant to the question of what to love is the question of what is worthy of love. It is better to love what is worthy of love than to love what is not.

Frankfurt's Avoidance of Objectivity

As I also mentioned at the beginning of this paper, this position, boring and commonsensical as it is, seems to me to go against the grain of Frankfurt's writings on what to love and care about. For the core of Frankfurt's message seems to be that it is important to care about, to love *something*, never mind what it is, and so, a fortiori, never mind whether it is worthy of love. At the same time, Frankfurt never explicitly rejects the position for which I have been arguing. Indeed, despite his claiming that one should care about what it is possible to care about, he admits that caring a lot about avoiding the cracks in the sidewalk would be in some way regrettable.[13] And when he says that "the importance to us of loving does not derive from an appreciation by us of the value of what we love," he inserts the parenthetical phrase "at least, not exclusively."[14] These remarks suggest that Frankfurt does not so much reject the thesis that objective value matters, as that he avoids, or deemphasizes, the subject. If this were right, then my difference with Frankfurt (on this issue, at least) would be merely one of emphasis—and a difference in emphasis need not be a *disagreement* about anything at all.

However, I suspect that there is a disagreement lurking behind the difference in emphasis. For the neglect or avoidance of considerations of objective value that I have been discussing in connection with the question of what to love and care about is part of a pattern in Frankfurt's work. There are a number of issues on which Frankfurt writes to which it seems to me a concern for objectivity is relevant. Since Frankfurt never expresses nor acknowledges such a concern, I suspect that he thinks it misguided or out of place.

One such issue concerns the desirability of wholeheartedness. In "The Faintest Passion,"[15] Frankfurt writes in glowing terms about the value of wholeheartedness, and in correspondingly negative terms about its opposite, ambivalence. Indeed, he writes "It is a necessary truth about us that we wholeheartedly desire to be wholehearted."[16]

I am inclined to describe myself as ambivalent about wholeheartedness (and correspondingly ambivalent about the opposite of wholeheartedness, ambivalence itself). For to be wholehearted about one's values, one's interests, or one's loves is to be fully and unwaveringly committed to them, to harbor no doubts, nor any inclination or willingness to doubt whether to continue in one's attachment to them. But if one believes that one's values might be wrong, or that it might be a mistake to care or to care so much about something, then it seems to me a certain degree of ambivalence, or at least openness to ambivalence, is called for. To be sure, to worry too much about whether one's values are right can be neurotic, and ambivalence and the indecisiveness that tends to go with it, can be paralyzing. On the other hand, wholeheartedness in the face or the context of objective reasons for doubt, seems indistinguishable from zealotry, fanaticism, or, at the least, close-mindedness. That Frankfurt shows no concern for this as a problem suggests either that he thinks people cannot be wrong about what to value and what to care about or that being wrong about such things does not matter. But it does matter—or, at least, it may.[17]

The second issue on which, I would argue, Frankfurt's views suffer from his neglect or rejection of the relevance of objectivity is that of free will. As is well known, Frankfurt believes that freedom of the will—which, with freedom of action, is "all the freedom it is possible to desire or to conceive"[18]—consists in the freedom to have the will that one wants (wholeheartedly) to have. Roughly, it is the freedom to act from one's deepest, most authentic, or "Real" Self, as opposed to acting on desires that are not affirmed and supported by one's deepest level of reflection and feeling.

A problem with this, also well known, is that there are examples of people who meet Frankfurt's condition who do not seem intuitively to have free will—and certainly not to have "all the freedom it is possible to desire or to conceive." A person with paranoid tendencies, for example, or one with an obsessive concern for cleanliness might be perfectly content with her values, and consequently with the will (say, to maintain twelve locks on her apartment door, or to avoid public places where germs are rampant) that flows from these values and cares. Such people will have problems with the world, no doubt, but not with themselves. They may act wholeheartedly, exercising the will they want to have. But far from being free (or from having a free will), they seem to me to be examples of people who are trapped, constrained, shackled by psychological problems the very nature of which makes their problems (their shackles) impossible for them to see.

Incompatibilists take such cases to indicate an incompatibilist condition on freedom—something like the condition that people be able to create or control or choose their own deepest selves. Like Frankfurt, I think this condition is unsatisfiable (and indeed, with Frankfurt, I do not think anything valuable would be gained if it could be satisfied). But in fact I think these examples show something else that a compatibilist can grant, and which when properly appreciated, may be able to explain away some of our incompatibilist impulses. Specifically, the problem with the paranoid and the cleanliness fanatic is not that they lack complete control of their deepest selves—perhaps we all lack that—but that what *is* in control, in their cases, are irrational forces that warp their victims' ability to appreciate what is true and worthwhile, that is, to see things aright. When we say, with Frankfurt, that freedom of the will is the freedom to have the will one wants, we take for granted that the one who is doing the wanting (the real self, as it were) is a sane person, able to understand and appreciate reasons (for example, reasons for valuing some things more than others) for what they are. The relevance of objectivity thus seems to me to lurk in the background of the problem of free will, as it lurks in the background of what to care about and of whether to be wholehearted.

Let me conclude with a highly speculative suggestion about why Frankfurt, a philosopher otherwise so insightful and perceptive about what is important in our lives, should have a blind spot when it comes to the importance of objectivity. Though Frankfurt is generally silent about the relevance of objective judgments in our lives, he is not silent about another topic: the importance of morality. At the beginning of "Duty and Love," for example, Frankfurt confesses that "it seems to (him) that many philosophers ... are excessively preoccupied with morality." "In my opinion," he goes on to say, "this pan-moralistic conception of practical normativity is mistaken."[19] As Frankfurt has also noted, philosophers have, in recent centuries, focused relatively little on other spheres of practical normativity, and for this and other reasons, talk of objective value and worth tends to be associated or identified with specifically moral value and moral worth. My speculation is that Frankfurt's distaste for moralism and his view that morality is less central to our lives than moral philosophers tend to think is behind Frankfurt's avoidance of considerations of objectivity, of truth and goodness, too. But this seems to me regrettable.

If one focuses on what Frankfurt urges us to focus on—on what is important to us, what gives our lives meaning, what makes us the persons we are—one will see that there is much that is valuable without being morally valuable, much that is worth doing and caring about that is not morally worth doing or caring about. Nonmoral value need not have any universal practical or even emotional implications—that an activity is valuable does not imply that everyone ought to engage in it, or even want to engage in it. That an individual is worth loving does not imply that everyone ought to love her. Nor do claims about what is nonmorally good need to be cashed out in terms of what is good *for* anyone. There is much, for example, that is worth doing despite its being of no particular benefit to humankind.

These last remarks seem to me to be in the spirit of Frankfurt's philosophy. But they use a vocabulary of objective value and worth that Frankfurt's own writing avoids. What I have tried to suggest in this paper is that if we want to get complete and adequate answers to the questions Frankfurt himself wants us to ask, we cannot avoid such language. We cannot in other words avoid the relevance and the value of objectivity.

Acknowledgments

I benefited greatly from the discussions of audiences at the University of Colorado, William and Mary, the Australian National University, and Johns Hopkins University, as well as to the participants of the Contours of Agency Conference who heard an earlier draft of this essay. In addition, I owe special thanks to Nomy Arpaly, Chris Grau, Sarah Buss, and Lee Overton, for detailed comments.

Notes

1. Harry Frankfurt, "The Importance of What We Care About," in *The Importance of What We Care About* (Cambridge: Cambridge University Press, 1988).

2. In personal correspondence, he explained that he has in mind things like background radiation or protein in one's diet that are important to something (such as health) that the person *does* care about. He did not intend to suggest that anything (even health, for example) might be important to a person independently of anything the person cares about. This is somewhat confusing in the text, for he writes that "the question of what to care about (construed as including the question of whether to care about anything) is one which must necessarily be important to him." Ibid., 92. He immediately qualifies this, however, with the comment that even this may not be *sufficiently* important to the person to make it worth his while to care about it.

3. Frankfurt, "The Importance of What We Care About," 94.

4. Harry Frankfurt, "Duty and Love," *Philosophical Explorations* 1 (1998): 4–9.

5. Though Frankfurt does not discuss the relation between love and care at length, he evidently regards loving to be a type of caring—or, more precisely, he takes the varieties of loving to be types of caring. See Frankfurt, "The Importance of What We Care About," 85.

6. Frankfurt, "Duty and Love," 7. I am more optimistic than Frankfurt about humans' capacity to find objects of love.

7. Frankfurt, "The Importance of What We Care About," 94.

8. This, however, appears to be at odds with our willingness to think "you can do better" in connection with a person's choice of partner, at least as I interpreted that remark earlier in this essay. I believe this reflects a serious tension or confusion in our thoughts on the value of persons that deserves more philosophical attention than it has received. One way of resolving this tension is to understand "you can do better" as a purely relational remark, referring not at all to how good a person the possible loved one is, but to how good it is *for the lover* to love that person. Another possibility is to distinguish two strands in our talk of the goodness or value of persons. In one sense, perhaps, all persons are of equal value, making them equally deserving of a kind of respect and certain forms of treatment; in another, some people are better than others, in virtue of their different qualities, and this may make them differentially deserving of certain kinds of love. I regret that I cannot do justice to this interesting issue here.

9. Michael Stocker, "The Schizophrenia of Modern Ethical Theories," *Journal of Philosophy* 73 (1976): 453–466.

10. Unashamed, that is, with respect to this issue. It is, of course, possible to be ashamed, unhappy, and conflicted about loving something or someone for reasons other than the unworthiness of the object of one's love. It may be inappropriate to love someone, or to love her in a particular way, for reasons other than worthiness.

11. See my "Meaningful Lives in a Meaningless World," *Quaestiones Infinitae* 19 (1997), publication of the Department of Philosophy, Utrecht University; "Happiness and Meaning: Two Aspects of the Good Life," *Social Philosophy and Policy* 14 (Winter, 1997): 207–225; and "Meaning and Morality," *Proceedings of the Aristotelian Society*, 97 (1997): 299–315.

12. Though I offer one in "Meaningful Lives in a Meaningless World," 17–21.

13. More precisely, he writes: "No doubt he is committing an error of some kind in caring about this. But his error is not that he cares about something which is not really important to him. Rather, his error consists in caring about, and thereby imbuing with genuine importance, something which is not worth caring about. The reason it is not worth caring about seems clear: it is not important to the person to make avoiding the cracks in the sidewalk important to himself. But we need to understand better just why this is so. . . ." Frankfurt, "The Importance of What We Care About," 94.

Frankfurt's claim to the contrary, it does not seem clear to me why, from Frankfurt's perspective, avoiding the cracks in the sidewalk is not worth caring about. (I leave aside the possibility that the person's care is based on a factual error—that he believes, for example, that if he steps on a crack he will break his mother's back.) Compare someone who cares about learning to play the Beethoven sonatas (I assume this would not be a mistake) with the person who cares about avoiding the cracks in the sidewalk. Why is it important *to* the former to make learning the Beethoven sonatas important to himself but not important *to* the latter to make avoiding the crack in the sidewalk important to himself? On my view, we may distinguish the worthiness of caring about these two aims by referring to the contrast between what is valuable about learning the Beethoven sonatas (it spurs the person to develop his skill at the piano, it brings him to a more intimate understanding of the beauty of the works, and so on) and what is valuable about avoiding the cracks in the sidewalk (precisely nothing). But this would not naturally be expressed in terms of its being important *to* the person to make the achievement in question important to himself. In any event, it does not seem to be what Frankfurt has in mind.

14. Frankfurt, "Duty and Love," 6.

15. Harry Frankfurt, "The Faintest Passion," in *Necessity, Volition, and Love* (Cambridge: Cambridge University Press, 1999).

16. Ibid., 106.

17. This is not an expression of ambivalence about my ambivalence about ambivalence. Rather, I mean to say that even if it would be unwarranted to say that

everyone ought to care about whether their values are sufficiently worthwhile and right, there is nothing wrong with people who do care about this. For those of us who do care, therefore, if not for anyone else, it is reasonable to be ambivalent about wholeheartedness.

18. Harry Frankfurt, "Freedom of the Will and the Concept of a Person," in *The Importance of What We Care About* (Cambridge: Cambridge University Press, 1988), 22.

19. Frankfurt, "Duty and Love," 4.

REPLY TO SUSAN WOLF

Harry Frankfurt

1. Wolf represents me as maintaining that "it is suitable ... to care about what it is possible for you to care about." She declares that the main purpose of her essay is to dispute this view, or at least to dispute "the suggestion lurking behind it that the question of whether something is *worthy* of our ... concern is out of place." The opposite suggestion would be just as unacceptable to her: it would be equally mistaken to assign worthiness a unique and definitive role in determining what it is suitable to care about. In her judgment, the "proper albeit unexciting" position "lies somewhere in between." Thus she maintains that "worth figures in, somehow, to what it is desirable to care about, but not exclusively or perhaps decisively." My response to her essay will be concerned largely with an attempt to clarify and to defend my position concerning these issues.[1]

2. Wolf asserts that "it is better to love what is worthy of love than to love what is not." Given her distinction between worth and affinity, I believe that there may actually be no advantage to a person in loving what is worthy as she understands it. People certainly do have an interest in loving things for which they have an affinity. They benefit by modes of loving that provide them with rich opportunities for fulfilling their most satisfying capacities, and that enable them to flourish. However, it may be no better for them to love something that is worthy by some measure other than affinity than to love something that is not.

The issues pertaining to love with which I have been concerned have to do most centrally with the fact that loving is valuable as such. It is a direct consequence of this fact that loving is in itself preferable (other things being equal) to not loving. Instances of loving have intrinsic value, which they possess regardless of their other characteristics and regardless of the characteristics of their objects. Since loving as such is valuable, it is reasonable to desire it for its own sake. It follows quite strictly that loving something is necessarily—given the customary assumption that other things are equal—better than not loving it and, of course, better than loving nothing.[2]

This does not mean that concern for the worthiness of an object is out of place in considering the suitability or desirability of caring about that object. It means only that there is always *something* to be said in favor of caring about any object, quite independent of considerations pertaining to whether the object is or is not—all things considered—worthy of being cared about. The desirability of any specific instance of loving is invariably supported in some measure by the value inherent in the loving as such, however overwhelmingly that loving may be rendered finally undesirable by the negative import of its more particular features and relationships.

.This is the basis for my claim that the mere possibility of loving something is invariably a reason for loving it. The possibility of loving something does not, to be sure, establish conclusively that it is desirable to love it. My claim is not that we should love whatever we can. After all, the intrinsic value of loving is not the only thing to take into account; and it will often be outweighed. Nonetheless, every possibility of loving is a possibility of bringing about a state of affairs that possesses some value, and the fact that a state of affairs would possess some value is always a reason—though not by itself, needless to say, a sufficient reason—for bringing it about.

3.   In saying that loving possesses intrinsic value I mean, of course, that loving as such is valuable to the lover. The lives of people are enhanced by loving. The fact that a person loves something, considered simply in itself, makes his life better for him. To be sure, loving certain things may not be good for a person; under certain conditions, loving may make a person's life worse. Moreover, his loving may not make life better for anyone else. These considerations bear upon the nature of the relationship between the desirability of loving and the worthiness of the object that is loved.

Consider the case of Adolf Hitler. The fact that Hitler cared deeply about the triumph of Naziism had consequences that made things worse for large numbers of people. It would have been far better for the world if Hitler had cared about nothing, and if he had accordingly led an empty and forlorn life. From a moral point of view, it would have been preferable for Hitler to have been idle and bored throughout his adult existence. However, being devoted to the Nazi ideal was very likely better for Hitler than just sitting around year after year, caring about nothing and hence with nothing interesting or important to him going on in his life.

Suppose that it had been possible for Hitler to care about something else, instead of about the triumph of Naziism. We know that as a young man he was interested for a time in being an artist. I have seen reproductions of some of his early drawings, and they are not bad at all. On the other hand, they are not remarkably good either. The chances are that life as an artist would not have brought Hitler benefits anything close in value to what Naziism brought him: a stimulating and enriching variety and intensity of experience, public acclaim, the gratifications of extraordinary achievement, and the pride of working creatively to overcome intimidating obstacles in an effort (as he saw it) to make fundamental contributions to the progress of civilization.

The career of an artist was plainly less worthy of choice, from Hitler's point of view, than the career he chose. I am not referring to the fact that he believed it to be more desirable morally or historically for his political goals to be attained than for his artistic ambitions to be indulged. We would, of course, disagree with him about that. Surely, however, we can recognize that choosing an artistic career would have been less reasonable for him in terms of how he could expect it to affect his own personal experience of life compared with how he could expect his life to be affected by devoting himself to Naziism.

Hitler could reasonably have expected that he would find experience as an artist less interesting, that it would provide him with fewer opportunities for developing the fullest range of his personal capacities and talents, that it would not enable him to make as much of a name for himself, and so on. Naziism promised Hitler a complex, exhilirating, and rewarding life. It offered him far more than was offered by the prospect of becoming a dreary failure as a third-rate artist, doubtless more or less impoverished, unappreciated, and ignored.[3]

4. The Naziism to which Hitler devoted his life was a dreadful evil. Is this a reason for regarding it as unsuitable to be loved? On Wolf's account, the immorality of what Hitler cared about counts against its suitability; and I suppose that it would count so strongly that she would judge it unsuitable no matter how much contentment and fulfillment and

joy his caring about Naziism brought to his life. On the other hand, the fact that his life was so dreadfully immoral might really have had no deleterious effect whatever on the value to him of living that life. It is possible, I am sorry to reveal, that immoral lives may be good to live. In my view, at least, the value to Hitler of living the life he chose would have been damaged by the immorality of that life only if morality was something that Hitler actually cared about, or if the immorality of his life somehow had a damaging effect on other matters that he cared about.

Wolf assumes that the immorality of an alternative counts against its suitability. It certainly counts against its moral suitability. That goes without saying. But do the essential nature or the consequences of immorality have any significant bearing on whether it would invariably be reasonable for a person to prefer a morally superior alternative over others? I am not convinced that the moral value of a person's life has any particular relevance in determining how good or how bad it is for the person to live that life. For well over two millennia, numerous philosophers and religious thinkers have endeavored assiduously, but without notable success, to show that only a moral life can be good to live. Wolf provides no basis for thinking that this can convincingly be shown, or for thinking that it is true. My guess is that it is not true, and that the goal of making it genuinely convincing is a will-o'-the-wisp.

Unless a person cares about being moral, or about something that depends on being moral, being moral will not make his life better for him. In that case, it will still be true that he should (in the moral sense) take moral considerations seriously in his deliberations concerning what to care about. He will still have a moral obligation to do that. However, it will not be reasonable for him to do what he is morally obliged to do, or to care that his conduct fails to meet the requirements of the moral law.[4] What reason would he have, after all, to care about something that makes no important difference to him?

Wolf suggests that it "should make us wary about Frankfurt's position" that nothing in it discourages taking up sadism, in preference to benevolence, if that would provide us with the greater rewards. I agree that my position should make us wary. What it should make us wary of, however, is not my claim that it may be unreasonable for a person who is rewarded by sadism to prefer benevolence. Rather, it should make us wary of doctrines that promulgate exaggerated estimates of the moral effectiveness of reason. Insofar as it is unreasonable to be immoral, it is not because somehow it inherently violates the canons of rationality. It is just because, for many of us, it tends to make our lives worse by its effects on things that we care about.

5.   There is some truth in Wolf's claim that "if you love something, or seriously care about it, it is hard not to think of it as good." We do often suppose that what we love is good. I believe that the primary explanation of this is that loving something entails identifying with it. Insofar as we are determined to think well of ourselves, we must therefore think well of what we love. We do not wish to be demeaned by loving what we or others consider to be ugly, or evil, or without charm, or worthless. However, this does not mean that we love things because we think that they are good. The loving itself is what is fundamental. Our evaluation of the beloved object, or our effort to persuade ourselves that what we love possesses value, is more often a response to the loving than its source.

Wolf's claim does strike me, in any case, as exaggerated. No doubt there are people who are especially anxious about being closely associated only with what they consider to be good. For others, it is not by any means difficult or uncommon to love something without giving any thought to its value. It is a familiar fact that some people seem unable to help believing that their children, or they themselves, possess various attractive or meritorious characteristics. Still, it is possible to love one's children or oneself without having any opinion about such matters and without caring about them. It is even possible—though it may be a misfortune—to love people whom one believes are really not good at all.

As I understand her, Wolf suggests that we want to love what is good because: (a) we are more or less indiscriminately bound to think that what we love is good, whether it is or not; and (b) our desire to avoid being deluded therefore implies that we should confine our loving to things that really are good. This sounds curiously like a claim that because we care about truth we must try to arrange that reality tracks our tendency to delude ourselves so that what we believe is not actually delusional. I believe that if we do care about truth, we would do better to resist our tendency to suppose that what we love must be good.

6.   I am similarly dubious about Wolf's notion that meaning in life depends upon a harmony between what one cares about and what one

thinks good. An enthusiastically meaningful life need not be connected to anything that is objectively valuable, nor need it include any thought that the things to which it is devoted are good. Meaning in life is created by loving. Devoting oneself to what one loves suffices to make one's life meaningful, regardless of the inherent or objective character of the objects that are loved.

There is, to be sure, a necessary connection of a sort between meaning and value; but it is not the sort of connection that Wolf evidently has in mind. In addition to making living meaningful, love also creates value. Things become valuable to us, however little value they would otherwise possess, in virtue of the fact that we love them. Therefore the fact that we love something, which creates possibilities of meaningful activity and experience, also ensures that the object upon which our meaningful experience and activity are focused is not worthless to us.

Given that our capacity for caring about things enables us to be creators of value, the possibility of meaningful life does not depend upon there being anything that is valuable independently of ourselves. To believe otherwise leads easily to despair, as efforts to make sense of "objective value" tend to turn out badly. Locating the source of meaning in the activity of loving renders opportunities for meaningful life much more readily accessible.

7.   Wolf says that she is "inclined to describe . . . [herself] as ambivalent about wholeartedness." Her basis for this attitude is that she is against "zealotry, fanaticism or . . . close-mindedness." I am against them too, but my attitude toward wholeheartedness is quite wholehearted. I suspect that the apparent disagreement between us on this matter is due to misunderstanding.

My view is just that it is intrinsically desirable to be wholehearted and that, other things being equal, being wholehearted is better than being ambivalent. This naturally does not mean that it is always a good idea to be wholehearted. After all, other things are intrinsically desirable too, and wholeheartedness may interfere with them. There are unquestionably circumstances, among them those of the sort Wolf cites, in which "a certain degree of ambivalence, or at least openness to ambivalence, is called for."

Acknowledging this is entirely consistent with regarding ambivalence as being, like many things that we would prefer to be able to do without, a sometimes necessary evil. It is hardly tantamount to being uncertain or ambivalent concerning whether, other things being equal, one prefers ambivalence as such to confident wholeheartedness. Wolf quite sensibly thinks that it is sometimes a good idea to remain ambivalent. I doubt, however, that she values ambivalence for its own sake. My guess is that, considering ambivalence and wholeheartedness strictly in themselves, she is not really uncertain or ambivalent concerning which is the more desirable.

8.   In her discussion of freedom, Wolf invites us to imagine paranoid individuals who are content with their values and who thus have no problems with themselves. Of such people she says: "They may act wholeheartedly, exercising the will they want to have. But far from being free ... they seem to me to be examples of people who are trapped, constrained, shackled by psychological problems the very nature of which makes their problems (their shackles) impossible for them to see." There are several confusions, I believe, in Wolf's position concerning this matter.

I do not believe that a truly paranoid individual can be content with his values, or that he can fail to have problems with himself. If paranoia is understood as a genuine pathology, it is a disease with which people cannot be comfortable. On the other hand, "paranoid" may be employed merely as a term of abuse; and in that case, I can indeed imagine people who are abused by being referred to as "paranoid" and who fit Wolf's description. However, the wholeheartedness of such people does not merit the reservations that Wolf expresses. They are not "trapped" or "shackled" by their condition, any more than the rest of us are constrained by the limits within which nature and nurture have confined us.

Wolf is aware of this point. Perhaps it is true, she concedes, that "the problem with the paranoid and the cleanliness fanatic is not that they lack complete control of their deepest selves—perhaps we all lack that— but that what is *in* their control ... are irrational forces that warp their victims' ability to appreciate what is true and worthwhile, that is, to see things right." Evidently, when Wolf denies that people of the kind she describes are free, what she really has in mind is that their lives are warped by irrational forces and for this reason are deficient and undesirable. She is correct, of course, about that. But the fact that their lives are bad implies nothing concerning whether they are free. Free lives may not be good lives. Freedom is not the only good thing, and there is no reason to deny that there may be circumstances in which it is actually not worth very much at all.

Notes

1. The notions of caring and of loving are not the same. For the sake of convenience, however, I shall use them interchangeably in my discussion of Wolf's essay.

2. Wolf evidently shares my view that loving is intrinsically desirable. I am uncertain whether she also shares my understanding of what that view entails. In any case, she seems not to appreciate the way in which the intrinsic desirability of loving figures in my account.

3. Of course, the life Hitler chose turned out to have a significant downside for him as well. His mission failed, he felt that he had been betrayed, and in the end he killed himself. Even from his own point of view, then, Hitler may perhaps have made a mistake in deciding what to care about.

4. Wolf insists that "we want what people care about to have some worth"—for example, to be neither egregiously trivial nor morally offensive. It is indeed a pity if someone wastes his life on inconsequential matters. But if there were someone so limited that he could really do nothing better with his life than devote it to avoiding the cracks in the sidewalk, then it would be better for him to care about that than to care about nothing. As for our desire that what people care about be morally worthy, this requires a warrant from a judgment that immorality on their part will harm either their interests or ours. Morality has no independent claim in determining what to care about. Its claim can derive only from what someone does in fact care about.

9

Bootstrapping

Barbara Herman

bootstrap, *v. trans.* 1. To make use of existing resources or capabilities to raise (oneself) to a new situation or state; to modify or improve by making use of what is already present.

bootstrap, *n.* A strap sewn on to a boot to help in pulling it on or looped around a boot to hold down the skirt of a lady's riding habit; a boot-lace.[1]

The attraction of bootstrapping is that you use a bit of what you already have to get some place you haven't been before, but need to go. As a strategy of argument, it is environmentally neutral. No new resources—new entities or capacities—are called for; little of what you start with is wasted. The most compelling philosophical bootstrapping arguments occur when the subject is basic—objects; the causally ordered items of experience; the choices of a perduring self—analyzed in the first instance in a theoretically plain way. The resources used in the first explanation are such ordinary items as perceptions and concepts, desires, beliefs, and the like. The bootstrapping move is prompted when further thought about what the basic subject is like reveals complexity, or some vulnerability to skeptical challenge, that outstrips the carrying capacity of the first explanation. The bootstrap is made of the same plain materials, only attached in a different place, so as to provide additional elements of argument. The idea is to provide just enough leverage in the argument to give a better account of the complexity and/or meet the skeptical challenge. Its ontological and theoretical abstemiousness make bootstrapping one of the more elegant modes of philosophical prestidigitation.

No doubt bootstrapping is as old as philosophy, and Descartes the historical hero of the art. In Harry Frankfurt's extensive work on the will and what we care about, he is revealed to be one of its premier modern practitioners. Frankfurt's bootstrapping enterprise is especially powerful because he brings to his subjects a rich and detailed account of the phenomena, a fiercely independent assessment of the issues marked out by philosophical tradition, and, balancing a commitment to account for the phenomena richly described with resources that demand as little theory as possible, remarkable argumentative ingenuity. In what follows, I want to try to pinpoint the bootstrapping in one central area of Frankfurt's work concerning the will, both because I think that there is much to be learned from its use there, but also because it is important to appreciate, as Frankfurt clearly does, its limits. The issue, at the end, is about costs: of the limits, on the one hand, and of the strong assumptions needed to get past them, on the other.

The subject of the will is a natural area for the employment of bootstrapping. There seem to be things one wants to say about choice and action that call for talk about will and willing. But it remains obscure what the will is, and whether, even if we have reason to regard human agents as having wills, thinking that they do requires that we add a special item to our catalogue of mental stuff. I think we do have wills (that we must) and that the will is a distinct kind of faculty or capacity, connected in an essential way to our rationality. In this I follow Kant. Frankfurt too thinks we have wills, but the will we have is a matter of something like desire plus attitude, raised to a new state by a little bootstrapping. That's enough, he holds, for anything it is sensible to want an account of will to do, and is, moreover, the real heart of the matter about what makes human action special. Indeed, he will argue that it is just this will—desire plus attitude—that is necessary for successful reasoning, not the other way around. Since I am skeptical that one can succeed with an account of the will severed from a robust idea of practical reason, this is for me a useful place to look at the strengths and limits of bootstrapping. After discussing Frankfurt's view, and looking briefly at what I have come to think is a very similar strategy of argument in Christine Korsgaard's recent work, I will turn (or return) to what I see as the compelling attraction of following Kant on these matters.

I

But first a little background. In most modern philosophy, it is a given that Kant's view of the will is the one to avoid. (I include among the avoiders many so-called Kantians.) There are indeed good reasons for being uneasy about any robustly Kantian view of the will. There are also, as I will try to argue, at least some good reasons for thinking it offers the more satisfactory account of rational action. Many who find Kant's notion of the will hard to take seriously do so in part because of what he says the will is, but also in part because they can't see anything sensible for it to do. As a nonnatural cause, it is metaphysically unpalatable. As the mental side of action, it seems to add nothing when we already have belief, desire, and intention. As the carrier of authoritative practical principle, bridging the gap between reason and desire, it appears to beg the question it is introduced to answer. And as practical reason itself, it either loses any distinctive identity, or if it remains essentially connected to judgment and choice, it may seem to provide evidence of a category mistake: no mode of reason can do what a faculty of choice does.

Though I am not unmoved by these worries, I do not think they survive close scrutiny. Moreover, worries, like arguments, begin in assumptions. In this case, the assumptions not only make it hard to see how there could be answers, it is not clear how there could be worries. Suppose one starts with the idea that the mental equipment relevant to action for a rational human being consists of belief, desire, and intention, and whatever faculties and capacities are necessary to arrive at beliefs, recognize desires, and form intentions. And then one looks for the place to add the will. There is then something quite natural about Hume's response that what we call will is no more than the subjective impression of the working of the other parts as they yield up action.[2] Or that will is what Frankfurt early on called an agent's "effective desire": "[the] one that moves a person all the way to action."[3] That is, talk about the will is a way of talking about aspects of the work done by other things. One comes to the same conclusion even with a view of will that is more complicated. Suppose one thought, as Frankfurt also does, that volitions play a special role in the activity of rational agents: for example, to order and sort the material of desires in light of an agent's regulative commitments. It is not clear why such volitions have to be anything more than desires of a special sort: higher-order, endorsed, or even rationally formed desires, but just desires all the same. There would be no reason to think this matters—there are often good reasons to specially denominate some of a class if they perform special functions—unless one could show that there is something the will is supposed to do or be that could not be done by anything that was a desire. And that is not so easily made out. Then, given the premises of the worry (here's the equipment of action, why do we need the will?), there is no room for much of an answer (given the equipment, we don't).

I think we can glimpse some advantage to be had in taking the will seriously if we follow out a related dynamic that occurs in the now frozen debate about internal and external reasons for action. Kant-friendly views are thought to be at a disadvantage since they cannot explain the normative force of the considerations they claim are reasons, since nothing counts as a reason in the relevant sense that does not connect to antecedent desires or desire-like states. Attempting to reverse the argument, some on the Kantian side of things argued that the best reason to posit a bit of responsive subjectivity is the conviction that there are reasons of a certain sort.[4] That is, if we are on solid ground in thinking that there is a certain class of reasons, then it must be that, as rational beings, we can act for them. It is in a way the right thing to say, but it is not a satisfying answer.

One source of dissatisfaction comes from the fact that the table-turning answer shares a structure of reasons and motives with the Humean critics: a theoretically concessive model of claim and response. As a result, arguments to reasons stop short because they depend on psychological states external to what the reason is. When we offer reasons, we are presenting claims whose legitimacy for an agent will depend on something else: something subjective, or receptive. *I* come to see what reasons I have by reasoning from what matters to me (construed however widely); when *you* claim I have a reason, if the claim is normative, you must consider how what the reason picks out is connected to what moves me. Given this, the further claim that what it is to be rational is to be responsive to the reasons there are just puts the issue on hold.

What is missing is the idea that the value a putative reason carries plays a role in the subjective condition that makes it a reason for me. My valuing X, or valuing something that leads me to value X, may connect me motivationally to X: that is, when these conditions obtain, I accept X as a reason. What my valuing X does not do is make the *value of X* my reason. Suppose one wants to say: it is the value of honesty that gives one a reason to tell the truth; or the value of human life that makes need a reason for beneficent action. And suppose we accept an argument that shows we do have a reason to speak truthfully and reason to offer help because there is something "in us" in virtue of which we directly or mediately care about truth telling and meeting needs. If it is the former, if we just do care about truth telling or need-meeting, then the *value* of what we care about does no work in the generation of reasons; and certainly if we don't directly care, if we care to tell the truth because we care about something else, the reasons we come to have do not express the value that honesty or persons have—in themselves. This is part of what I meant in saying that the concessive arguments *to* reasons stop short. We lack part of what makes a reason a reason—a story of its value. If we want to talk about value as something separate and reason-generating, it is not obvious that we can do this within the internalist framework of reasons and motives for action. There is no room for value, as there was no room for will.

Further, if the explanation of what gives us a motivating interest in a reason is something external to it, then there is always an extra thing, a feature of our subjectivity, that *gives* us an interest in the reason—even if this extra thing is Reason. In the end, there is some mere given— an element of passive receptivity. Now many will find in this a simple truth, not a source of worry at all. And they may do so out of the not in itself unreasonable conviction that something has to be a mere given: explanations run out. But the route to the truism leaves unexplained our relation to the given (or the givens, if there are more than one). The uncertain space left for rational reflection undermines the very idea of deliberative authority or governance.

What is wanted (or what is wanting) is a way to talk about reasons that satisfies the internalist's motivational strictures but without sacrificing the idea that reasons track values. And if part of the motivational story is to lie in the connection between reasons and values, value must make the connection without dependence on agents' independent subjective states, or without looping through them in the wrong sort of way. To get beyond the limited Humean connections, but without positing awkward new entities, a bit of a bootstrap could seem to be the right tool for the task. As I read him, in his later work Frankfurt offers just such a bootstrapping account of reasons, or of some reasons, that would establish a nonarbitrary and noncontingent connection to values (or, if not all the way to values, at least to what one cares about). Whether this tightening of the connection can meet the just-mentioned strictures and conditions is to be seen.

II

On Frankfurt's analytical view of a human self, rational agency consists in a system of beliefs and desires, organized hierarchically through a process—acts—of reflection and identification.[5] But even before there is a self there is will. The story of will begins in desires: specifically, the set of desires one happens to have as a function of physiology and circumstance. Originally, pre-reflectively, we desire in response to our needs. Thus the first objects of desire will perforce be of a certain kind, though their local specification is adventitious. This is enough for there to be will. For Frankfurt, an agent's will is that desire which, by virtue of its effectiveness, leads her to action. So there is even will in a creature who merely has desires of different strengths, if it is so constructed that a stronger desire "wins" and issues in action. Will can be present in a creature who has no capacity to learn or to modify its desires, and, a fortiori, no capacity to (in some way or other) opt for the satisfaction of one desire rather than another. Sufficient for identification of an entity's will is the manifestation of a desire-based pattern in its behavior. An entity whose will is set—so that it must act one way rather than another—is said to have a nature. In higher creatures, ones that are volitionally complex, we talk instead of having or being a self: something with a more or less stable, and more or less accessible identity.

The exercise of a capacity for reflection—the acquisition of conscious beliefs and the capacity to employ them reflexively—can produce higher-order desires and volitions. (Can, that is, in creatures capable of being altered in these ways by the process of reflection.) Closure of the chain of desires is secured either through brute identification with some one of them, or through some more reflective endorsement. We may or may not like what we find in our desires. But what we do like, and like ourselves liking, we can be said to care about. Part of our volitional complexity lies in the fact that in caring, we not only like what we like, but we make efforts to preserve as well as to satisfy our preferences. There is thus a co-development of self and will which, ideally, yields a non-accidental coincidence between who we are—what we care about—and what we will. If our will forms as we come to care about things, our will has autonomy as we are reflectively satisfied with what we care about, and will what we will wholeheartedly. (Wholeheartedness is, by design, the practical analogue of the Cartesian norm of clear and distinct perception.)[6]

This much is enough to set (some) normative parameters for willing. On the one hand, not all of the things we might desire are, for most of us anyway, things we are able to desire wholeheartedly: not everything we desire will we find important, and many of the things we take to be important will not survive further reflection or comparison with other things we find important. On the other hand, it is important that we find things that are important to us, things that make a difference we care about, and that we succeed, as much as we can, in willing and acting for them without ambivalence. Reflection introduces a practical burden. Its normative parameters, however, have no special rational or metaphysical authority: they arise from our biological and material circumstances. We have malleable desires, reflective abilities that we cannot refrain from using, and only limited powers to shape the world (and ourselves). This gives us a task of identifying things to care about and ways of acting that minimize stress. Stochastic disrupters are ambivalence about ends, conflicts of desires, unrealizable ideals, insufficiently rich or complex ends, guilt and shame, the various forms of bad luck, and so on. Some of these we can manage; some are unavoidable.[7] We have a free or autonomous will just in case we have the will we want to have, and we can say we have the will we want to have when we find no further reason to question or be ambivalent about the will we do have. To be a person is to have solved this set of problems to a reasonable degree.

In case it is not obvious, the bootstrapping is this. Starting with the plain stuff of desires, beliefs, and some facts about our reflective and practical capacities and needs, a project of self-construction is described, the norms for which emerge from the building-process they regulate (especially its need for stability). The end-product is a hierarchically ordered self whose volitional system is regulated by the emergent norm of wholeheartedness. Granted that this is a highly schematic presentation of a nuanced and complex view, I believe it contains sufficient detail to address my question. Can the bootstrapping in the account of normatively structured development—from desire to self and from self to person with freedom of the will—get us the connection between motivating reasons and value?[8]

Although my sketch of Frankfurt's hierarchical view of the self did not make use of any notion of value—at least not explicitly—Frankfurt avails himself of value talk, just as we should expect. Value attaches to things that can be cared about—for their own sakes or in virtue of their relation to other things we value. The view is abstemious. To talk of value is not to introduce any new thing. Things with value are important; and what makes something important is that its presence or absence matters: the parameters are harm, pleasure, satisfaction, and the like. Thus *our* values—the things we value—shape our actions, decisions, feelings, and deliberations in the usual way. It is an imperative of agency that we care about or value *some* things (as opposed to no thing). And if we did not have things we found or took to be ultimately important—call them final ends—that guided us in the adoption of ends for action, we would not be persons; we would lack a condition of identity.

There is a gap, however, between things that might be said to be *of value* and the things we value. One wants room to say: we may or may not value things that are of value. The bootstrapping story allows us to say: if we care about the wrong things, we will tend to find our ends and projects unsatisfying, either because they cannot bear the weight we put on them, or because we come to believe that what we care about is in some way not important, or not as important as we thought. Though this may be true, it is not the same as saying that what we have valued is not *of value*. For recall that what we value, what we care about, begins in our desire or need, and is shaped by rational reflection. But the norms of reflection do not pick out or track truth about value. Their goal is to eliminate, as much as possible, elements in a person's values that undermine their role in securing practical identity and reflective satisfaction with life. The norms of reflection are ultimately set by the conditions of agency and identity; they guide us in gaining assurance that what we value as ends, especially as final ends, can be willed wholeheartedly. Like norms of justified belief that do not track truth, but, when satisfied, give us reason to think we believe what we do for the best available reasons,

the norms of practical reflection are a guide to confidence, not truth—
that is, to confidence in ourselves as valuers, not to any truth about
value.

In response, one might argue that, nonetheless, the norms are sufficient
for value to play the requisite structuring role for will and action. The
formal nature of what we value provides all the critical balance between
value and reasons we need. Some of our values leave us a great deal of
volitional discretion. Some do not. I greatly value good food and wine,
but they are not so important in the scheme of things that I must drop
what I'm doing when the opportunity for a good meal comes along—not
if there are other more important things to attend to, and even not if I
simply don't want to. Other ends and values, however, present us with
imperatives; we cannot truly care about them and just ignore their reasons. And some of those imperatives, Frankfurt argues—especially ones
rooted in our loves—can be unconditional, giving reasons for action that
are not or no longer "up to us." We can no more abandon them, or decide we just don't care to attend to their demands, than we can cease
being who we are.

Now you might think that if such ends can give unconditional reasons
for action, then there is a direct connection between values and reasons
to be had within the bootstrapped framework—at least for some values.
It is certainly true that love for my child gives me immediate reasons to
act for the sake of his needs—or at least for the more urgent ones. And
as I love him, and cannot cease loving him at will or at all, his welfare
gives me motivating reasons that are not "up to me." This supports the
right transitivity: if when I love I value unconditionally, my reasons are
unconditional as well. So surely in loving, the motivating reasons that I
come to have are directly connected to value.

But are these reasons that I have when I love connected to value in the
way I was looking for? I don't think so. The problem is that in loving,
the support for reasons is not any value inherent in the loved person or
the loving relationship. The welfare of the loved other is reason-giving
for me because, and only because, I care about him. So, in a sense, the
unconditioned reasons that I have are only relatively so. Given who I am,
and so what I love, I do have reasons that are not up to me, that are
unconditioned, and so unconditionally attached to the valued object. But

the *authority* of the reasons derives from *my* caring, from my activity of valuing.

We should not go too quickly past this. What Frankfurt has shown is that the possibility of unconditioned reasons does not, as one might have thought, require external value, or anything outside the orbit of bootstrapping. They can arise from the nature of our sensitivity and capacity for love—the way we value some final ends. These unconditioned reasons are not mediated by attachment to any other end; their motivational force is secured directly with the recognition of a reason's applicability. And since the end that supports the reason is one I cannot abandon, it functions, volitionally, as unconditioned value. But there is still a condition. There is the value-to-us of unconditioned ends, paradoxically conditioned by our need for them—namely, if we are to be persons. When I do not abandon my final ends, it is not because of *their* value; it is because they have come to play a co-constitutive role in my identity as a person. The work is being done by inertia. It is inertia of a special sort, to be sure: for what I cannot abandon is myself.

So we are left with a limited result. Whether or not I love things for what I value in them, it is my loving them that makes them valuable to me. And loving is important, but not because of the value of the objects of love, but because of the value (to me) of loving. Granted, there is no third thing between my loving someone and my motivation to care about him. If I love I care. But a third thing is there, one step back, in what makes love important. This is where we reach the outer limit of the bootstrapping.

I am not at all supposing that Frankfurt would find this conclusion disturbing. Part of his project is to trace the limits of our rational powers, and to move into a more central place in our philosophical reasonings the idea that will is much more a function of where we begin as sensitive creatures than most rationalist accounts of agency allow. This shift is exhibited in his focus on the volitional structure of love (or caring), as opposed to that of morality, for he wants to show that many of the "special" features of moral reasons and value that drive rationalist accounts (their unconditional requirements, their status as final ends) are shared by the reasons of love and care. This explains, Frankfurt argues, why our loves may give us reasons that truly compete with the reasons of morality. There is an implicit claim as well. And that is that morality too must fit into the story of will, desire, and reflection, if it is to be important for us, and to offer us reasons we will find authoritative.

Even though this is not Frankfurt's issue, it is not unreasonable to press it. For if morality is not amenable to the same bootstrapping moves that work for love and care, both the explicit and implicit implications may need to be qualified. Frankfurt's bootstrapping is so very attractive because it succeeds in providing a robust account of volition that satisfies internalist strictures. We get an account of willing that, because it is responsive to the demands of complex ends and allows for imperatives, so situates the agent that she is normatively responsive to reasons. But this is not the same as an agent acting for reasons that track the value of what is valued. If acting from love is the best case, then although we get reasons connected to the value of what we value, that turns out not to be the same as having reasons derived from or responsive to what is of value. For Frankfurt, the value of what I value is, in the end, its value to me. This may or may not be a problem for understanding the norms of love and caring; it is an obstacle where moral norms are concerned. One fails to act morally unless the content of one's reasons is determined by nonrelative moral value.

III

This suggests an option within roughly the same space of argument that involves a more radical internalist move of a rationalist kind, one in which Reason itself is the subjective source of moral value, and so of reasons of the right sort. The option is tempting not just because subjective conditions are now given two jobs instead of just one (Frankfurt's bootstrapping had that), but because there is a rational source of values that supports reasons to which they are also motivationally responsive. What will make a consideration a reason is the connection of some fact with a Reason-derived value. And what will make the reason effective in producing action is the same imputed feature of our rational nature. If reasons track Reason, we are awfully close to the idea that reasons track value.

The in-principle advantages of such a rationalist subjectivism are many. It rebuts the question-begging charge against the practicality of reason; it makes the right sorts of connections between value and reasons, and between reasons and motives; and, given the foundation of reasons in values that express principles of Reason, it is a subjectivism that does not require an additional elaborate story about how to secure agreement—objectivity comes with the source of moral values. However, an additional story *is* required about *who we are* that explains the priority to us of our rational, value-generating natures. That is, something has to explain *why* we will or should take the deliverances of Reason to be determinative for our choices, since we obviously need not do so. It would do no good if it turned out that Reason has been cast (or miscast) in the role of a special sort of desire, requiring something additional and itself authoritative to identify and secure the authority of Reason's reasons. This is a variant of a familiar rationalist dilemma. And familiar, if problematic, strategies of resolution are available: more bootstrapping of the "nothing offers reasons that are better than Reason's reasons" sort; identity arguments to the effects that following the dictates of reason is the necessary condition for our being agents at all; and transcendental arguments that raise the identity arguments to a new level—that the authority of Reason's reasons is the necessary condition of our being, practically speaking, an "I."

One finds this kind of rationalist subjectivism in some of Christine Korsgaard's work.[9] Though she uses a fuller notion of rationality than Frankfurt allows in order to forge the connection between reasons and value, the style of argument is remarkably similar: a relatively flat Humean starting point and a bootstrapping rationalism that is more Cartesian than Kantian in spirit. Korsgaard's framing idea, which she also shares with Frankfurt, is to exploit the connection between identity and autonomy to secure a route to rational and moral norms for willing. She would argue that actions are not, properly speaking, ours—we are not their authors but the site for forces working through us—unless the way in which we come to act is under the evaluative command of reflective reason. Like Frankfurt, she sees this as the condition for being fully a person, not a wanton. But unlike Frankfurt, she wants to get both formal and substantive rational constraints. The formal constraint is universality: reasons, to be reasons at all, may not be fully particular. The substantive constraint is that our reasons be such that through them we acknowledge the status of persons as autonomous agents—that is, as independent sources of value. The universal form of reasons is a necessary condition of agency; the norm of reciprocal relations among autonomous agents introduces morality.[10] We cannot act as agents at all unless we satisfy the formal condition. We can, however, act without the norm of reciprocity. Although as rational agents we must take something as giving us a sufficient reason to act, this could involve, at the limit, no more than the satisfaction of the Frankfurtian reflexive requirement that we have some stable final ends. Again, a third thing is required to connect morality to agency.

The Kantian argument one might expect to bring morality into an account of agency would show that there cannot be any final end that gives sufficient support for action, properly speaking, except rational nature as an end in itself. But that's an argument Korsgaard thinks cannot be made with the materials at hand. Only so much can be built on the conditions that we should be one, or whole, or unambivalent, or author of our actions; none of these is sufficient to pick out any substantive final end.[11] Further acts of reflection (the Cartesian move) can clean up our system of ends and secure full generality of reasons. So while the normative extension to having our ends and ways of acting be ones that others can endorse or share (reciprocity) will strike some, perhaps most, as fitting with their sense of themselves as rational agents, it need not do so. And unless it is not only rational to embrace morality but also irrational to evade it, the account remains incomplete.

This may partly explain why Korsgaard is increasingly drawn to a more Platonic rationalism. Plato offers a richer story of the self or soul, where Justice, a principle of Reason, brings right-order to the disparate needs and wants of a human being so as to constitute her a unified, autonomous person, one capable of being a true cause of action.[12] And, of course, Justice unifies the parts of the self in the right way, with an eye to the good of the whole.[13] The building-in of the substantive requirement, conjoined with an argument to show the inadequacy of all other principles of final ends, would of course close the gap between reasons and reason-based value.

Now in Plato, as in Kant, closing the gap calls for an additional and I believe essential portion of metaphysics. In Kant it shows up in the account of why the only possible law of an autonomous will is the moral law, and in Plato, in the explanation of how the good of the person, or the state, is the good to which reason looks (or explains why a principle of unity is a principle of good for the whole). The former requires a more metaphysically contentful notion of will, the latter, the teleology of the theory of Forms. Whether one can have the advantages of the Platonic story without the Forms is not clear. It is clear, and, I should add, clear to Korsgaard, that *some* richer metaphysics is needed. Her preference is for a robustly teleological account of action: seeing what the essence of rational action is gives the connection between the formal and the substantive norms of reason. But whichever way one goes to close the gap, bootstrapping is left behind.

What follows? To the extent that Frankfurt or Korsgaard would bootstrap their way from essentially Humean materials, plus a more complex story of the needs and identity conditions of agency, to the autonomous will, their conception of autonomy cannot outstrip the carrying capacity of the elements with which they begin. Frankfurt is not disturbed by this: having extended the notion of willing through the hierarchical ordering of desires and volitions, and making the will responsive to imperatives, he has all the autonomy or freedom of will he wants. Korsgaard is less well served by this method. Wanting more from the will, or from the concept of action, in order to bridge the gap between reasons and value for the sake of a moral imperative, more has to be built into the start-up conditions. Bootstrapping is not alchemy.

When we leave bootstrapping behind, however, we appear to be caught between the twin misfortunes of moral skepticism and serious metaphysics. But before we contend with this dire prospect, I suggest we go back to the beginning of the discussion where we acceded to the elements of an essentially (and intentionally) anti-Kantian characterization of will and action. Since, after all, the problem of bridging reasons and value might be thought to be a distinctly Kantian one, a reassessment of the advantages and pitfalls of Kant's own account of the will looks like a reasonable next step. I admit that what one takes to be the worse problem matters: some might find the embrace of anything at all like Kant's account of will and action a move so fatal that, by contrast, the problems I have been pointing to are no problems at all. But I don't think so. My thought is that we have so quickly shied away from the basic elements of Kant's account of will and value, or tried to domesticate them while holding onto Kant's main conclusions, that we may not really see the force of what he tried to accomplish with his conception of practical reason. The ambition of Kant's rationalism of value can no more be cast in Cartesian or Platonic terms than his views about action fit a Humean or neo-Humean moral psychology. With this in mind, I want to spend some time looking at Kant's view, if only to indicate how dramatically different things look when one approaches action as he does. The account will perforce be sketchy; I don't think that will obscure its point.

IV

As you may recall, Kant begins the main argument of *Groundwork* II this way:

Everything in nature works according to laws. Only a rational being has the power to act according to his conception of laws, i.e., according to principles, and thereby has he a will. Since the derivation [*Ableitung*—drawing off] of actions from laws requires reason, the will is nothing but practical reason.[14]

Much that is attractive and impossible in Kant's view is captured here. The attractive part is the description of our freedom to act according to *our* conception of laws, to act according to principles we represent as sufficient, or justified. The impossible part: that to have a will is to have a special causal power—the power to act from representations of law ("a kind of causality belonging to living beings insofar as they are rational"[15]). And there are other problems. First Kant claims that the will is "nothing but practical reason"; just a few lines later, however, he talks about the human will as one that "does not in itself completely accord with reason." Surely he can't have it both ways: either the will *is* practical reason, or it is not. If it is, then we do not easily understand how what *is* practical reason can fail to accord with reason; and if it is not, then what the will is, and how it relates to practical reason, seems up in the air. Among other things, a normative connection is missing. Now some of these problems arise from the interpretive presupposition that the Kantian concepts of volition, practical necessity, maxim, and imperative, are just terminological variants of familiar notions. Others, from the commitment, at all costs, to avoid the idea of will as a cause. The former can be corrected by more careful reading of Kant. The latter—making sense of the idea of will as cause—will take some doing.

Now it might seem crazy to try to do anything with Kant's idea of "the will's causality." And perhaps it is. But whether the very idea is insupportable is not the question I think we should ask first. First we need to understand more about what "it" is, and why it demands the commitments it does.

Things tend to go awry as soon as the discussion turns to maxims. Maxims represent actions as-they-are-willed; as such, they are the proper objects of moral (and practical) assessment. Interpretive custom is to view maxims as the means-ends principles behind actions: to do some action, in such and such circumstances, for the sake of some end. The action figures in the principle under an end-relative description (a pumping water if that's my job; a poisoning if I'm part of a terrorist group). The primary question of moral assessment is: is the principle morally justified? It is if it is universalizable; not if it is not. Nothing so far requires that we talk about will at all, or about value until we reach the final step of justification. And nothing explains how a maxim relates to any actual doing. It is natural to suppose that what brings the agent to action, given her maxim, is some desire or motive waiting in the wings, connected somehow or other to her end, that is causally sufficient to bring about the right activity. The maxim proposes, the desire disposes.

But notice that once again we are working with the tools of belief, desire, intention, plus a principle of justification and a commitment to using it (another belief-desire pair). Reason enters in judgment determining means-end fit and in assessing the universalizability of the resulting maxim. Certainly no nonrational being can conceive of its action through a principle, or employ standards of evaluation. So it must be that to have a will is to be able to do *that*. Or, to be able to do that *and* care about the deliberative outcome. As before, "will" picks out nothing that cannot be captured in Humean terms. It is no surprise, then, that all the key issues remain. Whether the evaluative principle on offer is plausibly a principle of reason will be determined by independent debates about what reason's principles are. And the separate issue of motivational sufficiency is handled by the positing of a special desire or interest (the fabled "motive of duty"). Why, though, interpret Kant as if he embraced a Humean method—starting from basic, separate elements of mind brought together by iterations of simple combinatorial mechanisms to yield an account of acting on principle? As if when the agent fits together her ends, means, intentions, and desires, she acts (or tries to), and so she has a will, and a maxim. Kant is no such methodological atomist.

If we pay closer attention to Kant's exposition, we see that a maxim is not constructed from the bottom up. An agent's maxim is a principle that expresses a complex volitional judgment. The fact that maxims represent actions *as they are willed* introduces formal features beyond means-to-end fit that entail an essential evaluative component.[16] When an agent wills, and so has a maxim, she sets herself to act in a particular way, suited to promote an end, *as* she judges that-way-of-acting-for-that-end to be good. She therein conceives of herself acting in accord with a principle or standard of value. But that's not all. The standard of value or conception of the good in terms of which we conceive our actions cannot be alien to the will. If it were, we would be back where we started, with a gap between the material of action, its subjective side, and claims we might want to make about the reasons a person has.

Kant avoids the gap this way. To have a will is to have a capacity to be moved to action via a conception or representation (*Vorstellung*) of law. When one wills, that is how one is moved—by means of a conception. It is easy to think this means: *qua* rational agent, when I set myself to act, I make use of representations or conceptions of laws to determine how to reach my ends—bits of theoretical reasoning. And certainly, as a rational being, I do that. But that's not what it is to have a *rational* will. Kant's idea is that such a will, as a capacity to be moved to action by means of an agent's conception of a law, does not move us to action by means of a conception of just *any* law. Neither a representation of the law of gravity, nor of the lawlike connection between arsenic and poisoning would move one to action. There would have to be, in addition, a desire not to fall or not to die. And if one were moved in that way, one wouldn't need a will. (This seems to me exactly the point that Hume presses.)

However, among the laws we can and do represent to ourselves is the law constitutive of the will's own causal power. That law can only be, Kant argues, the moral law, a principle of best or sufficient reasons.[17] This is the idea of the moral law as a law of freedom. Now without defending either of these claims, I want to describe some of what they do to our understanding of willing. So Kant can say: in willing an action, one is moved by a perceived connection of an action to a representation of the principle of best reasons. There are not two things here that need to be matched up: the will and the principle of best reasons. The principle constitutive of the will's own activity *is* the principle of best reasons;

it is what we represent to ourselves as the basis of rational choice. When we get it right—when we correctly understand what the best reasons are—we act from the moral law as the final justificatory principle of our action. Of course we do not always get it right, or choose for the best; nonrational influences can affect the representation of the will's own law (as they can our representation of any law). Thus it is true both that the will is practical reason, and that, for us, willing may not always be in accord with reason.

Suppose this is right—about Kant, I mean. The connection he makes between will and value is then not something that can be constructed from or analyzed into Humean components. A being with a will is a certain kind of cause: one capable of initiating action by deriving it from her representation of the will's own principle. An action, so derived, is what a maxim represents. That is why, if the agent misrepresents the will's law, the maxim's failure under universalization will be imputable to the agent's willing. (And also why the mark of moral failure registers as a contradiction: if we think of the categorical imperative procedure as representing the constitutive law of the will, the faulty maxim presents as a law of willing a principle that cannot be a law.) When an agent acts "from duty," the action is derived from an accurate representation of the will's law (which is then the action's subjective principle; it was always the action's objective standard). Like the classical practical syllogism, the movement from principle to judgment to action is one. There is no separate motive. (Thus, we should thankfully note, no dour "motive of duty" either.)

Is there still room to talk about faulty action as free action? Faulty action is derived from misrepresented value, from an agent's defective volitional judgment about what is best. If by free action one means, as Kant does, action derived from the will's own principle, then the action is free in that sense. (Analogously, we say that mistakes in addition are mistakes *in addition*—that is, a result is derived from relevant arithmetic principles misapplied, perhaps, with self-serving lack of care. Unfree action is like a child's assertion of a sum, for no arithmetic reason.) Faulty action is thus imputable to the autonomous will, since the principle of the maxim is a representation—albeit a *mis*representation—of the will's own law.[18]

Looking back to the concerns that provoked this discussion, it may be useful to summarize some of what is novel in Kant's way of thinking about will and rational action. First, the derivation of action from the constitutive principle of *volition* provides a noncontingent connection between value and reasons. Failure to be moved by a reason is a sign of a deliberative error, not a lack of subjective connection to the reason's value. Second, action requires no separate motive. Because it is derived from the will's causal principle (as a specification of it), we get the normativity of reasons without having to add other motives or desires, even the special motives of rational agents.[19] Third, our rational nature is not a source of reasons in competition with anything else. No additional principle is needed to give warrant to reason's reasons. Interests we have may cause us to misrepresent what reason requires; they may cause us to be mistaken about what's best. This sets a task for practical and moral education to transform desires so that they are sensitive to reason, both by giving them appropriate objects, and by making them internally reason-responsive.[20] The good will is then the will whose willings are right—where the derivation of action gives rise to a maxim whose principle is the (correctly represented) law of a free will. (This rather neatly leaves room for empirical mistakes that do not undermine the moral worth of action.) That is why when one acts from the moral law, it is precisely the value of so acting that moves one—it is one's reason for action.

In contrast with the will of bootstrapping arguments, the Kantian will is not made up of or developed from simpler elements by identification or any kind of endorsement. The starting point is a different one. There needn't have been creatures with rational wills, but there are. And insofar as there are creatures with rational wills, there is a power to produce actions that there would otherwise not be. That is, if the rational will is a causal power, if it is a distinctive way of bringing things (actions) about, then its active principle will not be the mechanical principle of cause and effect (which, of course, does not bring things about but explains their occurrence), but a principle of the kind of cause it is—a rational principle of causality. In order to talk about the will of a rational agent, then, one has to introduce conceptual elements that would not be required except for the existence of the rational will. This is metaphysics, not bootstrapping. (Indeed, if it were bootstrapping, things would go much easier for Kant: no need for the third chapter of the *Groundwork* or for the Fact of Reason.)

And finally, there is the bridge problem. On Frankfurt's view the reasons one has ultimately depend on what one values. That is why there is no direct bridge from action or agency to morality at all. This is not a difficulty for Frankfurt. Morality will show up in due course as a condition (no doubt a very important condition) of various things that make human life go well. For Kant, the bridge is present in the idea that the law of the rational will's causal power is the moral law. The law of the Kantian rational will is, simply (!), the condition of free action, and thus is, *eo ipso*, the moral law. So it really is metaphysics all the way.

That leaves us with the elephant in the living room: the will as a kind of causality and all that. We need to be careful about what we take the problem to be. If we are worried about the will's causality because we do not countenance any mental causes, then I would hazard that the worry is not about Kant, and in any case depends on views about explanation and materialism or science that are not themselves compelling. I think we should argue that we have reason to accept the will as a cause because it provides the best explanation of what we do when we act morally, and, perhaps, whenever we act in a way that is directly responsive to value. I have tried to indicate why one might want such an explanation, and some of the costs of doing without it. If the worry is about the will as *noumenon*, we want to be sure we understand what Kant wants from this idea. It is one thing if he is committed to some higher or other reality beyond or behind ours. But it is doubtful he has any such idea (or that, consistent with his views, he could). Certainly, the idea of mental cause does not by itself require noumenal causality. That is why I take the will not to violate but to extend our "one world" account of what there is.[21] Some have argued that all this is easier if we adopt a "two standpoints" view of action. This leaves me uneasy. Either volitional judgment is sufficient for action or it is not. Of course much depends on what it means to think of ourselves as free causes "from a practical point of view." But unless the will's own law *is* the principle of rational action—not how we think of it, but what it is—then there is room for skeptical challenge to the authority of reason's reasons.

The point I would press is really one about methodological priority. I don't know whether there can be a metaphysically acceptable account of the kind of cause Kant thinks the will is. On the other hand, we don't understand much about this kind of cause apart from what we can say about the will. So trying to see what motivates Kant's idea of will and willing seems to me some kind of plain good sense. And I have tried to suggest that some things we want to say about reasons and value are available to us if we take Kant's account of the will seriously. It would be unfortunate to lose these insights because of premature metaphysical squeamishness. In arguing that what we want cannot be had with beliefs and desires and truly virtuoso bootstrapping, I hope to have offered some pragmatic reasons to be more open-minded about the will itself.

Notes

1. *The Oxford English Dictionary*, second ed., electronic text.

2. David Hume, *A Treatise of Human Nature*, second ed., ed. L. A. Selby-Bigge and P. H. Nidditch (Oxford: Clarendon Press, 1978), 399.

3. Harry Frankfurt, "Freedom of the Will and the Concept of a Person," in *The Importance of What We Care About*, 14.

4. The best examples of such arguments are in Thomas Nagel, *The Possibility of Altruism* (Oxford: Oxford University Press, 1970), and Christine M. Korsgaard, "Skepticism about Practical Reason," in her *Creating the Kingdom of Ends* (Cambridge: Cambridge University Press, 1996).

5. The summary of Frankfurt's view of agency is drawn primarily from the following set of his papers: "Freedom of the Will and the Concept of the Person," "The Importance of What We Care About, and "Identification and Whole-heartedness" in *The Importance of What We Care About* (Cambridge: Cambridge University Press, 1988); "On the Usefulness of Final Ends," "The Faintest Passion," "On the Necessity of Ideals," and the two lectures on caring, "Caring and Necessity," and "The Necessities of Love," all in *Necessity, Volition, and Love* (Cambridge: Cambridge University Press, 1999).

6. Doubt drives further reflection and the formation of higher-order desires and volitions; wholeheartedness is achieved when one can no longer see any reason to doubt or foresee conflict. So I might begin with an ambition-driven will to promote my career, but then be uncertain when I see that so willing might yield conflict with other things I care about or might come to care about. I cannot will wholeheartedly until this is resolved. It will be resolved when I am satisfied with what I will and I do not foresee disturbing conflicts.

7. It is not clear, for example, that things we can separately embrace whole-heartedly are things that together give unity to our wills, or that this is a reasonable ideal for an individual on her own. Given what we love, loss is not something extrinsic to it.

8. Where, if values do not directly support reasons, reasons at least nonaccidentally track values.

9. There are hints in "Skepticism about Practical Reason" and pieces of the view in "The Reasons We Can Share," both in *Creating the Kingdom of Ends* (Cambridge: Cambridge University Press, 1996), but what I am calling the rationalist

subjectivism begins to play a dominant role only in *The Sources of Normativity* (Cambridge: Cambridge University Press, 1996), Lecture III, and then in "Self-Constitution in the Ethics of Plato and Kant," *The Journal of Ethics* 3 (1999): 1–29.

10. This is put in Kantian language—ends and ways of acting must be possible subjects of universal legislation that all can endorse or share—but its separation from the formal constraint is a sign that it is not a move in a Kantian argument.

11. Korsgaard accepts this conclusion at the end of "The Normativity of Instrumental Reason," in *Ethics and Practical Reason*, eds. G. Cullity and B. Gaut (Oxford: Clarendon Press, 1997).

12. "The actions which are most truly a person's own are precisely those actions which most fully unify her and therefore most fully constitute her as their author." For this reason, Korsgaard considers Justice to be a principle of *self-constitution*. "Self-Constitution in the Ethics of Plato and Kant," 3.

13. Ibid., 19.

14. Immanuel Kant, *Grounding of the Metaphysics of Morals*, trans. J. Ellington (Indianapolis: Hackett, 1981), Ak. 412 (using the Prussian Academy numbering).

15. Ibid., Ak. 446.

16. One could represent the actions of animals in terms of means-ends principles, but they would not for that be acting on maxims—not even if they were somehow conscious of so acting.

17. My thanks here to Carol Voeller, whose recent work on Kant's metaphysics of action has helped me to understand many of these issues much more clearly.

18. A question remains about why one would care about getting one's willing right, since of course one can get it wrong, and indeed one will have interests that are better served if one does. Kant's answer is found in his curious discussion of the incentives of the will, where he argues that the interest in correctness of willing is *necessary* in any imperfectly rational being. This is a complicated business that I will take up elsewhere. The thing to note here, however, is the change in order of argument. When bootstrapping, absent the interest, one cannot get to reasons. Here, the connection between reasons and value is secured first. The appeal to interests comes after; it explains how one comes to care about oneself in doing what one in any case has to do. The caring is not necessary in order for us to act correctly; it is the causally necessary effect of the moral law on our sensible nature, transforming what counts as a life worth living.

19. Of course, strictly speaking, what follows on the derivation from principle is a *willed* action; whether bodily movement of the appropriate sort then occurs is a question for a different story.

20. The point of moral education is not just to make us good. It responds to a demand of our freedom—to express our capacity to make reason our rule.

21. It may be that the Kantian will is not an object of sense, and so not a possible object of experience. It would not be the only thing about ourselves we had a priori warrant to believe.

REPLY TO BARBARA HERMAN

Harry Frankfurt

1. Barbara Herman maintains that "it is the value of honesty that gives one a reason to tell the truth; or the value of human life that makes need a reason for beneficent action." That is a rather natural way of understanding our attitudes toward telling the truth and toward beneficence, and it sounds plausible. However, I think that it is misleading and philosophically obfuscatory. In my view, it is not to the value of honesty or to the value of life that we respond. We respond simply to honesty and to life themselves. Our response, if we are among those who do value honesty and life, is to care about truthfulness and to care about living.

What it is that makes us care about them is an interesting and important issue, which is worth more sustained consideration than it ordinarily receives. Truthfulness appeals to us in several ways. There is an unobstructed transparency in truthful relationships, which facilitates relaxed communication and a comfortable sense of immediacy; lying is frequently a cumbersome and unreliable maneuver; and, of course, the truth is often helpful and we depend upon it for our lives. As for our caring about living, which is so fundamentally determinative in establishing the criteria that guide and that justify our practical reasoning, there is hardly any reason to look further than the guarantee it derives from the workings of natural selection. We are simply built in such a way that living is important to us.

In any case, whatever explains our attitudes toward telling the truth and toward acting beneficently, there is no need to resort to construing value as being—in some metaphysically substantive sense—inherent in the things that it makes sense for us to value. Rather, the explanation derives from facts concerning what we care about. As I see it, the relationship between the value of honesty or of human life and our response to them is just the reverse of what Herman claims.

2. Against this way of looking at the matter, Herman objects that it makes reasons and reasoning depend on "some mere given—an element of passive receptivity ... [and this] undermines the very idea of

deliberative authority or governance." She fears that it leaves "room for skeptical challenge to the authority of reason's reasons." Now it is certainly true that, on my view, what counts for us as a reason depends on what we care about and thus on contingent aspects of what we ourselves are like. It does, as Herman says, depend on a given. However, I think that it is inappropriate to characterize this given as "mere."

In my view, there really is no authority for us other than the authority of what we care about—or, more particularly, the authority of love. What we love is what we care about in a way that is not up to us. It is its necessity, together with the fact that it defines our will, that provides it with authority. The authority of love is the authority for us of our own essential nature. This has very little to do with reasons or with a response to value. What is the authority that supports and vindicates our love for our infant children? Surely it is not from reason that this love derives its authority, nor is it from any perception that the infants are of value. Most of us are simply built in such a way that we cannot help loving our children. This love creates reasons for us to take care of them. Love is what explains and warrants our counting the fact that some course of action would be in the interests of our children as a reason for us to pursue it.

Herman supposes that reasons must track values. My view is that values track love and that love—if we look to the end of the story—has no reasons. Acknowledging that our vaunted rationality is grounded in "passive receptivity" may strike some as an abject and unacceptable confession of failure; but however we may feel about it, that's the way it is. This is especially obvious with respect to the value of life. As I have already noted, we consider life valuable because we are programmed by natural selection—that is, in virtue of our passive receptivity to the controlling influence of natural selection—to care a great deal about living. There is no other philosophically significant truth, so far as I can see, about the value of life. So I reject Herman's notion that our values must be understood as having some reality apart from our independent subjective states. We often do act for reasons that are independent of anything we happen to feel about what we are doing, but the fact that we count these things as reasons for acting does depend on our subjective states.

3.   After articulating my thesis that "the value of what I value is, in the end, its value to me," Herman says: "This may or may not be a problem

for understanding the norms of love and caring; it is an obstacle where moral norms are concerned. One fails to act morally unless the content of one's reasons is determined by moral or objective value." My own view is that we act morally when we are moved by love for a certain kind of world or a certain kind of life. The moral law may be in a sense objective, because it is an objective matter what sorts of conduct are required in order to promote the realization of that world. However, the objectivity of the reasons that these requirements generate is grounded in nothing but the subjective necessities of love.

4. Herman's account of my position is not only extraordinarily comprehensive and accurate. It is also sensitive and insightful, presenting my views in ways that bring out quite vividly just what they amount to and what they count for. This is especially the case when she observes that, on my account, "the norms of practical reason are a guide to confidence, not truth—that is, confidence in ourselves as valuers, not to any truth about value." That is exactly right. The problem of moral skepticism, with which Herman is concerned, is not a problem about truth. It is a problem about confidence.[1]

I do not need to prove to myself that it is okay for me to love my children and to regard them as exceptionally valuable to me. I have confidence in that, even though quite a large number of reasonable people do not love my children or consider them to be especially valuable. Many philosophers and other people think it is important to find ways of demonstrating conclusively such things as that it is reasonable to tell the truth, and to refrain from murdering people, and from inflicting pain gratuitously. They are not satisfied with the fact that many of us are moved lovingly—as a matter not of choice but of volitional necessity— by ideals of straightforwardness and of consideration for others.

But why are they not satisfied by this? If someone tries to interfere with my children, I will try to fight him off. If someone tries to interfere with our efforts to bring about or to sustain the kind of world we love, why should we not be as confidently disposed to fight him off? We do not need any knockdown reason for knocking him down, other than the reason that he is trying to damage something we love.

5. Confidence is more or less the same as what Spinoza refers to as "self-esteem" when he says (*Ethics* iv52s) that "self-esteem is really the

highest thing we can hope for." It is a matter of self-satisfaction or, what comes to the same thing, of wholeheartedness. It is readily understandable, of course, that we wish other people would try to achieve goals of greater interest to us than their own self-esteem. If they persist in caring about things to which we are indifferent, or that are inimical to what we love, there is likely to be trouble. Nonetheless, I find Spinoza's notion quite compelling. How could we hope to do anything better for ourselves, after all, than to live in such a way that we are satisfied with what we are?

Note

1. This is like what Descartes says, at the beginning of the *First Meditation*, about his struggle against skepticism with regard to knowledge. He does not there characterize the beliefs he wants as true, but as stable and permanent. Herman points out that my interest in wholeheartedness parallels Descartes's interest in clear and distinct perception. Although she says this is "by design," the fact is (at least as I recall) that it was inadvertent; I was not aware of the parallel until she pointed it out. I do not mean, of course, that it was a matter of chance. My philosophical thinking has been deeply influenced by the sustained effort that I made, many years ago, to understand what Descartes was up to.

10

Love's Authority

Jonathan Lear

I

Love, according to Harry Frankfurt, not only exerts power, it commands authority. In this way, love differs from "the mere pressures of emotions and desire." What is the nature of this authority? Frankfurt thinks it lies in a consideration of crucial features of the lover's will. "The authority for the lover of the claims that are made upon him by his love is the authority of his own *essential nature as a person*. It is in other words, the authority over him of the *essential nature of his own individual will*." Frankfurt says that the essential nature of a person is to be understood "as including the characteristics that define his essential identity." And, he elaborates: "Our essential natures as individuals are constituted ... by what we cannot help caring about. The necessities of love, and their relative order or intensity, define our volitional boundaries."[1]

Let us leave to one side precisely what is meant by these phrases, and simply assume we have a working understanding. Let us also leave to one side the details of Frankfurt's argument. For the moment all I want to do is state Frankfurt's thesis about the locus of love's authority. The reason for doing this is to make it clear what a striking thesis it is. However contentious the analytic-philosophical community tends to be, I think everyone would agree with this claim: that Harry Frankfurt is interesting. He is interested in interesting ways about interesting things. For over thirty years he has been delighting us with deep and fascinating thoughts about what is involved in being a person. And if we reflect on that delight, I think we shall see that Frankfurt has elicited a response that comes from the best part of ourselves.

Frankfurt's central idea about love's authority is this: The lover, in acting against the dictates of his love, ultimately betrays himself.

Now the fact that a person betrays himself entails, of course, a rupture in his inner cohesion and unity; it means there is a division within his will. There is, I believe, a quite primitive human need to establish and to maintain volitional unity.... It seems to me that the authority that love has for us is closely related to this compelling and irreducible need to protect the unity of the self. Since the commands of love derive from the essential nature of a person's will, a person who voluntarily disobeys those commands is thereby acting voluntarily against the requirements of his own will. He is opposing ends and interests that are essential to his nature as a person. In other words, he is betraying himself.[2]

To say that this person betrays himself is to put it mildly: the unity of his essential nature is at stake.

Note that the overall structure of Frankfurt's authorization bears a striking similarity to Kant's transcendental deduction. Kant sets out to show what authorizes the categories of judgment, and he concludes that authority ultimately resides in the unity of the individual ego. On the surface, this is a surprising result. One might have thought that authorization would have been found in the structure of judgment itself, rather than in the structure of the person who makes the judgments.

The analogous result is even more surprising in the case of love. Intuitively we take love to be one of the most important configurations of the soul, if not *the* most important, by which a person reaches out to the world. It is surprising that the authority for this reaching out should lie in the integrity of the individual will.

Is it too surprising? Might Frankfurt's argument be unselfconsciously entangled in a philosophical tradition that tends to justify all sorts of reachings out to the world—for knowledge, in judgment, morality, and in love—by appeal to the unity of the ego? Obviously, we cannot answer these questions without actually looking at the argument. Much will hang on how we are to understand our "essential natures as persons." But, for now, I should simply like to sketch, by way of contrast, an alternative picture of authorization.[3]

In Freud's last theory, love is one of the two basic instincts in human life.[4] Love is a fundamental force that promotes the growth of ever-more differentiated unities. One of the most significant differentiated unities is that of ego-and-world. For the mature Freud, the individual psyche is itself a psychological achievement. The biological infant is not born with an intact ego, nor with a clear sense of the boundaries between self and world. Rather, he is born into a less differentiated "infant-mother field."[5]

The infantile ego forms by differentiating itself out from the mothering world but does so in a way that keeps it in essential relation to that world. In general, the acquisition of psychological structure—for instance, the formation of a will capable of practical reason—is always itself a psychological process which occurs in ever more sophisticated relations to worldly objects. This whole process is, for Freud, a manifestation of love. And one of the most sophisticated developments is the formation of a will capable of structuring itself according to the dictates of the mature love that Frankfurt describes.

From this psychoanalytic point of view, the ego is always *essentially* in relation to objects. By "essentially" I do not merely mean that being in relation to objects is a central task of the ego, but that by reflecting on ego-development and function we come to see that "being in relation to objects" should be part of the very idea of the ego.[6] From this perspective what would authorize love, even for the lover, would not in the first instance be the essential unity of his will. Rather, it would be the essential unity of his relation to the world. Frankfurt says that there is a "quite primitive human need to establish and to maintain volitional unity"— and this does seem to be a psychological claim. From the current perspective, this primitive need is itself a manifestation of an even more fundamental need: to stay connected to the world. Volitional unity is of course important to those who have achieved it, but, developmentally speaking, it is the last in a series of psychic configurations of staying willfully connected to the world. From this point of view, what would be centrally important about volitional unity, even to the lover, would not be the unity of the will per se, but the types of connection to the world that that unity permitted. What would authorize love, even for the lover, would ultimately be love itself. (Obviously, much more needs to be said to fill out the picture.)

II

So far, I have not examined Frankfurt's argument. Perhaps there is something about it that will inescapably focus us on the essential nature of the individual will. The connection seems to come in his claim that (a certain form of) love is (a certain form of) autonomy. For Frankfurt, "the idea of autonomy is the idea of self-government": "individuals are autonomous to the extent that they govern themselves."[7] But Frankfurt differs significantly from Kant in what self-governance consists in. First, the autonomous will, for Frankfurt, need not be giving a law to itself. Individuals "are in fact governing themselves to the extent that the commands that they obey, whether based on rules or not, are their own commands."[8] Second, the autonomous will need not be a pure or a priori will. Indeed, Frankfurt thinks that the "pure will is a very peculiar and unlikely place in which to locate an indispensable condition of individual autonomy."[9] This is because the pure will is devoid of any of the contingent features which make the person the particular person she is. As Frankfurt says, "the pure will has no individuality whatsoever."

These emendations of Kant may be of great value in considering individual autonomy, but they also impose a burden. Frankfurt is working out a notion of autonomy in relation to Kant, but Kant was trying to work out the formal conditions under which a pure will could be said both to be free and subject to law. If we take away both the purity of the will and the subjection to law, it is not clear what is left of the Kantian notion of autonomy. That is fine, *if* Frankfurt can give a substantial characterization of what he means by autonomy. That is the burden. If autonomy is "self-governance," we need to know what, for Frankfurt, this self-governance is.

It is at this point, though, that Frankfurt's argument becomes dense to the point of obscurity. Let me quote the passage and then offer an interpretation:

Someone is *heteronomous* when what he wills is not determined exclusively by *the inherent nature of his will* but at least partly by considerations that are *conceptually* inessential to it. These *conceptually* inessential considerations are *separable* from his will, and in that respect they are *logically external* to it. Now insofar as a person's will is affected by considerations that are external to it, the person is being acted upon. To that extent he is *passive*. The person is *active*, on the other hand, insofar as his will determines itself. The distinction between heteronomy and autonomy coincides, then, with the distinction between being passive and being active. If it is indeed possible to be autonomous by virtue of submitting to the ruling passion of love, it must be possible to be ruled by love without thereby being passive.

In many of its instances, love is fundamentally passive. It is passive when the lover is motivated by an expectation that obtaining or continuing to possess the object of his love will be beneficial to him.... In one way or another ... the object strikes the lover as being capable of providing him with gratification or with joy or with some desirable state. This is the essential basis upon which his loving the object depends: his love is conditional upon his attribution to his beloved of a capacity to improve his condition in life. What mainly binds him to the object of his love, whether he is prepared to acknowledge this or not, is a preoccupation with his own good.[10]

This much is clear: the aim of the argument is to link *heteronomy* with *conceptually inessential* with *logically external* with *passive* with *self-interested love*. Correlatively, it aims to link *autonomy* with *conceptually essential* with *active* with *self-disinterested love*. But what do these terms mean and how are they related? My problem is that what I take to be the best interpretation is not, I think, the one Frankfurt himself adopts.

Here is an interpretation that will make the claims come out true. Let us assume that it is part of *the very idea* of the will that a will is constituted by its final ends. Then what is *conceptually essential* to the will are the final ends that are essential to it. There are various ways to parse this, but let us assume that essential final ends are those final ends that the will cannot help but have. (Granted, we still need to give content to what is meant by "cannot help but.") Then what is conceptually inessential to the will are its means, nonfinal ends, and final ends that the will could abandon. (Similarly, we still need to give content to what we mean by "could.") Given this sense of *conceptual* inessentiality, we can stipulate that these features are *logically* external to the will. And then we can define *passivity* in terms of externality: anything that "affects" the will from "outside."

How, on this interpretation, does ultimately self-interested love come out as passive? Suppose that what essentially motivates Brad is the joy he feels in loving. Then he may genuinely fall in love with Jennifer. He may spend all his time thinking and acting for her well-being. But, given that his essential motivation is the joy of loving, Jennifer is only a conditional end. We can *imagine* him giving Jennifer up and loving someone else as a different means to his essential final end. What Brad really cannot give up is the joy-in-loving. And we can give some intuitive sense to the idea that this kind of love is passive. For having an essential final end of joy-in-loving, Brad is now dependent on the world for finding ways to attain it. In finding Jennifer, he is affected by her: thus his love is passive.

This interpretation has the virtue of making all of Frankfurt's claims come out true. But it depends on stressing the *conceptual* nature of this inessentiality. For suppose we take into account some humanly realistic sense of *psychological* necessity. And suppose Brad is ultimately and essentially motivated by his own joy-in-loving, but that as a matter of psychological fact, he cannot help but get it through Jennifer. As Neil Sedaka memorably put it, "breaking up is hard to do." This is, I think, a very plausible human situation, though we may still lack the conceptual resources to describe it adequately. For what we want to say is that, as a matter of psychological fact, Brad cannot help but love Jennifer, but that nevertheless that love is not essential to him in the sense that that love is pursued for the sake of a more ultimate and essential end: his own joy-in-loving. We want to say that Brad has gotten entangled in his own psychological necessities, but that what really motivates him is the pursuit of his own joy.

A gap seems to have opened between what, for lack of better terms, I shall call conceptual essentiality and psychological necessity. In this latter case, Brad's love of Jennifer is both conceptually inessential and psychologically necessary. It is conceptually inessential in the sense that we can imagine—perhaps even Brad can imagine—him pursuing his essential final end without Jennifer. But it is psychologically necessary in the sense that as a matter of brute psychological fact, Brad cannot possibly give her up. (Thus we have both a conceptual and a psychological sense of "cannot help but" and "could.")

In conversation Frankfurt has said that he did not mean to stress the conceptual nature of the essentiality or nonessentiality. Rather, he meant to speak in the broadest terms about what a person cannot help but will. On this construal, psychological necessities would count as part of the will's essential nature. But then there is no basis for linking ultimately self-interested love with passivity or with heteronomy. Brad's love would now come out as essential to his will, and thus as autonomous and active. But it would remain ultimately self-interested.

Frankfurt has to choose: *either* he has to give up the correlations he is trying to establish between autonomy, essential nature of the will, activity and disinterested love, on the one hand, and heteronomy, inessential nature, passivity and self-interested love on the other; *or* he has to restrict his conception of the essential nature of the will so as to exclude many psychological necessities. Frankfurt would then have to admit that there are many things we "cannot help but" will psychologically speaking, but which are nevertheless not part of our essential natures. And he would have to give a substantial account of which necessities count as part of our essential natures and which do not.

In terms of the overall argument of this essay, the important point is that Frankfurt has not yet worked out a fully satisfactory conception of autonomy. He has made potentially valuable emendations of Kant: allowing an autonomous will to be shaped by contingent particularities and not especially concerned with law. But, in the short run, at least, these changes have left it unclear what, precisely, an autonomous will is. And if we do not yet know what an autonomous will is, then there is no particular argumentative pressure for us to locate love's authority in the individual autonomous will.

III

Active love, for Frankfurt, is selfless.

Loving of any variety implies conduct that is designed to be beneficial to the beloved object. In *active love*, the lover values this activity for its own sake instead of for the sake of advantages that he himself may ultimately derive from it. He is motivated by an interest in serving the interests and ends of his beloved rather than by an interest in serving his own.[11]

Again, to make this correlation come out right, it seems we need to be thinking in terms of what is conceptually essential to the will rather than what is psychologically necessary. Otherwise, Brad's love for Jennifer would come out as active, yet ultimately self-interested. So let us pursue this notion of active love in the sense that makes Frankfurt's claim come out true. That is, although more work needs to be done to clarify the revised notions of autonomy, activity, and so forth, I am nevertheless going to work within Frankfurt's overall framework.

The paradigm of active love, for Frankfurt, is a certain kind of parental love for a child. Though an actively loving parent will have an interest in the child, that interest is not itself motivated by any anticipation of benefits for the parent. What motivates the parent is the welfare of the child. Thus the parent's interest in the child is itself "entirely disinterested." "The interest that moves the devoted parent is unquestionably *personal* but it is also utterly *selfless*."[12]

Now this seems to have an odd consequence:

Although active love as such is valuable to the lover only for the sake of the benefits that it provides to his beloved, it is also true that it is valuable to him for its own sake. The loving is valuable to him for its own sake, however, *precisely* and *only* because of its utility. Serving the ends and interests of his beloved is something that he values as an end in itself. If he did not consider his loving devotion to be instrumentally valuable in providing benefits to his beloved, it would not be intrinsically valuable to him.[13]

But let us imagine a person, Abelard, held totally incommunicado in prison, actively in love with his Heloise. Abelard knows that Heloise will never even know of his love and will certainly never benefit by it. Does his love thereby lose intrinsic value for him? Or, are we to conclude that if Abelard continues to love, it must after all be ultimately self-interested? This seems wildly counterintuitive. Abelard *may* accrue certain benefits from his love: it may keep him sane, organize his life, give him something to live for. But it seems wrong to conclude that these *must* be his ultimate motivations if he continues to love in these circumstances. Surely, it must be possible for Abelard to continue actively to love Heloise precisely because he actively loves her: she is an essential final end. In these circumstances, Abelard's love may indeed be a source of great pain: because he cannot benefit her, yet continues to love her, he suffers. He would then accrue no benefit for himself and he would know that his love conferred no benefit on his beloved, yet he would continue to love.

Think of our love for the dead. Our continuing love for the dead can be a source of unbearable pain. It is not out of the question for a person to conclude that, when it comes to his own self-interest, he would be better off dead too. And yet he continues to live and continues to love. It must be possible for this to be active love. And it must be possible for the lover to treat that love as having intrinsic value, even though he recognizes that it no longer has utility for his beloved. It seems to me that we need a conception of active and autonomous love that fits these conditions.

IV

In conclusion, I should like to share two intuitions in the hope of reviving a Platonic idea: that love's authority derives from the fact that it is aimed onto the good.

The first intuition comes from reflecting on the relation of slave and master. Intuitively, this is the paradigm of lack of freedom: the slave's will is entirely subservient to the will of the master. Still, on Frankfurt's account, a solution to the slave's predicament is to fall actively, autonomously, selflessly in love with his master. He then makes his master's ends his own ends—and not for any selfish benefit, but simply for the sake of his master.

Of course, the slave cannot choose to fall in love in this way: it is not up to him. It is important to Frankfurt that "the unconditional importance to the lover of what he loves is not a voluntary matter. The [active] lover cannot help being selflessly devoted to his beloved. In this respect he is not free. On the contrary, he is in the very nature of the case *captivated* by his beloved and by his love."[14] In this way, we *fall* into active love. But, then, if this should happen to the slave, it would seem on Frankfurt's view to be his lucky day. Indeed, if he does so fall in love, then, on Frankfurt's account, he violates his own essential nature if he acts to end his enslavement. We arrive at the unusual conclusion that the slave violates his own self-respect if he acts to free himself.

I suspect that Frankfurt might be somewhat sympathetic to this position, for there is a distinguished philosophical tradition according to which freedom consists in falling in love with necessity. Thus we are at home in the world when we freely choose to live according to its necessary principles. I do not want to go into the details of this position. I only want to remark that insofar as this position looks plausible it is because the necessities at issue are not transparently evil.

Slavery, by contrast, is a transparent evil. That is why I am inclined to say that even if the slave can fall autonomously in love with the master (in Frankfurt's sense), even if he gains real psychological benefit from so falling in love, even if his love constitutes the essential nature of his will, nevertheless love has no authority here. The reason is that love by its nature aims at the good, and in this case the aim of love has been thoroughly perverted.

Of course, the slave may well think that his love aims at the good. Indeed, the slave may even *think* that his love is authorized by the essential nature of his will—but he would be mistaken. And he would be mistaken even if he were correct about the shape of his will. The reason is that he has unified his will around aiming toward a conception of the good that is not simply mistaken, but *absolutely perverted*. In our understanding of aiming, we need to distinguish distortion from absolute perversion. Since Plato's Cave, at least, it has been a familiar idea that human beings often live their lives distorted by fantastic images of the good. Even so, we can recognize that these prisoners of fantasy are aiming at some distorted image of the good. The prisoners in the Cave are *imprisoned* at a certain level: and each of them has at least the possibility of a painful ascent. None of them is in freefall.[15] When we see a person who is actively aiming at *descent*, though he thinks he is in the process of *ascent*, we realize that nothing can authorize this. Even for the slave: his will may be unified, but he mistakenly takes himself to be aiming toward the good. If he were to understand his true position, he would know that it is better for him to have a disunited will, and be conflictedly struggling toward a good.

In short, an essentially unified will *looks* like it might be the basis of love's authority for the lover, but only because there is a background assumption that the lover is aiming toward something good.

Furthermore, it is worth noting that when philosophers talk about the unity of the will, they tend to be concerned with a synchronic unity—unity at a given moment. Psychoanalysts, by contrast, tend to be concerned with some peculiar form of diachronic unity. Freud took very seriously an obvious fact about humans: that we need to construct narratives of our lives that make a certain kind of sense. We strive to have some kind of understanding of ourselves as enduring in more or less consistent fashion over time. Often, significant parts of an analysis will consist in an analysand revising her account of who she is and how she got to be where she is. In the search for self-understanding, there is always a danger that the search itself will become a defense: that one will end up "finding" more unity than in fact exists. Indeed, to find the genuine unity of a person's will over time, I think one needs to accept that there will often be moments of serious disruption, breakdown, and regression. Some of these disruptions may be self-induced, others may be imposed—but the upshot in both cases may be an occasion for growth and reconfiguration. It is not uncommon for a person to discover an essential final end by betraying it. One betrays an ideal, one betrays a love—and in so doing discovers how essential that ideal or love is to one's very being. One deepens not only one's self-understanding, one deepens one's will through an act of self-betrayal. In this way, the unity of the will *over time* may be achieved precisely by betraying one's essential nature in a moment.

Of the slave in love I want to say that even if in breaking with his master he betrays himself, he does not thereby fail to respect himself. Quite the contrary, in betraying himself—and thus in disrupting the unity of his will—he acts in the service of a better unity that may become his will after he has broken through his (currently self-imposed) enslavement.

V

Finally, I should like to consider the phenomenon of envy.

Frankfurt contrasts love with an emotion like jealousy, and claims that while jealousy may have great power to grip us, it has no authority.[16] "However imposing or intense the motivational *power* that the passions [like jealousy] mobilize may be, the passions have no inherent motivational *authority*. In fact, the passions do not really make any *claims* upon us at all. Considered strictly in themselves ... their effectiveness in moving us is entirely a matter of *sheer brute force*."[17] Though the feelings may be powerful, an emotion like jealousy is no more than "volitional raw material."

> The volitional attitudes that a person maintains towards his own elementary motivational tendencies are entirely up to him. Passions such as jealousy and craving provide him with psychic raw material, as it were, out of which he must design and fashion the character and structure of his will.... Whether a person identifies himself with these passions, or whether they occur as alien forces that remain outside the boundaries of his volitional identity, depends upon what he himself wants his will to be.[18]

Clearly, it is important to distinguish passions from structuring principles of the will and to distinguish mere pressure from authority. But when we look to the actual phenomenology of love and jealousy, we see that the situation is more complicated than the one Frankfurt describes.

Love and jealousy can both exist at different psychic levels. Love can be a feeling, I think, and as such a question can arise for the person what, if anything, to do about it. But love can also, as we have seen, be a structuring principle of the will. Something similar is true for jealousy. Psychoanalysis teaches us that the formation of the capacity for practical

reason in an individual occurs in the context of core unconscious fantasies which structure a world-outlook. Thus a person may not only *feel*
jealous, he may *be* a jealous person. And by this I mean not merely someone who is disposed to feel jealous. Rather, his core unconscious fantasy
structures a world-outlook in which jealousy is often the appropriate
emotion. So, for instance, as soon as a friend has something, Henry is
disposed to see it as something he *really* wants. He can therefore feel
jealous and deprived. However, if that friend had not acquired that
thing, Henry would have had no interest in that possession. It is in the
context of this world-outlook that Henry forms his ends and means. If
we *start* to investigate Henry's essential nature by investigating the
essential nature of his will, then there is something important about
Henry we can never know.

Frankfurt says that whether a person identifies with his jealousy or
whether it remains outside his volitional identity "depends on what he
himself wants his will to be." This does not seem to be true. Of course,
there is a possible situation in which a person with a developed capacity for practical reason feels a pang of jealousy and decides what to
do about it. But in the universe of human-psychological events, such an
occurrence is sophisticated and rare. In general, identification is a nonrational, unconscious mental activity. The psyche—in particular, the
capacity for practical reason—is formed in part by innumerable projec-
tions and introjections which constitute the environment in which the
will operates. As a matter of psychological fact, the will is always already
constituted by identifications. These identifications are not a matter of
what a person wants his will to be. Rather, they supply the background
context against which any such wants are formed. By the time Henry can
decide whether to identify with or reject a particular feeling of jealousy,
he has already been constituted as a jealous person.

Jealously, like love, is still aiming toward the good. A jealous person
may do great harm to others and to himself, but he is still aiming to get
some good. If he gets angry and destructive it is because he wants a good
that someone else has.

Envy is different. At least as psychoanalysts use the term, envy differs
from jealousy in that envy aims for the bad.[19] Envy too can be both
an emotion and a structuring principle of the soul. The envious person
wants to harm another because it is bad for him. In this sense, envy provides a horrific mirror image of love. It is even possible to use Frankfurt

to formulate conditions for heteronomous and autonomous envy. The envy is heteronomous when a person seeks the bad for another, but is ultimately motivated by a personal satisfaction in obtaining that bad. The heteronomously envious person not only takes pleasure in the demise of another, the obtaining of that pleasure is ultimately the reason he is doing it. The autonomously envious person, by contrast, has set the harm to another as an essential final end. He may or may not obtain satisfaction from the harm of another, but that is not why he is doing it.

Does envy have authority? Let us simply assume that a person can structure his essential will around envy. He takes the harm of another as an essential final end. And let us further assume that as he reflects on his envy he correctly sees that the essential unity of his will is at stake. He therefore concludes that his envy has authority for him. Is he right about that? I cannot speak with confidence here, but I would like to suggest that the answer is "no." The suggestion is this: envy essentially aims at the destruction of one's connection to the world. Envy is not another way of staying connected to the world, it is a way of disrupting that connection. But the will is *essentially* a connecting-to-the-world, so that in acting enviously one is attacking the will itself. This is so even in the case where the will has envy as an essential final end. Indeed, I want to make the paradoxical claim that *especially* in the case in which envy is an essential final end that envy itself has no authority. The reason is that the will's essential need for connectedness is even more primitive and fundamental than its need for internal unity. When it comes down to a limiting case like envy, openness to the world trumps internal coherence. These remarks do not constitute an argument, but they do, I think, point in the direction of one.

It seems to me particularly appropriate to end on a note of suggestion. There is no more fertile thinker at work today on what is involved in being a person than Harry Frankfurt. I hope that this paper stands as some small testament to the kinds of thinking that Frankfurt's own thought can provoke in another.[20]

Notes

1. All quotes in this paragraph are from "Autonomy, Necessity, and Love," in *Necessity, Volition, and Love* (Cambridge: Cambridge University Press, 1999), 138 (my emphasis).

2. Ibid., 139.

3. I do not argue for it here, though I do make at least a first attempt at arguing for it in *Love and Its Place In Nature: A Philosophical Interpretation of Freudian Psychoanalysis* (New Haven: Yale University Press, 1999). See also my introduction to Hans Loewald, *The Essential Loewald: Collected Papers and Monographs* (Hagerstown, Maryland: University Publishing Group, 2000).

4. Or drives (*Triebe*).

5. See Loewald, *The Essential Loewald*; and D. W. Winnicott, *Maturational Process and the Facilitating Environment* (New York: International Universities Press, 1965); *Through Paediatrics to Psycho-Analysis* (London: Hogarth Press, 1975). Perhaps a word about terminology is appropriate. I have recently heard committed fathers object to the characterization the "infant-*mother*" field—in a way that is reminiscent of earlier feminist objections to the use of "he" as the indefinite third person pronoun. And, to them, it is not an adequate response to say that by "mother" one does not mean the biological mother, but anyone, of any gender, who performs mothering functions. For them, even to characterize these functions as "mothering," as opposed to "parenting" or "nurturing," is to distort the true picture. I suppose it is nice to live in a time of changing conceptualizations and shifting vocabulary. I am tempted to follow the lead of a rock star and say that what Loewald and Winnicott are talking about is "the function (formerly known as mothering)." But in fact the vocabulary has not (yet) undergone such a shift—though it may. So perhaps what we are talking about is "the function (which may soon be formerly known as mothering)." For short, I shall continue to follow Loewald and Winnicott and call it "mothering."

6. See Loewald, "Ego and Reality," in *The Essential Loewald*.

7. Frankfurt, "Autonomy, Necessity, and Love," 131.

8. Ibid., 131.

9. Ibid., 132.

10. Ibid., 132–133 (my emphasis).

11. Ibid., 133 (my emphasis).

12. Ibid., 134 (Frankfurt's emphasis).

13. Ibid. (Frankfurt's emphasis).

14. Ibid., 135 (Frankfurt's emphasis).

15. I discuss the significance of the structure of the Cave in *Happiness, Death, and the Remainder of Life* (Cambridge: Harvard University Press, 2000).

16. Frankfurt, "Autonomy, Necessity, and Love," 136.

17. Ibid., 137.

18. Ibid.

19. Melanie Klein, *Envy and Gratitude: A Study of Unconscious Sources* (New York: Basic Books, 1957).

20. I would like to thank Gabriel Richardson for helping me to think through some of the central issues in this essay.

REPLY TO JONATHAN LEAR

Harry Frankfurt

1. The account of ego-formation that Lear sketches is, on the whole, one that I accept. In any case, I have no quarrel with his notion that the ego is essentially related to objects. I agree that it cannot exist outside of such relationships, and that this is the most primitive or fundamental condition of its existence. Moreover, I have no particular quarrel with the suggestion that the development of relations to objects may appropriately be construed as "a manifestation of love." To be sure, the more elementary modes of this development are not manifestations of the sort of disinterested love with which I have mainly been concerned. Nonetheless, it seems reasonable to think of the latter as more sophisticated formations that depend upon and that may derive from the former.

Of course, human beings are not the only creatures that have relations to objects. Lesser animals have them as well. If subhuman creatures that have relations to objects do not have egos, it is because they are not self-conscious or reflective in the particular ways that are distinctive of human life. The formation of a fully developed human ego, with a robust sense of self and a capacity for disinterested love, obviously requires not only a relationship to objects but the formation of a certain complex structure within the psyche as well. This psychic structure too is a condition of the existence of the ego, which implicates not only a person's connection to the world but his connection to himself as well. Lear insists that the most fundamental need of the ego is to stay connected to worldly objects. Acknowledging the priority of this need is entirely consistent with my claim that the ego must also maintain the integrity of its inner structure. Whichever need is more basic, it is essential to satisfy both.

2. I understand autonomy to entail subjection to the essential requirements of the self, not as defined in legislation promulgated by the pure will (as for Kant) but as defined by the dictates of love. Lear has led me to recognize an error in what I said, in the essay he discusses, concerning the relationship between autonomy and love. In that essay, I distinguished two modes of love—active and passive—and I argued that being

ruled by love counts as being autonomous only insofar as the love that rules is active rather than passive. I should not have made this a condition of autonomy.

Following the dictates of love does not constitute acting autonomously because the love is active rather than passive. It constitutes acting autonomously simply because love is essential to the nature of the self. When it is being moved by love, the self is moving itself rather than being moved by something external to its own nature. The distinction between active and passive love is an important one, but it was a mistake on my part to invoke it as critical to the understanding of autonomy. The commands of love are issued to the person by himself, regardless of whether the love is active or passive, just in virtue of the fact that love defines the boundaries of the self.

There is no "gap ... between ... conceptual essentiality and psychological necessity." Volitional necessity is a form of psychological necessity. Love is volitionally necessary and, for that reason, it is a defining and hence essential (though not, of course, a logically necessary) feature of the will. Needless to say, it is not a defining feature of will as such. The will that love defines, and to which it is "conceptually essential," is the particular will of the lover.

3.   A person acts autonomously when he is moved by love, since he is then moved by the essential character of his own will. Now what about the issue of authority? Loving is one of the most important ways in which a person reaches out to the world. Lear finds it surprising that I locate "the authority for this reaching out" in the integrity of the individual will. But I have never said much—certainly not in the essay with which he deals—about the authority *for* love. What I located in the integrity of the will is the authority *of* love, which is a different matter entirely. In speaking of the authority of love, I was not referring to whatever authority may provide a warrant for love but to the authority that love itself deploys. Much of Lear's critique of my views is due, I believe, to his neglect of this distinction.

Let us consider his discussion of the slave who falls in love with his master. My account implies that this slave would act autonomously when, out of love for his master, he serves his master's ends. I see nothing wrong with accepting this implication. When the slave comes to love his master, he embraces his fate and finds joy in loving its maker. This is quite analogous to Spinoza's escape from the bondage of passivity in a deterministic world through an intellectual love of God. Of course, whether the slave is to be regarded as lucky for falling in love with his master depends partly on what his master is like. Loving a person who takes advantage of the love leads to trouble for anyone. On the other hand, loving a benign and competent master, who has the interests of the slave genuinely at heart, might turn out very well.

Another relevant consideration in evaluating the slave's love for his master is whether a superior alternative is available to him. The determinism with which Spinoza was concerned has its source in God or Nature, from which there is no escape. However, the slave might be able to do better than by identifying his master's will as his own. The autonomy he achieves by coming to love his master is genuine autonomy. But it might also be possible for him to achieve autonomy through escaping from his master; or his life might be better, though perhaps more stressful and shorter, if he defied his master and refused to obey him. Autonomy is not the only good thing in life, nor should it be assumed that it is in itself so good that nothing else matters.

Lear anticipates some such response from me, and he acknowledges that "there is a distinguished philosophical tradition according to which freedom consists in falling in love with necessity . . . [and] we are at home in the world when we freely choose to live according to its necessary principles." I have indicated that Spinoza belongs to this tradition and, I cannot help adding, so does Freud. Nonetheless, Lear has reservations about it. "Insofar as this position looks plausible," he says, "it is because the necessities at issue are not transparently evil"; but slavery is a transparent evil. I will certainly not dispute that slavery, considered simply as such, is transparently evil. However, it seems obvious to me that a slave who achieves autonomy within his slavery may thereby improve his life.

Apparently, Lear is prepared to admit this. The point he wishes to make does not concern whether there is a benefit to the slave in loving his master. It concerns the authority of love. "Even if [the slave] gains real psychological benefit from so falling in love . . . , nevertheless love has no authority here. The reason is that love by its nature aims at the good, and in this case the aim of love has been thoroughly perverted." Since the slave's love for his master brings "real psychological benefit," one might think that it does aim at something good even if it does not aim at "the good." Presumably, we are supposed to understand that the aim of love is somehow "thoroughly perverted" by the slave insofar as he aims at preserving (albeit while improving) something—his slavery— that is inherently evil. However, Lear offers no argument for his claim that "love by its nature aims at the good," and the claim is in any case so vague that it is difficult to know how to evaluate it.

4.   What does Lear have in mind when he claims that the love of the slave for his master "has no authority"? His basis for making the claim is that slavery is a transparent evil. But how is this supposed to be relevant? When I say that love has authority, I do not mean to be saying anything at all about the quality of its aims, or about whether it is on the whole a good thing or a bad thing. I mean only to say something about the structural role of love in a person's life and, more particularly, something concerning the sort of impairment a person will suffer if he fails to accede to its dictates. One might well say that if a certain love is not a good thing, then it is unfortunate for it to have this authority. But nothing in the notion of authority rules out the possibility that genuine authority may be possessed by something that is unwholesome or evil and that, all things considered, its authority should be defied.

I do not know to what extent Lear and I actually disagree here, because it often appears that the issue pertaining to authority with which he deals is quite different than the one with which I have been concerned. Thus, he says: "When we see a person who is actively aiming at descent, though he thinks he is in the process of ascent, we realize that nothing can authorize this.... If ... [the slave] were to understand his true position, he would know that it is better for him to have a disunited will, and be conflictedly struggling toward a good." In my view it *might* be better for the slave to have a disunited will than to identify his master's will as his own. My point about the authority of love is just that our basic and natural resistance to having a disunited will is what gives love its authority over us. I never suggested that this resistance should always have the last word and that it can never be a good idea, all things considered, to accept a disunited will.

The issue of authority that concerns Lear has to do with what authority there is *for* loving. He believes that the authority for loving derives from a presumed relationship between love and the good. Be that as it may, it is not pertinent to my view regarding the authority *of* loving. My view does not bear on the question of how love is to be justified. Rather, it concerns the nature of the claim that love makes upon us. Identifying the nature of this claim implies nothing as to whether, or under what conditions, it may be reasonable for the claim to be resisted or defied.

5. In his remarks about jealousy, Lear recalls my statement that whether a person identifies with his jealousy is up to him; and he objects that "identification is a nonrational, unconscious activity." He is certainly right about this. Identifying or declining to identify with a certain feeling or inclination may be accomplished nonrationally and unconsciously, and I regret not having acknowledged this more explicitly.

Lear observes that "envy essentially aims at the destruction of one's connection to the world . . . , but the will is essentially a connecting-to-the-world, so that in acting enviously one is attacking the will itself." It is not so clear to me that envy does in fact have the aim that Lear ascribes to it. What he says about envy is more plausible, I would have thought, as a characterization of hatred. Hatred does aim, at least in many instances, at the destruction of what is hated. Insofar as the aim of hatred is to eliminate its object, it aims at eliminating itself. Someone who hated everything, or who experienced no attitude other than hatred, would therefore be committed to undermining his own psychic survival. Perhaps this shows that hatred is essentially irrational.

11

On Frankfurt's Explanation of Respect for People

Joseph Raz

Harry Frankfurt's writings aspire to the condition of jewelry. He crafts his work not merely, as most of us do, to facilitate understanding, but to give his insights such consummate shape that their wisdom will shine on all who behold them. Is it the result of his early fascination with Descartes? Is that why he practices philosophy as if philosophical truths worth knowing can be, and should be made to be, *clara et distincta*? Or is it an older ideal at work, the ideal that the true is also the beautiful, and to attain its goal philosophy must be beautifully shaped?

One example, to me a particularly tantalizing one, of the craftsman at work is his essay "Equality and Respect."[1] Within its typically small frame it is really two essays: the first and main one, a sequel to his justly famous "Egalitarianism as a Moral Ideal,"[2] explains his rejection of equality as a moral ideal. In the second, subsidiary one, Frankfurt explores for the first time the moral role of respect for people. Having long agreed with his rejection of egalitarianism, I was glad to join him in his exploration of respect, a subject that for many years I found elusive and slippery. This essay is an account of that personal exploration, an account of where it started, and where it led, of its balance of success and failure.

I Starting Point: The Question of the Independence of Respect

The basic question is whether there are any reasons for respecting people.[3] Granted that sometimes we respect people and sometimes we do not, that some of our actions express respect, some others express disrespect (and others still may express neither), still the question is: do we have reasons to respect people so that our respect for them is a response to specific reasons to respect them. "What else could they be?" you may wonder. Of course there are specific reasons to respect and to show respect for people. Doffing one's hat may be something that respect for another requires on certain occasions. Or, standing up in class before speaking may be required as a mark of respect for the teacher, or for the class itself. Similarly, people show their respect for their hosts by dressing up to go to their dinner party, and they show how little they think of their hosts by failing to do so, by turning up slovenly and unkempt. All these are symbolic actions that we have reason to take, when appropriate, in order to show our respect for some people or institutions or causes, and so on. I will refer to them as cases of symbolic respect.

There is no doubt that we often have reasons to take such actions, and that those reasons are to show respect where respect is due. They are reasons for respect. We ought to respect certain people or institutions, and we ought to take such symbolic actions to manifest our respect. It is equally clear that where respect for people is thought to be a central feature of moral thought, symbolic respect is not what people have in mind. First, the meaning and appropriateness of symbolic actions are determined by social practices and are not among the immutable precepts of morality. They can, of course, be applications to specific circumstances of general moral precepts. But second, the moral doctrine of respect for people claims that we owe respect to people *qua* people, whereas symbolic respect typically distinguishes between people by their skills and accomplishments, social position, or some other contingent criteria. Some instances of symbolic respect may be applications of a universal doctrine of respect for people, but not all cases of symbolic respect can be accounted for in this way. To make sense of *respect for people* we need an account of respect that is independent of symbolic respect. It should explain how we can respond to reasons to respect people (or other objects), and how we can manifest our respect for people and other objects other than by symbolic actions. And it must explain how there could be reasons to respect people and other objects for what they are, for aspects of their essential nature, as well as other reasons to respect them for their contingent accomplishments. Only then will it be possible for *some* cases of symbolic respect to be explained as instances of respect for persons.

This reflection helps explain that in searching for a moral doctrine of respect for people we cannot be confident that there is some common, familiar concept of respect whose explanation, when it takes people as its object, constitutes a statement of the doctrine we are looking for. Our search is guided by some inchoate understanding derived from our studies of moral philosophy. The search is internal to moral philosophy. It does not arise directly from the notion of respect as used in everyday life. Its difficulty derives from the fact that we are not happy with what previous writers wrote on the subject, yet we feel that there was some elusive truth they were after. Most specifically, we owe much of our thought about respecting people to Kant's doctrine of people as ends in themselves and members of the kingdom of ends. There is much in Kant's views on these matters that we reject, yet we feel that he half got hold of a significant moral truth that we are struggling to grasp.

Struggling, and often failing at the first hurdle. For many people suppose that there are duties of respect, that there are reasons to treat people in some ways or not to treat them in some ways simply because they are to be respected, and treating them in those ways is what respect for them requires of us. Yet it is not easy to see how this could be so. After all we respect people if we treat them as they should morally be treated.[4] But that means that the way they should morally be treated is determined by other considerations (they should not be made to suffer, should be helped in their valuable endeavours, should be protected from destitution, and so on). Once these considerations are determined we know what we ought to do. They are moral reasons, and we should follow them. A byproduct of following them, a byproduct of doing our moral duty, is that we will be respecting people.

If that is so then there are no duties of respect as such. Respect is what we show when we do what we otherwise have to do. We need not worry about respect. We will respect people willy nilly, simply by doing what we have non-respect-based reasons to do. The conclusion is to deny the existence of a moral doctrine of respecting people as a source of reasons or duties toward people.

Some see the special role of a doctrine of respect for people as determining status. It determines not how to treat people morally, but that people are of moral concern. They enjoy a moral status, and therefore one should look for moral reasons, moral duties or prohibitions regarding their proper treatment. Plants, according to some, differ from people in that regard. There is no doctrine of respect for plants, and that means that they do not enjoy moral standing. They do not count, as people say.

Therefore, we need not seek for moral prohibitions, or duties, regarding the ways they must or must not be treated.

Such doctrines of status are not, however, easy to understand. David Copperfield, when a child, is forbidden to play with Peggotty, because one should not play with servants. We can imagine that his case, as understood by his stepfather, is governed by two kinds of considerations, call them considerations of intrinsic merit and of status. Considerations of intrinsic merit determine that an appropriate playmate is one who is willing to play in a friendly, cooperative spirit, abide by the rules, be fun, and so on. In all these ways Peggotty is a very suitable playmate. However, considerations of status determine that one should not associate with members of a social class lower than one's own, and therefore, even though intrinsically she is a good playmate, one may not play with her. This is the way that some people understand doctrines of moral standing, and they reject them for the same reasons that make us suspicious of the social status rule that helped to ruin part of Copperfield's childhood, and was so unfair to Peggotty. According to them: people can suffer from pain, hunger, and other afflictions, and so can other mammals. Intrinsic considerations show that it is wrong to cause pain and other afflictions to mammals, human or otherwise. The only possible effect of introducing a separate doctrine of status is to deny the application of reasons where they do in fact apply. Although we must respect people, there is no similar doctrine of respect regarding other mammals, and therefore, we must not cause pain to people; but there is no reason not to cause pain to other mammals, since they do not count. But if the reason for not causing pain applies to all animals, how could a doctrine of status absolve us from following it? If, as some may think, there is no reason to refrain from causing pain to animals of other species, would not that have to be a result of the content of the reason to refrain from causing pain (i.e., it would be a reason that does not apply to other animal species), and not a result of a doctrine of status whose effect is to exempt us from following reasons where they apply?

The question is: once a reason to treat someone in some way is established, what room is there for a doctrine of respect to determine who counts? Is it not plain that so far as that reason goes all those to whom it applies count and that is the end of the matter? And the same goes for any other reason. So if there is reason not to hurt, that reason applies to those who can be hurt; a duty not to kill would apply to all those who can be killed. Of course, if the duty not to kill is explained by reasons that do not apply to all living creatures, then it would not apply to all. If we should not kill because we should not abbreviate people's expectation of life, or because we should not prevent people from conceiving and engaging in worthwhile enterprises, then we should not kill any animal whose expectations of life would thereby be curtailed, or whose ability to conceive and engage in worthwhile activities would be interrupted. Not all animals, indeed not all human animals, will meet this condition, and therefore not all of them are protected by the injunction against killing. The details of the example do not matter. What matters is that there is no room, or so the argument goes, for a doctrine of status to determine the scope of application of reasons or duties. The grounds of those reasons or duties determine their scope.

Some readers may be nodding wisely: it all shows, they may say, that if you forget that the doctrine of respect is a product of constructivism in ethics you will never be able to understand it. Personally, I am not confident that constructivists have an easier time in explaining the meaning and role of the doctrine of respect for people. But as I have difficulty in understanding constructivism in any case, I am no fair judge of the matter. Perhaps the conclusion should be just that: one has no room for a doctrine of respect except within a constructivist account of morality. But it is premature to conclude so as yet. All we need is some understanding of respect for people as a source of special moral reasons or duties (I'll not distinguish here between types of moral considerations). With that in mind we may turn to Frankfurt to see how he understands the doctrine.

II Frankfurt's Respect

Frankfurt's concern with respect is secondary. His main aim is to reinforce his objection to egalitarianism as a moral ideal. In the course of doing so he distinguishes between concern for equality and other, more legitimate, concerns. Thus he invites us to consider that a person who has enough of something may still object to having less of it than others have, not because he minds the inequality as such, but because, in the circumstances, its existence offends him for "it suggests to him that whoever is responsible for the discrepancy has failed to treat him with a certain kind of respect."[5] "Treating a person with respect," Frankfurt explains, "means, in the sense that is pertinent here, dealing with him exclusively on the basis of those aspects of his particular character or circumstances that are actually relevant to the issue at hand" (150). Respect, therefore, "entails impartiality and the avoidance of arbitrariness." "Those who wish to treat people with respect aim at outcomes that are matched specifically to the particularities of the individual" (150).[6]

In these initial remarks Frankfurt is following the natural road that regards respect as a byproduct of following right reason. Frankfurt emphasizes impartiality and absence of arbitrariness. One can, of course, fail to act for all relevant aspects of a case without acting arbitrarily and without displaying partiality. But absence of arbitrariness and partiality are—like respect—byproducts of following sound reasons. There are no special duties of avoidance of arbitrariness. One avoids it by acting as one should, for independent reasons, act.[7] Similarly, these remarks suggest, there are no special duties of respect. One respects people by treating them as one should, for independent reasons, treat them.[8] Frankfurt as much as makes the point himself when he remarks that treating people with respect is "an elementary aspect of being rational" (152). But at this point his exploration takes a new direction.

Frankfurt remarks that the importance of respecting people is moral and therefore cannot be explained by the desirability of acting rationally, since irrationality as such is not immoral, whereas failing to respect people is. So while in respecting people we do nothing more than act as reason requires, there must be moral reasons for respecting people, reasons other than the fact that doing so is rationally required:

The lack of respect consists in the circumstances that some important fact about the person is not properly attended to or is not taken appropriately into account. In other words, the person is dealt with as though he is not what he actually is.... Pertinent aspects of how things are with him are treated as though they had no reality. It is as though, because he is denied suitable respect, his very existence is reduced.

This sort of treatment, at least when it has to do with matters of some consequence, may naturally evoke painful feelings of resentment. It may also evoke a more or less inchoate anxiety; for when a person is treated as though significant elements of his life count for nothing, it is natural for him to experience this as in a certain way an assault upon his reality. What is at stake for him, when people act as though he is not what he is, is a kind of self-preservation. It is not his biological survival that is challenged, of course, when his nature is denied. It is the reality of his existence for others, and hence the solidity of his own sense that he is real. (153)

The notion of respect, which seemed about to disappear in the capacious embrace of a requirement of rationality, appears to be saved, and assume life of its own when examined not from the point of view of the agent, but from the point of view of the recipient, and—as often—when we turn our gaze from what is achieved by compliance, to what is lost in violation. For its recipients, lack of respect is a denial of their existence for others, and thereby their own sense that they are real. The psychological drama these words evoke matches our intuitive understanding of respect, as the elementary, the basic duty we owe even complete strangers, the moral duty that does not presuppose any personal ties, any loyalties, any undertakings and commitments for its existence, the one that presupposes no more than the common humanity of all those to whom it is owed.

III   The Questions: Morality and Rationality

The rhetorical force of Frankfurt's remarks notwithstanding, his discussion is bound to raise as many questions as it answers. Some, to do with the way his account of respect fits with other of his views, are of no concern here. I will assume some appropriately "objectivist" understanding of reasons, or considerations. Respect is then understood by reference to following reason where it leads, or something like that. The connection between respect and reason leads Frankfurt to what I find a puzzling remark. It needs to be examined before I return to the basic question. For until clarified, it may suggest the possibility of another line of thought, which I believe to be illusory.

Having asked: "What is it about impartiality and about what I have been referring to as 'respect' that makes them morally imperative?" (152), Frankfurt remarks that while being respectful is a special case of being rational, that cannot be the answer since it is not immoral not to be rational. There must, therefore, be another, a moral reason for being respectful, other than that this is a requirement of rationality.

I find this argument tantalizing, for it seems to me both right and totally misleading. Frankfurt is right to say that being irrational or acting irrationally is not in itself immoral, and he is right that there must be some explanation of why we ought to be respectful, other than that it is rationally required. And yet as stated his remarks suggest a misleading relationship between reason and morality, as if reason or rationality is one kind of requirement or source of requirements for action, whereas morality is another.

It is wrong to say either that Reason or that Rationality is a reason for action. There is therefore no straightforward answer to Frankfurt's question "what is the moral importance of avoiding irrationality?" (152), for there is no straightforward answer to the question "why avoid irrationality?" People act rationally if they conform with (undefeated) reasons for action that apply to them. They are irrational (roughly speaking) if knowingly, recklessly, or negligently, they fail to conform with undefeated reasons.[9] The importance is not in avoiding irrationality, or in being rational as such. It is (where it is important) the importance of not flouting the undefeated reasons that apply to the case. And these are different on different occasions. That is why Frankfurt is right to look for reasons people have to respect others, reasons other than that failure to do so is irrational: it is irrational only if there are such undefeated reasons, and only (partly) because of such reasons.

As Frankfurt remarks, irrationality is not essentially immoral.[10] Whether or not it is depends on whether the reasons that are being irrationally disregarded are moral ones or not. When one irrationally fails to respect people, knowing that that is what one has undefeated reason to do, that is immoral. It is immoral because it is an irrational defiance of *a moral* reason.

Frankfurt's own reason for respecting people is that otherwise their very reality is denied. Suppose John accepts that and yet, knowing what he is doing, John fails to respect another person. Should we condemn John for being irrational or for denying the existence of another? We should do both. In denying the existence of another, knowing that he should not do so, John is irrational. But is it not true that criticizing John for undermining the reality of another, rather than for being irrational, is the relevant moral criticism of his action? His immorality, even in these circumstances, is a factor apart from his irrationality.

This observation may mislead. In the circumstances, his irrationality is his immorality. But as in all cases, telling someone, or telling others of someone, that he is irrational may not bring out the salient facts. It may repeat what is known and obvious, but not explain why it is so, what it is that makes the act irrational (and immoral). Where that explanation is required, mere assertion of John's irrationality will miss the point. That is all.

These questions of the relation between morality and reason are fascinating and I raised them for that reason, and to avoid the temptation to develop Frankfurt's observations about the relations between respect, morality, and rationality, in spite of their sound core, in a misleading way. It is, of course, impossible here to provide and defend a complete account of the matter. So let us now return to the basic question, and Frankfurt's reply to it.

IV   The Questions: The Independence of Respect

In my introductory remarks I raised the question, which I will call the question of the independence of respect for people, whether there are specific reasons for respecting people, or whether respecting people is a byproduct of doing as one ought anyway to do. I suggested that we are torn both ways on this point. Frankfurt's essay offers a solution that, if successful, also helps explain why the puzzle arises in the first place.

On the one hand, according to Frankfurt, respecting people is merely a byproduct of acting for undefeated reasons. But on the other hand, when our action can count as treating a person one way or another, and we fail to follow undefeated reasons, our action causes a particular kind of hurt, arising out of the fact that that person's very reality is denied. Undermining people's sense of the solidity of their own existence is a hurt we should avoid inflicting on them, and that now gives us an independent reason to respect them, an additional reason to conform to undefeated reasons when we treat people.[11]

Of course, Frankfurt does not express the view I have just attributed to him. Nor does he ask my question regarding the independence of respect for people. But I think that it is fair to say that what he wrote about respect commits him to such a view, if certain natural assumptions are allowed. Is this a correct explanation of the autonomy of respect? Does the tempting combination of respect being both no more than conforming to reason, and being a response to a specific concern, the concern not to deny the reality of the other, constitute the correct account of respecting people?

For the account to stand any chance of making sense, we must assume a background where evaluative ignorance does not occur. We must assume that *we* all know what sound reasons confront agents, and that they know that respect consists in following reason. Perhaps a somewhat weaker set of assumptions would do. But without some such assumptions the Frankfurt account does not work. Without them, at most, it shows what hurt is caused to people when they *think* that they are treated wrongly, not when they actually are treated wrongly.

Is it not unrealistic, however, to assume that everyone reacts in the same way to people's failure to follow reason in treating them? To be sure, some insecure people may indeed feel their very reality denied any time anyone fails to conform to reason when treating them. But others may have a robust sense of their own worth and will not feel threatened however wrongly they are treated. Others fill the full gamut of possibilities in between.

To circumvent this difficulty it may be best to shift the emphasis from the psychological, on which Frankfurt focuses, to the normative. What matters is not whether anyone actually feels the hurt of his very reality being denied when people fail to conform to reason in treating him, but that people are entitled to feel that hurt. Failing to conform to reason in the way they are treated constitutes a normative = symbolic denial of their reality, and they are entitled to feel so, regardless of whether they do or not. We should respect people because we should not deny their reality. That duty may be more stringent when the people concerned are more liable to suffer from the hurt, but it is there whether or not they are actually likely to suffer.

Even so doubts persist. Is it credible to think that any deviation from sound reasons constitutes an assault on the reality of people? In the preceding discussion I have already narrowed down the condition: people ought to follow reason in all they do, but their conduct, even when conforming with reason, is respectful of a person only if it is conduct that treats that person one way or another.

When does one person, when acting, "treat another"? This is no easy question. Let me assume as a holding answer that one does so if one's action has nonnegligible consequences for that other. This answer itself is far from clear. Some cases that are clearly ways of treating people are not clearly cases of actions with consequences for others: any time I insult someone I treat him insultingly. But such actions do not always have consequences. What of actions others object to on principle? Does the fox hunter treat the antihunting protestors one way or another by ignoring their protests, and carrying on with the hunt? Difficulties abound, but we will put such worries on one side in order to confront another.

It does not seem plausible that whenever (a) we act in a way that treats another, and (b) we fail to conform to reason, we are disrespectful of that person. A simple illustration will do: I drive my friend into town, and in order to bring him close to the shop he wishes to visit, I park my car on a double yellow line next to the shop. I should not have done so. It is a violation of a sensible parking regulation, and I have no adequate reason to disregard it. Was I disrespectful to my friend by doing this to him? Not if the circumstances were the ordinary circumstances we assume.

We need to narrow down the way we fail to conform to reason in order to reach that core of nonconformity which constitutes disrespect. An obvious amendment is that the reasons we disregard somehow relate to features of the person concerned. But this is so vague as to be of little help without much further clarification. Frankfurt is happy to intimate that only violating reasons of some importance could constitute disrespect. It does not seem to me that the solution to the difficulties lies in that direction.

I open a large grocery store in the neighborhood, predictably causing a local trader to go bankrupt. As it turns out I lose money and am forced to close the store only a couple of months later. My failure was predictable, and I acted rashly and irrationally in opening the store. But even though my action was irrational and had significant effects on the local trader, it is doubtful that I was disrespectful of him. I acted within my rights as a merchant, pursuing what he takes to be the best business decision.[12]

I do not wish to deny that someone may argue that in making business decisions we should be careful not to hurt other people, at least unless we will actually gain something ourselves. According to this view, in my example, I failed to discharge that duty, and therefore failed to treat the local trader with respect. My point is merely that this argument presupposes an independent duty to the other trader. It does not derive my disrespect simply from the fact that my act affected him and was irrational.

It seems that we fail in duties of respect for another only when we fail in our duties toward him. Those duties have to be established independently of the doctrine of respect.

Nor is that the end of the trouble. Suppose that I have a duty to competitors not to jeopardize their commerce unless I am going to make a profit from doing so. And suppose that I fail to discharge this duty. Does it follow that they are entitled to think that my action denies their reality? The answer seems to depend on my motives, and state of belief. If I believed that I have such a duty toward them, but concluded irrationally that I will make a profit, and therefore that I am not in breach of duty toward them, then once they know that that was my state of belief at the time, they are not entitled to think that I am denying their existence. My irrationality is a simple case of a rash mistake. No hostility to them is expressed. Similarly, suppose I conclude that I should not go ahead with the new store, that my duty to them precludes doing so, but I succumb to some irrational temptation and do so all the same. Why should my action be construed as denying the reality of my competitors? I acknowledged their reality and my own irrationality. Perhaps the right conclusion is that in my action I threaten my own reality, for I am being irrational. But I do not threaten my competitors' reality, for I acknowledge my duty toward them, even in the breach.

I find it difficult to know what conclusions to draw from the examples concerning the relevance of agents' state of beliefs and motives, except that, whatever one makes of this or that example, it is difficult to avoid the conclusion that the agents' beliefs and motives matter, that without taking them into account it would be wrong to understand their actions as the denial of the reality of another. But if so then denial of the reality of another cannot be that closely connected to failure of respect. For, Frankfurt must be right in seeing the expression of respect or its denial in the meaning of the action, a meaning that cannot be just a reflection of the intentions and beliefs that happen to inform it in one set of circumstances or another.[13]

V   The Road Ahead[14]

Herein lies the difficulty I feel in following Frankfurt. I share his view that there are reasons for respect. I find it difficult to combine that view, the affirmation of the independence of respect, with the byproduct view that is implied by his initial comment that we respect others if when treating them we act for sound undefeated reasons. Moreover, if acts that express disrespect for others are acts whose meaning is "a denial of the reality of the other," when this phrase is properly understood, they must be special acts. They cannot be just actions that fail to treat others as reason requires. There are just too many different ways in which that failure can happen, and not all of them have the required meaning. But Frankfurt fails to identify any particular failures as bearing the required meaning.

I believe that there are acts whose meaning is something like Frankfurt's denial of the reality of another, and which are wrong because they infringe special reasons, not just because of any failure to conform with reasons. They are acts that deny that people are of value in themselves. The thought that people are of value in themselves is an old one, and, in Kant's writing, it is tied to the origins of the modern understanding of the moral injunction of respect for people. An act denies that a person, or people of a class, and so forth are of value in himself or in themselves if its performance is inconsistent with such a belief. The doctrine of respect for people enjoins us not to perform such acts.

Without regarding the classification as hard and fast, we could distinguish three stages of correct response to value, and to the presence of good-making properties in objects. First, and at the most basic level, comes appropriate psychological response: regarding objects in ways consistent with their value, in one's thoughts, understood broadly to include imaginings, emotions, wishes, intentions, and so forth. I do not mean to imply that we should believe that whatever is of value is of value. There is no general reason to know or believe that what is of value is of value, any more than there is a general reason to know or to believe in all the propositions that are in fact true. But there is a general reason that if we think of an object that is of value, we should think of it in ways consistent with its value. This applies to our fantasies, imaginings, wishes, emotions, as well as to our plain beliefs. For example, despising someone as worthless, or mean, when he is in fact generous and kind is having an emotion inconsistent with his value, and inconsistent with the general reason I have in mind here: the reason that in our thoughts we should regard objects in ways consistent with the value they in fact have.

Given the close relations of thought and its expression in language and other symbolic actions, I will regard expression of recognition of respect in language and other symbolic actions as also belonging with the first stage of relating to value.

Second, there is a general reason to preserve what is of value. Naturally, the strength of the reason varies with the value of the object. But in general we have reason not to destroy, and furthermore, to preserve what is of value. There are difficult questions here: is the reason to preserve as stringent as the reason not to destroy? Or is the latter more stringent? Is there also a general reason to bring into existence things of value? If so, does it derive from the same considerations, and is it of the same stringency as the reason not to destroy what is of value? I will say nothing of them, except to assume that reasons of respect enjoin us not to destroy, and possibly to preserve, but not to create new objects of value.

Third, we can engage with value in appropriate ways. We do so when we listen to music with attention and discrimination, read a novel with understanding, climb rocks using our skill to cope, spend time with friends in ways appropriate to our relationships with them, and so on.

The first two stages of relating to value contrast with the third. Ultimately value is realized when it is engaged with. There is a sense in which music is there to be appreciated in listening and playing, novels to be read with understanding, friendships to be pursued, dances to be joined in, and so on. Merely thinking of valuable objects in appropriate ways and preserving them is a mere preliminary to engaging with value. Similarly, people are fulfilled, their virtues express themselves in their lives, and their lives are rewarding only if they engage with values in their lives. Merely not destroying or helping with the preservation of valuable objects, and thinking of them appropriately, is not enough for having a fulfilled life.[15] Yet, obviously, not everyone must engage with any valuable object. We need not read all the novels, listen to all the music, climb all the mountains, go to all the parties, dance in all the dances, which are worthwhile. On the other hand, even though the first two stages are in a sense preparatory or preliminary only, they do involve duties that apply to all. Not everyone has much time for Picasso's paintings, and there is nothing wrong in not caring for them (so long as it does not involve false beliefs about them or their value). But no one should destroy them, or treat them in ways inconsistent with the fact that they are aesthetically valuable. No one need care for dancing. But no one should spoil (possibly other people's) dances. And so on.[16]

The road I am pointing to is by now all too obvious. Reasons of respect are reasons belonging to the first two stages: reasons regarding the way we treat objects of value in thought and expression, and reasons for preserving them. These differ from reasons for engaging with valuable objects. But while in one way ultimately our lives are about engaging with value, the rest being mere preliminaries, in another way the reasons of respect are more basic. They are also more categorical, in not depending to the same degree on people's tastes and inclinations.

According to this view respect for people is merely a special case of respect for value: respect for the fact that people are of value. If respect for people differs from respect for works of art, this is partly because the value of people differs from the value of works of art. It is also because people, unlike works of art, the comatose and other animals, have a sense of their own identity, a sense that they are of value, and therefore are hurt by disrespect, a fact that lends special stringency to duties of respect for people. How do they differ in value? What are the special ways in which respect for people must be manifested? How does it differ from engaging with people? All these, and others, are the questions that must be answered in order to understand the role of the doctrine of respect for people within the larger framework of morality.[17] Such explorations will have to await another occasion. I hope, however, that enough has been said to show how an account of reasons of respect along the lines suggested here can explain why failure of respect can plausibly be taken by its victims as challenge to their reality.

Acknowledgments

I am grateful to Penelope Bulloch and Ulrike Heuer for helpful comments on a draft of this essay, and for the many suggestions and criticisms by the editors of this volume.

Notes

1. In *Necessity, Volition, and Love* (Cambridge: Cambridge University Press, 1999).

2. In *The Importance of What We Care About* (Cambridge: Cambridge University Press, 1988).

3. I will call "reasons for respect" reasons that one has to respect another, or to express that respect. I will not normally distinguish between these two, assuming that reasons to respect yield reasons to express respect on appropriate occasions. They are, I will therefore assume, reasons to take actions which express or manifest that respect. Though, as will become clear below, the actions may not bear that character on their sleeves.

4. In *The Morality of Freedom* (Oxford: Oxford University Press, 1986) I expressed that thought simply by saying that we respect people by treating them in accordance with sound moral principles (157). I now think that this statement is misleading for reasons that are partly explained in this essay.

5. Frankfurt, "Equality and Respect," 150. Subsequent page numbers in the text refer to this paper.

6. I will not take this last remark too literally. Taken literally it may forbid following rules such as "first come first served," or "last in first out." These rules, one may say, disregard the particularities of the individuals they apply to. That is, in a way, their very purpose. Nevertheless, in many circumstances there is nothing wrong in following them or many other considerations that literally violate Frankfurt's remark here.

7. Acting for sound reasons guarantees absence of arbitrariness, though not the other way round. That is, one can act wrongly without acting arbitrarily. Frankfurt emphasizes both elements: acting for the relevant reasons, i.e., for sound reasons, and acting impartially and nonarbitrarily, without analyzing their relationship.

8. The case of impartiality can be interpreted in a similar way, with the complication that, while there are no special duties of impartiality, there are special duties to appear impartial. But the case of impartiality is more complex, and I will not consider it in detail.

9. My *Engaging Reason* (Oxford, Oxford University Press, 2000), chap. 4, esp. 68–75, provides a slightly fuller sketch of elements in an account of rationality, which explains why failure to follow reasons that one is not aware of can be irrational (as is here implied). However, my comments in the next few paragraphs are formulated to avoid relying on this point, and to command the assent even of those who reject it.

10. Nor does immorality always involve irrationality.

11. It will be evident that Frankfurt must mean "denying the reality of another" metaphorically. Literally speaking, a torturer is fully aware of the existence of the tortured. He may plan his actions taking full account of the susceptibilities of his victim to maximize his suffering. But that is not what is meant here by the expression. It means, as I will claim below, something like "a typical experience one has when realizing that another person is denying the *value* of one's existence." But that, it will turn out, is inconsistent with central aspects of Frankfurt's account.

12. Nothing in this example should be taken to imply any moral shortcoming in the market institutions within which I act. However just the institutions may be, they would not exclude the possibility of decisions like the one used in this example.

13. This is not meant to be a highly theoretical claim to be justified by an account of respect, or of our duty to respect people. Rather it is meant as part of our common ("pretheoretical") understanding of the concept, part of the platitudes that a philosophical account of respect has to accommodate and explain. You can test it by looking at the expression of respect in symbolic actions. If you stand up before speaking in class (see the example at the beginning of section I) you (or your action) express respect for the teacher, whatever your view of the matter. To express disrespect, your action, not only your intention, must change and acquire the character of a mocking pseudo-gesture, which subverts its meaning. If only your intention changes, but your action remains the same, then you express respect without meaning to do so.

14. The argument of this section is developed further in chapter 4 of *Value, Respect, and Attachment* (Cambridge: Cambridge University Press, 2001).

15. This should be qualified to allow that one can have a fulfilling career as a conservator of objects of value of some kind or another. There is no need here to develop the qualifications and details that show how this is consistent with the general view expressed in the text.

16. The point requires careful unpacking. For example, everyone has reason to engage with whatever is of value, if he or she can do so, other things being equal. Engaging with what is of value is an intelligible and, other things being equal, good thing to do. Roughly speaking, this is what we say when we say that we have reason to engage with what is of value. But, special circumstances apart, there is no fault in one in not engaging with this or that valuable thing or activity. On the other hand, we have a duty to treat valuable things as indicated in the first two stages of responding to value, and we are (prima facia) at fault when we do not do so.

17. Throughout the discussion, I have tried to bear in mind the lessons of Frankena's "The Ethics of Respect for Persons," *Philosophical Topics* 14 (1986): 149–167, which successfully shows that one cannot regard duties of respect as the foundation of morality if that means that the rest of morality is no more than the working out of the implications of the doctrine of respect.

REPLY TO JOSEPH RAZ

Harry Frankfurt

1. Let me begin with a small point that is of hardly more than terminological significance. My conception of respect for a person entails, as Raz observes, aiming at "outcomes that are matched specifically to the particularities of the individual." He supposes that this cannot be taken literally; for he thinks that it would in that case condemn as disrespectful anyone following a rule like "first come first served," the whole point of which is to ignore the particular characteristics of the individuals to whom the rule applies. However, I intended the notion of someone's "particularities" to refer to everything about him—to transient features of his situation as well as to those relatively stable personal characteristics that belong more intimately to his individual character. So the fact that someone was the first to arrive is, in my sense of the term, among his particularities.

2. The issues Raz raises concerning the relationship between respect and rationality are more troublesome, although here too much of the apparent disagreement between us may be due just to failures in communication. I have argued that being respectful is a special case of being rational but that, since failing to be rational is not as such immoral, this cannot be what makes respect morally imperative.[1] Of this argument, Raz says that it "seems to me both right and totally misleading." On the one hand, he agrees that being irrational is not in itself immoral and that, accordingly, there must be an explanation of why we ought to be respectful other than that respect is required by reason. On the other hand, he thinks that I "suggest a misleading relationship between reason and morality, as if reason or rationality is one kind of requirement or source of requirements for action, whereas morality is another."

In saying that being respectful is a special case of being rational, what I had in mind was that it consists in giving due consideration to whatever facts about people are relevant, and that this is an a priori condition of rationality. That is, I was maintaining that treating people with respect is part of what it means to be rational. Here is the relevant passage:

Why is it important to be guided in dealing with people only by whatever it is about them that is genuinely relevant? There is a sense in which being guided by what is relevant—thus treating relevantly similar cases alike and relevantly unlike cases differently—is an elementary aspect of being rational. Being impartial and respectful is a special case of being rational in this sense.[2]

It is inherently irrational to violate the principle that conduct should be guided by what is relevant. This principle is a priori. I was concerned that some people might think (and I believe some philosophers have actually thought) that it is some such a priori principle, articulating a general condition of rationality, that supports the requirement that people be treated with respect.

My purpose in pointing out that irrationality is not in itself immoral was to make it clear that the immorality of failing to treat people with respect cannot be explained by observing that disrespect contravenes an a priori principle and is therefore irrational. When we fail to respect someone we tend to cause, in my view, a particular kind of hurt—a hurt that is a response to the fact that we deny some aspect or feature of the person's reality.[3] On my account, avoiding this tendency to hurt that is due to denying their reality provides the morally pertinent reason for treating people with respect.

Raz does not find it plausible that we are disrespectful of people whenever (a) we do something that affects them in an important way and (b) what we do fails to conform to reason. Neither do I. I agree with him entirely concerning the example in which someone opens a store on the basis of judgments and decisions that fly in the face of reason, and in which this has as an outcome (perhaps unanticipated and unintended) that another store is driven out of business. It is stipulated in the example that the person who opens the store acts irrationally in doing so, and that his conduct has an important harmful effect on the person whose business is ruined. In my judgment, as in Raz's, these circumstances do not imply that the person who is driven out of business has been treated disrespectfully. Unlike Raz, however, I do not see that there is anything in my account of respect that requires me to judge the matter differently.

Treating people disrespectfully is not a matter simply of acting in a way that has important effects on them and that fails to conform to reason. Raz attributes to me the view that "we respect others if when treating them we act for sound undefeated reasons." But that has never been my view. Treating someone disrespectfully entails, on my account, something rather more specific than flouting the requirements of rationality or ignoring sound undefeated reasons. It entails acting in a way that denies the person's reality—for example, acting as though the person lacks some characteristic that he actually possesses, or acting as though some fact about the person is not a fact. As Raz points out, the person who opens the store harms the person whom he drives out of business but does not in any way deny that person's reality. On my view, then, he is not guilty of failing to treat him with respect.

3.   I am not so confident as Raz that respect is *entirely* separate from motives and beliefs. He says that if you stand up in class before speaking, you express respect for the teacher "whatever your view of the matter"; if you stand up without intending thereby to show respect, "you express respect without meaning to do so." Let us suppose that a student who stands up before speaking has just joined the class from a culture in which standing up is a well-established way of expressing defiance of the teacher, and that he is unaware of what standing up expresses in his present environment. Perhaps it is nonetheless true, as Raz maintains, that in standing up before speaking he inadvertently expresses respect for the teacher. But now suppose further that everyone who observes what is going on knows both that he is unaware that in his present environment standing up is customarily accepted as an expression of respect, and that he understands standing up to express nothing but defiance. In that case I doubt that, when he stands up, he would either be taken to be expressing respect or that he would in fact be doing so.

4.   Perhaps the most significant difference between Raz and me has to do with the relationship between respect and value. I cannot accept his suggestion that treating people without respect, as I understand it, is "something like" performing acts that "deny that people are of value in themselves." While there undoubtedly must be similarities, as there are between any two things, there are no distinctively close or philosophically important relationships between them.

What does it mean to deny that people are in themselves of value? It would be quite natural to understand an assertion that some object has no value as implying that the object can be discarded without loss.

That is hardly what is conveyed about a person by any but the most extraordinarily disrespectful actions. No doubt Raz understands the assertion that people have value in a different way—as conveying, along the Kantian lines to which he alludes, the importance of treating people as ends rather than only as means. But however important or fundamental to morality treating people as ends may be, it is not very pertinent to the sort of respect with which I have been concerned. There is no reason to assume that actions in which some relevant fact about a person is ignored must invariably imply that the person may appropriately be treated merely as a means. Ignoring something about a person (even ignoring him entirely) is not tantamount to focusing exclusively on his utility.

I doubt that there is, on my account of respect, any inherent connection between respecting people and acknowledging their value. Suppose I am making a list of people who weigh exactly 160 pounds, and suppose I decline to add the name of a certain person to that list despite the fact that I have conclusive evidence that he belongs on it. Weighing exactly 160 pounds is a feature without any inherent value. In acting as though the person lacks that feature, I am therefore not acting as though he lacks something valuable. Nor am I acting as though he is a person of no value, or as though he is to be treated as a means rather than as an end. I am simply, with regard to a quite limited matter, not taking him seriously.

This may be, of course, because I do not value him; or it may be for some other reason. For whatever reason, and perhaps for no reason at all, I am refusing to acknowledge that he is what he is. To be sure, he might not care about what I am doing. It might cause him concern only if there is some benefit to be gained by getting on the list; or he might be upset about it just because he is in general a person who is very sensitive to being ignored. Nonetheless, whether my offense is regarded as grave or as inconsequential, the fact is that although I am not denying his value, I am treating him without respect.

Notes

1. Cf. "Equality and Respect," collected in my *Necessity, Volition, and Love* (Cambridge: Cambridge University Press, 1999), p. 152.

2. Ibid.

3. Raz assumes that in referring to the hurt caused by denying the reality of another person, I am thinking of "a typical experience one has when realizing that another person is denying the value of one's existence." However, I do not think of the sort of hurt in question as linked especially to a person's realization that someone denies the value of his existence. I construe the denial of reality more literally than that. It consists in acting as though a person lacks some characteristic that he actually possesses, and thus in denying the reality of something that is in fact a reality. This entails no evaluation. I will have more to say below concerning the relationship between respect and value.

12

Deeper into Bullshit

G. A. Cohen

bullshit n. & v. *coarse sl.*—*n.* **1** (Often as *int.*) nonsense, rubbish. **2** trivial or insincere talk or writing.—*v. intr.* (**-shitted**, **-shitting**) talk nonsense; bluff. **bullshitter** *n.*
—*Oxford English Dictionary*

It is just this lack of connection to a concern with truth—this indifference to how things really are—that I regard as the essence of bullshit.
—*Harry Frankfurt*

I

Harry Frankfurt's essay "On Bullshit"[1] is a pioneering and brilliant discussion of a widespread but largely unexamined cultural phenomenon. On being honored by an invitation to contribute to the present volume, I decided to focus on Frankfurt's work on bullshit, partly because it is so original and so interesting, and partly because bullshit, and the struggle against it, have played a large role in my own intellectual life. They have played that role because of my interest in Marxism, which caused me to read, when I was in my twenties, a great deal of the French Marxism of the 1960s, deriving principally from the Althusserian school.

I found that material hard to understand, and, because I was naive enough to believe that writings that were attracting a great deal of respectful, and even reverent, attention could not be loaded with bullshit, I was inclined to put the blame for finding the Althusserians hard entirely on myself. And when I managed to extract what seemed like a reasonable idea from one of their texts, I attributed to it more interest and/or importance (so I later came to see) than it had, partly, no doubt, because I did not want to think that I had been wasting my time. (That psychological mechanism, a blend, perhaps, of "cognitive dissonance reduction" and "adaptive preference formation," is, I believe, at work quite widely. Someone struggles for ages with some rebarbative text, manages to find some sense in it, and then reports that sense with enthusiasm, even though it is a banality that could have been expressed in a couple of sentences instead of across the course of the dozens of paragraphs to which the said someone has subjected herself.)[2]

Yet, although I was for a time attracted to Althusserianism, I did not end by succumbing to its intoxication, because I came to see that its reiterated affirmation of the value of conceptual rigor was not matched by conceptual rigor in its intellectual practices. The ideas that the Althusserians generated, for example, of the interpellation of the individual as a subject, or of contradiction and overdetermination, possessed a surface allure, but it often seemed impossible to determine whether or not the theses in which those ideas figured were true, and, at other times, those theses seemed capable of just two interpretations: on one of them they were true but uninteresting, and, on the other, they were interesting, but quite obviously false. (Failure to distinguish those opposed interpretations produces an illusory impression of interesting truth.)

No doubt at least partly because of my misguided Althusserian dalliance, I became, as far as bullshit is concerned, among the least tolerant people I knew. And when a set of Marxists or semi-Marxists, who, like me, had come to abhor what we considered to be the obscurity that had come to infest Marxism—when we formed, at the end of the 1970s, a Marxist discussion group that meets annually, and to which I am pleased to belong, I was glad that my colleagues were willing to call it the Non-Bullshit Marxism Group. Hence the emblem at the head of this article, which says, in Latin, "Marxism without the shit of the bull." (The group is also called, less polemically, and as you can see, the September Group, since we meet each September, for three days.)

II

I should like to explain how this essay reached its present state. I read Frankfurt's article in 1986, when it first appeared. I loved it, but I didn't think critically about it.

Having been asked to contribute to the present volume, I reread the article, in order to write about it. I came to realize that its proposal about the "essence" of bullshit worked quite badly for the bullshit (see section I) that has occupied me. So I wrote a first draft that trained counterexamples drawn from the domain of the bullshit that interests me against Frankfurt's account. But I then realized that it was inappropriate to train those examples against Frankfurt, that he and I are, in fact, interested in different bullshits, and, therefore, in different *explicanda*. Frankfurt is interested in a bullshit of ordinary life,[3] whereas I am interested in a bullshit that appears in academic works, and, so I have discovered, the word "bullshit" characteristically denotes *structurally* different things that correspond to those different interests. Finally, and, belatedly, I considered, with some care, the OED account of "bullshit," and, to my surprise, I discovered (and this was, of course, reassuring) that something like the distinct *explicanda* that I had come to distinguish are listed there under two distinct entries.[4]

So, instead of citing cases of the bullshit that interests me in disconfirmation of Frankfurt's account, I now regard it as bullshit of a different kind[5]—which is not to say that I have no criticism of Frankfurt's treatment of the kind of bullshit that interests him.

Frankfurt is partly responsible for my original, misdirected, approach. For he speaks, after all—see the second epigraph at the beginning of this article—of the "essence" of bullshit, and he does not acknowledge that the *explicandum* that attracted his interest is just one flower in the lush garden of bullshit. He begins by saying that the term "bullshit" is very hard to handle, analytically, but, as we shall see, he rather abandons caution when he comes to offer his own account of it.

Consider, then, the OED reading of "bullshit":

bullshit n. & v. *coarse sl.*—*n.* **1** (Often as *int.*) nonsense, rubbish. **2** trivial or insincere talk or writing.[6]—*v. intr.* (**-shitted**, **-shitting**) talk nonsense; bluff. **bullshitter** *n.*

The bullshit that interests me falls under definition 1 of the noun, but the bullshit that interests Frankfurt is closer to what falls under definition 2 of the noun. And that is because of the appearance of the word "insincere" in that second definition of "bullshit." In definition 2 of the noun "bullshit," bullshit is constituted as such through being the product of discourse governed by a certain state of mind. In this activity-centered definition of bullshit, the bull, conceptually speaking, wears the trousers: bullshit is bullshit because it was produced by a bullshitter, or, at any rate, by someone who was bullshitting at the time. Bullshit is, by nature, the product of bullshitting, and bullshitting, by nature, produces bullshit, and that biconditional, so understood that "bullshitting" enjoys semantic primacy, is true of Frankfurt's view of the matter.[7]

Definition 1, by contrast, defines "bullshit" without reference to the bullshit-producer's state of mind. The defect of this bullshit does not derive from its provenance: almost any state of mind can emit nonsense or rubbish, with any old mix of sincerity and its lack. Here the shit wears the trousers, and *if* there are indeed "bullshitters," and "bullshittings," that correspond to the bullshit of definition 1, then they are defined by reference to bullshit. But it may be the case, as I meant to imply by that "*if*," that the words "bullshitting" and "bullshitter" don't have a stable place on this side of the *explicandum* divide.[8] However that may be, definition 1 supplies an output-centered definition of the noun: the character of the process that produces bullshit is immaterial here.

Note, moreover, how the alternatives in the brief entry on the verb "to bullshit" match alternatives 1 and 2 in the definition of the noun (even though that entry isn't, as it perhaps should have been, subnumbered "1" and "2"). One can "talk nonsense" with any intentions whatsoever, but one cannot unknowingly or inadvertently "bluff": bluffing is a way of intending to deceive. (I'm not sure, by the way, that the dictionary is right in its implication that it suffices for bullshitting, in the nonbluff sense, that you produce bullshit, in sense 1: innocent producers of bullshit might be said not to be bullshitting when they produce it.)[9]

It is a limitation of Frankfurt's article that, as we shall see, he took for granted that the bull wears the semantic trousers: he therefore focused on one kind of bullshit only, and he did not address another, equally interesting, and academically more significant, kind. Bullshit as insincere talk or writing is indeed what it is because it is the product of something like bluffing, but talking nonsense is what it is because of the character of its output, and nonsense is not nonsense because of features of the nonsense-talker's mental state.

III

At the beginning of his article, Frankfurt describes a complexity that afflicts the study of bullshit:

Any suggestion about what conditions are logically both necessary and sufficient for the constitution of bullshit is bound to be somewhat arbitrary. For one thing, the expression *bullshit* is often employed quite loosely—simply as a generic term of abuse, with no very specific literal meaning. For another, the phenomenon itself is so vast and amorphous that no crisp and perspicuous analysis of its concept can avoid being procrustean. Nonetheless it should be possible to say something helpful, even though it is not likely to be decisive. Even the most basic and preliminary questions about bullshit remain, after all, not only unanswered but unasked. (117)

I have no problem with Frankfurt's first remark, to wit, that "bullshit" has a wide use in which it covers almost any kind of intellectual fault. To circumvent this problem, to identify a worthwhile *explicandum*, we could ask what "bullshit" denotes where the term does carry (as Frankfurt implies that it sometimes does) a (more or less) "specific literal meaning," one that differs, in particular, from the meanings carried by words that are close to "bullshit," but instructively different in meaning from it, such as the word "horseshit," which, at least in the United States, denotes, I believe, something characteristically produced with less deviousness than characterizes the production of (OED-2) bullshit. And I think that, for one such meaning, Frankfurt has provided an impressively discriminating (though not, as we shall see, fault-free) treatment: much of what he says about one kind of bullshit is true of it but false, for example, of horseshit.

Frankfurt's second remark, about the difficulty caused by the fact that "the phenomenon itself is so vast and amorphous," is more problematic.

Notice that this remark is meant to be independent of the first one (hence the words "For another ..."), as indeed it must be, since no *phenomenon* could be thought to correspond to "bullshit" where it is an undifferentiated term of abuse. In making this remark, Frankfurt must suppose, if, that is, he supposes, as he appears to do, that he will command the reader's agreement, that the reader has some "specific, literal meaning" of "bullshit" implicitly in mind. But that is extremely doubtful, partly because it is a gratuitous assumption (and, indeed, as the OED reveals, a false one) that "bullshit" has some *single* "specific, literal meaning." In a word: how can we be expected to agree, *already*, that bullshit is "vast" and "amorphous," when no specification of "bullshit" has yet been provided?

However that may be, Frankfurt leaves these preliminary problems behind, and plunges right into his subject, by reviewing, refining, and developing a definition that Max Black once gave of "humbug" (which is close to bullshit of the OED-2 kind), and then by commenting on an example of real or feigned rage expressed by Ludwig Wittgenstein against (putative) bullshit uttered by Fania Pascal.

Emerging from the Black and Wittgenstein discussions, Frankfurt very surprisingly says, that "the essence of bullshit ... is ... lack of connection to a concern with truth— ... indifference to how things really are ..." (125), where that indifference (see the Frankfurt passage quoted in the paragraph that follows here) is concealed by the speaker. It's the word "essence" that surprises me here: it seemed to be implied by Frankfurt's preliminary remarks that the term "bullshit," considered comprehensively, denotes no one thing whose essence one might try to specify,[10] and Frankfurt had not in the interim indicated a particular *region* of bullshit, whose bullshit might, perhaps, be identified by an essence.

Frankfurt later elaborates his definition as follows:

This is the crux of the distinction between him [the bullshitter] and the liar. Both he [the bullshitter] and the liar represent themselves falsely as endeavoring to communicate the truth. The success of each depends upon deceiving us about that. But the fact about himself that the liar hides is that he is attempting to lead us away from a correct apprehension of reality; we are not to know that he wants us to believe something he supposes to be false. The fact about himself that the bullshitter hides, on the other hand, is that the truth-values of his statements are of no central interest to him; what we are not to understand is that his intention is neither to report the truth nor to conceal it. This does not mean that his speech is anarchically impulsive, but that the motive guiding and controlling it is unconcerned with how the things about which he speaks truly are. (130)

Notice that, when Frankfurt elaborates what is supposed to be a proposal about bullshit, he speaks not of "bullshit" but of the "bullshitter." This confirms that, in Frankfurt's account, it is the bull that wears the trousers. But he wrongly takes for granted that that is the only important or interesting bullshit that there is.

Now, in the light of the semantic promiscuity of "bullshit" that was discussed at the outset of this section, it was, so I have suggested, unwise of Frankfurt to cast his claim as one about the "essence" of bullshit, as he does in the page 125 passage. He should have submitted his indifference-to-truth thesis as an attempt to characterize (at least) one interesting kind of bullshit, whether or not there are other interesting kinds of it. Let us assess his thesis as such, that is, not with the ambitiously generalizing status that Frankfurt assigns to it, but as an attempt to characterize one kind of bullshit, and, in particular, an activity-centered kind of bullshit. I return to the distinct bullshit-*explicandum*, which corresponds to OED definition 1, in section 4 below.

Consider Frankfurt's statement, with which we may readily agree, that:

[t]he realms of advertising and of public relations, and the nowadays closely related realm of politics, are replete with instances of bullshit so unmitigated that they can serve among the most indisputable and classic paradigms of the concept. (122)

I find it hard to align this remark with Frankfurt's proposal about the essence of bullshit: advertisers and politicians are often very concerned indeed "to lead us away from a correct apprehension of reality" (130) and to design what we might well call "bullshit" to serve that end (yet the quoted page 130 words are used by Frankfurt to characterize the purpose of liars *as opposed* to bullshitters). Is it not a problem for Frankfurt's proposal about the essence of bullshit that those whom he designates as paradigm bullshitters engage in a great deal of what is not, for Frankfurt, bullshitting?

Frankfurt might say (as he must, to sustain his proposal) that, when advertisers and politicians seek to cover up the truth, they are doing something *other* than bullshitting. But when we are inclined to agree with Frankfurt that advertising and politics supply paradigms of bullshit, it is not the subset of their doings to which his proposal points that induces our inclination to agree. I think we are induced to agree partly because we recognize at least some lying to be also bullshitting.[11] Frankfurt's contrast between lying and bullshitting is malconstructed, and he erred, I believe, because he failed to distinguish two dimensions of lying, which we must separate if we are to determine the relationship between lying and Frankfurt's bullshitting.

Standardly, a liar says what he believes to be false: let us call that his standard *tactic* (or, for short, his tactic). Liars also standardly seek to deceive their listeners about some fact (other than the fact that they disbelieve what they say): we can call that the liar's (standard) *goal*. And normally a liar pursues the stated *goal* by executing the stated *tactic*: he says something that he believes to be false *in order to* induce his listener to believe something false. (Usually, of course, what I have called the liar's "standard goal" is not also his ultimate or final goal, which may be to protect his reputation, to sell a bill of goods, to exploit his listener, or whatever.[12] But the liar standardly pursues such further goals by pursuing the goal which liars standardly seek. None of these further goals *distinguish* the liar from nonliars.)

Now, what I have called the "standard tactic" and the "standard goal" of lying can come apart. Consider what was one of Sigmund Freud's favorite jokes:

Dialogue between two travelers on a train from Moscow:
"Where are you going?"
"To Pinsk."
"Liar! You say you are going to Pinsk in order to make me believe you are going to Minsk. But I *know* you are going to Pinsk. So whom are you trying to fool?"[13]

Suppose that the first traveler's diagnosis of the purpose of the second traveler's uttering "To Pinsk" is correct: let us therefore call the second traveler Pavel (because of the "P" in Pinsk), and let us call the first traveler Trofim. On the indicated supposition, Trofim is right to call Pinsk-bound Pavel a liar, since, as Frankfurt says, the liar is someone who tries "to lead us away from a correct apprehension of reality" (130), and that's what Pavel is trying to do to Trofim. The peculiarity of the present example is that Pavel here seeks to deceive by telling the truth. Pavel does not, in my view, lie, on this occasion, but he nevertheless proves himself to be a liar. Pavel's goal is the standard goal of the liar, but his tactic, here, is to speak the truth. (The important and entirely nonverbal point is that the standard goal and the standard tactic of lying lose their normal association here, not whether Pavel is lying, or telling a lie, etc.)

A converse case, in which the standard tactic subserves a nonstandard goal, would go as follows. Pavel knows that Trofim knows that Pavel habitually lies, at any rate when it comes to disclosing his intended destinations. But, on the present occasion, it is very important to Pavel that Trofim should believe the truth about where Pavel is going. So Pavel, once again travelling to Pinsk, says that he is going to Minsk, precisely because he wants Trofim to believe the truth, which is that Pavel is going to Pinsk. I don't know, or very much care, whether Pavel thereby lies, but he is not here "attempting to lead [Trofim] away from a correct apprehension of reality," save with respect to his own state of mind: he wants him to think he's trying to get Trofim to believe something false, when he's not.

We must, accordingly, distinguish two respects in which liars characteristically traffic in falsehood. Liars usually intend to utter falsehoods, while intending that they be thought to be speaking truthfully; but that is quite separate from their standard goal, which is to cause a misrepresentation of reality in the listener's mind.

What is the bearing, if any, of this distinction, on Frankfurt's distinction between lying and bullshitting?

The root difficulty for Frankfurt's bullshitting/lying distinction, the difficulty underlying the problem with his advertiser example, is that, while Frankfurt identifies the liar by his goal, which is to mislead with respect to reality, he assigns no distinctive goal to the bullshitter, but, instead, identifies the bullshitter's activity at the level that corresponds to what I have called the liar's tactic. The standard liar pursues his distinctive goal by asserting what he believes to be false and concealing that fact. Frankfurt's bullshitter asserts statements whose truth-values are of no interest to him, and he conceals *that* fact. But Frankfurt assigns no distinctive goal to the bullshitter that would distinguish him from the liar. And, in fact, Frankfurt's bullshitters, as he identifies them, have no distinguishing goal: they have a variety of goals, one of which can be precisely to mislead with respect to reality, and that, indeed, is the goal of bullshit advertising.[14] Advertisers and politicians spew a lot of bullshit, and they indeed seek to induce false beliefs about reality, but those are not, as Frankfurt must have it, separate but, typically, coincident activities on their parts.

The failure to distinguish the level of tactic from the level of goal runs throughout the discussion. Frankfurt writes at page 128:

Bluffing too is typically devoted to conveying something false. Unlike plain lying, however, it is more especially a matter not of falsity but of fakery. This is what accounts for its nearness to bullshit. For the essence of bullshit is not that it is *false* but that it is *phony*. (my emphases)

The problem is that this falsehood is at the level of tactic, whereas phoniness is at the level of goal. If bluffing is like bullshit, that is partly because bullshitting, too, is often devoted to conveying something false— although often not by saying that false thing itself.

As Frankfurt says, the bullshitter may not care whether or not what he says is true. But Frankfurt has confused that with the bullshitter's not caring whether his audience is caused to believe something true or false. That explains an error that Frankfurt makes about the Fourth of July orator whom he describes at pages 120–121:[15]

Consider a Fourth of July orator, who goes on bombastically about "our great and blessed country, whose Founding Fathers under divine guidance created a new beginning for mankind." This is surely humbug.... the orator is not lying. He would be lying only if it were his intention to bring about in his audience beliefs which he himself regards as false, concerning such matters as whether our country is great, whether it is blessed, whether the Founders had divine guidance, and whether what they did was in fact to create a new beginning for mankind. But the orator does not really care what his audience thinks about the Founding Fathers, or about the role of the deity in our country's history, or the like. At least, it is not an interest in what anyone thinks about these matters that motivates his speech.

It is clear that what makes Fourth of July oration humbug is not fundamentally that *the speaker regards his statement as false.* Rather ... the orator intends these statements to convey a certain impression of himself. *He is not trying to deceive anyone concerning American history.* (my emphases)

The orator's unconcern about truth is, mistakenly, identified at the level of his goal, rather than, in line with page 130, merely at the level of his immediate tactic. For the bullshitting orator, as Frankfurt describes him, might well care a lot about what the audience thinks about the Founding Fathers.[16] If the orator had been Joseph McCarthy, he would have wanted the audience to think that the "new beginning" that the Founding Fathers "created" should persuade the audience to oppose the tyranny supposedly threatened by American communism. The fact that it is not "fundamental" that "the speaker regards his statements as false" in no way implies that "he is not trying to deceive anyone concerning American history." (Similarly, advertisers may not care whether or not what they say is true, but they do care about what their audience is caused to believe, or, rather, more generally, about the thought-processes that they seek to induce in people.)[17]

IV

Unlike Frankfurt's bullshitting, lying is identified in terms of the defect at which it aims, namely, falsehood. We clarify what a liar is by reference to falsehood, rather than the other way around; we do not, that is, when asked to characterize what falsehood is, say that falsehood is what a liar aims to say. In parallel, we might, unlike Frankfurt, seek to clarify what a bullshitter is by reference to what he aims at, to wit, bullshit. We might start with the shit, not with the bull. And that would induce us to consider OED definition 1 ("nonsense, rubbish") the one that fits the bullshit that interests me, rather than the bullshit that interests Frankfurt. My bullshit belongs to the category of *statement* or *text*. It is not primarily an activity but the result of an activity (whether or not *that* activity always qualifies as an activity of bullshitting).[18]

A liar who tries to say something false may inadvertently speak the truth, whether or not he is then lying, and whether or not what he then says is a lie. And there is also the opposite case in which an honest person, by mistake, speaks falsely. The bullshit that interests me is relevantly parallel. I countenance a bullshitter who has tried, but failed, to produce bullshit—what comes out, by accident, is good sense—and I also countenance a lover of truth who utters what he does not realize is bullshit. A person may avow, in full honesty, "I'm not sure whether what I'm about to say is bullshit." These are not possibilities for the bullshit that interests Frankfurt. But they are possibilities. So the bullshit that interests Frankfurt doesn't cover the waterfront.

A person who speaks with Frankfurtian indifference to the truth might do so yet *happen* to say something true, and, in at least one sense of the term, the one that interests me, what he says could not then be bullshit.[19]

And, oppositely, an honest person might read some bullshit that a Frankfurt-bullshitter wrote, believe it to be the truth, and affirm it. When that honest person utters bullshit, *she*'s not showing a disregard for truth. So it is neither necessary nor sufficient for every kind of bullshit that it be produced by one who is informed by indifference to the truth, or, indeed, by any other distinctive intentional state.

The honest follower, or the honest confused producer of bullshit, may or may not count as a bullshitter,[20] but she is certainly honest, and she certainly utters (one kind of) bullshit. There exists bullshit as a feature of utterances that does not qualify as bullshit by virtue of the intentional state of the utterance's producer (although that state may, of course, causally explain why the bullshit is there, and/or why what's there is bullshit).

But what *is* that feature of utterances? *One thing it can be*, at least to a first approximation, is what the OED calls it, to wit, *nonsense*. But what particularly interests me is a certain variety of nonsense, namely, that which is found in discourse that is by nature *unclarifiable*, discourse, that is, that is not only obscure but which cannot be rendered unobscure, where any apparent success in rendering it unobscure creates something that isn't recognizable as a version of what was said. That is why it is frequently an appropriate response to a charge of bullshit to set about trying to clarify what was said. (Think of attempts to vindicate Heidegger, or Hegel. The way to show that they weren't bullshitters is not by showing that they cared about the truth, but by showing that what they said, resourcefully construed, makes sense. Those who call them bullshitters do not doubt that they cared about the truth, or, at any rate, it is not *because* of any such doubt that they think Hegel and Heidegger were bullshitters.[21] That Frankfurt issue isn't the issue here.)

Something is unclarifiable if and only if it cannot be made clear, but I shall not try to say what "clear" means in this essay. (I'm inclined to think it's not possible to do so, in an illuminating way.) Note, however, that there are relevantly different forms of unclarity, all of which have bearing here. There is the unclarity of a sentence itself, and then there is the unclarity as to why a certain (possibly perfectly clear) sentence is uttered in a given context. So, for example, the meaning of Wittgenstein's "If a lion could speak, we would not understand him" is in one way perfectly clear, but it might nevertheless be judged obscure, and unclarifiably obscure, by one who doubts that it carries, in context, a graspable point. There is also the unclarity of why one statement should be taken to lend credence to another statement. And there are no doubt other pertinent unclarities too.

Note that it is not an objection to the proposed sufficient condition of bullshit that different people might, in the light of different background beliefs, impose different standards of clarity, and, therefore, identify different pieces of texts as bullshit. Some of the people might, of course, be wrong.

I emphasized "one thing it can be" three paragraphs back because defects other than unclarifiable unclarity can suffice to stigmatize a text as bullshit. I focus on this variety of the phenomenon because it commands a greater academic following than other varieties do. In the various varieties of bullshit, what is wanting, speaking very generally, is an appropriate connection to truth, but not, as in Frankfurt's bullshit, as far as the state of mind of the producer is concerned, but with respect to features of the piece of text itself. Unclarifiable unclarity is one such feature. Rubbish, in the sense of arguments that are grossly deficient either in logic or in sensitivity to empirical evidence, is another. A third is irretrievably speculative comment, which is neither unclear nor wanting in logic, such as David Miller's excellent example, "Of course, everyone spends much more time thinking about sex now than people did a hundred years ago."

I focus on unclarifiable unclarity in particular in preparation for a further inquiry into bullshit that addresses the question why so much of that particular kind of bullshit is produced in France. This kind of academic bullshit, unlike the two contrasting types of bullshit, be they academic or not, mentioned in the previous paragraph, comes close to being celebrated for its very unclarity by some of its producers and consumers. What some of them certainly celebrate is a disconnection with truth: in what perhaps ranks as the consummation of the development of unclarity-type bullshit, a consummation that Hegel might have called "bullshit risen to consciousness of itself," truth is, in much postmodernism, *expressly* disparaged.

Although I foreswear a definition of "clarity," I can offer a sufficient condition of unclarity. It is that adding or subtracting (if it has one) a negation sign from a text makes no difference to its level of plausibility[22]:

no force in a statement has been grasped if its putative grasper would react no differently to its negation from how he reacts to the original statement. The deliberate bullshit published by Alan Sokal no doubt comes out as unclarifiable, by that criterion.[23] Note that this test does not apply to the different sorts of bullshit reviewed a couple of paragraphs back, and, being a merely sufficient condition of unclarifiability, it does not characterize *all* cases of the latter either.

An objection that faces my account is that it appears to classify good poetry that isn't bullshit as bullshit, since a piece of good poetry may be unclarifiable. A tempting way of acquitting such poetry of the charge of bullshit is by reference to its designation *as* poetry, rather than *as* some sort of contribution to knowledge in a more straightforward sense. But then the same text would be bullshit or not according, Frankfurt-like, to its, as it were, intentional encasement, and I am trying to characterize an intention-independent sense of the term.

An unclarifiable text can be valuable because of its suggestiveness: it can stimulate thought, it can be worthwhile seeking to interpret it in a spirit which tolerates multiplicity of interpretation, and which therefore denies that it means some one given thing, as a clarifiable piece of text does. So let us say, to spare good poetry, that the bullshit that concerns me is not only unclarifiable but also lacks this virtue of suggestiveness.[24] (I am sure that many academic bullshitters get away with a lot of bullshit because *some* of their unclarifiabilia are valuably suggestive, and therefore not bullshit. Their readers then mistakenly expect more, or most, of it to be so.)

So much by way of a preliminary attempt to identify the *bullshit* that interests me. But what reading of "bullshitter," if any, corresponds to the bullshit that I have tried to identify? Producers of Cohen-bullshit are clearly not by nature bullshitters, in Frankfurt's sense, though Frankfurt-bullshitters often produce Cohen-bullshit, at least in the academy. Rather, I would say that the word "bullshitter" that corresponds to my bullshit has two readings. In one of its readings, a bullshitter is a person who is *disposed* to bullshit: he tends, *for whatever reason*, to produce a lot of unclarifiable stuff. In a second acceptable reading of the term, a bullshitter is a person who *aims* at bullshit, however frequently or infrequently he hits his target.[25] (Notice that other nouns that signify that their denotations engage in a certain activity display a similar pair of readings: a killer may be a being that tends to kill, with whatever intention or lack of it [a weed-killer, for example, is a killer, and a merely careless human stomper on flowers is a (flower-) killer]; or he may be a being who intends to kill, whether or not he ever does.) Aim-(Cohen)-bullshitters *seek* and *rely* on unclarifiability, whereas innocent speakers of bullshit are merely victims of it. Aim-bullshitters resort to bullshit when they have reason to want what they say to be unintelligible, for example, in order to impress, or in order to give spurious support to a claim: the motives for producing bullshit vary. (And just as a person might sometimes kill, without being a killer in either of the senses I distinguished, so a person who is in neither of the senses I distinguished a bullshitter might, on occasion, produce bullshit.)

What about the verb, "to bullshit"? Does the producer of my bullshit, always bullshit when she produces bullshit, as Frankfurt's does? I see no reason for saying that an innocent does, especially if she's not even a disposition-bullshitter. But an aim-bullshitter who produces bullshit indeed bullshits.[26]

V

It matters that bullshit can come in the non-intention-freighted form by which I am exercised. For there is, today, a great deal of my kind of bullshit in certain areas of philosophical and semi-philosophical culture, and if, as we should, we are to conduct a struggle against it, the sort of struggle that, so one might say, Alan Sokal has inaugurated,[27] then it is important not to make false accusations, and not, therefore, for example, to charge possibly innocent traffickers in bullshit of lacking a concern for truth, or of deliberately conniving at obscurity.[28] Our proper polemical target is bullshit, and not bullshitters, or producers of bullshit, as such. So while it's lots of fun for people like me, who have a developed infantile streak, to talk about bullshit, and even just to write "bullshit" over and over again, in an academic essay, there is nevertheless, in my opinion, something important at stake here, and the character of what is at stake makes the bullshitter/bullshit distinction important.

To prevent misunderstanding, let me add that I do believe that there is quite a lot of *aiming* at obscurity in the production of philosophical bullshit, and a lot, to boot, in this region, of lack of concern with truth.[29]

But these moral faults should not be our primary focus. For reasons of
courtesy, strategy, and good evidence, we should criticize the product,
which is visible, and not the process, which is not.[30]

Acknowledgments

For comments on an earlier draft, I thank Malcolm Anderson, Annette
Barnes, Jerry Barnes, Sarah Buss, Paula Casal, John Davis, Jon Elster,
Cécile Fabre, Diego Gambetta, Grahame Lock, Ian Maclean, David
Miller, Alan Montefiore, Michael Otsuka, Lee Overton, Derek Parfit,
Rodney Peffer, Mark Philp, Saul Smilansky, Alan Sokal, Hillel Steiner,
Tracy Strong, and Arnold Zuboff.

Notes

1. Harry Frankfurt, "On Bullshit," in his *The Importance of What we Care
About* (Cambridge University Press, 1988).

2. As Diego Gambetta has pointed out to me, a mechanism merits mention that
is different from the "sunk cost" one that figures above. You can be so happy
that you've got *something* (after whatever amount of labor, or lack of it, you've
expended) from someone who is reputed to be terrific that you overvalue it. In
both mechanisms you misattribute the pleasure of getting *something* to the quality of the text you got it from.

3. His essay begins as follows: "One of the most salient features of our culture is
that there is so much bullshit. Everyone knows this. Each of us contributes his
share."

4. Frankfurt himself cites the OED, but mainly with respect to meanings and
uses of the word "bull": he touches on its definition of "bullshit" only in its use
as a verb. I disagree with his discussion of the entries he cites, but it would be an
imposition on the reader's capacity to endure tedium to explain why.

5. Four differences between the kinds of bullshit that exercise Frankfurt and me
are listed in note 26 below. The import of those differences will emerge in due
course, but the reader will probably follow me better if he or she glances ahead
now to note 26.

6. "Trivial" is very different from "insincere," partly because it has weaker
implications for the state of mind of the speaker/writer. I shall take 2 with the
accent on "insincere."

7. Frankfurt certainly believes that a person bullshits if he produces bullshit,
since he thinks it a necessary condition of bullshit that it was produced with a
bullshitting intention. He (in effect) raises the question whether that intention is
also sufficient for bullshit at p. 119. But, although he doesn't expressly pursue

that question, his definition of "bullshit" (125), and its elaboration (130), show that he holds the sufficiency view as well. It is because Frankfurt asserts sufficiency that he can say (129) that a piece of bullshit can be true.

8. See, further, the last two paragraphs of section IV below.

9. See, once again, the last two paragraphs of section IV below.

10. Does Frankfurt think that the phenomenon of "indifference to how things really are" is "vast and amorphous"? Surely not. Then *what*, again, is he asserting to be "vast and amorphous," in his second preliminary remark, which I criticized two paragraphs back?

11. I suppose all lying is insincere talk, and I do not think all lying is bullshitting: at least to that extnt, the OED-2 definition is too wide. But *some* lying is undoubtedly also bullshitting, so Frankfurt's definition of activity-centered bullshit is too narrow.

12. Few liars care about nothing more than inducing false beliefs: that is the ultimate goal of only one of the eight types of liar distinguished by St. Augustine. See "On Bullshit," 131.

13. See Sigmund Freud, *Jokes and their Relation to the Unconscious.* In *The Basic Writings of Sigmund Freud* (New York: Modern Library, 1965).

14. It is not, of course, the ultimate goal of that advertising, which is to cause (some of) its audience to buy what's advertised.

15. Strictly, the orator's oration is presented as an example of humbug, rather than bullshit. But it's clear that Frankfurt would also say that he is a bullshitter, precisely in virtue of what makes him a purveyor of humbug, whatever difference between humbug and bullshit Frankfurt might want to affirm.

16. I do not think Frankfurt means to be *stipulating* otherwise: we are meant to agree with what he says about the orator on the basis of his initial, first-sentence of the passage, description of him. "Surely," in the second sentence, would otherwise make no sense.

17. Although this is not, again (see the text to note 13 above), their ultimate goal.

18. See the final paragraph of this section.

19. Perhaps in contrast with Frankfurt's sense, and certainly in contrast with what Frankfurt says about that sense (see p. 129).

20. That question is addressed in the penultimate paragraph of this section.

21. For the record, I do not believe that Hegel was a bullshitter, and I am too ignorant of the work of Heidegger to say whether or not he was a bullshitter. But I agree with my late supervisor Gilbert Ryle that Heidegger was a *shit*. I once asked Ryle whether he had continued to study Heidegger after he had written a long review of *Being and Time* in *Mind*. Ryle's reply: "No, because when the Nazis came to power, Heidegger showed that he was a shit, from the heels up, and a shit from the heels up can't do good philosophy." (Experience has, alas, induced me to disagree with the stated Rylean generalization.)

22. This criterion of bullshit was devised by Professor Arthur J. Brown, to whom I am indebted.

23. In his wonderful spoof, "Transgressing the Boundaries: Towards a Transformative Hermeneutics of Quantum Gravity," *Social Text* 46 (1996): 217–252 (which was published as a nonspoof in the thereby self-condemning *Social Text*).

24. I am allowing that the unclarifiable may be productively suggestive, but I would not go as far as Fung Yu-lan does: "Aphorisms, allusions, and illustrations are ... not articulate enough. Their insufficiency in articulateness is compensated for, however, by their suggestiveness. Articulateness and suggestiveness are, of course, incompatible. The more an expression is articulate, the less it is suggestive—just as the more an expression is prosaic, the less it is poetic. The sayings and writings of the Chinese philosophers are so inarticulate that their suggestiveness is almost boundless." *A Short History of Chinese Philosophy* (New York, 1960), 12.

25. Michael Otsuka comments insightfully on a familiar academic "case in which the two come apart: i.e., in which someone is disposed to unclarifiable unclarity without aiming at it. Many academics (including perhaps an especially high proportion of graduate students) are disposed to produce the unclarifiable unclarity that is bullshit, not because they are aiming at unclarifiable unclarity, but rather because they are aiming at profundity. Their lucid utterances are manifestly unprofound, even to them. Their clarifiable unclear utterances can be rendered manifestly not profound through clarification. But their unclarifiably unclear utterances are unmanifestly not profound. Hence it is safe for them to think that they are profound. These utterances are not profound either because they are meaningful (in some subtle way, should there be one, that is consistent with their unclarifiable unclarity) but unprofound or because they are meaningless. They are *unmanifestly* not profound because it is hard to demonstrate that they are not profound, given their unclarifiability. By aiming at profundity, these academics tend to produce obscurity. But they do not aim at obscurity, not even as a means of generating profundity" (Private communication, September 2, 1999).

26. Let me now list some central differences between the two kinds of bullshit that I have distinguished:

	Typical context of Utterance	Corresponding OED Definition	Primary Locus	Essence
Frankfurt's bullshit	everyday life	2	activity	indifference to truth
Cohen's bullshit	the academy	1	output	unclarifiability

27. Initially in the article referenced in note 23, and then more comprehensively in *Intellectual Impostures*, which he wrote with Jean Bricmont (London: Profile Books, 1998).

28. Consider this sentence from the work of Etienne Balibar: "This is precisely the first meaning we can give to the idea of dialectic: a logic or form of explanation specifically adapted to the determinant intervention of class struggle in the very fabric of history." *The Philosophy of Marx*, trans. Chris Turner (New York: Verso, 1995). If you read that sentence quickly, it can sound pretty good. The remedy is to read it more slowly, and you will then recognize it to be a wonderful paradigm of bullshit: yet I know Balibar to be an honest thinker.

29. The evidence assembled in Sokal and Bricmont's *Intellectual Impostures* proves, so I think, the truth of those beliefs.

30. We may hope that success in discrediting the product will contribute to extinguishing the process. I try to contribute to the project of discrediting the product in an unpublished discussion of Why One Kind of Bullshit Flourishes in France, a copy of which will be supplied upon application to me.

REPLY TO G. A. COHEN

Harry Frankfurt

1. Cohen's essay is, so far as I am aware, the first significant attempt either to criticize or to extend my work on bullshit. So I welcome it with particular appreciation and interest. Let me say at once that I am by no means inclined to resist his suggestion that there are important varieties of bullshit other than the one I discussed in my essay.[1] It is true that I did speak there of "the essence" of bullshit. That was perhaps misleading, insofar as it may have suggested that all genuine instances of bullshit must be of the kind I discussed. If I am reluctant to endorse Cohen's claim that the sort of bullshit on which my attention was focused "is just one flower in the lush garden of bullshit," it is not because I doubt that his claim is true. It is only because I cannot help recalling that bullshit is an animal product and not a plant. In any case, I am neither surprised nor dismayed that Cohen believes he has identified a type of bullshit that was, by the sort of procrustean maneuver that I acknowledged I would be unable to avoid, cut out of the concept as I analyzed it.

2. As Cohen correctly points out, my account of bullshit is activity-centered, rather than output-centered. On my account, the mental state of the person who creates some piece of discourse is a crucial factor in determining whether or not what is created is bullshit. The defining feature of the sort of bullshit that I considered is a lack of concern with truth, or an indifference to how things really are. This does not mean that something can count as bullshit only if it is uttered by a person who is, at least on that occasion, lacking in concern for truth. It is possible for a sincere and honest person to believe some bullshit that has been created by another, and to repeat it without manifesting any indifference to how things really are. What he repeats is bullshit as he repeats it, insofar as it was originated by someone who was unconcerned with whether what he was saying was true or false. A person who believes a lie may repeat it without lying, but what he is repeating is nonetheless a lie. The situation is the same with regard to bullshit, which may be repeated as bullshit even by someone who is not a bullshitter.

    The relationship between bullshit and lies is not as problematic on my account, it seems to me, as Cohen maintains. It is certainly true that

advertisers may qualify as liars, since they may know that they are pur-
veying falsehoods with an intention to deceive. However, in the sort of
case that I had in mind, their most fundamental commitment is as bullshitters. They are liars only, as it were, incidentally or by accident. My
presumption is that advertisers generally decide what they are going to
say in their advertisements without caring what the truth is. Therefore,
what they say in their advertisements is bullshit. Of course, they may
sometimes also happen to know, or they may happen subsequently to
discover, disadvantageous truths about their product. In that case what
they choose to convey is something that they know to be false, and so
they end up not merely bullshitting but telling lies as well.

Cohen suggests that what he refers to as the "root difficulty" for my
distinction between bullshit and lying is that I identify the liar by his goal
(i.e., the goal of misleading his hearers) whereas I assign no distinctive
goal to the bullshitter that distinguishes him from the liar. But the bullshitter is distinguished from the liar precisely insofar as he lacks any goal
such as that by which the liar is defined. In his effort to stimulate sales,
the bullshitting advertiser probably wouldn't mind if what he tells people
is true; on the other hand, he doesn't really care one way or the other.
The cigarette company conveys in its advertisements the message that
smoking Marlboros makes men as manly as cowboys. I suppose it is
reasonable to assume that the company believes that this is false and
that it knows it is trying to mislead people; but it is not motivated
primarily by an intention to deceive. Its advertising campaign is not
designed especially to conceal a truth. The company is willing to deceive, but the fact that it finds itself undertaking to do so is in a
way supererogatory. Its advertising campaign is designed and planned
without any real attention to the actual relationship between Marlboros
and manliness.[2]

3.   Cohen maintains that there is a kind of bullshit "equally interesting, and academically more significant" than the kind with which I have
dealt. This variety consists of discourse that is "by nature unclarifiable."
He does not say much about what he means by "unclarifiable." Indeed,
he declares that he will "not try to say what 'clear' means in this essay,"
and goes on to confess that he is "inclined to think it's not possible to do
so, in an illuminating way." This comes pretty close to conceding that
"clear" is unclarifiable, and hence to hoisting Cohen's account of bullshit

by its own petard. But perhaps construing what he says in this way is somehow too harsh.

Be that as it may, it must surely be conceded that there are no generally accepted or authoritative criteria of what counts as meaningful. Standards of clarity are quite impressionistic, most discourse is by some standards and in some respects and to some extent unclear, and Cohen does not explain how clear a text must be in order to escape condemnation. Moreover, and perhaps even more serious, it is quite problematic what it means to say of some text that it is "unclarifiable," and it is comparably problematic how the unclarifiability of a text is to be established. It is not so easy, accordingly, to know just what sort of discourse it is that Cohen proposes to identify as bullshit.

The only actual example of unclarifiable discourse that he offers is the following sentence from a work by Etienne Balibar: "This is precisely the first meaning we can give to the idea of dialectic: a logic or form of explanation specifically adapted to the determinant intervention of class struggle in the very fabric of history." I find this very unconvincing as an example of unclarifiable discourse. For one thing, it occurs to me that the meaning of the sentence might be much more readily apparent within the context from which Cohen detaches it than it is when taken by itself. Second, even without knowing its context, I think I can make a fairly good stab at understanding what the sentence means. My guess is that it means something like this: "The most distinctive point of dialectical explanations is precisely that they are supposed to be particularly helpful in illuminating how class struggle has significantly determined the course of history." This is, to be sure, a bit vague; but it is no more vague than most of what is generally accepted not only as intelligible but as reasonably clear. Have I succeeded, then, in clarifying a text that Cohen finds unclarifiable?

4. Anyhow, I am not sure that I want to dismiss as bullshit every utterance that I regard as unclarifiable. People who intend to say something meaningful, and who make conscientious efforts to do so, may nonetheless fail because of deep conceptual problems that do not reflect any reprehensible intellectual negligence or confusion on their part. The problems may not be due to them at all, but rather to the inadequacies of a system of thought that is currently standard and that is confidently assumed by everyone to be entirely reliable. These inadequacies may be

hidden and unsuspected even by the best thinkers. Thus it may one day be discovered that statements accepted for generations by all responsible authorities actually involve obscurities or logical flaws that vitiate their intelligibility, that cannot be repaired, and that are therefore unclarifiable. It seems inappropriate to insist that those statements were always bullshit. Characterizing something as bullshit is naturally construed as seriously pejorative, and in the kind of case I have imagined, the opprobrium is not warranted.

5. The species of bullshit that interests Cohen may well be, as he says, more significant in the academic world than the species I have discussed. Whether or not that is so, it is certainly worth trying to understand the phenomenon of unclarifiable discourse better than we do. On the other hand, I do not consider that phenomenon to be as important a threat to our culture as the species of bullshit with which I have been concerned. For one thing, while what goes on in the academic world may sometimes have considerable influence elsewhere, it very often does not. For another, it is difficult to suppose that an author is likely to do very drastic harm when no one can understand what he is talking about. The occurrence of discourse that is genuinely without meaning may be offensive, or even infuriating, especially when for some reason people appear to take it seriously or profess to admire it. Nevertheless, texts that are genuinely unintelligible will very likely not be widely read, and it is even less likely that much will for very long be based on them.

In contrast, indifference to the truth is extremely dangerous. The conduct of civilized life, and the vitality of the institutions that are indispensable to it, depend very fundamentally on respect for the distinction between the true and the false. Insofar as the authority of this distinction is undermined by the prevalence of bullshit and by the mindlessly frivolous attitude that accepts the proliferation of bullshit as innocuous, an indispensable human treasure is squandered. Unintelligibility bears its fault on its face in a way that falsehood does not. For this reason, even apart from anything else, it is less insidious. The nonsense generated by negligent or pretentious or silly academics can be an irritating distraction from productive inquiry and an impediment to intellectual progress. I do not mean to dismiss it as inconsequential. It seems to me, however, that the harm promulgated by a lack of concern for the truth is a deeper and a more urgent issue.

Notes

1. Moreover, I welcome the provocative references that he makes to related deformities of discourse and thought, such as horseshit, which also merit serious inquiry and discussion.

2. My understanding of the Fourth of July orator is similar. He may know that what he says about American history is false, and he may intend his listeners to be deceived about it, but while this may make him a liar it does not imply that he is any less a bullshitter.

Bibliography of Harry Frankfurt's Work

Books

Demons, Dreamers, and Madmen: The Defense of Reason in Descartes's "Meditations." Indianapolis: Bobbs-Merrill, 1970.

Leibniz: A Collection of Critical Essays. Edited by Harry Frankfurt. Notre Dame, Ind.: University of Notre Dame Press, 1976.

The Importance of What We Care About. Cambridge: Cambridge University Press, 1988.

Necessity, Volition, and Love. Cambridge: Cambridge University Press, 1999.

Articles

"Realism and the Objectivity of Knowledge." *Philosophical Quarterly* 7 (1957).

"The Dependence of Mind." *Philosophy and Phenomenological Research* 19 (1958).

"The Logic of Omnipotence." In *Necessity, Volition, and Love.* First published in *Philosophical Review* 73 (1958).

"Memory and the Cartesian Circle." *Philosophical Review* 71 (1958).

"Peirce's Account of Inquiry." *Journal of Philosophy* 55 (1958).

"Peirce's Notion of Abduction." *Journal of Philosophy* 55 (1958).

"Science and Philosophy: A Reply to Mr Pasch." *Philosophical Studies* 9 (1958).

"Meaning, Truth, and Pragmatism." *Philosophical Quarterly* 10 (1960).

"Philosophical Certainty." *Philosophical Review* (1962).

"Descartes's Validation Of Reason." *American Philosophical Quarterly* 2 (1965).

"A Reply to Mr. Nelson's Comments on 'Memory and the Cartesian Circle.'" *Dialogue* (1965).

"Descartes's Discussion of His Existence in the Second Meditation." In *Necessity, Volition and Love.* First published in *Philosophical Review* 75 (1966).

"Functional Analyses in Biology." With Brian Poole. *British Journal of Philosophy of Science* 17 (1966).

"Alternate Possibilities and Moral Responsibility." In *The Importance of What We Care About*. First published in *Journal of Philosophy* 66 (1969).

"Freedom of the Will and the Concept of a Person." In *The Importance of What We Care About*. First published in *Journal of Philosophy* 68 (1971).

"The Anarchism of Robert Paul Wolff." *Political Theory* 1 (1973).

"Coercion and Moral Responsibility." In *The Importance of What We Care About*. First published in Ted Honderich, ed., *Essays on Freedom of Action* (London: Routledge and Kegan Paul, 1973).

"Three Concepts of Free Action." In *The Importance of What We Care About*. First published in *Proceedings of the Aristotelian Society*, Suppl 49 (1975): 113–125.

"Descartes on the Creation of the Eternal Truths." In *Necessity, Volition, and Love*. First published in *Philosophical Review* 86 (1977).

"Identification and Externality." In *The Importance of What We Care About*. First published in Amelie Rorty, ed., *The Identities of Persons* (Los Angeles: University of California, 1977).

"The Problem of Action." In *The Importance of What We Care About*. First published in *American Philosophical Quarterly* 15 (1978).

"Comments on MacIntyre's 'How Moral Agents Became Ghosts.'" *Synthese* 53 (1982).

"The Importance of What We Care About." In *The Importance of What We Care About*. First published in *Synthese* 53 (1982).

"What We Are Morally Responsible for." In *The Importance of What We Care About*. First published in Leigh Cauman, ed., *How Many Questions? Essays in Honor of Sydney Morgenbesser* (Indianapolis: Hackett, 1983).

"Necessity and Desire." In *The Importance of What We Care About*. First published in *Philosophy and Phenomenological Research* 45 (1984): 1–14.

"On Bullshit." In *The Importance of What We Care About*. First published in *Raritan* 6 (1986).

"Two Motivations for Rationalism: Descartes and Spinoza." In *Necessity, Volition, and Love*. First published in A. Donagan and A. N. Perovich, eds., *Human Nature And Natural Knowledge* (Dordrecht: D. Reidel, 1986).

"Equality as a Moral Ideal." In *The Importance of What We Care About*. First published in *Ethics* 98 (1987).

"Continuous Creation, Ontological Inertia, and the Discontinuity of Time." In *Necessity, Volition, and Love*. Originally published in French as "La creation continue, l'inertie ontologique, et la discontinuite du temps," *Revue de Metaphysique et de Morale*, no. 4 (1987). First published in English in Georges Moyal, ed., *Rene Descartes: Critical Assessments*, vol. 3 (London: Routledge, 1991).

"Identification and Wholeheartedness." In *The Importance of What We Care About*. First published in Ferdinand Schoeman, ed., *Responsibility, Character and the Emotions: New Essays in Moral Psychology* (New York: Cambridge University Press, 1987).

"Les Desordres du Rationalisme." In *Le Discourse et sa Methode*, edited by N. Grimaldi and J. L. Marion. Paris: Presses Universitaires de France, 1987.

"Rationality and the Unthinkable." In *The Importance of What We Care About* (Cambridge University Press, 1988).

"Concerning the Freedom and Limits of the Will." In *Necessity, Volition, and Love*. First published in *Philosophical Topics* 17 (1989).

"The Faintest Passion." In *Necessity, Volition, and Love*. First published in *Proceedings and Addresses of the American Philosophical Association* (1992).

"On the Usefulness of Final Ends." In *Necessity, Volition, and Love*. First published in *Iyyun, The Jerusalem Philosophical Quarterly* 41 (1992).

"On God's Creation." In *Necessity, Volition, and Love*. First published in E. Stump, ed., *Reasoned Faith* (Ithaca: Cornell, 1993).

"On the Necessity of Ideals." In *Necessity, Volition, and Love*. First published in G. C. Noam and T. Wren, eds., *The Moral Self* (Cambridge, Mass: MIT Press, 1993).

"An Alleged Asymmetry between Actions and Omissions." In *Necessity, Volition, and Love*. First published in *Ethics* 104 (1994).

"Autonomy, Necessity, and Love." In *Necessity, Volition, and Love*. First published in H. F. Fulda and R.-P. Horstmann, eds.,*Vernunftbegriffe in der Moderne: Stuttgarter Hegel-Congress 1993* (Stuttgart: Klett-Cotta, 1994).

"Equality and Respect." In *Necessity, Volition, and Love*. First published in *Social Research* 64 (1997).

"Comments on Gillian Brock's Essay 'Morally Important Needs.'" *Philosophia* 26 (1998).

"Duty and Love." *Philosophical Explorations* 1 (1998).

"Gleichheit und Achtung." *Deutsche Zeitschrift fur Philosophie* 47 (1999)

"Responses." *Journal of Ethics* 3 (1999).

References

Albritton, Rogers. "Freedom of Will, and Freedom of Action." Presidential address delivered in 1985 to the Pacific Division APA, in *Proceedings of the American Philosophical Association* (1985).

Allison, Henry E. *Kant's Theory of Freedom*. New York: Cambridge University Press, 1990.

Andrews, John D. W. *The Active Self in Psychotherapy: An Integration of Therapeutic Styles*. Boston: Allyn and Bacon, 1991.

Anscombe, Roderick. "The Myth of the True Self." *Psychiatry* 52 (1989): 209–217.

Arpaly, Nomy and Schroeder, Timothy. "Alienation and Externality." *Canadian Journal of Philosophy* 29 (1999): 371–387.

Austen, Jane. *The Oxford Illustrated Jane Austen*, third ed., edited by R. W. Chapman. Oxford: Oxford University Press, 1932–1954.

Benhabib, Seyla. "The Generalized and the Concrete Other: The Kohlberg-Gilligan Controversy and Moral Theory." In *Women and Moral Theory*, edited by Eva Feder Kitty and Diana T. Meyers. Totowa, NJ: Rowman and Littlefield, 1987.

Berofsky, Bernard. *The Metaphysical Basis of Responsibility*. New York: Routledge and Kegan Paul, 1987.

Beyer, Lawrence. "The Disintegration of Belief." Ph.D. thesis, Stanford University, 1999.

Blumenfeld, David. "The Principle of Alternate Possibilities." *Journal of Philosophy* 67 (1971): 339–344.

Bok, Hilary. *Freedom and Responsibility*. Princeton: Princeton University Press, 1999.

Bratman, Michael. "Identification, Decision, and Treating as a Reason." In *Faces of Intention: Selected Essays on Intention and Agency*. New York: Cambridge University Press, 1999. First published in *Philosophical Topics* 24 (1996): 1–18.

Bratman, Michael. "Reflection, Planning, and Temporally Extended Agency." *Philosophical Review* (2000): 35–61.

Bratman, Michael. "Review of Korsgaard's *The Sources of Normativity*." In *Faces of Intention: Selected Essays on Intention and Agency*. New York: Cambridge University Press, 1999. First published in *Philosophy and Phenomenological Research* 58 (1998): 699–709.

Bratman, Michael. "Valuing and the Will." *Philosophical Perspectives* 14 (2000): 249–265.

Bratman, Michael. *Faces of Intention: Selected Essays on Intention and Agency*. New York: Cambridge University Press, 1999.

Bratman, Michael. *Intention, Plans, and Practical Reason*. Cambridge: Harvard University Press, 1987. Reissued by CSLI Publications, 1999.

Buss, Sarah. "Autonomy Reconsidered." In *Midwest Studies in Philosophy XIX: Philosophical Naturalism*, edited by Peter A. French, Theodore E. Uehling Jr., and Howard K Wettstein. Notre Dame, Ind.: University of Notre Dame Press, 1994.

Buss, Sarah. "Review of *The Metaphysics of Free Will*, by John Martin Fischer." *Philosophical Books* (1997): 117–121.

Churchland, Patricia. "Epistemology in the Age of Neuroscience." *Journal of Philosophy* 84 (1987): 548–549.

Cohen, G. A. "Reason, Humanity, and the Moral Law." In *The Sources of Normativity*, by Christine Korsgaard.

Cohon, Rachel. "Internalism about Reasons for Action." *Pacific Philosophical Quarterly* 74 (1993): 265–288.

Davidson, Donald. "Freedom to Act." In *Essays on Actions and Events*.

Davidson, Donald. *Essays on Actions and Events*. Oxford: Oxford University Press, 1980.

Della Rocca, Michael. "Frankfurt, Fischer, and Flickers." *Nous* 32 (1998): 99–105.

Dennett, Daniel. "Conditions of Personhood." In *Brainstorms: Philosophical Essays on Mind and Psychology*. Cambridge, Mass.: MIT Press, 1981.

Dennett, Daniel. "How to Change Your Mind." In *Brainstorms*.

Dennett, Daniel. "Where Am I?" In *Brainstorms*.

Dennett, Daniel. *Elbow Room*. Cambridge, Mass.: MIT Press, 1984.

Descartes, Rene. *The Passions of the Soul*. In *The Philosophical Works of Descartes*, volume I, trans. Elizabeth S. Haldane and G. R. T. Ross. Cambridge: Cambridge University Press, 1911–1912 and 1931.

Dillon, Robin. "Respect and Care: Toward Moral Integration." *Canadian Journal of Philosophy* 22 (1992): 105–132.

Dupre, John. *The Disorder of Things*. Cambridge, Mass.: Harvard University Press, 1993.

Eagle, Morris. "Psychoanalysis and the Personal." In *Mind, Psychoanalysis, and Science*, edited by P. Clark and C. Wright. Oxford: Blackwell, 1988.

Eagle, Morris. "Psychoanalytic Conceptions of the Self." In *The Self: Interdisciplinary Approaches*. New York: Springer-Verlag, 1991.

Ekstrom, Laura. "Protecting Incompatibilist Freedom." *American Philosophical Quarterly* 35 (1998): 281–291.

Epstein, Mark. *Thoughts without a Thinker: Psychotherapy from a Buddhist Perspective*. New York: Basic Books, 1995.

Erikson, Erik. *Identity, Youth, and Crisis*. New York: W.W. Norton, 1968.

Feinberg, Joel. "The Interest of Liberty on the Scales." In *Rights, Justice, and the Bounds of Liberty: Essays in Social Philosophy*. Princeton, NJ: Princeton University Press, 1980.

Fischer, John Martin and Ravizza, Mark. "When the Will Is Free." In *Agents, Causes, and Events*, edited by Timothy O'Connor. New York: Oxford University Press, 1995.

Fischer, John Martin and Ravizza, Mark. *Responsibility and Control: A Theory of Moral Responsibility*. Cambridge: Cambridge University Press, 1998.

Fischer, John Martin. *The Metaphysics of Free Will: An Essay on Control*. Oxford: Blackwell Publishers, 1994.

Fischer, John Martin. "Recent Work on Moral Responsibility." *Ethics* 110 (1999): 93–139.

Fischer, John Martin. "Responsibility and Self-Expression." *Journal of Ethics* 3 (1999): 277–297.

Foot, Philippa. "Moral Arguments." In *Virtues and Vices*. University of California Press, 1978.

Frankena, William. "The Ethics of Respect for Persons." *Philosophical Topics* 14 (1986).

Freud, Anna. *The Ego and the Mechanisms of Defense*. London: Hogarth Press, 1937. Reprinted in *Pivotal Papers on Identification*, edited by George H. Pollock (Madison, CT: International Universities Press, 1993).

Freud, Sigmund. "Notes upon a Case of Obsessional Neurosis." In *The Standard Edition of the Complete Psychological Works of Sigmund Freud*, vol. X, edited by James Strachey et al. London: Hogarth Press and the Institute of Psycho-Analysis, 1953–1974.

Freud, Sigmund. *Jokes and Their Relation to the Unconscious*, translated by James Strachey. New York: Norton, 1960.

Gass, William. "The Stylization of Desire." *Fiction and the Figures of Life*. Boston: David Godine, 1980.

Gibbard, Allan. *Wise Choices, Apt Feelings*. Cambridge, Mass.: Harvard University Press, 1990.

Ginet, Carl. "In Defense of the Principle of Alternative Possibilities: Why I Don't Find Frankfurt's Argument Convincing." *Philosophical Perspectives* 10 (1996): 403–417.

Grice, H. P. "Intention and Uncertainty." *Proceedings of the British Academy* 57 (1971): 263–279.

Hampshire, Stuart. *Freedom of the Individual*. New York: Harper and Row, 1965.

Hampshire, Stuart. *Freedom of the Individual*. Princeton, NJ: Princeton University Press, 1975. Expanded edition.

Harman, Gilbert. "Desired Desires." In *Value, Welfare and Morality*, edited by R. G. Frey and C. W. Morris. Cambridge: Cambridge University Press, 1993.

Harman, Gilbert. "Practical Reasoning." *Review of Metaphysics* 29 (1979): 431–463.

Harré, Rom. *The Singular Self: An Introduction to the Psychology of Personhood*. London: Sage Publications, 1998.

Horgan, Terence. "'Could,' Possible Worlds, and Moral Responsibility." *Southern Journal of Philosophy* 17 (1979): 345–358.

Hume, David. *A Treatise of Human Nature* (second edition), edited by L. A. Selby-Bigge and P. H. Nidditch. Oxford: Clarendon Press, 1978.

Hunt, David P. "Moral Responsibility and Unavoidable Action." *Philosophical Studies* 97 (2000): 195–227.

James, William. "The Dilemma of Determinism." In *The Will to Believe and Other Essays*. New York: Dover, 1956.

Johnson, Edward. "Ignoring Persons." In *Respect for Persons*, edited by O. H. Green, *Tulane Studies in Philosophy* 31 (1982).

Kane, Robert. *Free Will and Values*. Albany, NY: State University of New York Press, 1985.

Kane, Robert. *The Significance of Free Will*. New York and Oxford: Oxford University Press, 1996.

Kant, Immanuel. *Grounding of the Metaphysics of Morals*, translated by J. Ellington. Indianapolis: Hackett, 1981.

Kihlstrom, J. F. and Cantor, N. "Mental Representations of the Self." In *Advances in Experimental Social Psychology*, vol. 17, edited by Leonard Berkowitz. New York: Academic Press, 1984.

Korsgaard, Christine. "Self-Constitution in the Ethics of Plato and Kant." *The Journal of Ethics* 3 (1999): 1–29.

Korsgaard, Christine. "Skepticism about Practical Reason." In *Creating the Kingdom of Ends*. Cambridge: Cambridge University Press, 1996.

Korsgaard, Christine. "The Normativity of Instrumental Reason." In *Ethics and Practical Reason*, edited by G. Cullity and B. Gaut. Oxford: Clarendon Press, 1997.

Korsgaard, Christine. "The Reasons We Can Share." In *Creating the Kingdom of Ends*. Cambridge: Cambridge University Press, 1996.

Korsgaard, Christine. *The Sources of Normativity*. Cambridge: Cambridge University Press, 1996.

Kosslyn, Stephen and Koenig, Oliver. *Wet Mind: The New Cognitive Neuroscience.* New York: Macmillan, 1992.

Lehrer, Keith. "'Can' in Theory and Practice: A Possible Worlds Analysis." In *Action Theory: Proceedings of the Winnipeg Conference on Human Action,* edited by M. Brand and D. Walton. Dordrecht: D. Reidel, 1976.

Levine, Frederic J. and Kravis, Robert. "Psychoanalytic Theories of the Self: Contrasting Clinical Approaches to the New Narcissism." In *The Book of the Self: Person, Pretext, and Process,* edited by Polly Youaang-Eisendrath and James A. Hall. New York: New York University Press, 1987.

Lewis, David. *Counterfactuals.* Cambridge, Mass.: Harvard University Press, 1973.

Logothetis, Nikos. "Vision: A Window on Consciousness." *Scientific American* (November 1999).

Marks, Isaac. *Fears, Phobias, and Rituals.* New York: Oxford University Press, 1987.

Mele, Alfred R. "Flickers of Freedom." *Journal of Social Philosophy* 29 (1998): 144–156.

Mele, Alfred R. "Kane, Luck, and the Significance of Free Will." *Philosophical Explorations* 2 (1999): 96–104.

Mele, Alfred R. "Soft Libertarianism and Frankfurt-Style Scenarios." *Philosophical Topics* 24 (1996): 123–142.

Mele, Alfred R. and Robb, David. "Rescuing Frankfurt-Style Cases." *Philosophical Review* 107 (1998): 97–112.

Melville, Joy. *Phobias and Obsessions.* London: George Allen and Unwin, 1977.

Nagel, Thomas. "Moral Luck." In *Mortal Questions.* Cambridge: Cambridge University Press, 1979.

Nagel, Thomas. *The Possibility of Altruism.* Princeton, NJ: Princeton University Press, 1970.

Nozick, Robert. *Philosophical Explanations.* Cambridge, Mass.: Harvard University Press, 1981.

O'Connor, Timothy, ed. *Agents, Causes, and Events.* New York: Oxford University Press, 1995.

Parfit, Derek. *Reasons and Persons.* Oxford: Oxford University Press, 1984.

Pereboom, Derk. "Alternative Possibilities and Causal Histories." Chapter 1 of *Living without Free Will,* unpublished manuscript, Department of Philosophy, University of Vermont, Burlington.

Pettit, Philip and Smith, Michael. "Backgrounding Desire." *Philosophical Review* 96 (1990): 565–592.

Plantinga, Alvin. "An Evolutionary Argument against Naturalism." *Logos* 12 (1992): 27–49.

Prichard, H. A. "Acting, Willing, Desiring." In *Moral Obligation.* Oxford: Clarendon Press, 1949.

Raz, Joseph. *Engaging Reason*. Oxford: Oxford University Press, 2000.

Raz, Joseph. *The Morality Of Freedom*. Oxford: Oxford University Press, 1986.

Robert Kane, "Two Kinds of Incompatibilism." *Philosophy and Phenomenological Research* 50 (1989).

Rorty, Richard. "Untruth and Consequences." *The New Republic* (July 31, 1995).

Rubin, Jeffrey. "Does the True Self Really Exist? A Critique of Winnicott's True Self Concept." In *A Psychoanalysis for our Time: Exploring the Blindness of the Seeing "I."* New York: New York University Press, 1998.

Sartre, Jean-Paul. *Being and Nothingness: An Essay on Phenomenological Ontology*, translated by Hazel E. Barnes. New York: Philosophical Library, 1956.

Sass, Louis. "Introspection, Schizophrenia, and the Fragmentation of the Self." *Representations* 19 (1987).

Scanlon, T. M. *What We Owe to Each Other*. Cambridge: Harvard University Press, 1998.

Schafer, Roy. *Aspects of Internalization*. New York: International Unversities Press, 1968.

Skinner, B. F. *Walden Two*. New York: MacMillan, 1962.

Smith, Angela. *Agency, Attitude, and Responsibility*. Ph.D. thesis, Harvard University, 1999.

Smith, Michael. *The Moral Problem*. Oxford: Blackwell, 1994.

Sokal, Alan. "Transgressing the Boundaries: Towards a Transformative Hermeneutics of Quantum Gravity." *Social Text* 46 (1996): 217–252.

Solomon, Andrew. "Anatomy of Melancholy." *The New Yorker* (January 12, 1998): 46–58.

Spelman, Elizabeth. "On Treating Persons as Persons." *Ethics* 88 (1977): 150–161.

Stalnaker, Robert. "A Theory of Conditionals." In N. Rescher, ed., *Studies in Logical Theory. American Philosophical Quarterly Series*. Oxford: Blackwell, 1968.

Stump, Eleonore. "Alternative Possibilities and Responsibility: The Flicker of Freedom." Unpublished manuscript delivered at the American Philosophical Association Pacific Division Meetings, March 1998, Los Angeles, Calif.

Stump, Eleonore. "Aquinas's Account of Freedom: Intellect and Will," *The Monist* 80 (1997).

Stump, Eleonore. "Augustine on Free Will." In *The Cambridge Companion to Augustine*, edited by Norman Kretzmann and Eleonore Stump. Cambridge: Cambridge University Press, 2000.

Stump, Eleonore. "The Direct Argument for Incompatibilism." *Philosophy and Phenomenological Research* 61 (2000): 459–466.

Stump, Eleonore. "Intellect, Will, and the Principle of Alternate Possibilities," in *Christian Theism and the Problems of Philosophy*, edited by Michael Beaty (Notre Dame: University of Notre Dame Press, 1990), 254–285. Reprinted in *Moral Responsibility*, ed. John Martin Fischer and Mark Ravizza (Ithaca, NY: Cornell University Press, 1993).

Stump, Eleonore. "Libertarian Freedom and the Principle of Alternate Possibilities." In *Faith, Freedom, and Rationality: Philosophy of Religion Today*, edited by Daniel Howard-Snyder and Jeff Jordan. Lanham, Maryland: Rowman and Littlefield, 1996.

Stump, Eleonore. "Non-Cartesian Dualism and Materialism with Reductionism." *Faith and Philosophy* 12 (1995): 505–531.

Stump, Eleonore. "Persons: Identification and Freedom." *Philosophical Topics* 24 (1996): 183–214.

Stump, Eleanore. "Sanctification, Hardening of the Heart, and Frankfurt's Concept of Free Will." In *Perspectives On Moral Responsibility*, edited by John Martin Fischer and Mark Ravizza. Ithaca, NY: Cornell University Press, 1993.

Stump, Eleonore and Fischer, John Martin. "Transfer Principles and Moral Responsibility." *Philosophical Perspectives* 14 (2000): 47–55.

van Inwagen, Peter. "The Incompatibility of Responsibility and Determinism." In *Bowling Green Studies in Applied Philosophy 2: Action and Responsibility*, edited by Michael Bradie and Myles Brand. Bowling Green, Ohio: Bowling Green State University Press, 1980, 30–37. Reprinted in John Martin Fischer, ed., *Moral Responsibility* (Ithaca, NY: Cornell University Press, 1986).

van Inwagen, Peter. "When Is the Will Free?" *Philosophical Perspectives* 3 (1989). Reprinted in Timothy O'Connor, ed., *Agents, Causes, and Events* (New York: Oxford University Press, 1995).

van Inwagen, Peter. *An Essay on Free Will*. Oxford: Oxford University Press, 1983.

Velleman, J. David. "Love as a Moral Emotion." *Ethics* 109 (1999): 338–374.

Velleman, J. David. "On the Aim of Belief." In *The Possibility of Practical Reason*. Oxford: Clarendon Press, 2000.

Velleman, J. David. "Self to Self." *Philosophical Review* 105 (1996): 39–76.

Velleman, J. David. "The Guise of the Good." *Nous* 26 (1992): 3–26.

Velleman, J. David. "What Happens When Someone Acts?" In *The Possibility of Practical Reason*. First published in *Mind* 101 (1992): 462–481.

Velleman, J. David. *The Possibility of Practical Reason*. Oxford: Oxford University Press, 2000.

Wallace, R. Jay. *Responsibility and the Moral Sentiments*. Cambridge, Mass.: Harvard University Press, 1994.

Watson, Gary. "Disordered Appetites: Addiction, Compulsion, and Dependence." In *Addiction: Entries and Exits*, edited by Jon Elster. Russell Sage Foundation, 1999.

Widerker, David. "Libertarian Freedom and the Avoidability of Decisions." *Faith and Philosophy* 12 (1995): 113–118.

Widerker, David. "Libertarianism and Frankfurt's Attack on the Principle of Alternative Possibilities." *Philosophical Review* 104 (1995): 247–261.

Williams, Bernard. "Deciding to Believe." In *Problems of the Self*. Cambridge: Cambridge University Press, 1973.

Williams, Bernard. "Internal and External Reasons." In *Moral Luck*. Cambridge: Cambridge University Press, 1981.

Williams, Bernard. "Moral Incapacity." In *Making Sense of Humanity*. Cambridge: Cambridge University Press, 1995. First published in *Proceedings of the Aristotelian Society* 92 (1992–1993).

Winnicott, D. W. "Ego Distortion in Terms of True and False Self." In *Collected Papers: Through Paediatrics to Psycho-analysis*. London: Tavistock Publications, 1958.

Wolff, Robert Paul. "There's Nobody Here but Us Persons." In *Women and Philosophy: Toward a Theory of Liberation*, edited by Carol C. Gould and Marx W. Wartofsky. New York: G. P. Putnam's Sons, 1976.

Wollheim, Richard. "Imagination and Identification." In *On Art and the Mind*. Cambridge, MA: Harvard University Press, 1974.

Wollheim, Richard. *The Thread of Life*. Cambridge, MA: Harvard University Press, 1984.

Wyma, Keith D. "Moral Responsibility and Leeway for Action." *American Philosophical Quarterly* 34 (1997): 57–70.

Index